Microsoft® EXCEL
FUNCTIONS AND FORMULAS

Second Edition

BERND HELD

T0204775

MERCURY LEARNING AND INFORMATION
Dulles, Virginia

Publisher: David Pallai

MERCURY LEARNING AND INFORMATION
22841 Quicksilver Drive
Dulles, VA 20166
info@merclearning.com
www.merclearning.com
1-800-758-3756

This book is printed on acid-free paper.

B. Held. *Microsoft EXCEL FUNCTIONS AND FORMULAS, Second Edition*.
ISBN: 978-1-9364200-1-8

Microsoft, Excel, Visual Basic, and Windows are registered trademarks of Microsoft Corporation in the U.S. and other countries.

The publisher recognizes and respects all marks used by companies, manufacturers, and developers as a means to distinguish their products. All brand names and product names mentioned in this book are trademarks or service marks of their respective companies. Any omission or misuse (of any kind) of service marks or trademarks, etc. is not an attempt to infringe on the property of others.

Library of Congress Control Number: 2010941257 ·

101112 3 2 1

Our titles are available for adoption, license, or bulk purchase by institutions, corporations, etc. For additional information, please contact the Customer Service Dept. at 1-800-758-3756 (toll free).

Microsoft® EXCEL
FUNCTIONS AND FORMULAS

Second Edition

CONTENTS

ACKNOWLEDGMENTS

I would like to thank all of the individuals at Mercury Learning International who worked on this book for their hard work and dedication to quality books.

Introduction

Microsoft Excel is the well-known standard spreadsheet application that allows you to easily perform calculations and recalculations of data by using numerous built-in functions and formulas. Although you may be familiar with simple functions such as SUM, this is just one of the many Excel functions and formulas that can help you simplify the process of entering calculations. Because there are so many other useful and versatile functions and formulas inside Excel that most users haven't discovered yet, this book was written to help readers uncover and use its wide range of tools.

For each function or formula, we started with a simple task that can be solved with Excel in an efficient way. We added tips and tricks and additional features as well to provide deeper knowledge and orientation. After you have stepped through all the lessons, you will have a great toolbox to assist you with your projects and make many everyday workbook tasks much easier.

The content of the book is as follows:

Chapter 1 describes practical tasks that can be solved by using formulas.

In Chapter 2 you learn the usage of logical functions that are often used in combination with other functions.

Chapter 3 shows how text functions are used. You will often need these functions when working with text in tables or if the text needs to be changed or adapted, especially when it is imported into Excel from other applications.

In Chapter 4 you learn about the date and time functions in Excel. Times and dates are automatically converted inside Excel to the number format, which makes it easier to perform calculations.

With Chapter 5 you delve into the secrets of working with statistics in Excel.

Chapter 6 describes the most commonly used functions for mathematics and trigonometry along with easy-to-follow tasks. The most common function here is the SUM function, with which you may already be familiar. However, you may be surprised about the additional possibilities shown.

If you want to learn more about functions for financial mathematics, take a look at Chapter 7. Here you will find examples of how to calculate depreciation of an asset and how long it takes to pay back a loan using different interest rates.

With Chapter 8 you get into the secrets of database functions. There are a variety of functions explained that can be used for evaluation of data especially when using different criteria.

Chapter 9 is about lookup and reference functions inside Excel. With these functions you can address data in various ranges and look up values in a reference.

Chapter 10 goes into the secrets of conditional formatting. This feature has been available since Excel 97, but there are still some tips and tricks on enhancing the built-in features — just take a look at the possibilities.

Chapter 11 provides an introduction to array formulas. With these you learn how to perform multiple calculations and then return either a single result or multiple results. This special feature is similar to other formulas except you press Ctrl+Shift+Enter after entering the formula.

Chapter 12 shows interesting solutions with formulas, such as creating a function to color all cells containing formulas inside an Excel spreadsheet.

Chapter 13 goes even deeper into user-defined functions by using Visual Basic for Applications inside Excel. This chapter will show you how to solve tasks even when Excel cannot calculate an answer.

With Chapter 14 we present some tasks that combine several functions shown in the previous chapters. Use these to get more experience. Read the description of the task first and try to determine the functions that are needed to get the desired result. Check your solution with the one shown beneath the task.

Examples are provided on the companion CD-ROM. These are organized into Excel workbooks for each chapter and allow you to enter your data and perform calculations without having to enter the formulas yourself.

If you have further questions or would like to provide feedback about the book in general, visit http://held-office.de or send an e-mail to b.held@held-office.de.

Have fun reading the book and in the continuous usage of the functions and formulas you will discover here.

Chapter 1   FORMULAS IN EXCEL

PRODUCTION PER HOUR

Data for some employees is recorded in a worksheet. They work a varied number of hours each day to produce clocks. By calculating the number of pieces each employee produces per hour, it can be determined who is the most productive employee.

To See Who is the Most Productive Employee:

1. In a worksheet, enter your own data or the data shown in Figure 1–1.
2. Select cells D2:D7.
3. Enter the following formula: **=C2/(B2*24)**.
4. Press **<Ctrl+Enter>** to fill the selected cell range with the current entry.
5. From the toolbar select **Home** and go to **Number**.
6. Click the dropdown arrow and select **Format Cells**.
7. Select the **Number** tab and then select **Number** from the Category list.
8. Set Decimal places to **2**.
9. Click **OK**.

D2		▼	f_x	=C2/(B2*24)	
	A	B	C	D	E
1	employee	time	pieces	pieces/hour	
2	Clark	3:50	60	15.65	
3	Miller	4:15	80	18.82	
4	Austin	5:55	98	16.56	
5	Beckham	7:04	155	21.93	
6	Butcher	8:35	180	20.97	
7	Field	6:30	85	13.08	
8					
9					
10					

FIGURE 1–1

Mr. Beckham is the most productive. He produces an average of nearly 22 clocks per hour.

CALCULATE THE AGE OF A PERSON IN DAYS

A worksheet lists the names of friends in column A and their birth dates in column B. To calculate the number of days each person has been alive, enter the current date in cell B1 and perform the following steps:

▶ **To Calculate the Age of a Person in Days:**

1. In a worksheet, enter your own data or the data shown in Figure 1–2.
2. Select cells C5:C9.
3. Enter the following formula: **=$B$1-B5**.
4. Press **<Ctrl+Enter>**.
5. From the toolbar select **Home** and go to **Number**.
6. Click the dropdown arrow and select **Format Cells**.
7. Select the **Number** tab and then select **General** from the **Category** list.
8. Click **OK**.

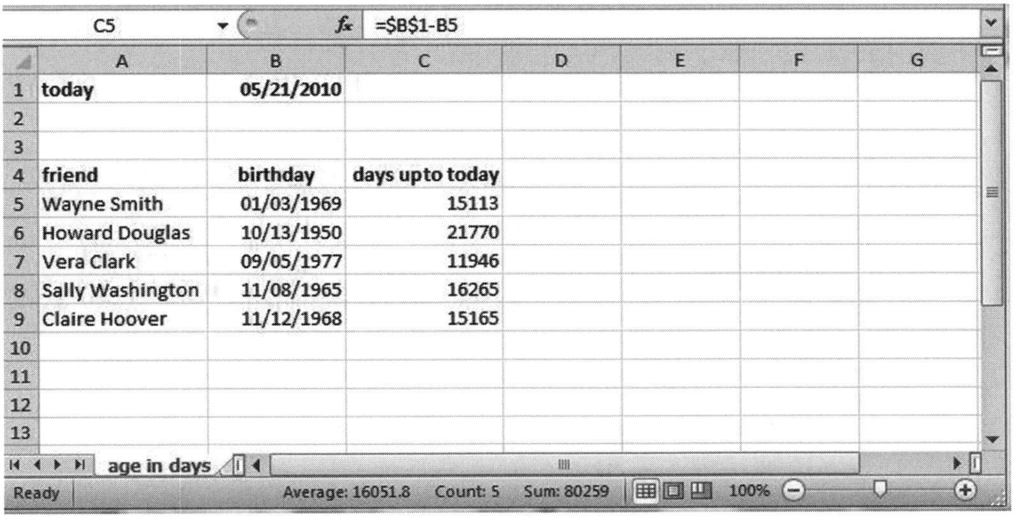

	C5			f_x	=$B$1-B5			
	A	B	C	D	E	F	G	
1	today	05/21/2010						
2								
3								
4	friend	birthday	days up to today					
5	Wayne Smith	01/03/1969	15113					
6	Howard Douglas	10/13/1950	21770					
7	Vera Clark	09/05/1977	11946					
8	Sally Washington	11/08/1965	16265					
9	Claire Hoover	11/12/1968	15165					
10								
11								
12								
13								

age in days

Ready   Average: 16051.8   Count: 5   Sum: 80259   100%

FIGURE 1–2

NOTE *The formula must have an absolute reference to cell B1, which is available by going to the formula bar, highlighting the cell reference, and pressing F4 until the appropriate reference appears.*

CALCULATE A PRICE REDUCTION

All prices in a price list have to be reduced by a certain percentage. The amount of the price reduction is 15% and is entered in cell C1.

▶ **To Reduce All Prices by a Certain Percentage:**

1. In a worksheet, enter your own data or the data shown in Figure 1–3.
2. Select cell C1 and type **-15%**.
3. Select cells C4:C8.
4. Enter the following formula: **=B4+(B4*$C$1)**.
5. Press **<Ctrl+Enter>**.

	C4		▼		f_x	=B4+(B4*$C$1)			
	A	B	C	D	E	F	G	
1	pricelist	price reduction	-15%					
2								
3	product name	old price	new price					
4	M11	11.45	9.73					
5	M12	14.00	11.90					
6	M13	18.90	16.07					
7	M14	34.67	29.47					
8	M15	131.99	112.19					
9								
10								
11								
12								
13								

◄ ◄ ► ►|	price reduction							
Ready		Average: 35.87	Count: 5	Sum: 179.36		100%		

FIGURE 1–3

NOTE *Please note that the formula must have an absolute reference to cell C1. Also, columns B and C are formatted with the Currency style, which is available by clicking on the $ button in the Home ribbon toolbar.*

CONVERT CURRENCY

In a worksheet, currency has to be converted from dollars (column B) to euros (column C). The rate of exchange from dollars to euros is placed in cell C1; here we use 0.747.

▶ **To Convert Currency:**

1. In a worksheet, enter your own data or the data shown in Figure 1–4.
2. Select cells C4:C8.
3. Enter the following formula: **=B4*$C$1**.
4. Press **<Ctrl+Enter>**.
5. Press **<Ctrl+1>** to show the dialog Format Cells.
6. Select the **Number** tab and then select **Currency** from the Category list.
7. Choose the required € **Euro** format.
8. Click **OK**.

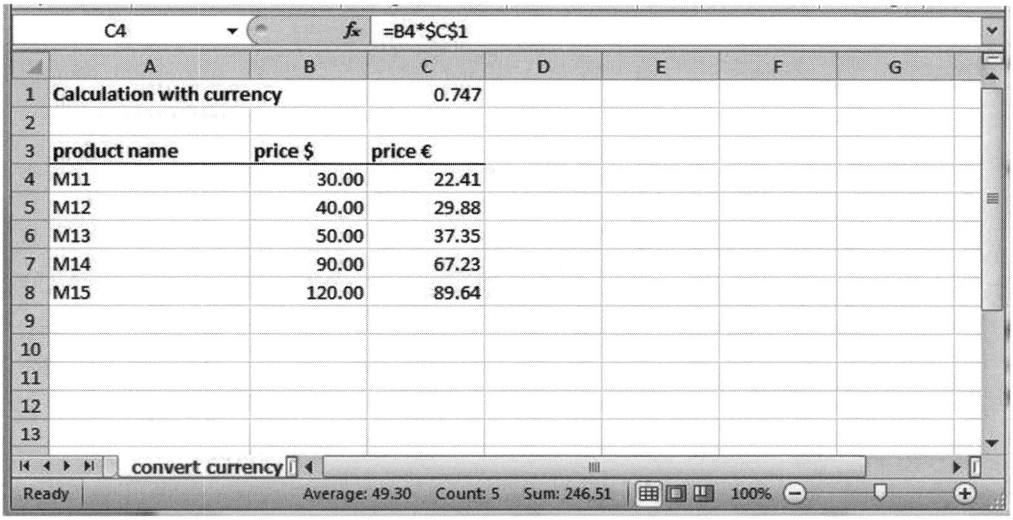

FIGURE 1–4

NOTE   *To convert euros back to dollars, use the following formula:* **=C4/$C$1**.

CONVERT FROM HOURS TO MINUTES

As a task, time in a timesheet has to be converted from hours to minutes.

▶ **To Convert Time to Minutes:**

1. In a worksheet, enter your own data or the data shown in Figure 1–5.
2. Select cells B4:B8.
3. Enter the following formula: **=A4*24*60**.
4. Press **<Ctrl+Enter>**.
5. Format cells B4:B8 as general by pressing **<Ctrl+1>** and then selecting from the **Number** tab **General** in the Category list.
6. Click **OK**.

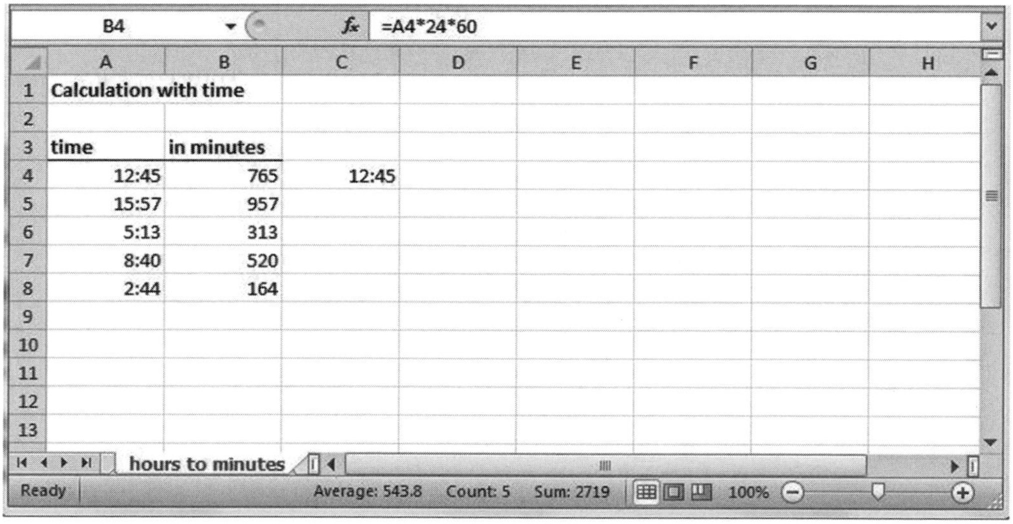

FIGURE 1–5

NOTE *To convert minutes to hours and minutes format, use the formula* **=B4/24/60**. *Remember to format the cells with a time format, as shown in cell C4 in Figure 1–5.*

DETERMINE FUEL CONSUMPTION

In a worksheet, fuel consumption data is recorded. Each time you refill your gas tank, record the following data: date, miles traveled, and gallons purchased. Then reset the mileage counter. To calculate the fuel consumption of your vehicle, perform the following steps:

▶ **To Determine Fuel Consumption:**

1. In a worksheet, enter your own data or the data shown in Figure 1–6.
2. Select cells D5:D10.
3. Enter the following formula: **=B5/C5**.
4. Press **<Ctrl+Enter>**.

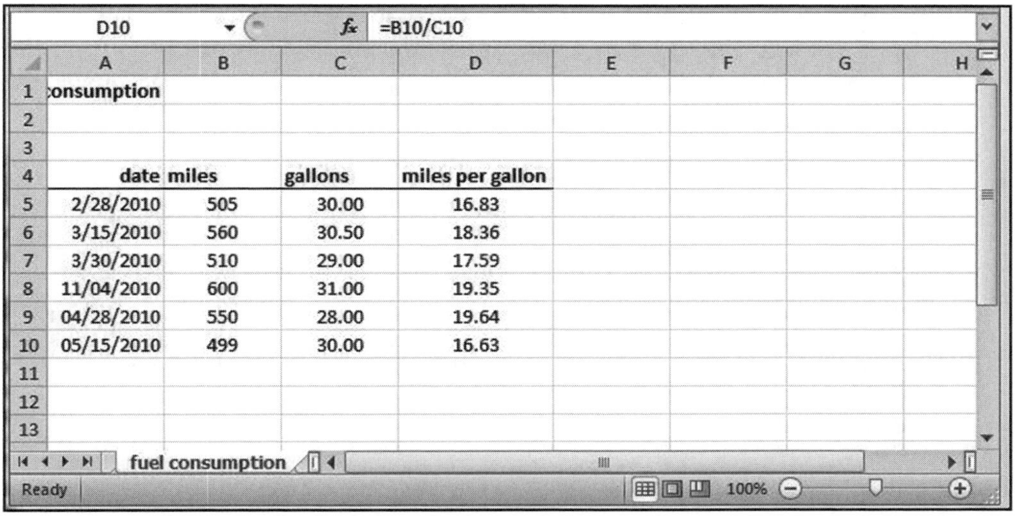

	D10		▼		*fx*	=B10/C10				▼
	A	B	C	D	E	F	G	H	
1	:onsumption								
2									
3									
4	date	miles	gallons	miles per gallon					
5	2/28/2010	505	30.00	16.83					
6	3/15/2010	560	30.50	18.36					
7	3/30/2010	510	29.00	17.59					
8	11/04/2010	600	31.00	19.35					
9	04/28/2010	550	28.00	19.64					
10	05/15/2010	499	30.00	16.63					
11									
12									
13									

fuel consumption

Ready 100%

FIGURE 1–6

CALCULATE YOUR IDEAL AND RECOMMENDED WEIGHTS

Formulas for calculating ideal body weight first came into existence in 1871 when a French surgeon, Dr. P.P. Broca, created this formula (known as Broca's index):

Weight (in kg) should equal height (in cm)–100,
plus or minus 15% for women or 10% for men

In recent years, the body mass index (BMI) has become the standard for calculating ideal weight.

▶ **To Determine Ideal and Recommended Weights:**

1. In a worksheet, enter your own data or the data shown in Figure 1–7.
2. Select cell B6 and type the following formula to determine your ideal weight (BMI = body mass index): **=(B4-100)*0.9**.
3. Select cell B7 and type the following formula to calculate your recommended weight: **=B4-100**.
4. Calculate the total difference in cells D6 and D7 by simple subtraction.
5. Calculate the difference in percentage in cells E6 (**=1-B5/B6**) and E7 (**=1-B5/B7**).

6. Press **<Ctrl+Enter>** to show the dialog Format Cells.
7. Select the **Number** tab and then select **Percentage** from the Category list.
8. Set Decimal places to **2** and click **OK**.

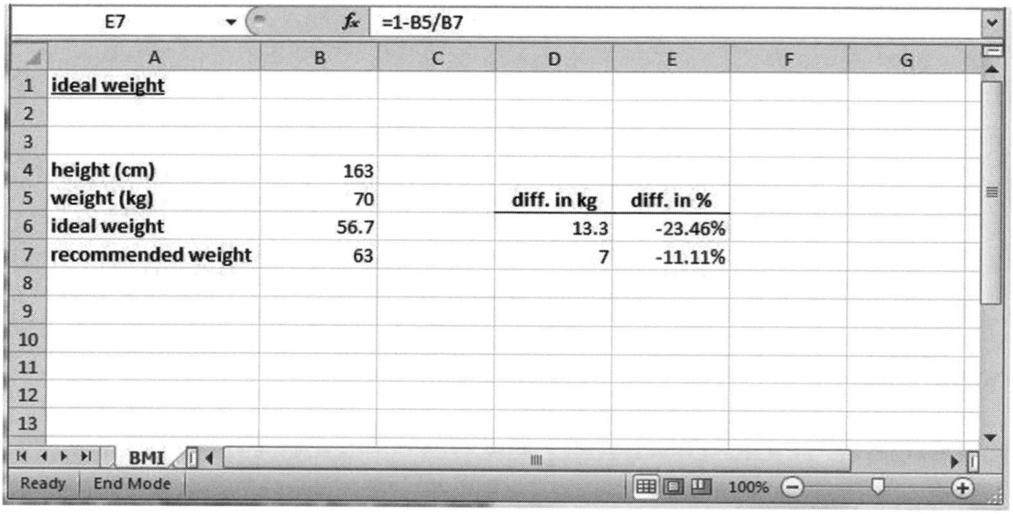

	E7			f_x	=1-B5/B7			
	A	B	C	D	E	F	G	
1	ideal weight							
2								
3								
4	height (cm)	163						
5	weight (kg)	70		diff. in kg	diff. in %			
6	ideal weight	56.7		13.3	-23.46%			
7	recommended weight	63		7	-11.11%			
8								
9								
10								
11								
12								
13								

BMI

Ready   End Mode   100%

FIGURE 1–7

THE QUICK CALENDAR

To create a simple calendar, use the Fill command in combination with a formula.

▶ **To Create a Quick Calendar:**

1. Select cell A1 and type the following formula: **=TODAY()**.
2. Select cell B1 and type the following formula: **=A1+1**.
3. Select cells B1:G1.
4. From the **Edit** menu, select **Fill** and **Right**.
5. In cell A2, type **=A1**.
6. Drag the bottom-right corner of cell A2 with the mouse cursor rightward through cell E2.
7. Press **<Ctrl+1>** to show the dialog Format Cells.
8. Select **Custom** under Category.
9. Enter the custom format **ddd** and press **OK**.

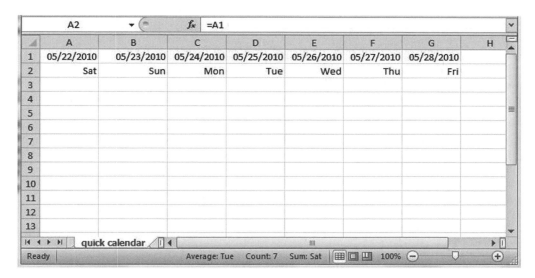

FIGURE 1–8

DESIGN YOUR OWN TO-DO LIST

Generate your own to-do list by entering the hours of the day in column A and your daily tasks in column B.

▶ **To Generate Your Own To-Do List:**

1. Select cell B1 and type **=TODAY()**.
2. Select cell A3 and type **7:00**.
3. Select cell A4 and type the following formula: **=A3+(1/24)**.
4. Select cells A4:A13.
5. Go to the **Editing** group and choose the downward arrow.

6. Click on **Down**.

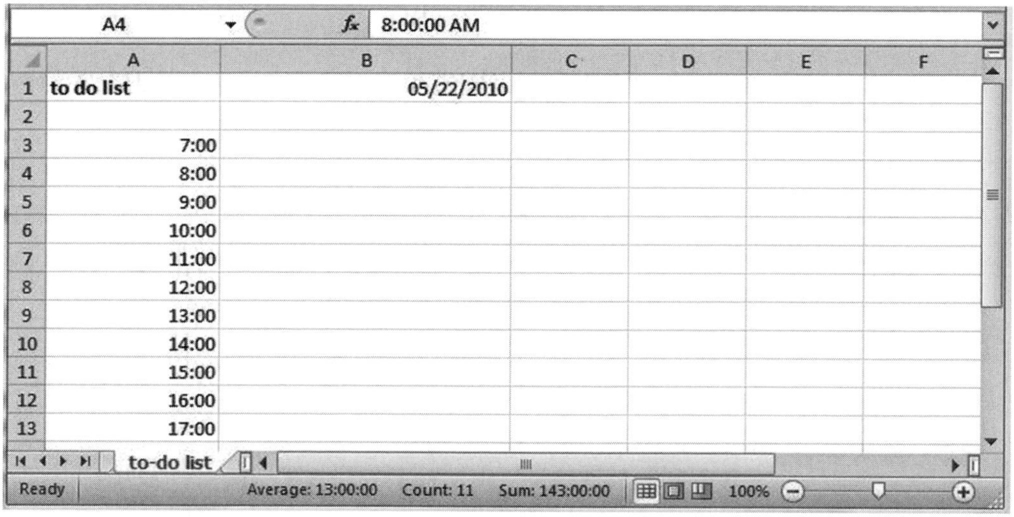

FIGURE 1–9

NOTE   *To get increments of half an hour, use the formula =A3+(1/48). To display column A as shown in Figure 1–9, select Cells from the Home tab, click the Number group, select Time from the Category list, select 1:30 PM, and click OK.*

INCREMENTING ROW NUMBERS

Standard row numbering in Excel is often used, but you can also create your own numbering system in a table, such as incrementing by 10 as described below.

▶ **To Increment Row Numbers by 10:**

1. Select cell A2 and type **0**.
2. Select cell A3 and type the following formula: **=A2+10**.
3. Select cells A3:A12.
4. Select **Editing** from the ribbon, choose the downward button, and select **Down**.

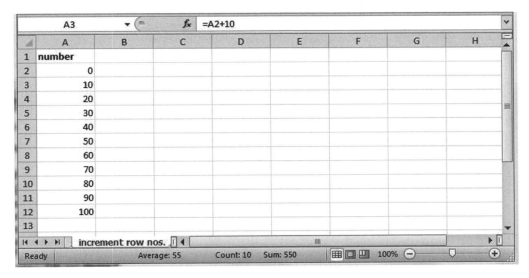

FIGURE 1–10

NOTE *If the value of cell A2 is changed, the values in all other cells change, too.*

CONVERT NEGATIVE VALUES TO POSITIVE

A worksheet contains negative values. To convert all of the negative values to positive values, perform the following steps.

▶ **To Convert Negative Values to Positive Values:**

1. Enter a series of negative values in cells B1:B10.
2. Select cell C1 and type **-1**.
3. Copy this cell.
4. Select cells B1:B10.
5. In the **Home** tab, in the **Clipboard** group, click **Paste** and then click **Paste special**.
6. In the **Paste Special** dialog box, under **Paste**, select **Multiply**.
7. Click **OK**.

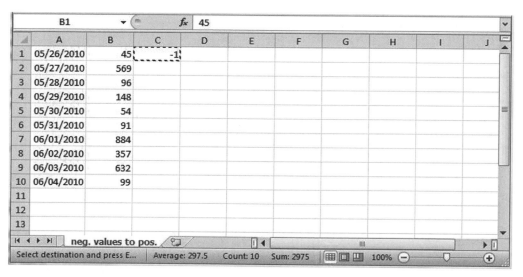

FIGURE 1–11

NOTE   *After this, C1 can be cleared.*

CALCULATE TAXES

In this exercise, tax on an item has to be calculated. We can also find the original price given the tax rate and the final price.

▶ **To Calculate the Price with Tax:**

    1. Select cell A2 and type **8%**.
    2. Select cell B2 and type **120**.
    3. Select cell C2 and type the following formula: **=B2+B2*A2**.

▶ **To Calculate the Original Price:**

    1. Select cell A4 and type **8%**.
    2. Select cell C4 and type **129.60**.
    3. Select cell B4 and type the following formula: **=C4/(1+A4)**.

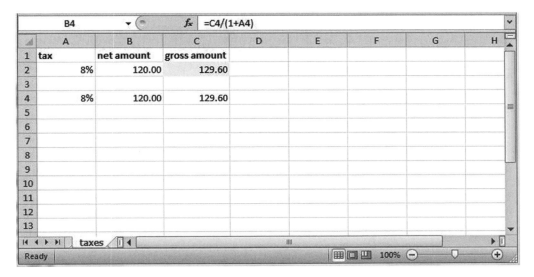

FIGURE 1–12

COMBINE TEXT AND NUMBERS

In this example, we want to combine text and numbers. Use the & operator to accomplish this.

▶ **To Combine Cells Containing Text and Numbers:**

1. Select cell B1 and type **computers**.
2. Select cell B2 and type **5**.
3. Select cell B4 and type the following formula:
   ="You ordered" & B2 & " " & B1 & "today!".

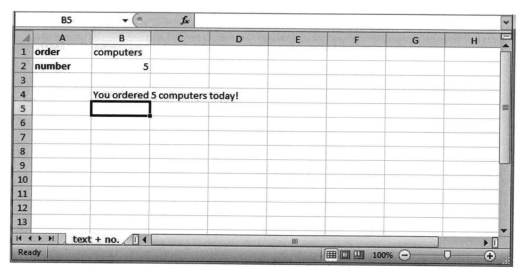

FIGURE 1–13

NOTE *Each cell reference must be placed between & operators, and additional text must be surrounded by quotation marks.*

COMBINE TEXT AND DATE

Excel has a problem combining cells that contain text and dates. This results in the date showing up as a number value because Excel has lost the format. To get the desired result, use the following workaround.

▶ **To Combine Text and Date:**

1. Select cell A1 and type **actual status**.
2. Select cell D1 and type the following formula: =**TODAY**().
3. Select cell A3 and type the following formula: =**A1& " " &TEXT(D1, "MM/DD/YYYY")**.

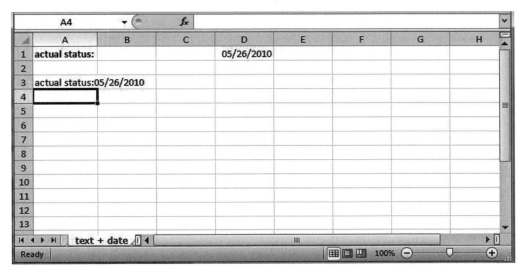

FIGURE 1–14

COMBINE TEXT AND TIME

This example shows how to combine text and time successfully.

▶ **To Combine Text and Time:**

1. Select cell A5 and type **shutdown**.
2. Select cell D5 and press **<Ctrl+Shift+:>** to insert the current time.
3. Select cell A7 and type the following formula: **= "Today" & A5 & "at" & TEXT(D5,"hh:mm PM")**.

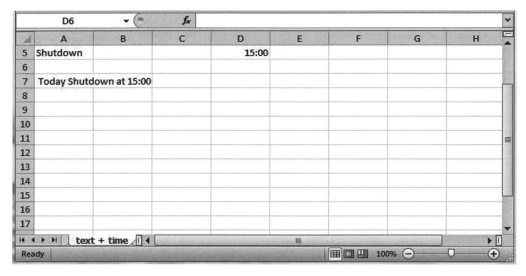

FIGURE 1–15

A SPECIAL RANKING LIST

You can use Excel to generate a special ranking list. Let's say a worksheet contains a few values, some of which are repeated. To rank the list in a particular order, follow these instructions.

▶ **To Rank a List in a Particular Order:**

1. Select cell A1 and type **Value**.
2. In cells A2:A13, enter values from 10 to 20.
3. Select cell A2.
4. In the **Home** tab click on the **AZ** icon in the **Editing** group.
5. Select **Sort Smallest to Largest**.
6. Select cell B2 and type **1**.
7. Select cells B3:B13 and type the following formula: **=B2+(A2<A3)**.
8. Press **<Ctrl+Enter>**.

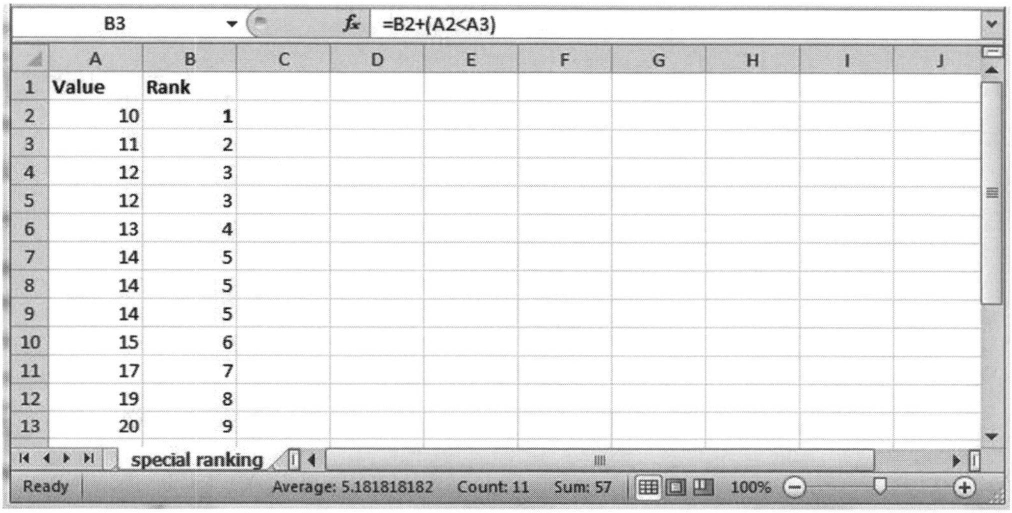

| | B3 | | ▾ | ● | | *fx* | =B2+(A2<A3) | | | | | | | ▾ |

◢	A	B	C	D	E	F	G	H	I	J
1	Value	Rank								
2	10	1								
3	11	2								
4	12	3								
5	12	3								
6	13	4								
7	14	5								
8	14	5								
9	14	5								
10	15	6								
11	17	7								
12	19	8								
13	20	9								

| ◄ ◄ ► ►| | special ranking | ▌◄ | | | | | |
| Ready | | | Average: 5.181818182 | Count: 11 | Sum: 57 | | 100% | ⊖ | ⊕ |

FIGURE 1–16

DETERMINE THE AVERAGE OUTPUT

In a worksheet, the start and end production dates of a machine are given, as well as the output during this period. How do you calculate the average daily production?

▶ **To Calculate the Average Daily Production:**

1. Select cell B1 and type **10/18/2004**.
2. Select cell B2 and type **11/13/2002**.
3. Type **55,900** in cell B3.
4. Select cell B5 and type the following formula: **=B3/(B1-B2)**.

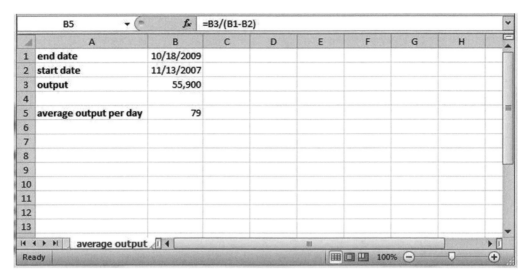

FIGURE 1–17

STOCKS — GAINS AND LOSSES

Imagine your stocks have fallen 11.5% in value in one day. What is the percentage of gain that will be needed the next day to compensate for the loss?

▶ **To Determine the Gain/Loss of a Stock:**

1. Select cell C2 and type **1000**.
2. Select cell B3 and type **11.50%**.
3. Select cell C3 and type the following formula: **=C2-(C2*$B$3)**.
4. Select cell B4 and type the following formula: **=B3/(1-B3)**.
5. Select cell C4 and type the following formula: **=C3+(C3*$B$4)**.
6. Be sure to format column C as Currency.

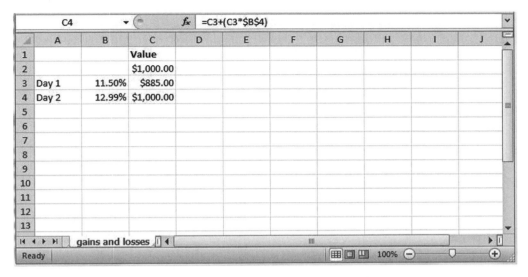

FIGURE 1–18

EVALUATE PROFITABILITY

You have some products for sale and you want to know which one is the most profitable. Use conditional formatting for this purpose.

▶ **To Determine the Most Profitable Product:**

1. In a new worksheet, type the cost of each product in column B and the corresponding price in column C.
2. Select cells D2:D6 and type the following formula: **=1-(B2/C2)**.
3. Press **<Ctrl+Enter>**.
4. In the **Home** tab, in the **Styles** group, click the arrow next to **Conditional Formatting**.
5. Select **New Formatting Rule** and enter the following formula: **=D2=max($D$2:$D$6)**.

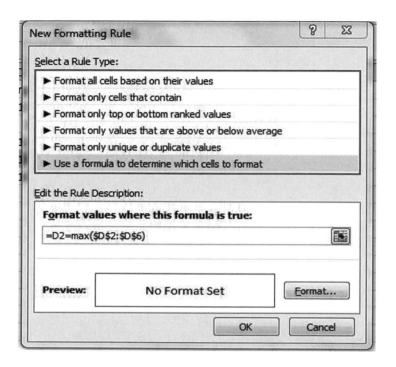

6. Click **Format**, select the **Fill** tab, choose a color, and click **OK**.

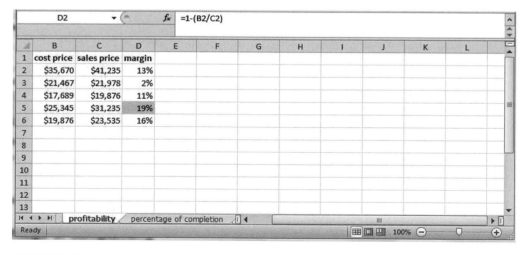

FIGURE 1–19

NOTE   *Product pr04 has the greatest profit margin as calculated in column D. The conditional formatting highlights the cell automatically.*

DETERMINE PERCENTAGE OF COMPLETION

To manage a project it is necessary to determine the percentage of completion. This can be accomplished with the following calculation.

▶ **To Calculate Percentage of Completion:**

1. In a worksheet, enter data in columns A, B, and D as shown in Figure 1–20.
2. Select cell E2 and type **=B2+B3**.
3. Select cell E3 and enter the target value of **200**.
4. In cell E5, type the formula **=E3-E2** to get the difference between the target and the number already produced.
5. Calculate the percentage of missing products in cell E6 with this formula: **=1-E2/E3**.
6. Select cell E8 and calculate the percentage of production by using this formula: **=100%-E6**.

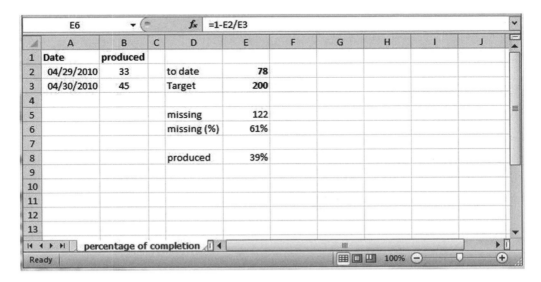

FIGURE 1–20

CONVERT MILES PER HOUR TO KM PER HOUR

A worksheet contains speed in miles per hour. To convert the data to kilometers per hour, use the following calculation.

▶ **To Convert Miles Per Hour to Kilometers Per Hour:**

1. In a worksheet, enter the data shown in Figure 1–21.
2. Select cell D1 and enter the conversion value **0.621371**.
3. Select cells B2:B8 and type the following formula: **=A2/$D$1**.
4. Press **<Ctrl+Enter>**.

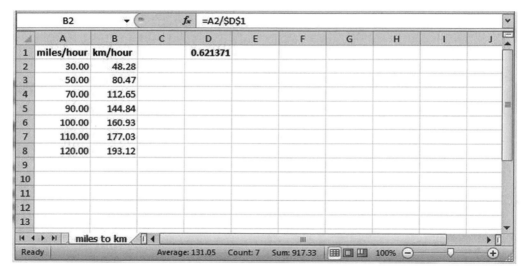

FIGURE 1–21

NOTE *To convert the other way around, from kilometers per hour to miles per hour, use the formula =B2*$D$1.*

CONVERT FEET PER MINUTE TO METERS PER SECOND

A worksheet contains speed data. To convert feet per minute to meters per second, use the calculation described as follows.

▶ **To Convert Feet/Minute to Meters/Second:**

1. In a worksheet, enter the data shown in Figure 1–22, or use your own data.
2. Select cell D1 and enter the conversion value **196.858144**.
3. Select cells B2:B10 and type the following formula: **=A2/$D$1**.
4. Press **<Ctrl+Enter>**.

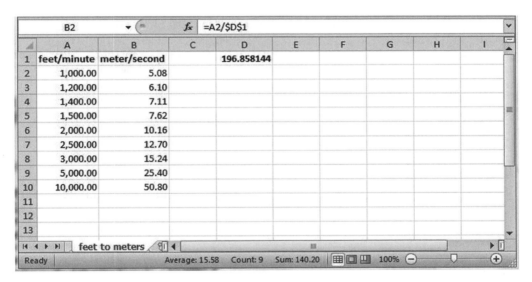

	A	B	C	D	E	F	G	H	I
1	feet/minute	meter/second		196.858144					
2	1,000.00	5.08							
3	1,200.00	6.10							
4	1,400.00	7.11							
5	1,500.00	7.62							
6	2,000.00	10.16							
7	2,500.00	12.70							
8	3,000.00	15.24							
9	5,000.00	25.40							
10	10,000.00	50.80							
11									
12									
13									

FIGURE 1–22

NOTE *To convert the other way around, from meters per second to feet per minute, use the formula =B2*$D$1.*

CONVERT LITERS TO BARRELS, GALLONS, QUARTS, AND PINTS

In a worksheet, data is input as liters. To convert the value to different scales, use the following formulas.

▶ **To Convert Liters to Barrels, Gallons, Quarts, and Pints:**

1. Select cell B1 and enter **150**.
2. Select cell B3 and type the formula **=$B$1/158.98722** to convert to barrels.
3. Select cell B4 and type the formula **=$B$1/3.78541** to convert to gallons.
4. Select cell B5 and type the formula **=$B$1/1.101241** to convert to quarts.
5. Select cell B6 and type the formula **=$B$1/0.5506** to convert to pints.

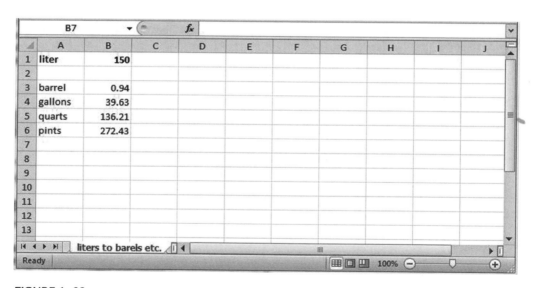

FIGURE 1–23

CONVERT FROM FAHRENHEIT TO CELSIUS

To convert temperatures from Fahrenheit to Celsius, you can use the formula =(Fahrenheit–32)*5/9, or you can use the calculation described here.

▶ **To Convert from Fahrenheit to Celsius:**

1. In a worksheet, enter a few temperatures in Fahrenheit in column A.
2. Select cells B2:B14 and type the following formula: **=(A2*1.8)+32**.
3. Press **<Ctrl+Enter>**.

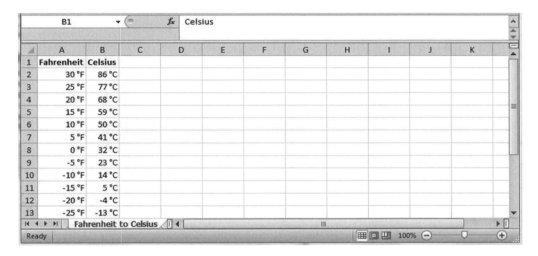

	B1			f_x	Celsius						
	A	B	C	D	E	F	G	H	I	J	K
1	Fahrenheit	Celsius									
2	30 °F	86 °C									
3	25 °F	77 °C									
4	20 °F	68 °C									
5	15 °F	59 °C									
6	10 °F	50 °C									
7	5 °F	41 °C									
8	0 °F	32 °C									
9	-5 °F	23 °C									
10	-10 °F	14 °C									
11	-15 °F	5 °C									
12	-20 °F	-4 °C									
13	-25 °F	-13 °C									

FIGURE 1–24

NOTE *You can create a user-defined format to insert the degree sign (°). Go to the Format menu, and select Cells, Number, Custom. In the Type box, select General and press OK. Select a cell, hold down the <Alt> key, type 0176 on the numeric keypad, then release <Alt> and type either "F" or "C" without the quotes.*

CONVERT FROM CELSIUS TO FAHRENHEIT

To convert temperatures from Celsius to Fahrenheit, you can use the formula = (Celsius *9/5)+32, or you can use the calculation described here.

▶ **To Convert from Celsius to Fahrenheit:**

1. In a worksheet, enter a few temperatures in Celsius in column A.
2. Select cells B2:B14 and type the following formula: **=(A2-32)/1.8**.
3. Press **<Ctrl+Enter>**.

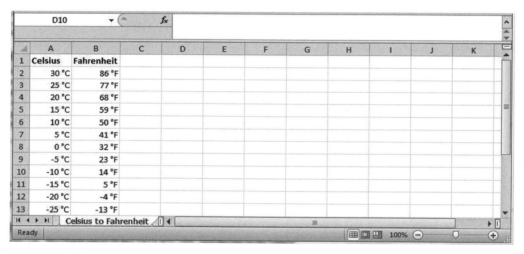

FIGURE 1–25

| | NOTE | *You can create a user-defined format to insert the degree sign (°). Go to the Format menu, and select Cells, Number, Custom. In the Type box, select General and press OK. Select a cell, hold down the <Alt> key, type 0176 on the numeric keypad, then release <Alt> and type either "F" or "C" without the quotes.* |

CALCULATION WITH PERCENTAGE

Let's say you want to buy a new car. The listed price of the car is $25,500, and the tax to be added is 8%. After negotiating a sales discount of 10%, the final price has to be calculated.

▶ **To Calculate the Final Price:**

1. Select cell B1 and enter **25500**.
2. Select cell B2 to enter the tax rate of **8%**.
3. Select cell B3 and enter the discount rate of **10%**.
4. Select cell B5 and type the following formula: **=B1*(1+B2)*(1-B3)**.

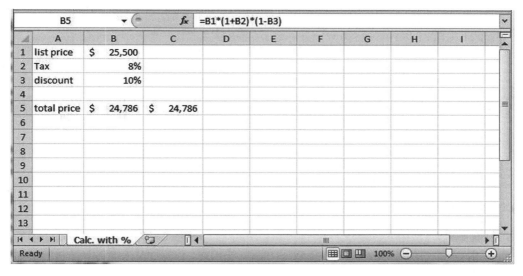

FIGURE 1–26

NOTE *As you see in cell C5 in Figure 1–26, the formula =B1*(1–B3)*(1+B2) also works. The order of multiplication does not matter.*

MONITOR THE DAILY PRODUCTION PLAN

A worksheet is used to monitor daily production. The target is defined as 1,500 pieces per day. To calculate the percentage produced of the daily goal, perform the following steps.

▶ **To Monitor Daily Production:**

1. Select cell B1 and enter the predefined target: **1500**.
2. Select cells C4:C11 and type the following formula: **=B4/$B$1**.
3. Press **<Ctrl+Enter>**.
4. In the **Home** tab go to the **Number** group and click on the % sign.
5. In the same group click the lowest left button "**Increase Decimal**" twice.
    That way you set decimal places to 2.

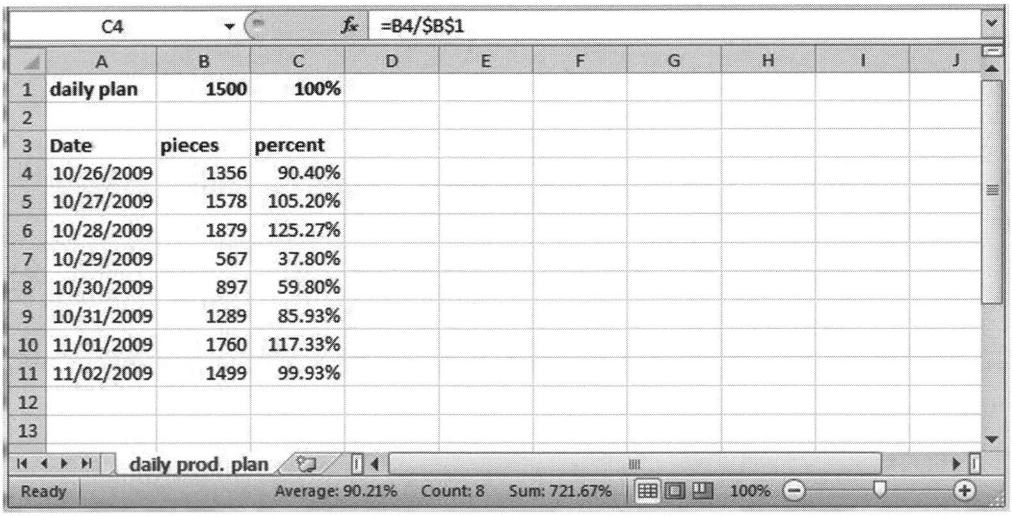

	C4	▾		fx	=B4/$B$1					
	A	B	C	D	E	F	G	H	I	J
1	daily plan	1500	100%							
2										
3	Date	pieces	percent							
4	10/26/2009	1356	90.40%							
5	10/27/2009	1578	105.20%							
6	10/28/2009	1879	125.27%							
7	10/29/2009	567	37.80%							
8	10/30/2009	897	59.80%							
9	10/31/2009	1289	85.93%							
10	11/01/2009	1760	117.33%							
11	11/02/2009	1499	99.93%							
12										
13										

daily prod. plan

Ready   Average: 90.21%   Count: 8   Sum: 721.67%   100%

FIGURE 1–27

CALCULATE THE NUMBER OF HOURS BETWEEN TWO DATES

Excel has a problem calculating the difference between two dates in hours. Try this by opening a new worksheet and typing the starting date including time (3/20/2006 13:42) in cell A2. In cell B2, type the end date and time (3/24/2006 7:42). Then subtract B2 from A2 in cell C2. The calculation generates 1/3/1900 18:00, which is incorrect. If your result displays #####, you'll need to extend the width of column C. Cells A2 and B2 have to be formatted as follows:

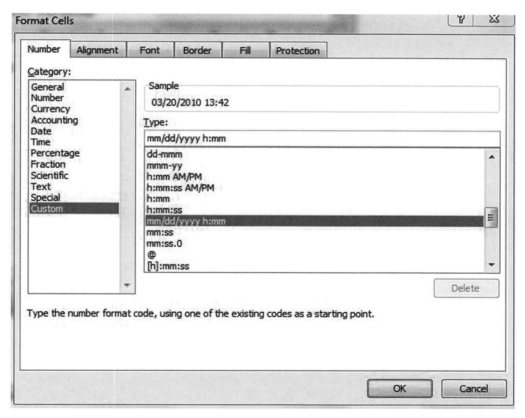

FIGURE 1–28

▶ **To Properly Format the Difference in Hours:**

1. Select cell C2.
2. In the **Home** tab go to the **Number** group and click on the right bottom arrow.
3. In the **Number** tab click on **Custom** from Category.
4. Type the custom format **[hh]:mm**.
5. Click **OK**. This gives the correct answer.

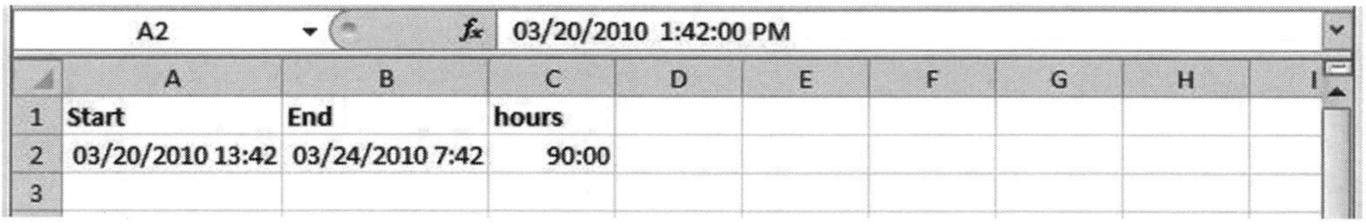

	A2			f_x	03/20/2010 1:42:00 PM					
	A	B	C	D	E	F	G	H	I
1	Start	End	hours						
2	03/20/2010 13:42	03/24/2010 7:42	90:00						
3									

FIGURE 1–29

DETERMINE THE PRICE PER POUND

A worksheet lists food products in column A. Column B shows the corresponding weight in pounds, and column C contains the total price. What is the price per pound?

▶ **To Calculate the Price per Pound:**

1. In a workshop, enter the data shown in Figure 1–30, or use your own data.
2. Select cells D2:D8.
3. Type the following formula: **=C2/B2**.
4. Press **<Ctrl+Enter>**.

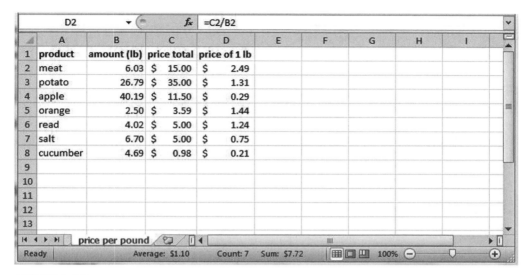

	D2			f_x	=C2/B2					
	A	B	C	D	E	F	G	H	I	
1	product	amount (lb)	price total	price of 1 lb						
2	meat	6.03	$ 15.00	$ 2.49						
3	potato	26.79	$ 35.00	$ 1.31						
4	apple	40.19	$ 11.50	$ 0.29						
5	orange	2.50	$ 3.59	$ 1.44						
6	read	4.02	$ 5.00	$ 1.24						
7	salt	6.70	$ 5.00	$ 0.75						
8	cucumber	4.69	$ 0.98	$ 0.21						
9										
10										
11										
12										
13										

price per pound

Ready   Average: $1.10   Count: 7   Sum: $7.72   100%

FIGURE 1–30

DETERMINE HOW MANY PIECES TO PUT IN A BOX

Let's say a container can hold 10 boxes and each box can hold up to 300 items. The customer requires a total of 500 items. How many items must be packed in each box, given a number of boxes?

▶ **To Determine the Number of Pieces in Each Box:**

1. Select cell A2 and enter **10**.
2. Select cell B2 and enter **50**.
3. Select cell D2 and type =**B2*A2**.
4. In cells A4:A7 enter the number of boxes from 2 to 9.
5. Select cells B4:B7 and type the following formula: =**$B$2*($A$2/A4)**.
6. Press **<Ctrl+Enter>**.
7. Select cells D4:D7 and type the formula =**B4*A4**.
8. Press **<Ctrl+Enter>**.

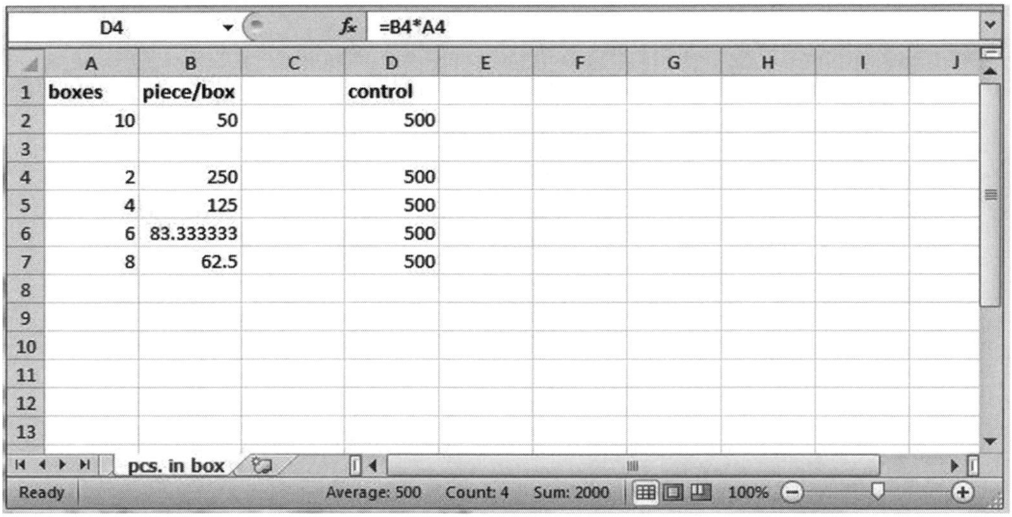

			fx	=B4*A4							

	A	B	C	D	E	F	G	H	I	J
1	boxes	piece/box		control						
2	10	50		500						
3										
4	2	250		500						
5	4	125		500						
6	6	83.333333		500						
7	8	62.5		500						
8										
9										
10										
11										
12										
13										

pcs. in box

Ready   Average: 500   Count: 4   Sum: 2000   100%

FIGURE 1–31

NOTE   *Some entries in column A may result in a number with a decimal point in column B. These will require additional calculations on your part to determine exactly how many pieces fit in the given number of boxes so that the customer receives exactly 500 pieces.*

CALCULATE THE MANPOWER REQUIRED FOR A PROJECT

The number of employees needed for a project has to be calculated. To do this, enter the available time (14 days) for the project in cell A2. Cell B2 contains the number of working hours per day (8.5). Cell C2 shows the current number of employees. Now we can calculate how many employees are needed to reduce the project duration or change the number of daily working hours of the employees.

▶ **To Calculate the Desired Number of Employees:**

1. Enter different combinations of desired days in column A and daily working hours in column B.
2. Select cell E2 and insert the formula **=A2*B2*C2** to calculate the total working hours of the project.

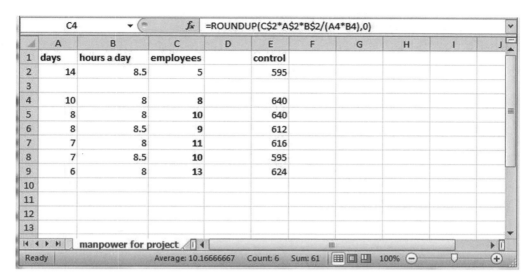

	C4			f_x	=ROUNDUP(C$2*A$2*B$2/(A4*B4),0)					
	A	B	C	D	E	F	G	H	I	J
1	days	hours a day	employees		control					
2	14	8.5	5		595					
3										
4	10	8	8		640					
5	8	8	10		640					
6	8	8.5	9		612					
7	7	8	11		616					
8	7	8.5	10		595					
9	6	8	13		624					
10										
11										
12										
13										

manpower for project

Ready   Average: 10.16666667   Count: 6   Sum: 61   100%

FIGURE 1–32

3. Select cells C4:C9 and type the following formula:
   =ROUNDUP(C$2*A$2*B$2/(A4*B4),0).
4. Press **<Ctrl+Enter>**.
5. Select cells E4:E9 and type the following formula: **=A4*B4*C4**.
6. Press **<Ctrl+Enter>**.

DISTRIBUTE SALES

In a company each sale is assigned to a particular salesperson. The sale of 30 pieces totals $199,000. Each salesperson sold an individual amount of goods. Calculate the corresponding sales for each person.

▶ **To Calculate the Total Amount of Sales for Each Employee:**

1. Select cell B1 and enter the total amount of sales: **$199,000**.
2. Select cell C1 and enter the total amount of sold goods: **30**.
3. In columns A and B, enter the names of the salespeople and the number of pieces they sold.
4. Select cells C5:C11 and type the following formula: **=B5*$B$1/$B$2**.
5. Press **<Ctrl+Enter>**.

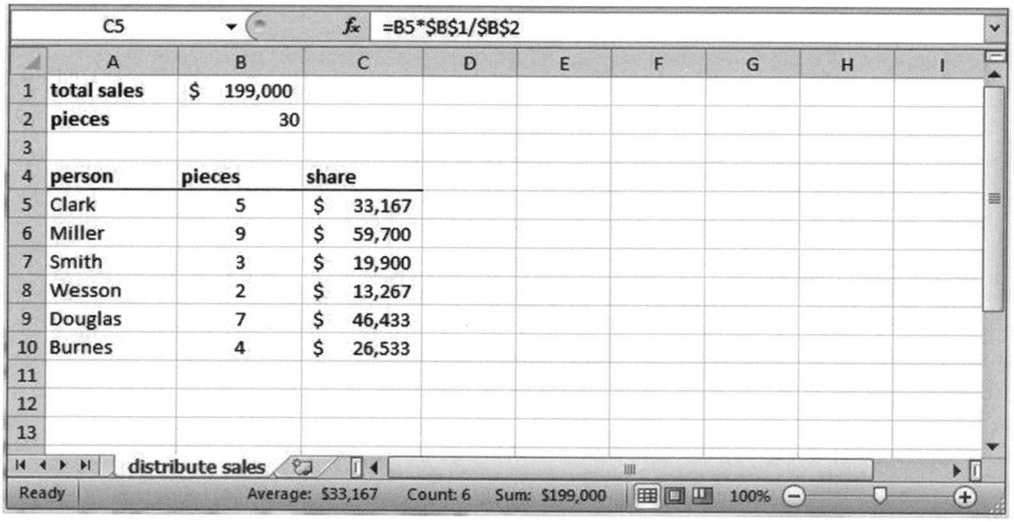

	C5		▾	fx	=B5*$B$1/$B$2					
	A	B	C	D	E	F	G	H	I
1	total sales	$ 199,000							
2	pieces	30							
3									
4	person	pieces	share						
5	Clark	5	$ 33,167						
6	Miller	9	$ 59,700						
7	Smith	3	$ 19,900						
8	Wesson	2	$ 13,267						
9	Douglas	7	$ 46,433						
10	Burnes	4	$ 26,533						
11									
12									
13									

distribute sales

Ready   Average: $33,167   Count: 6   Sum: $199,000   100%

FIGURE 1–33

NOTE   *Check out the AutoSum of the selected range in the status bar.*

CALCULATE YOUR NET INCOME

People often talk about their gross income. To calculate net income, it is necessary to consider the tax percentage using the following calculation.

▶ **To Calculate Net Income:**

1. Select cell B1 and enter the tax as a percentage: **33%**.
2. In cell B2, enter the gross income: **$3500**.
3. Select cell B3 and type the formula **=B2*B1** to calculate the tax amount.
4. Determine the net income in cell B4 with the formula **=B2-B3**.

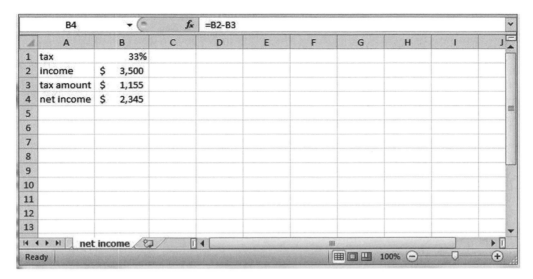

FIGURE 1–34

NOTE *The amounts in cells B1 and B2 can be changed.*

CALCULATE THE PERCENTAGE OF PRICE REDUCTION

A digital camera is on sale. The camera's original price is $250, but it is now available for $131. What is the percentage of the reduction?

▶ **To Calculate the Price Reduction as a Percentage:**

1. Select cell B2 and enter the original price: **$250**.
2. In cell B3, enter the sales price: **$131**.
3. Calculate the absolute difference in cell B4 with the formula **=B2-B3**.
4. Determine the percentage of price reduction in cell B5 using the following formula: **=B4/B2**.
5. Go to the **Number** group in the **Home** tab and select **Percentage** in the uppermost category.

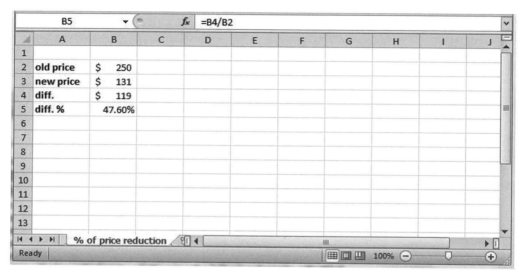

FIGURE 1–35

DIVIDING AND DOUBLING EVERY THREE HOURS

In an experiment, bacteria divides and doubles every three hours. How many bacteria will there be at the end of one day (24 hours)?

▶ **To Calculate the Total Amount of Bacteria After 24 Hours:**

1. Enter values from 1 to 4 in cells B2:B8.
2. Select cells C2:C8 and type the following formula: **=A2^(24/B2)**.
3. Press **<Ctrl+Enter>**.
4. Press Ctrl+1 and select the **Number** tab and **Number** in Category.
5. Set Decimal places to **0**, and tick the **Use 1000 Separator** check box.
6. Click **OK**.

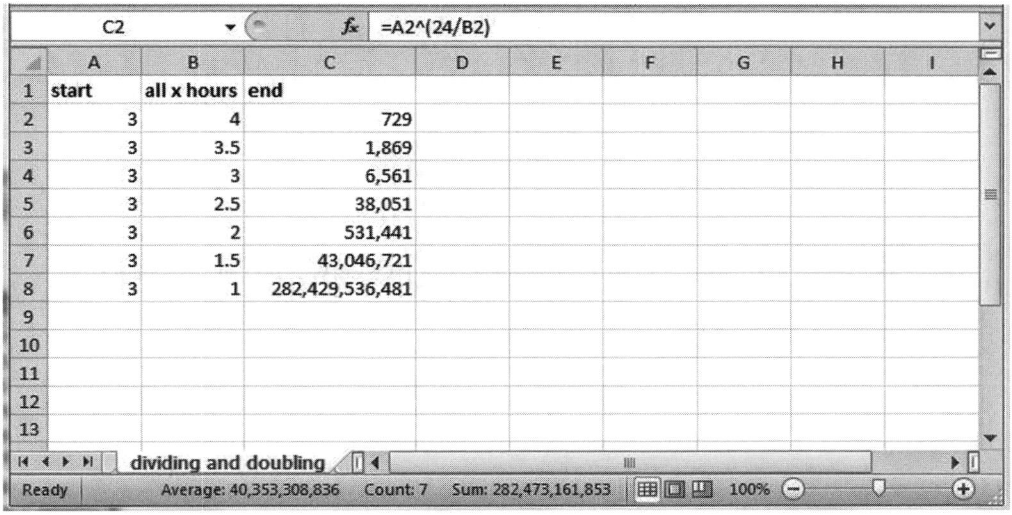

	C2			f_x	=A2^(24/B2)					
	A	B	C	D	E	F	G	H	I	
1	start	all x hours	end							
2	3	4	729							
3	3	3.5	1,869							
4	3	3	6,561							
5	3	2.5	38,051							
6	3	2	531,441							
7	3	1.5	43,046,721							
8	3	1	282,429,536,481							
9										
10										
11										
12										
13										

dividing and doubling

Ready   Average: 40,353,308,836   Count: 7   Sum: 282,473,161,853   100%

FIGURE 1–36

NOTE   *To insert the ^ character, press the <^> key on the keyboard followed by a <Space>.*

CALCULATE THE AVERAGE SPEED

In this example, someone travels from New York to Los Angeles with an average speed of 90 miles per hour. On the way back, the average speed is 75 miles per hour. What is the overall average speed?

To calculate the average speed, the speed in each direction has to be taken into consideration.

▶ **To Calculate the Overall Average Speed:**

      1. In cell C2, enter **90**.

      2. In cell C3, enter **75**.

      3. In cell C4, type the following formula: **=(C2+C3)/2**.

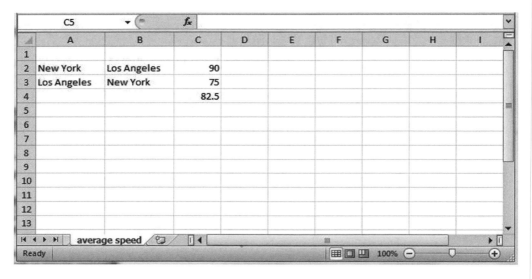

FIGURE 1–37

Chapter 2 — LOGICAL FUNCTIONS

USE THE AND FUNCTION TO COMPARE TWO COLUMNS

Two columns in a worksheet have to be evaluated. If the value in column A is greater than 20 and the value in column B is greater than 25, both values are valid.

▶ To Compare Two Columns:

1. In cells A2:A10, enter values from 1 to 100.
2. In cells B2:B10, enter values from 1 to 100.
3. Select cells C2:C10 and type the following formula: **=AND(A2>20,B2>25)**.
4. Press **<Ctrl+Enter>**.

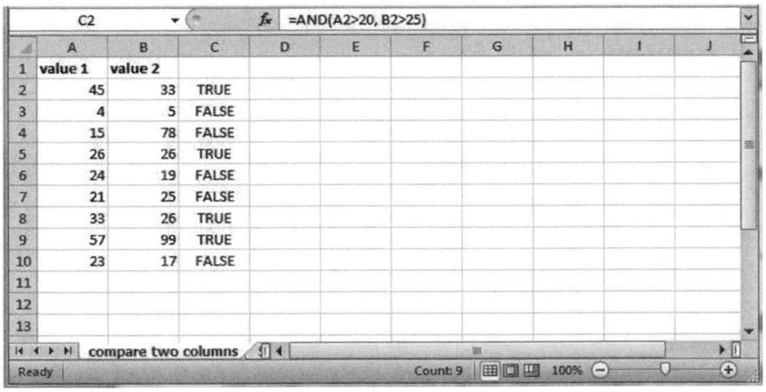

	A	B	C
1	value 1	value 2	
2	45	33	TRUE
3	4	5	FALSE
4	15	78	FALSE
5	26	26	TRUE
6	24	19	FALSE
7	21	25	FALSE
8	33	26	TRUE
9	57	99	TRUE
10	23	17	FALSE

FIGURE 2–1

> NOTE *If both criteria are valid, Excel shows the value as TRUE; otherwise, it is FALSE.*

USE THE AND **FUNCTION TO SHOW SALES FOR A SPECIFIC PERIOD OF TIME**

This example checks all rows for a specific time period using the AND function. The function returns TRUE if the arguments are TRUE and FALSE if one or more arguments are FALSE.

> NOTE *Up to 30 conditions can be used in one formula.*

▶ **To Show Sales in a Period of Time:**

1. Select cell B1 and enter the start date.
2. Select cell B2 and enter the end date.
3. The range A5:A16 contains dates from 09/13/04 to 09/21/04.
4. The range B5:B16 contains sales amounts.
5. Select cells C5:C16 and type the following formula:
   =AND(A5>=$B$1,A5<=$B$2).
6. Press **<Ctrl+Enter>**.

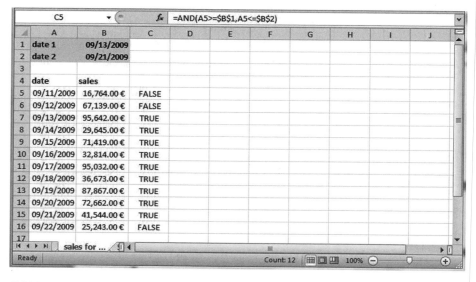

FIGURE 2–2

USE THE OR **FUNCTION TO CHECK CELLS FOR TEXT**

A worksheet contains several words in column A. Each row has to be checked for the words "new" or "actual" in column A. The OR function is used for this task. The function returns TRUE if either argument is true and FALSE if the arguments are not true.

NOTE   *Up to 30 conditions can be used in one formula.*

▶ **To Use the OR Function to Check for Two or More Criteria:**

1. Enter in range A2:A11 words like "new," "actual," and "old."
2. Select cells B2:B11 and type the following formula:
   =OR(A2="New",A2="actual").
3. Press **<Ctrl+Enter>**.

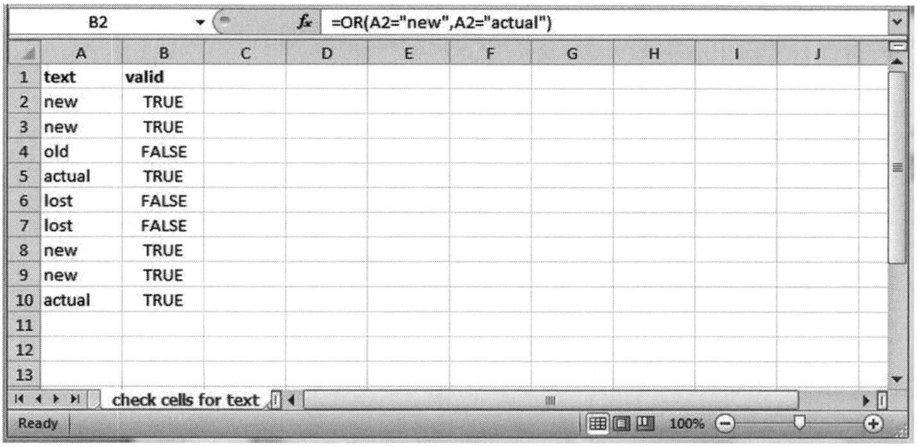

	A	B	C	D	E	F	G	H	I	J
1	text	valid								
2	new	TRUE								
3	new	TRUE								
4	old	FALSE								
5	actual	TRUE								
6	lost	FALSE								
7	lost	FALSE								
8	new	TRUE								
9	new	TRUE								
10	actual	TRUE								
11										
12										
13										

B2   *fx* =OR(A2="new",A2="actual")

check cells for text

Ready   100%

FIGURE 2–3

USE THE OR **FUNCTION TO CHECK CELLS FOR NUMBERS**

A worksheet contains several values in column A. Each row has to be evaluated based on certain criteria in column A. The OR function is used for this task. The function returns TRUE if any argument is TRUE and FALSE if all arguments are FALSE.

NOTE *Up to 30 conditions can be used in one formula.*

▶ **To Check for Two or More Criteria:**

1. Enter in range A2:A12 values from –43 to 100.
2. Select cells B2:B12 and type the following formula:
   =OR(A2=1,A2>=99,A2<0).
3. Press **<Ctrl+Enter>**.

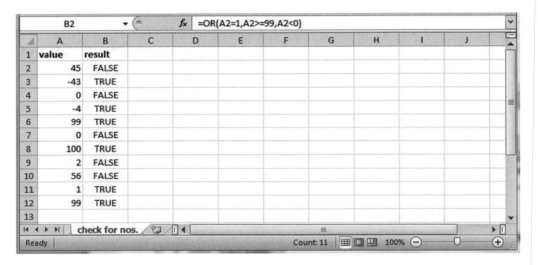

	B2	▾	*fx*	=OR(A2=1,A2>=99,A2<0)							
	A	B	C	D	E	F	G	H	I	J	
1	value	result									
2	45	FALSE									
3	-43	TRUE									
4	0	FALSE									
5	-4	TRUE									
6	99	TRUE									
7	0	FALSE									
8	100	TRUE									
9	2	FALSE									
10	56	FALSE									
11	1	TRUE									
12	99	TRUE									
13											

check for nos.   Count: 11   100%   Ready

FIGURE 2–4

USE THE IF FUNCTION TO COMPARE COLUMNS AND RETURN A SPECIFIC RESULT

As shown in earlier examples, Excel returns the value TRUE or FALSE when using the OR and AND functions. The IF function can also be used to conduct conditional tests on values and formulas.

This example compares two columns and shows the result in column C.

▶ **To Return Specific Text After Comparing Values:**

1. Enter in range A2:A12 values from 1 to 1000.
2. Enter in range B2:B12 values from 1 to 1000.

3. Select cells C2:C12 and type the following formula:
=IF(A2>=B2,"Column A is greater or equal","Column B is greater").
4. Press **<Ctrl+Enter>**.

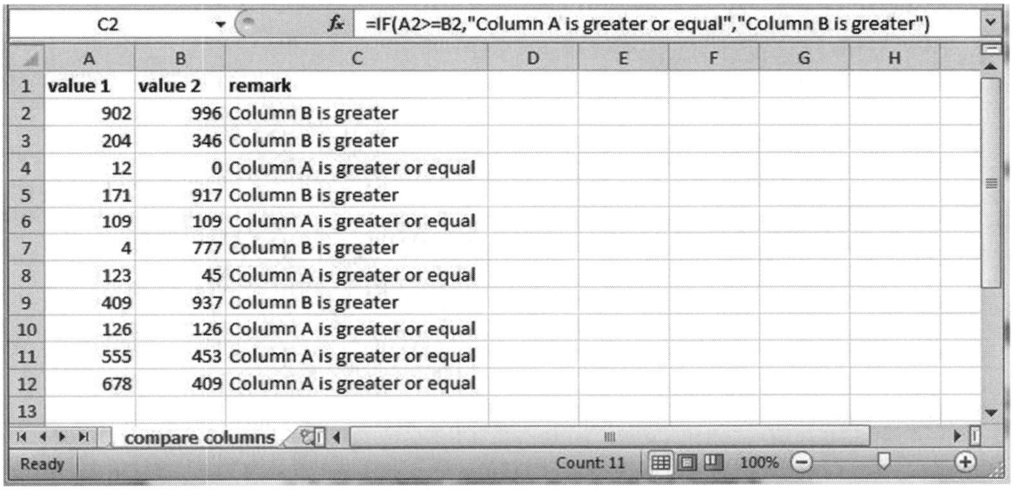

	C2		▼	fx	=IF(A2>=B2,"Column A is greater or equal","Column B is greater")				
	A	B	C	D	E	F	G	H	
1	value 1	value 2	remark						
2	902	996	Column B is greater						
3	204	346	Column B is greater						
4	12	0	Column A is greater or equal						
5	171	917	Column B is greater						
6	109	109	Column A is greater or equal						
7	4	777	Column B is greater						
8	123	45	Column A is greater or equal						
9	409	937	Column B is greater						
10	126	126	Column A is greater or equal						
11	555	453	Column A is greater or equal						
12	678	409	Column A is greater or equal						
13									

compare columns · Ready · Count: 11 · 100%

FIGURE 2–5

USE THE IF FUNCTION TO CHECK FOR LARGER, EQUIVALENT, OR SMALLER VALUES

In the previous example, two different messages were used as the result for comparing values. To check for three conditions in column A and present the result as "Column A is larger," "equal," or "Column A is smaller," perform the following steps.

▶ **To Compare Columns and Show the Result:**

1. Copy the previous example.
2. Select cells C2:C12 and type the following formula:
=IF(A2>B2,"Column A is larger",IF(A2=B2,"equal", "Column A is smaller")).
3. Press **<Ctrl+Enter>**.

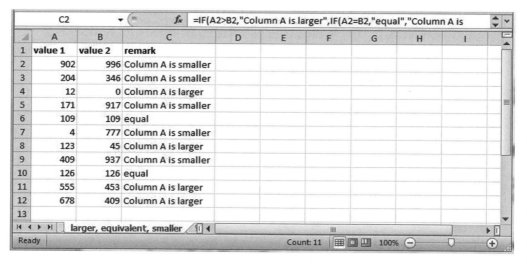

FIGURE 2–6

NOTE *Up to seven IF functions can be combined in one cell. To combine more than seven functions, use the customized solution near the end of this chapter.*

COMBINE IF WITH AND TO CHECK SEVERAL CONDITIONS

In this example, Excel evaluates which condition meets the criteria and returns the result in the same row.

▶ **To Combine the IF and AND Functions:**

1. Copy the content of cells C2 to C5 in Figure 2–7 to your Excel table.
2. Frame the table as shown in the screenshot.
3. Select cell A2 and enter any kind of sales value, e.g., 120.
4. In cell B2, type the following formula:
   =IF(AND($A$2<=100,$A$2),"Sales value is","").
5. In cell B3, type the following formula: **=IF(AND($A$2>100,$A$2<= 150),"Sales value is","").**
6. In cell B4, type the following formula: **=IF(AND($A$2>150,$A$2<= 200),"Sales value is","").**
7. In cell B5, type the following formula: **=IF($A$2>200,"Sales value is","").**

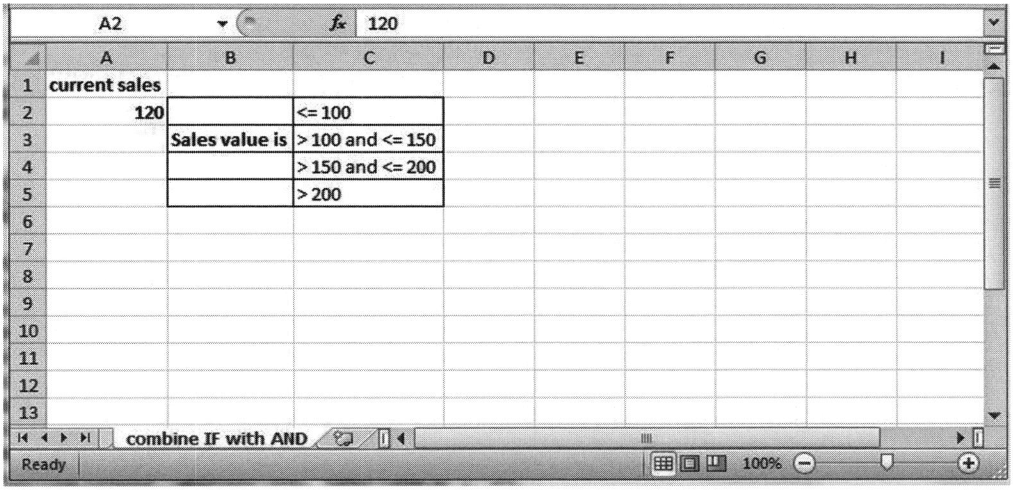

FIGURE 2–7

USE THE IF FUNCTION TO DETERMINE THE QUARTER OF A YEAR

After entering an initial value, Excel can automatically fill worksheet cells with the names of weekdays or months. Open a new worksheet and type the word "January" in cell A2. Then drag the lower-right point of this cell down to A13 to let Excel create a list containing the months of the year. In this example, we want to indicate which months fall into which quarter.

▶ **To Determine the Quarter of a Year in Which a Particular Month Falls:**

　　1. Select cells B2:B13 and type the following formula:
　　　 **=IF(OR(A2="January",A2="February",A2="March"),
　　　 "1st quarter",IF(OR(A2="April",A2="May",
　　　 A2="June"),"2nd quarter",IF(OR(A2="July",A2="August",
　　　 A2="September"),"3rd quarter","4th quarter"))).**
　　2. Press **<Ctrl+Enter>.**

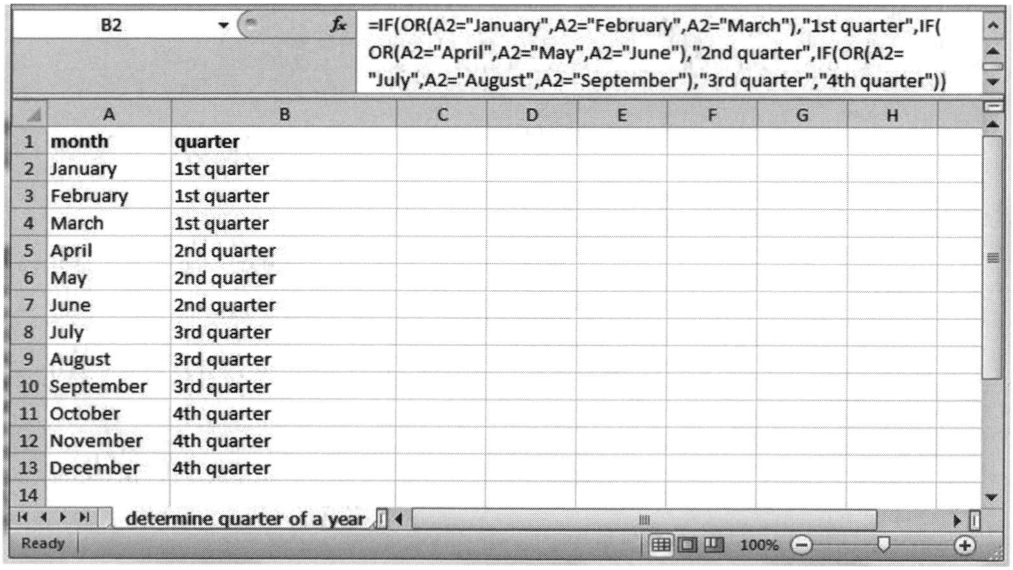

	B2			f_x	=IF(OR(A2="January",A2="February",A2="March"),"1st quarter",IF(OR(A2="April",A2="May",A2="June"),"2nd quarter",IF(OR(A2= "July",A2="August",A2="September"),"3rd quarter","4th quarter"))					
	A	B		C	D	E	F	G	H	
1	month	quarter								
2	January	1st quarter								
3	February	1st quarter								
4	March	1st quarter								
5	April	2nd quarter								
6	May	2nd quarter								
7	June	2nd quarter								
8	July	3rd quarter								
9	August	3rd quarter								
10	September	3rd quarter								
11	October	4th quarter								
12	November	4th quarter								
13	December	4th quarter								
14										

determine quarter of a year

Ready   100%

FIGURE 2–8

USE THE IF FUNCTION TO CHECK CELLS IN WORKSHEETS AND WORKBOOKS

To use an IF statement not only in a worksheet but also in a linked worksheet or workbook, start typing part of the formula, for example, "=IF(," then navigate to another worksheet or open up a workbook, select the desired cell, and go back to the first worksheet to finish the formula.

▶ **To Use the IF Function to Check Out Cells in Another Worksheet:**

Type **=IF(Sheet8!A2"january","wrong month","OK").**

▶ **To Use the IF Function to Check Out Cells in Another Workbook:**

Type **=IF('C:\Held\Formulas\Files\[Formulas.xls]
Sheet35'!$A$1<>1,"wrong","OK").**

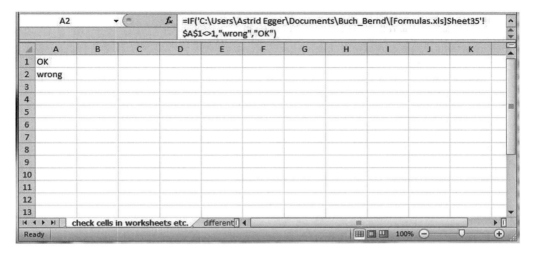

| | A2 | ▾ | | *fx* | =IF('C:\Users\Astrid Egger\Documents\Buch_Bernd\[Formulas.xls]Sheet35'! $A$1<>1,"wrong","OK") |

	A	B	C	D	E	F	G	H	I	J	K
1	OK										
2	wrong										
3											
4											
5											
6											
7											
8											
9											
10											
11											
12											
13											

check cells in worksheets etc.   different

Ready   100%

FIGURE 2–9

USE THE IF FUNCTION TO CALCULATE WITH DIFFERENT TAX RATES

If two or more different tax rates have to be handled, you can use the IF function to calculate each one individually. Simply combine several IF functions, depending on the calculation.

▶ **To Calculate the Price After Tax:**

1. In column A, enter some prices.
2. In column B, enter different tax percentages (0, 8, or 10 for this example).
3. Select cells C2:C10 and type the following formula: **=IF (B2=8,A2/100*8,IF(B2=10,A2/100*10,A2/100*0))**.
4. Press **<Ctrl+Enter>**.
5. Select cells D2:D10 and type the formula **=A2+C2**.
6. Press **<Ctrl+Enter>**.

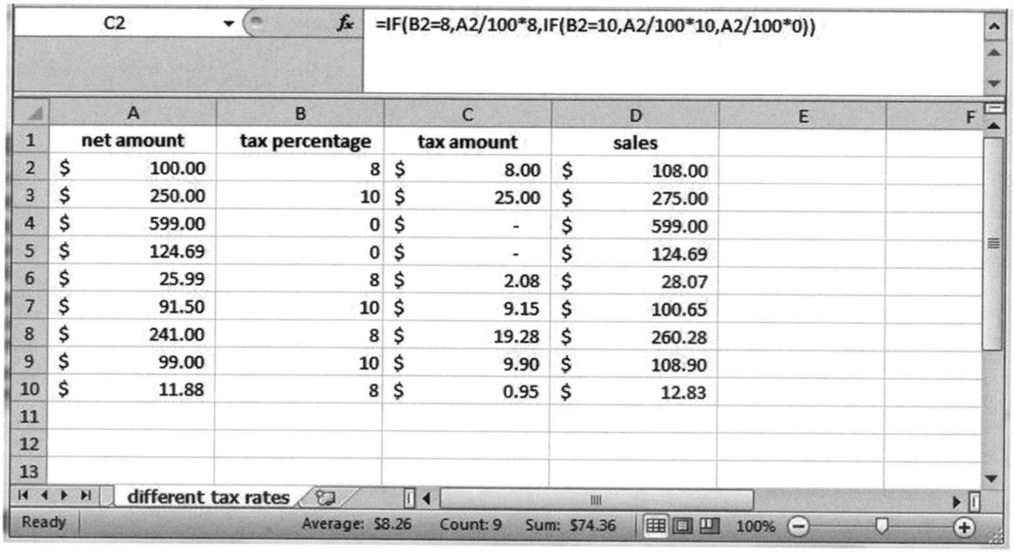

	C2			f_x	=IF(B2=8,A2/100*8,IF(B2=10,A2/100*10,A2/100*0))		

	A	B	C	D	E	F
1	net amount	tax percentage	tax amount	sales		
2	$ 100.00	8	$ 8.00	$ 108.00		
3	$ 250.00	10	$ 25.00	$ 275.00		
4	$ 599.00	0	$ -	$ 599.00		
5	$ 124.69	0	$ -	$ 124.69		
6	$ 25.99	8	$ 2.08	$ 28.07		
7	$ 91.50	10	$ 9.15	$ 100.65		
8	$ 241.00	8	$ 19.28	$ 260.28		
9	$ 99.00	10	$ 9.90	$ 108.90		
10	$ 11.88	8	$ 0.95	$ 12.83		
11						
12						
13						

different tax rates				

Ready   Average: $8.26   Count: 9   Sum: $74.36   100%

FIGURE 2–10

USE THE IF FUNCTION TO CALCULATE THE COMMISSIONS FOR INDIVIDUAL SALES

A company has a policy for individual commissions depending on sales, as shown below:

Sale < $100   3%
Sale => $100 and < $500   5%
Sale >= $500   8%

▶ **To Calculate the Commissions:**

1. Enter different possible sales amounts in column A.
2. Select cells B2:B12 and type the following formula:
   =A2*IF(A2>=500,0.08,IF(A2>=100,0.05,0.03)).
3. Press **<Ctrl+Enter>**.

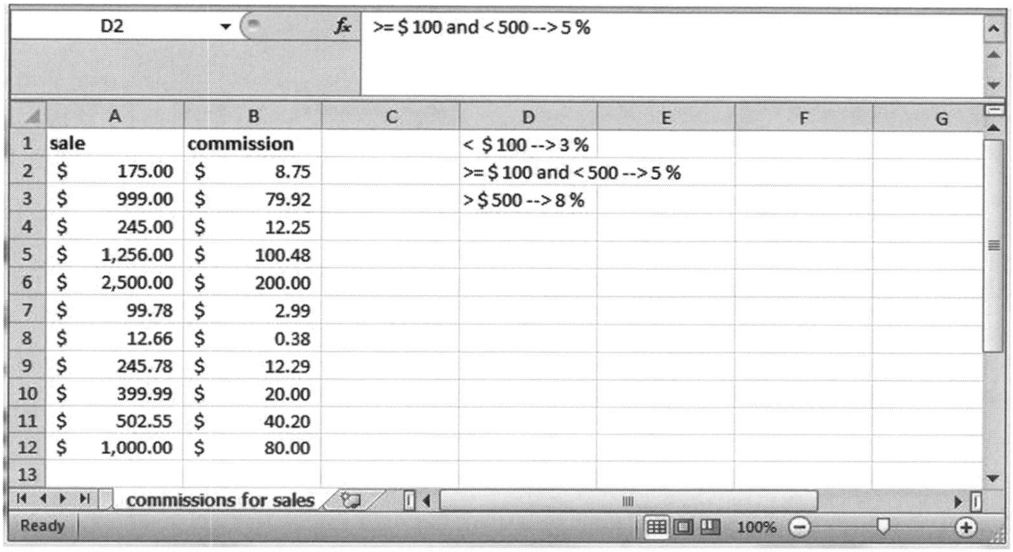

D2 | f_x >= $ 100 and < 500 --> 5 %

	A	B	C	D	E	F	G
1	sale	commission		< $ 100 --> 3 %			
2	$ 175.00	$ 8.75		>= $ 100 and < 500 --> 5 %			
3	$ 999.00	$ 79.92		> $ 500 --> 8 %			
4	$ 245.00	$ 12.25					
5	$ 1,256.00	$ 100.48					
6	$ 2,500.00	$ 200.00					
7	$ 99.78	$ 2.99					
8	$ 12.66	$ 0.38					
9	$ 245.78	$ 12.29					
10	$ 399.99	$ 20.00					
11	$ 502.55	$ 40.20					
12	$ 1,000.00	$ 80.00					
13							

FIGURE 2–11

USE THE IF FUNCTION TO COMPARE TWO CELLS

The following tip is a solution for comparing two cells line by line. Prepare a new worksheet, filling the first two columns with the values 0 and 1 as shown in Figure 2–12.

▶ To Compare Cells Line by Line:

1. Select cells C2:C11 and type the following formula: **=IF(A2&B2="11","OK",IF(A2&B2="10","First Value is OK", IF(A2&B2="01","Second Value is OK","Both Values are FALSE")))**.
2. Press **<Ctrl+Enter>**.

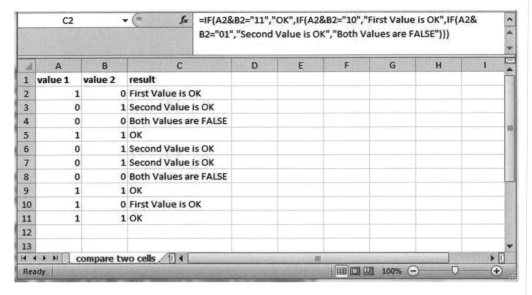

	A	B	C	D	E	F	G	H	I
1	value 1	value 2	result						
2	1	0	First Value is OK						
3	0	1	Second Value is OK						
4	0	0	Both Values are FALSE						
5	1	1	OK						
6	0	1	Second Value is OK						
7	0	1	Second Value is OK						
8	0	0	Both Values are FALSE						
9	1	1	OK						
10	1	0	First Value is OK						
11	1	1	OK						
12									
13									

FIGURE 2–12

USE THE INT FUNCTION WITH THE IF FUNCTION

To see if one value is a whole number and can be divided by another value, use the IF function in combination with the INT function.

▶ **To See If a Whole Number can be Divided by 4:**

1. Select cells B2:B10 and type the following formula:
    =IF(INT(A2/4)=A2/4,"whole number divisible by 4",FALSE).
2. Press **<Ctrl+Enter>**.

Or

1. Select cells C2:C10 and type the following formula:
    =IF(A2/4-INT(A2/4)=0,"whole number divisible by 4", FALSE).
2. Press **<Ctrl+Enter>**.

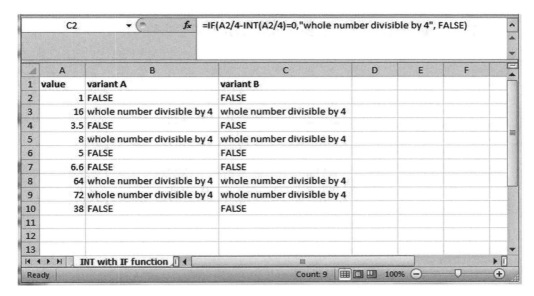

	A	B	C	D	E	F
1	value	variant A	variant B			
2	1	FALSE	FALSE			
3	16	whole number divisible by 4	whole number divisible by 4			
4	3.5	FALSE	FALSE			
5	8	whole number divisible by 4	whole number divisible by 4			
6	5	FALSE	FALSE			
7	6.6	FALSE	FALSE			
8	64	whole number divisible by 4	whole number divisible by 4			
9	72	whole number divisible by 4	whole number divisible by 4			
10	38	FALSE	FALSE			
11						
12						
13						

C2 fx =IF(A2/4-INT(A2/4)=0,"whole number divisible by 4", FALSE)

INT with IF function

FIGURE 2–13

USE THE TYPE FUNCTION TO CHECK FOR INVALID VALUES

Sometimes Excel cannot interpret some values, especially imported data. As an example, let's say a cell contains an apparent value but the calculation leads to an incorrect result. To prevent this, use the IF function in combination with TYPE to check for invalid data in the worksheet. This example will enter the text "invalid value" in column B if the value entered in column A is not numeric.

▶ **To Show Invalid Values in a Worksheet:**

1. Enter some values or text in column A.
2. Select cells B2:B10 and type the following formula:
   =IF(AND(TYPE(A2)=1,A2<>""),A2,"invalid value").
3. Press **<Ctrl+Enter>**.

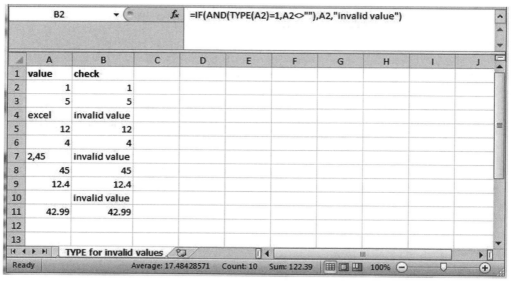

FIGURE 2–14

USE THE IF FUNCTION COMBINED IN ONE CELL MORE THAN SEVEN TIMES

The Excel online help says that it is not possible to combine the IF function more than seven times. However, that is not true, as shown below.

▶ **To Insert More than Seven Conditions:**

1. Select cell A2 and enter **12**.
2. Select cell B2 and type the following formula:
   =IF(A2=1,A2,IF(A2=2,A2*2,IF(A2=3,A2*3,IF(A2=4,A2*4, IF(A2=5,A2*5,IF(A2=6,A2*6,IF(A2=7,A2*7,)))))))+ IF(A2=8,A2*8,IF(A2=9,A2*9,IF(A2=10,A2*10,)))+ IF(A2=11,A2*11,IF(A2=12,A2*12,)).
3. Press **<Enter>**.

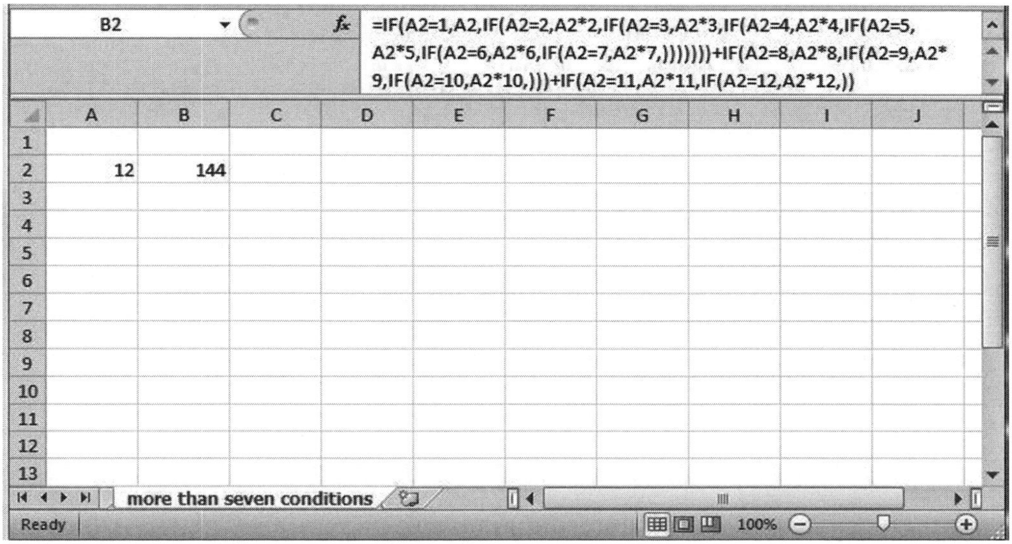

FIGURE 2–15

USE THE IF FUNCTION TO CHECK WHETHER A DATE IS IN THE PAST OR FUTURE

In this example we want to check whether a particular date is in the past or the future. To do so, the TODAY() function is used with IF to compare dates with the actual date and show its result.

▶ **To Compare Dates — Variant A:**

1. Select cell B2:B11 and type the following formula:
   =IF(NOT(A2>TODAY()),"past","future").
2. Press **<Ctrl+Enter>**.

▶ **To Compare Dates — Variant B:**

1. Select cell B2:B11 and type the following formula:
   =IF(A2>=TODAY(),IF(A2=TODAY(),"Today","Future"),"Past").
2. Press **<Ctrl+Enter>**.

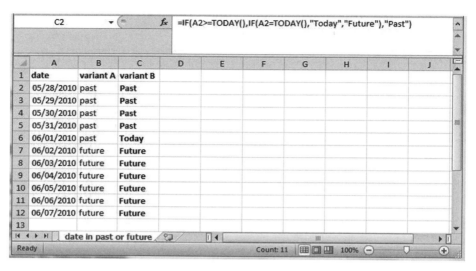

FIGURE 2–16

USE THE IF FUNCTION TO CREATE YOUR OWN TIMESHEET

In this last example we create our own timesheet, step by step. First, press <Shift+F11> to insert a new worksheet. Then create the following timesheet as an example:

We have to consider that the daily target of eight hours is still fulfilled when an employee is ill (IL), on holiday (HO), or in training (TR). For other days, the number of working hours has to be calculated.

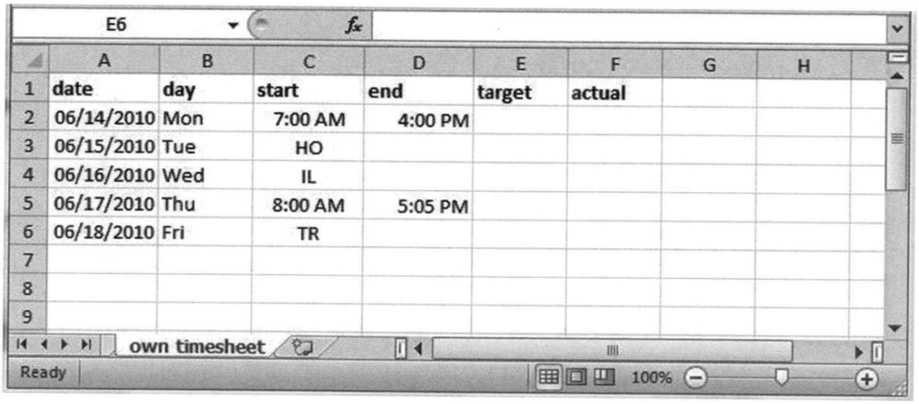

date	day	start	end	target	actual
06/14/2010	Mon	7:00 AM	4:00 PM		
06/15/2010	Tue	HO			
06/16/2010	Wed	IL			
06/17/2010	Thu	8:00 AM	5:05 PM		
06/18/2010	Fri	TR			

FIGURE 2–17

▶ **To Calculate the Daily Working Hours:**

    1. Select cell F2:F6 and type the following formula:
       =IF(OR(C2="TR",C2="IL",C2="HO"),E2,D2-C2).

    2. Press **<Ctrl+Enter>**.

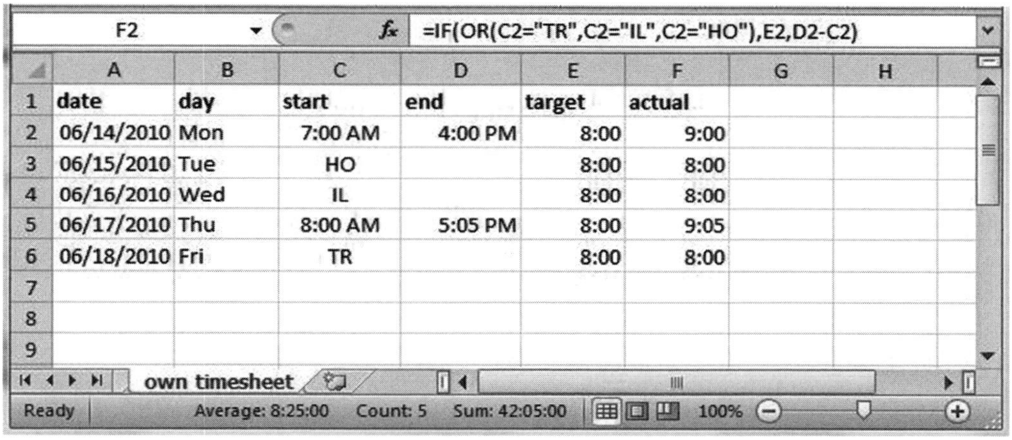

	F2		▼	f_x	=IF(OR(C2="TR",C2="IL",C2="HO"),E2,D2-C2)			
	A	B	C	D	E	F	G	H
1	date	day	start	end	target	actual		
2	06/14/2010	Mon	7:00 AM	4:00 PM	8:00	9:00		
3	06/15/2010	Tue	HO		8:00	8:00		
4	06/16/2010	Wed	IL		8:00	8:00		
5	06/17/2010	Thu	8:00 AM	5:05 PM	8:00	9:05		
6	06/18/2010	Fri	TR		8:00	8:00		
7								
8								
9								

own timesheet

Ready   Average: 8:25:00   Count: 5   Sum: 42:05:00   100%

FIGURE 2–18

Chapter 3 TEXT FUNCTIONS

USE THE LEFT AND RIGHT FUNCTIONS TO SEPARATE A TEXT STRING OF NUMBERS

A worksheet contains a list of 10-digit numbers that have to be separated into two parts: a three-digit part and a seven-digit part. Use the LEFT and RIGHT functions to do this. The LEFT function returns the first character or characters in a text string, based on the number of characters specified. The RIGHT function returns the last character or characters in a text string based on the number of characters specified.

▶ **To Separate a Text String of Numbers:**

1. In a worksheet, enter a series of 10-character numbers in cells A2:A10. The numbers can also contain letters.
2. Select cells B2:B10 and type the following formula: **=LEFT(A2,3)**.
3. Press **<Ctrl+Enter>**.
4. Select cells C2:C10 and type the following formula: **=RIGHT(A2,7)**.
5. Press **<Ctrl+Enter>**.

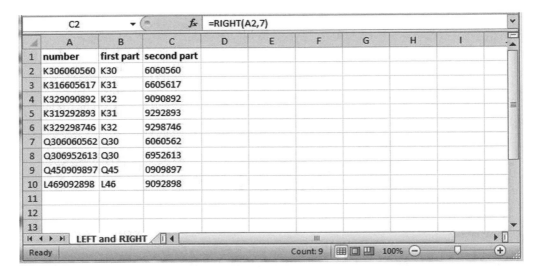

FIGURE 3–1

USE THE LEFT FUNCTION TO CONVERT INVALID NUMBERS TO VALID NUMBERS

In this example, invalid numbers have to be converted to valid numbers. The invalid numbers contain a minus sign at the right end of the text. Excel cannot interpret this, so the last digit of the text needs to be moved to the left of the numbers. First, check the length of each number with the LEN function. This function returns the number of characters in a text string. Then use the LEFT function to move the minus sign.

LEN(*text*)

> *text*: The text whose length you want to be determined. A space is considered a character.

▶ **To Cut Off the Last Digit and Display a Negative Value:**

1. In a worksheet, enter a series of numbers in cells A2:A10 that have a minus sign at the end.
2. Select cells B2:B10 and type the following formula:
   =-LEFT(A2,LEN(A2)-1).
3. Press **<Ctrl+Enter>**.

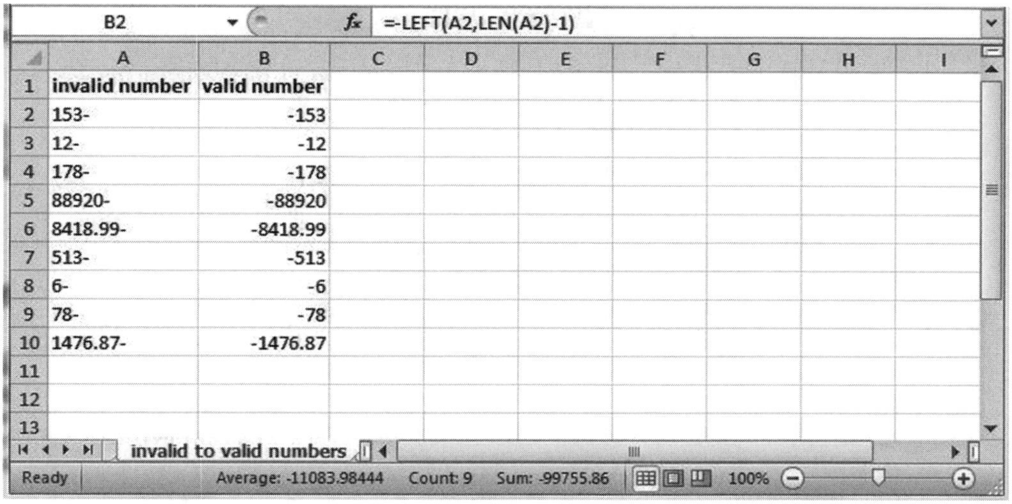

	A	B	C	D	E	F	G	H	I
1	invalid number	valid number							
2	153-	-153							
3	12-	-12							
4	178-	-178							
5	88920-	-88920							
6	8418.99-	-8418.99							
7	513-	-513							
8	6-	-6							
9	78-	-78							
10	1476.87-	-1476.87							
11									
12									
13									

FIGURE 3–2

USE THE SEARCH FUNCTION TO SEPARATE FIRST NAME FROM LAST NAME

This task demonstrates how to separate first and last names. In a worksheet, full names are listed in column A. We want to copy the first name to column B. The SEARCH function can be used to determine the space between the parts of the text string. This function returns the position of the searched character inside a text string.

SEARCH(*find_text*, *within_text*, *start_num*)

find_text: The text or character for which you are searching. Wild-card characters, question marks (?), and asterisks (∗) can be used in find_text. A question mark matches any single character, and an asterisk matches any sequence of characters. To find a question mark or asterisk, type a tilde (~) before the character.

within_text: The text you want to search for find_text.

start_num: The start position for the search function within the text; if there is no start_num defined inside the function, Excel sets it to 1.

▶ **To Separate the First and Last Names:**

1. In a worksheet, enter a series of full names in cells A2:A11.
2. Select cells B2:B11 and type the following formula:
   =LEFT(A2,SEARCH(" ",A2)-1).
3. Press **<Ctrl+Enter>**.

	A	B	C	D	E	F	G	H	I
B11			*fx*	=LEFT(A11,SEARCH(" ",A11)-1)					
1	names	first name							
2	Will Smith	Will							
3	Vera Miller	Vera							
4	Pat Most	Pat							
5	Steve McNamara	Steve							
6	Andy Garcia	Andy							
7	Tom Stone	Tom							
8	Sandy Beach	Sandy							
9	Walter King	Walter							
10	Alexander Walton	Alexander							
11	Patricia York	Patricia							
12									
13									

FIGURE 3–3

USE THE MID FUNCTION TO SEPARATE LAST NAME FROM FIRST NAME

In a worksheet, names are listed in column A, and the last name has to be copied to column B. As in the previous example, the space between the first and last names has to be determined with the SEARCH function. This function returns the position of the desired character inside a text string starting from start_num. The MID function then returns a specific number of characters starting from a desired position inside a text string.

MID(*text, start_num, num_chars*)

text: Text string containing the desired characters.

start_num: Position of the first character to extract from the text.

num_chars: Number of characters to be extracted.

▶ **To Separate the Last Name from the First Name:**

1. In a worksheet, enter a series of full names in cells A2:A11.
2. Select cells B2:B11 and type the following formula:
   =MID(A2,SEARCH(" ",A2)+1,100).
3. Press **<Ctrl+Enter>**.

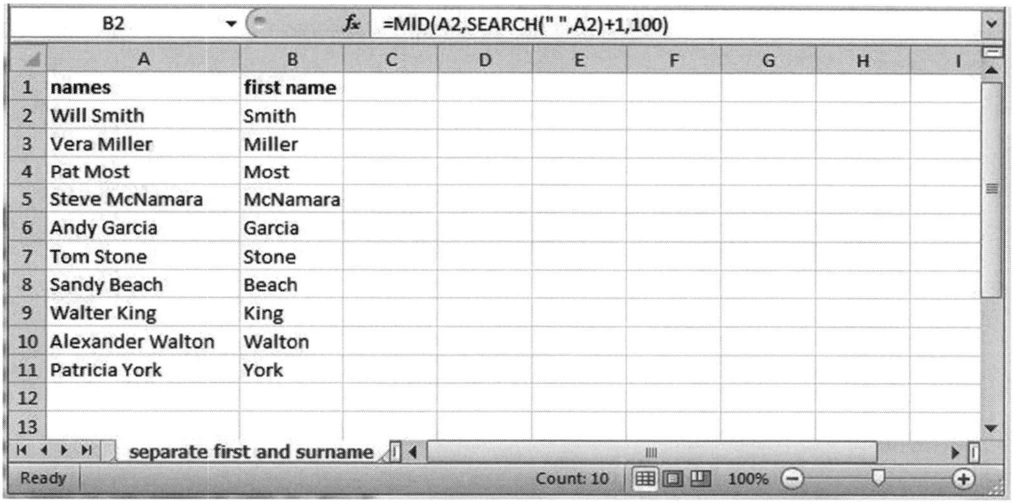

	B2	▾	fx	=MID(A2,SEARCH(" ",A2)+1,100)					
	A	**B**	**C**	**D**	**E**	**F**	**G**	**H**	**I**
1	names	first name							
2	Will Smith	Smith							
3	Vera Miller	Miller							
4	Pat Most	Most							
5	Steve McNamara	McNamara							
6	Andy Garcia	Garcia							
7	Tom Stone	Stone							
8	Sandy Beach	Beach							
9	Walter King	King							
10	Alexander Walton	Walton							
11	Patricia York	York							
12									
13									

separate first and surname

Ready — Count: 10 — 100%

FIGURE 3–4

USE THE MID FUNCTION TO SUM THE DIGITS OF A NUMBER

A worksheet contains four-digit numbers in column A. Each of the four digits has to be added and the result shown in column B. To do so, the four digits of a cell are extracted by the MID function and summed.

▶ **To Determine the Cross Sum:**

1. In a worksheet, enter a series of four-digit numbers in cells A2:A10.
2. Select cells B2:B10 and type the following formula:
   =MID(A2,1,1)+MID(A2,2,1)+MID(A2,3,1)+MID(A2,4,1).
3. Press **<Ctrl+Enter>**.

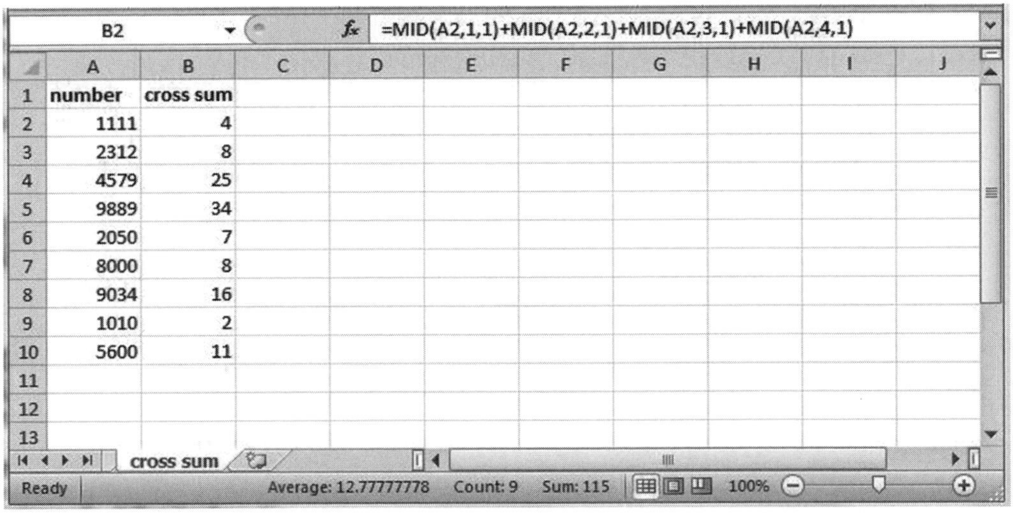

	B2			f_x	=MID(A2,1,1)+MID(A2,2,1)+MID(A2,3,1)+MID(A2,4,1)						
	A	B	C	D	E	F	G	H	I	J	
1	number	cross sum									
2	1111	4									
3	2312	8									
4	4579	25									
5	9889	34									
6	2050	7									
7	8000	8									
8	9034	16									
9	1010	2									
10	5600	11									
11											
12											
13											

cross sum

Ready   Average: 12.77777778   Count: 9   Sum: 115   100%

FIGURE 3–5

USE THE EXACT FUNCTION TO COMPARE TWO COLUMNS

There are two ways to compare two columns. With the IF function, it doesn't matter if the text is written in upper- or lowercase. The EXACT function, on the other hand, can distinguish between upper- and lowercase.

EXACT(*text1*, *text2*)

text1: The first text string.

text2: The second text string.

▶ **To Compare Two Columns:**

1. In a worksheet, copy columns A and B from Figure 3–6.
2. Select cells C2:C10 and type the following formula: **=EXACT(A2,B2)**.
3. Press **<Ctrl+Enter>**.
4. Select cells D2:D10 and type the following formula: **=IF(A2=B2,TRUE,FALSE)**.
5. Press **<Ctrl+Enter>**.

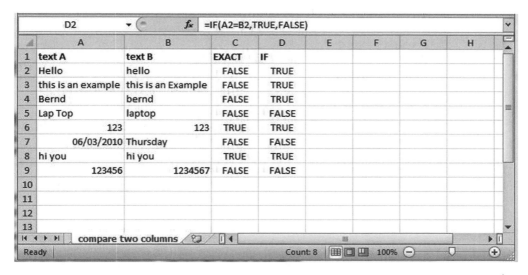

FIGURE 3–6

Differences in formatting don't matter. The function will still work, as shown in cells A7 and B7; B7 contains the numeric value of the date in A7. Extraneous blanks in cells, as shown in row 8, also don't matter.

USE THE SUBSTITUTE FUNCTION TO SUBSTITUTE CHARACTERS

A worksheet contains values in column A that cannot be summed up because the first character in each cell is an apostrophe. How do you solve this problem? Use the SUBSTITUTE formula to replace specific characters in text or a cell.

SUBSTITUTE(*text, old_text, new_text, instance_num*)

text: The text or the reference to a cell containing text in which characters are substituted.

old_text: Text that should be replaced.

new_text: Text that replaces *old_text*.

instance_num: Specifies which instance of *old_text* is to be replaced by *new_text*. If omitted, every instance of *old_text* is replaced.

▶ **To Use SUBSTITUTE and Force Excel to Calculate:**

1. Format column A as text.
2. Enter a series of numbers in cells A2:A10. Notice that Excel tags them with green triangles in the upper-left corner to indicate the numbers have been entered as text.
3. Select cells B2:B10 and type the following formula:
   =VALUE(SUBSTITUTE(A2,"","")).
4. Press **<Ctrl+Enter>**.
5. Select cell A12, type the following formula: **=SUM(A2:A10)**, and press **<Enter>**.
6. Select cell B12, type the following formula: **=SUM(B2:B10)**, and press **<Enter>**.

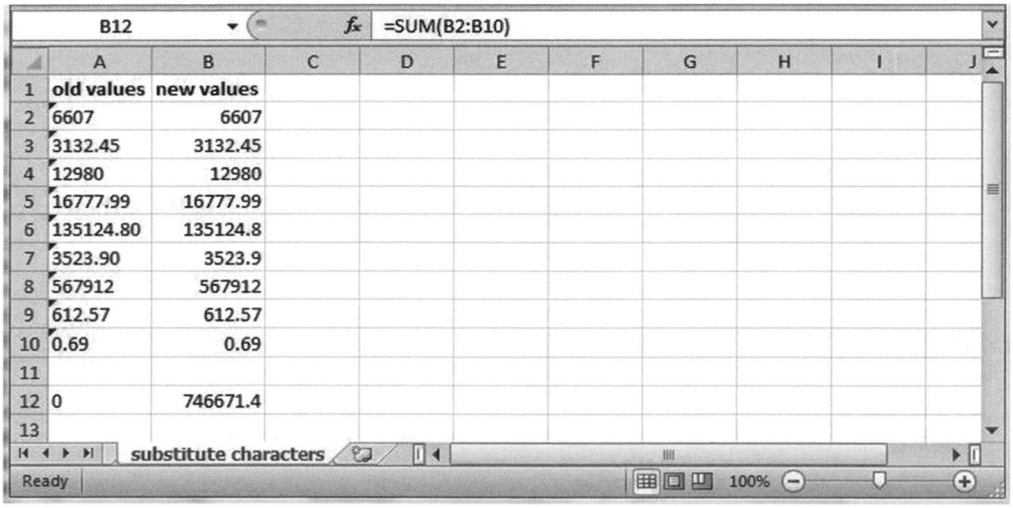

	B12				*fx*	=SUM(B2:B10)						
	A	B	C	D	E	F	G	H	I	J		
1	old values	new values										
2	6607	6607										
3	3132.45	3132.45										
4	12980	12980										
5	16777.99	16777.99										
6	135124.80	135124.8										
7	3523.90	3523.9										
8	567912	567912										
9	612.57	612.57										
10	0.69	0.69										
11												
12	0	746671.4										
13												

substitute characters

Ready   100%

FIGURE 3–7

USE THE SUBSTITUTE FUNCTION TO SUBSTITUTE PARTS OF A CELL

In this example, the "-" character needs to be replaced with a blank space. But only the first occurrence of this character should be replaced. To do this, type any kind of text and numbers in column A, as shown in the following screenshot, using the "-" character in different positions and in a variety of occurrences.

▶ **To Substitute Parts of a Cell:**

1. Select cells B2:B10 and type the following formula: **=SUBSTITUTE(A2,"-","",1)**.
2. Press **<Ctrl+Enter>**.

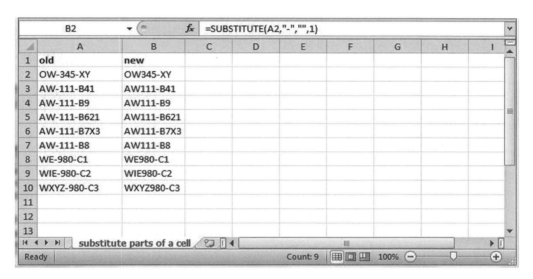

FIGURE 3–8

NOTE *If you want to substitute the second occurrence of this character, use the following formula: =SUBSTITUTE(A2,"-","",2).*

USE THE SUBSTITUTE FUNCTION TO CONVERT NUMBERS TO WORDS

A worksheet contains the numbers 1 to 5 in column A. Use the SUBSTITUTE function to change each number to a word. For example, change 1 to one, 2 to two, 3 to three, 4 to four, and 5 to five.

▶ **To Convert Each Number to a Word:**

1. In column A, type a series of numbers using 1, 2, 3, 4, and 5.
2. Select cells B2:B10 and type the following formula:
   =(SUBSTITUTE(SUBSTITUTE(SUBSTITUTE(SUBSTITUTE (SUBSTITUTE(A2,1,"one-"),2,"two-"),3,"three-"), 4,"four-"),5,"five-")).
3. Press **<Ctrl+Enter>**.

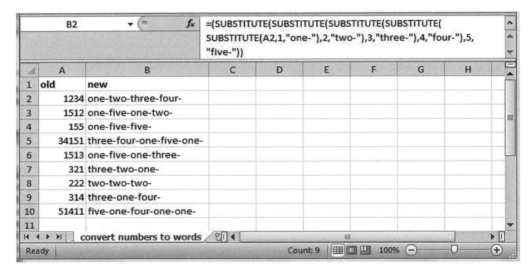

FIGURE 3–9

USE THE SUBSTITUTE FUNCTION TO REMOVE WORD-WRAPPING IN CELLS

To wrap text in a cell, you can select Cells from the Format menu, select the Alignment tab, and tick the Wrap text check box. Another way to do this is to type the first row of a cell, then press <Alt+Enter>, type the next line, and continue as desired.

If you want to disable word-wrap, the SUBSTITUTE and CHAR functions can be used together. CHAR returns the character specified by a number. The ASCII character numerical equivalent for word-wrap is 10.

▶ **To Delete Word-Wrap:**

1. In cells A2 and A3 type text with word-wraps.
2. Select cells B2:B3 and type the following formula:
   =SUBSTITUTE(A2,CHAR(10)," ").
3. Press **<Ctrl+Enter>**.

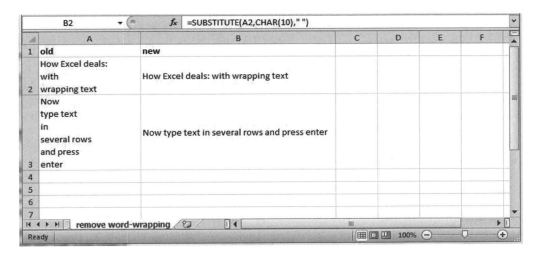

FIGURE 3–10

USE THE SUBSTITUTE **FUNCTION TO COMBINE AND SEPARATE**

The & operator is used to combine several columns into one column. To include a separator between each part in addition to blank spaces, you can specify the separator just once while using the SUBSTITUTE function as follows.

▶ **To Combine and Separate at the Same Time:**

1. In columns A to E, type any kind of data.
2. Select cells F2:F10 and type the following formula:
   =SUBSTITUTE(A2&" "&B2&" "&C2&" "&D2 & " " &E2," ","-").
3. Press **<Ctrl+Enter>**.

	F2			▼	f_x	=SUBSTITUTE(A2&" "&B2&" "&C2&" "&D2 & " " &E2," "," - ")					
◢	A	B	C	D	E	F	G	H	I	J	
1	part1	part2	part3	part4	part5	result					
2	KI	125	HI1	18	CIA	KI - 125 - HI1 - 18 - CIA					
3	KO	456	HI2	18	CIA	KO - 456 - HI2 - 18 - CIA					
4	KL	124	HI3	18	CIA	KL - 124 - HI3 - 18 - CIA					
5	KP	567	HI4	18	TIA	KP - 567 - HI4 - 18 - TIA					
6	LU	987	HI5	18	TIA	LU - 987 - HI5 - 18 - TIA					
7	GW	656	HI6	19	TIA	GW - 656 - HI6 - 19 - TIA					
8	DA	578	HI7	19	TIA	DA - 578 - HI7 - 19 - TIA					
9	TR	678	HI8	19	HGH	TR - 678 - HI8 - 19 - HGH					
10	WW	789	HI9	19	HGH	WW - 789 - HI9 - 19 - HGH					
11											
12											
13											
14											

combine and separate

Ready   Count: 9   100%

FIGURE 3–11

USE THE REPLACE FUNCTION TO REPLACE AND CALCULATE

The following worksheet contains an employee's work hours.

	C11			▼	f_x						
◢	A	B	C	D	E	F	G	H	I	J	K
1	date	start	end								
2	03/20/2010	7.50	13.51								
3	03/21/2010	6.50	8.30								
4	03/22/2010	7.00	16.00								
5	03/23/2010	10.21	14.33								
6	03/24/2010	08.09	15.11								
7	03/25/2010	7.57	17.55								
8	03/26/2010	10.44	13.12								
9	03/27/2010	9.0	14.33								
10	03/28/2010	7.01	18.55								
11											
12											
13											
14											

replace and calculate

Ready   100%

FIGURE 3–12

The format of columns B and D cannot be used to calculate time. Note that the triangle in the upper-left corner indicates the numbers have been entered as text. Rather than a period, a colon needs to be placed between the numbers to indicate time. Therefore, the period has to be replaced using the REPLACE function in combination with SEARCH. The REPLACE function replaces part of a text string with a different text string, based on the number of characters specified. The syntax for the SEARCH function was provided earlier in this chapter.

REPLACE(*old_text*, *start_num*, *num_chars*, *new_text*)

old_text: Original text in which some characters are to be replaced.

start_num: Position of the character in old_text that is to be replaced with new_text.

num_chars: Number of characters in old_text to be replaced.

new_text: Text that will replace characters in old_text.

▶ **To Replace Periods with Colons and Calculate:**

1. In a worksheet, copy the data shown in Figure 3–12.
2. Select cells D2:D10 and type the following formula:
   =(REPLACE(C2,SEARCH(".",C2),1,":")-
   REPLACE(B2,SEARCH(".",B2),1,":")).
3. Press **<Ctrl+Enter>**.

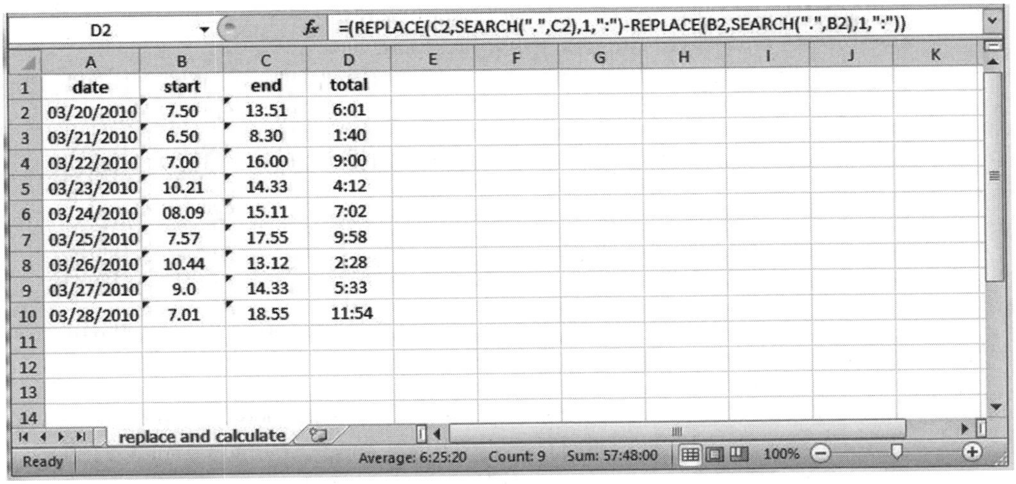

	D2			fx	=(REPLACE(C2,SEARCH(".",C2),1,":")-REPLACE(B2,SEARCH(".",B2),1,":"))							
	A	B	C	D	E	F	G	H	I	J	K	
1	date	start	end	total								
2	03/20/2010	7.50	13.51	6:01								
3	03/21/2010	6.50	8.30	1:40								
4	03/22/2010	7.00	16.00	9:00								
5	03/23/2010	10.21	14.33	4:12								
6	03/24/2010	08.09	15.11	7:02								
7	03/25/2010	7.57	17.55	9:58								
8	03/26/2010	10.44	13.12	2:28								
9	03/27/2010	9.0	14.33	5:33								
10	03/28/2010	7.01	18.55	11:54								
11												
12												
13												
14												

replace and calculate

Ready   Average: 6:25:20   Count: 9   Sum: 57:48:00   100%

FIGURE 3–13

USE THE FIND FUNCTION TO COMBINE TEXT AND DATE

The following worksheet contains daily tasks in column A and their corresponding dates in column B. The task here is to combine the data and change the format of the dates. Take a closer look at the following screenshot:

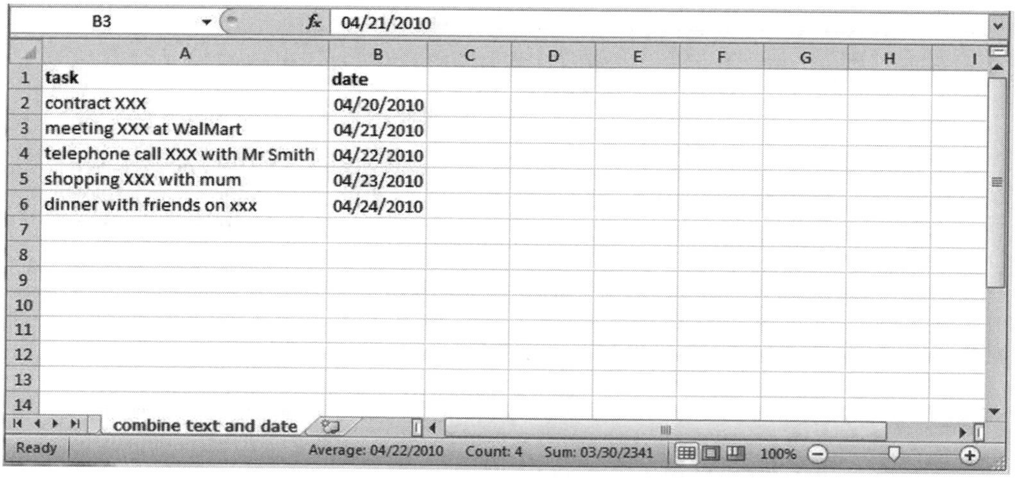

FIGURE 3–14

The text string XXX has to be replaced by the dates in column B. To do so, the starting position of the text string has to be determined by using the FIND function. The REPLACE function will replace the XXX text string with the date.

FIND(*find_text*, *within_text*, *start_num*)

find_text: Text to find. Wildcard characters are not allowed.

within_text: Text containing find_text.

start_num: Specifies the first character in the search. If omitted, Excel sets start_num to 1.

▶ **To Combine and Format Data at the Same Time:**

1. In a worksheet, copy the data shown in Figure 3–14.
2. Select cells C2:C6 and type the following formula: **=REPLACE (A2,FIND("XXX",A2,1),3,TEXT(B2,"MM-DD-YYYY"))**.
3. Press **<Ctrl+Enter>**.

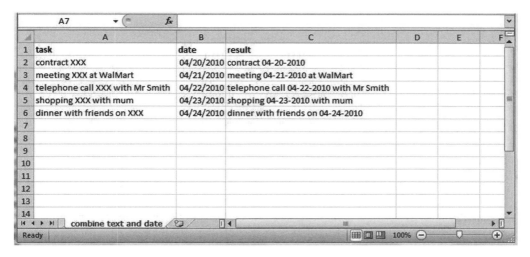

FIGURE 3–15

USE THE UPPER FUNCTION TO CONVERT TEXT FROM LOWERCASE TO UPPERCASE

The UPPER function is used to convert a text string to all uppercase letters. This function has the following syntax:

UPPER(*text*)

> *text*: Text to be converted to all uppercase letters. The text can be either a reference or a text string.

▶ **To Convert a Text String to Uppercase:**

1. In cells A2:A8 type any text in lowercase letters.
2. Select cells B2:B8 and type the following formula: **=UPPER(A2)**.
3. Press **<Ctrl+Enter>**.

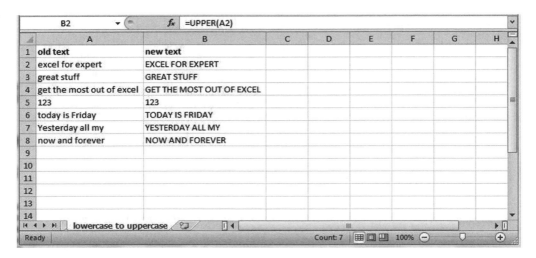

FIGURE 3–16

USE THE LOWER FUNCTION TO CONVERT TEXT FROM UPPERCASE TO LOWERCASE

To convert all letters to lowercase in a text string, use the LOWER function. This function has the following syntax:

LOWER(*text*)

> *text*: Text to be converted to all lowercase letters. The text can be either a reference or a text string.

▶ To Convert a Text String to Lowercase:

1. In cells A2:A8 type any text in uppercase letters.
2. Select cells B2:B8 and type the following formula: **=LOWER(A2)**.
3. Press **<Ctrl+Enter>**.

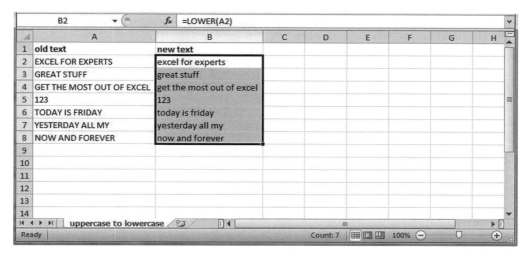

FIGURE 3–17

USE THE PROPER **FUNCTION TO CONVERT INITIAL CHARACTERS FROM LOWERCASE TO UPPERCASE**

To convert the first letter in each word to uppercase and all other letters to lowercase, the PROPER function is used. This function capitalizes the first letter in a text string and any letters that follow characters other than a letter (such as a space). All other letters will be changed to lowercase.

This function has the following syntax:

PROPER(*text*)

> *text*: Text enclosed in quotation marks, a formula that returns text, or a reference to a cell that contains the text that should have an initial capital letter.

▶ **To Convert a Text String to Proper Case:**

1. In cells A2:A7 type any kind of text.
2. Select cells B2:B7 and type the following formula: **=PROPER(A2)**.
3. Press **<Ctrl+Enter>**.

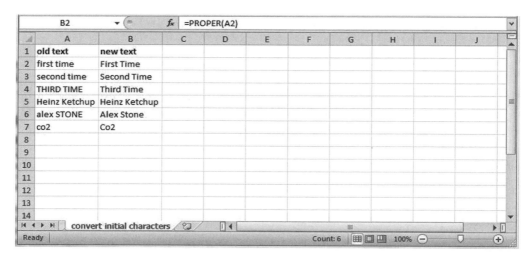

FIGURE 3–18

USE THE FIXED FUNCTION TO ROUND AND CONVERT NUMBERS TO TEXT

To round numbers and return the result as text, use the FIXED function. This function rounds a number to the specified number of decimals, returning the result as text with or without commas.

FIXED(*number, decimals, no_commas*)

> *number*: The number to round and convert to text.

> *decimals*: The number of digits to the right of the decimal point. If omitted, Excel sets it to 2.

> *no_commas*: A logical value that prevents FIXED from including commas when set to TRUE. If *no_commas* is FALSE or omitted, the returned text includes commas.

▶ **To Round and Convert Numbers to Text:**

1. In cells A2:A10, type values with decimals.
2. Select cells B2:B10 and type the following formula:
   =FIXED(A2,-1,FALSE).
3. Press **<Ctrl+Enter>**.

4. Select cells C2:C10 and type the following formula:
   =FIXED(A2,-2,FALSE).
5. Press **<Ctrl+Enter>**.

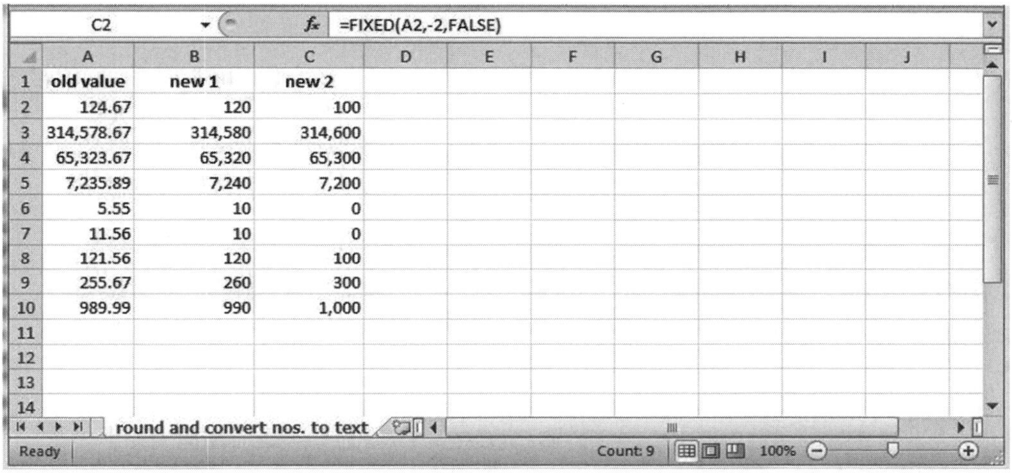

	C2	▼	f_x	=FIXED(A2,-2,FALSE)							
	A	B	C	D	E	F	G	H	I	J	
1	old value	new 1	new 2								
2	124.67	120	100								
3	314,578.67	314,580	314,600								
4	65,323.67	65,320	65,300								
5	7,235.89	7,240	7,200								
6	5.55	10	0								
7	11.56	10	0								
8	121.56	120	100								
9	255.67	260	300								
10	989.99	990	1,000								
11											
12											
13											
14											

round and convert nos. to text

Ready   Count: 9   100%

FIGURE 3–19

USE THE TRIM **FUNCTION TO DELETE SPACES**

Column A of a worksheet contains text with spaces at the left and right side of the text. This could be a problem if, for example, data is used for evaluation. Use the TRIM function to remove all spaces from a text string except for the single spaces between words.

▶ **To Delete Unneeded Spaces from Text:**

1. In cells A2:A5, type text with leading and trailing spaces.
2. Select cells B2:B5 and type the following formula: **=TRIM(A2)**.
3. Press **<Ctrl+Enter>**.

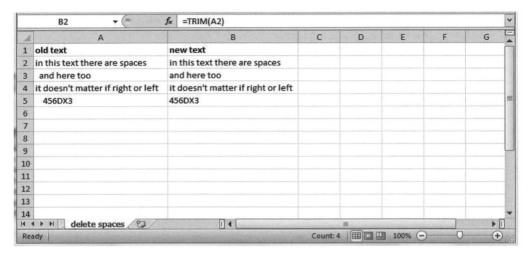

FIGURE 3–20

USE THE TRIM FUNCTION TO CONVERT "TEXT-NUMBERS" TO REAL NUMBERS

In this example, numbers entered as text have to be converted to values. To do this, use the VALUE and TRIM functions in combination to get the correct result. The VALUE function converts a text string that represents a number to a number, and the TRIM function deletes all leading and trailing spaces.

▶ **To Convert Text that Represents a Number to a Value:**

1. Format column A as text.
2. In cells A2:A10, type a series of numbers with leading spaces.
3. Select cells B2:B10 and type the following formula: **=VALUE(TRIM(A2))**.
4. Press **<Ctrl+Enter>**.

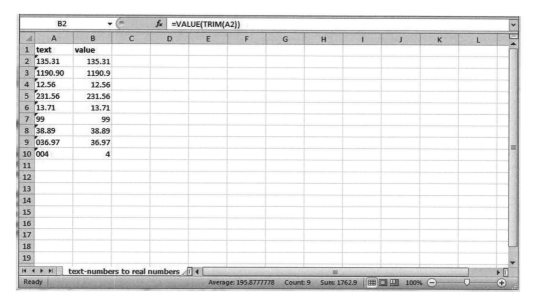

FIGURE 3–21

USE THE CLEAN FUNCTION TO REMOVE ALL NON-PRINTABLE CHARACTERS

If data is imported from other applications, it is possible for this data to contain characters that may not be printable. In this case, the CLEAN function can be used to remove all non-printable characters from text.

▶ **To Delete Non-Printable Characters:**

1. Type any text in cells A2:A5. Make sure that some of the cells contain non-printable characters.
2. Select cells A2:A5 and type the following formula: **=CLEAN(A2)**.
3. Press **<Ctrl+Enter>**.

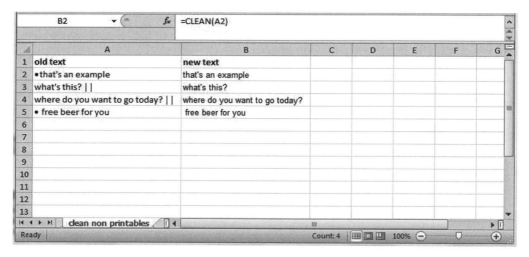

FIGURE 3–22

USE THE REPT FUNCTION TO SHOW DATA IN GRAPHIC MODE

To demonstrate data in a chart-like view, you can use a special character in a symbol font and repeat the character. To do so, use the REPT function. This function repeats a character a given number of times.

▶ **To Show Data in a Simple Chart:**

1. In cells A2:A10, type numbers from 1 to 10.
2. Select cells B2:B10 and type the following formula: **=REPT("n",A2)**.
3. Press **<Ctrl+Enter>**.
4. Press Ctrl + 1.
5. Select the **Font** tab.
6. Select **Wingdings** from the Font list and click **OK**.

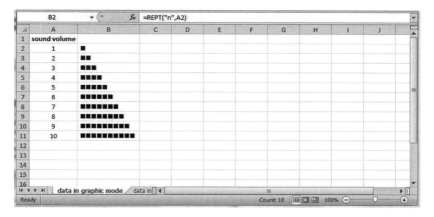

FIGURE 3–23

USE THE REPT FUNCTION TO SHOW DATA IN A CHART

To show data in a chart-like view, you can define a character and repeat this character a specified number of times using the REPT function.

▶ **To Show Data in a Chart:**

1. In cells B2:B10, type percentages in the range of 1% to 100%.
2. Select cells C2:C10 and type the following formula:
    =REPT("|",B2*100).
3. Press **<Ctrl+Enter>**.

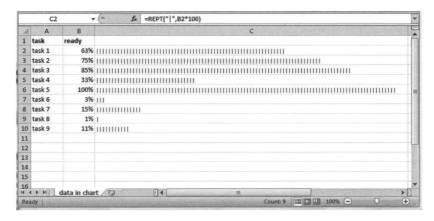

FIGURE 3–24

USE THE CHAR FUNCTION TO CHECK YOUR FONTS

To check a few fonts at the same time, open a new worksheet and format columns B to E with the Arial, Wingdings, Webdings, and Terminal fonts. Use the CHAR function to return the character specified by a number in column A.

▶ **To Check Installed Fonts:**

1. In cell A2, type **1**.
2. Press **<Ctrl>** and drag the right corner of cell A2 down to cell A256.
3. Select cells B2:E256 and type the following formula: **=CHAR($A2)**.
4. Press **<Ctrl+Enter>**.

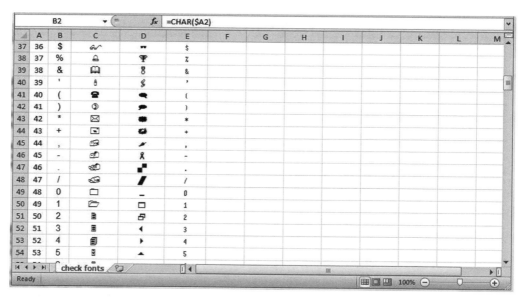

FIGURE 3–25

USE THE CHAR FUNCTION TO DETERMINE SPECIAL CHARACTERS

To use special characters, it is necessary to figure out how to get them. The CHAR function will return the character specified by a number in column A. Note that some fonts may have different special characters.

▶ **To Determine Special Characters:**

1. Copy column A as shown below to your worksheet.
2. Select cells B2:B16 and type the following formula: **=CHAR(A2)**.
3. Press **<Ctrl+Enter>**.

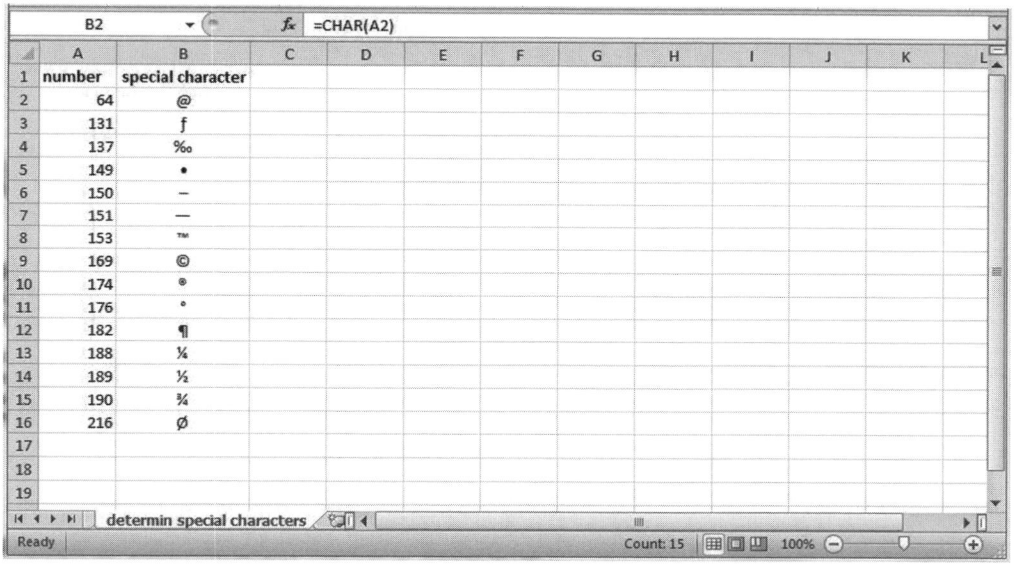

	A	B	C	D	E	F	G	H	I	J	K	L
	B2			f_x	=CHAR(A2)							
1	number	special character										
2	64	@										
3	131	ƒ										
4	137	‰										
5	149	•										
6	150	–										
7	151	—										
8	153	™										
9	169	©										
10	174	®										
11	176	°										
12	182	¶										
13	188	¼										
14	189	½										
15	190	¾										
16	216	Ø										
17												
18												
19												

determin special characters   Count: 15   100%

FIGURE 3–26

USE THE CODE FUNCTION TO DETERMINE THE NUMERIC CODE OF A CHARACTER

To return the numeric, or ASCII, code for the first character in a text string, use the CODE function. This function returns the code corresponding to the currently used character set.

▶ **To Determine the Numeric Code of a Character:**

1. In cells A2:A10, type letters of the alphabet in both upper- and lowercase.
2. Select cells B2:B10 and type the following formula: **=CODE(A2)**.
3. Press **<Ctrl+Enter>**.

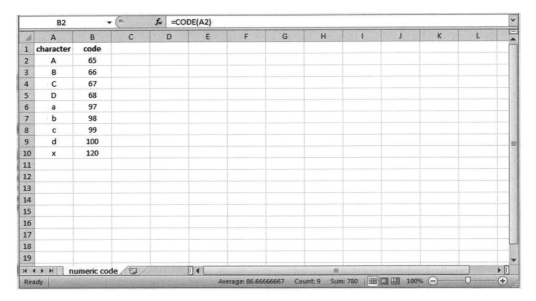

FIGURE 3–27

USE THE DOLLAR FUNCTION TO CONVERT NUMBERS TO CURRENCY IN TEXT FORMAT

The DOLLAR function converts a number to text format and applies a currency symbol. The currency format will be rounded to the specified decimal place.

DOLLAR(*number, decimals*)

> *number*: A number and a reference to a cell that contains a number, or a formula that calculates a value.

> *decimals*: The number of digits to the right of the decimal point. If negative, the number is rounded to the left of the decimal point. If omitted, Excel sets it to 2.

▶ **To Convert Numbers to Currency:**

1. In cells A2:A10, type numeric values.
2. Select cells B2:B10 and type the following formula: **=DOLLAR(A2,2)**.
3. Press **<Ctrl+Enter>**.

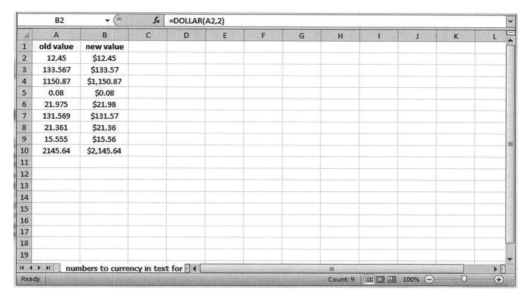

FIGURE 3–28

USE THE T FUNCTION TO CHECK FOR VALID NUMBERS

Take a look at Figure 3–29. Notice that some numbers are listed, but there are also references to text and other values. You can check whether a number is a real value in an Excel worksheet by using the T() function. This function checks whether a value is text. If it is text, T returns the text; if it is not, T returns empty text.

▶ **To Check for Valid Numbers:**

1. Enter some values in column A and change the format for some of them to text (using the Cells option from the Format menu).
2. Select cells B2:B10 and type the following formula: **=T(A2)**.
3. Press **<Ctrl+Enter>**.

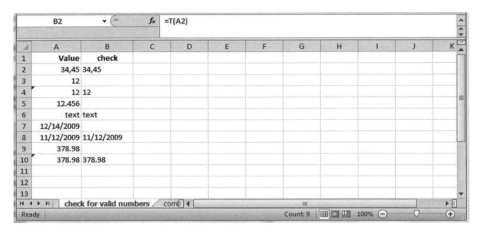

FIGURE 3–29

USE THE TEXT FUNCTION TO COMBINE AND FORMAT TEXT

In a daily sales record, employee names are listed in column A and their daily sales are entered in column B. There are two tasks here: We need to determine the percentage of the weekly sales goal ($1,000) that was met by the daily sales, and we want to combine the information from columns A and B.

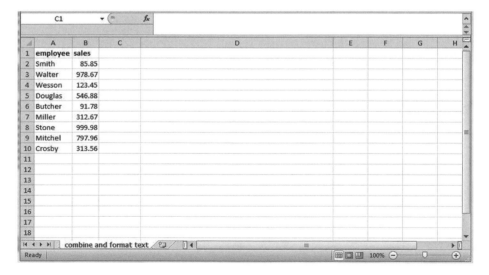

FIGURE 3–30

▶ **To Combine and Format Text:**

1. In a worksheet, copy the data shown in Figure 3–30.
2. Select cells C2:C10 and type the formula **=B2/1000**.
3. Press **<Ctrl+Enter>**.
4. Select cells D2:D10 and type the following formula: **=A2&" sold "&TEXT(B2,"$0.00")&"today. That's "&TEXT(C2,"0.0%")&" of weekly goal"**.
5. Press **<Ctrl+Enter>**.

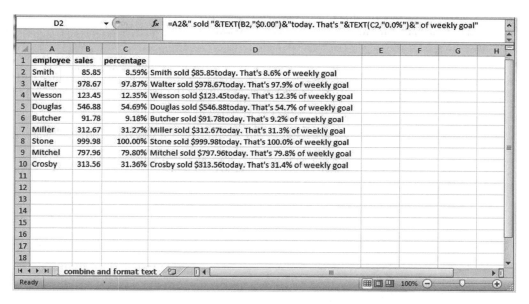

FIGURE 3–31

4 DATE AND TIME FUNCTIONS

USE CUSTOM FORMATTING TO DISPLAY THE DAY OF THE WEEK

A worksheet contains dates in column A. Use this tip to get the corresponding day of the week of these dates.

▶ **To Display Weekdays Using Customized Formatting:**

1. Select cells B2:B10 and type the formula **=A2**.
2. Press **<Ctrl+Enter>**.
3. Press Ctrl + 1.
4. Select the **Number** tab and click **Custom** in Category.
5. In the Type box, change the number format to **dddd**.
6. Press **OK**.

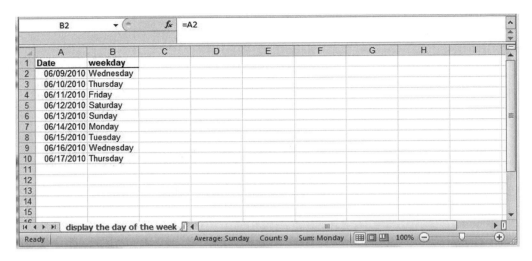

FIGURE 4–1

USE THE WEEKDAY FUNCTION TO DETERMINE THE WEEKEND

How do you find out whether or not a date falls on a weekend? To answer this question you can either use the previous tip or use the more convenient WEEKDAY function. This function returns the day of the week as a number corresponding to a date. The returned number is given as an integer, ranging from 1 (Sunday) to 7 (Saturday), by default.

▶ **To Determine the Weekend:**

1. Using the worksheet from the previous example, select cells C2:C10 and type the following formula: **=IF(OR(WEEKDAY(A2)=7, WEEKDAY(A2)=1),"weekend","").**
2. Press **<Ctrl+Enter>**.

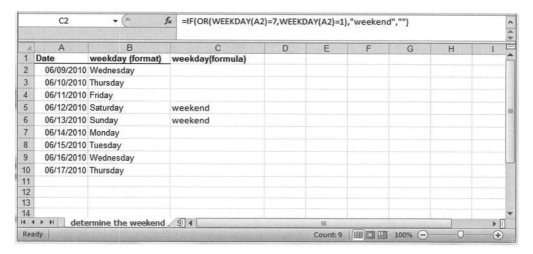

FIGURE 4–2

NOTE   *In column B use the custom format dddd to check the result of column C.*

USE THE TODAY FUNCTION TO CHECK FOR FUTURE DATES

In a worksheet, dates in column A have to be checked to see if they are in the future. The actual date can be determined by using the TODAY function and can be compared with the dates in the worksheet using the IF function. If dates are in the future, the result in column B should be Y; otherwise, it should be N.

▶ **To Check for Future Dates:**

1. In cell D1, type the formula **=TODAY()** to show the current date.
2. Select cells B2:B10 and type the following formula:
   =IF(A2<=TODAY(),"n","y").
3. Press **<Ctrl+Enter>**.

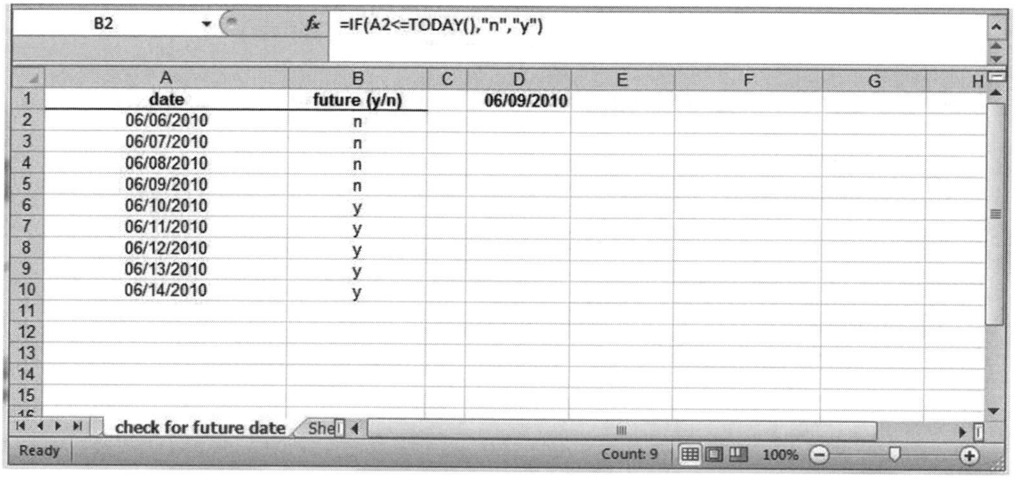

	B2	▾	*fx*	=IF(A2<=TODAY(),"n","y")					
	A	B	C	D	E	F	G	H
1	date	future (y/n)		06/09/2010				
2	06/06/2010	n						
3	06/07/2010	n						
4	06/08/2010	n						
5	06/09/2010	n						
6	06/10/2010	y						
7	06/11/2010	y						
8	06/12/2010	y						
9	06/13/2010	y						
10	06/14/2010	y						
11								
12								
13								
14								
15								

check for future date / She

Ready   Count: 9   100%

FIGURE 4–3

USE THE TEXT FUNCTION TO CALCULATE WITH THE TODAY FUNCTION

A project starts today and ends 10 days later. These dates are shown in cells B1 and B2. The end date has to be calculated based on the start date, and the dates have to be combined with additional text to form the message shown in cell A4.

▶ **To Calculate with the TODAY Function:**

1. In cell B1 type the formula **=TODAY()**.
2. In cell B2 type the formula **=TODAY()+10** to add ten days to the current date.
3. Select cell A4 and type the following formula: **="The project starts on " & TEXT(B1,"MM/DD/YYYY") & " and ends on " & TEXT(B2,"MM/DD/YYYY")**.
4. Press **<Enter>**.

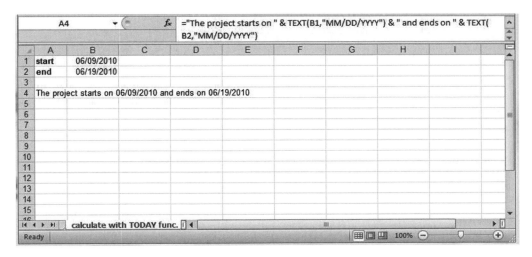

FIGURE 4–4

NOTE *The TEXT function (TEXT(value, format_text)) converts a value to text in a specific number format. In this example, format_text is shown as MM = month (two digits), DD = day (two digits), and YYYY = year (four digits).*

USE THE NOW FUNCTION TO SHOW THE CURRENT TIME

The previous tip described how to get the current date. Now we want to determine the current time. The NOW function returns the serial number of the current date and time. Microsoft Excel stores dates as sequential numbers so they can be used in calculations. By default, January 1, 1900, is number 1, and January 1, 2006, is number 38718 because it is 38,717 days after January 1, 1900. Numbers to the right of the decimal point in the number represent the time; numbers to the left represent the date. For example, the serial number .5 represents the time 12:00 noon. The NOW() function is not updated continuously.

▶ **To Show the Current Time:**

1. In cell A1 type the formula **=NOW()** and press **<Enter>**.
2. Ensure that cell A1 is selected and choose **Cells** from the Format menu.

3. In the **Number** tab, select **Date** under Category.
4. Select the format **3/14/01 1:30 PM**.
5. Press **<Enter>**.

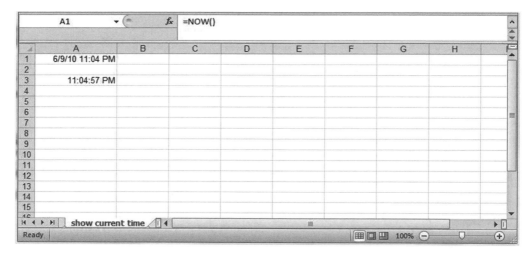

FIGURE 4–5

USE THE NOW **FUNCTION TO CALCULATE TIME**

To calculate with time, it is helpful to know that Excel stores the time as a decimal value. For example, 0.5 is 12:00 noon, 0.75 is 18:00, and so on.

▶ **To Calculate with Time:**

1. In cell B1 type the formula **=NOW()**.
2. In cell B2 type the formula **=B1+0.25** to add six hours to the current time in cell B1.
3. Type the following formula in cell C1: **="The meeting starts at " & TEXT(B1,"hh:mm") & " and ends at " & TEXT(B2,"hh:mm")**.
4. Press **<Enter>**.

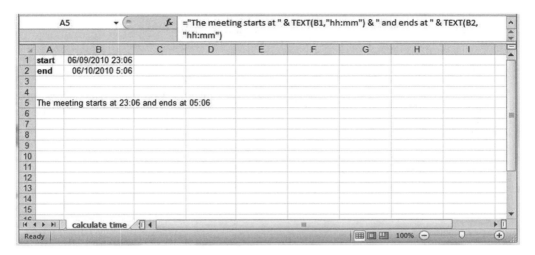

FIGURE 4–6

USE THE DATE FUNCTION TO COMBINE COLUMNS WITH DATE PARTS

The worksheet shown in Figure 4–7 uses three columns showing dates. Column A lists years, column B lists months using numbers from 1 to 12, and column C contains the days of a month from 1 to 31. These columns have to be combined to show one formatted date. To do so, use the DATE function.

DATE(*year, month, day*)

year: This argument can be from one to four digits. Microsoft Excel for Windows uses the 1900 date system.

month: A number representing the month of the year (1 to 12).

day: A number representing the day of the month (1 to 31).

▶ **To Combine Values of Cells into One Date:**

1. Select cells D2:D10 and type the following formula:
   =DATE(A2,B2,C2).
2. Press **<Ctrl+Enter>**.

NOTE *Excel knows which years are leap years, and thus provides correct results even when incorrect data is entered, as in row 3.*

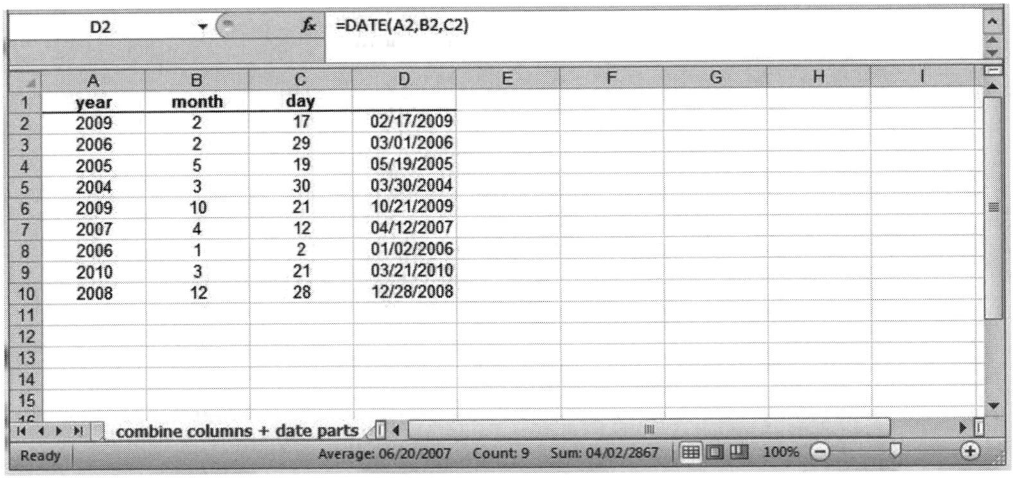

	A	B	C	D	E	F	G	H	I
	D2	▼		f_x =DATE(A2,B2,C2)					
1	year	month	day						
2	2009	2	17	02/17/2009					
3	2006	2	29	03/01/2006					
4	2005	5	19	05/19/2005					
5	2004	3	30	03/30/2004					
6	2009	10	21	10/21/2009					
7	2007	4	12	04/12/2007					
8	2006	1	2	01/02/2006					
9	2010	3	21	03/21/2010					
10	2008	12	28	12/28/2008					
11									
12									
13									
14									
15									

combine columns + date parts

Ready   Average: 06/20/2007   Count: 9   Sum: 04/02/2867   100%

FIGURE 4–7

USE THE LEFT, MID, AND RIGHT FUNCTIONS TO EXTRACT DATE PARTS

The worksheet in Figure 4–8 contains date values in column A. Excel cannot interpret these values as dates. To show the date in a correct format, the values of column A have to be extracted to year, month, and day.

▶ **To Extract, Combine, and Display the Correct Format:**

1. Select cells B2:B10 and type the following formula:
   =DATE(LEFT(A2,4),MID(A2,FIND(".",A2,1)+1,2), RIGHT(A2,2)).
2. Press **<Ctrl+Enter>**.

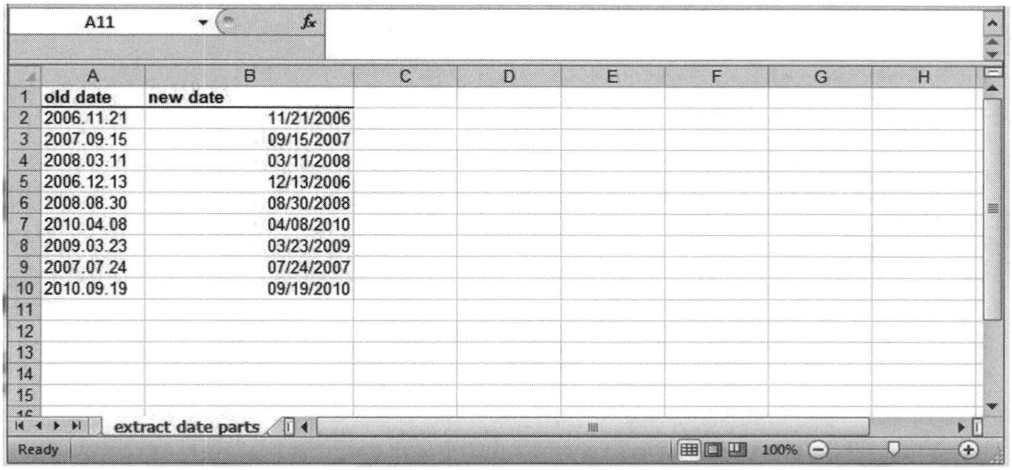

	A	B
1	old date	new date
2	2006.11.21	11/21/2006
3	2007.09.15	09/15/2007
4	2008.03.11	03/11/2008
5	2006.12.13	12/13/2006
6	2008.08.30	08/30/2008
7	2010.04.08	04/08/2010
8	2009.03.23	03/23/2009
9	2007.07.24	07/24/2007
10	2010.09.19	09/19/2010

FIGURE 4–8

NOTE *The first four digits have to be transferred with the LEFT function. Then use the FIND function to detect the decimal point. On the right of the first decimal point (+1), two digits are interpreted as the month using the MID function. On the right side of the second decimal point, use the RIGHT function to extract two digits as the day value.*

USE THE TEXT FUNCTION TO EXTRACT DATE PARTS

A worksheet contains date values in column A as text that cannot be interpreted by Excel as date values. As in the previous example, the text has to be extracted, but the result should be specially formatted as shown in the screenshot below.

▶ To Extract, Combine, and Show a Specially Formatted Date:

1. Select cells B2:B10 and type the following formula: **=TEXT(DATE(RIGHT(A2,4),MID(A2,3,2), MID(A2,1,2)),"YYYY-MM-DD")**.
2. Press **<Ctrl+Enter>**.

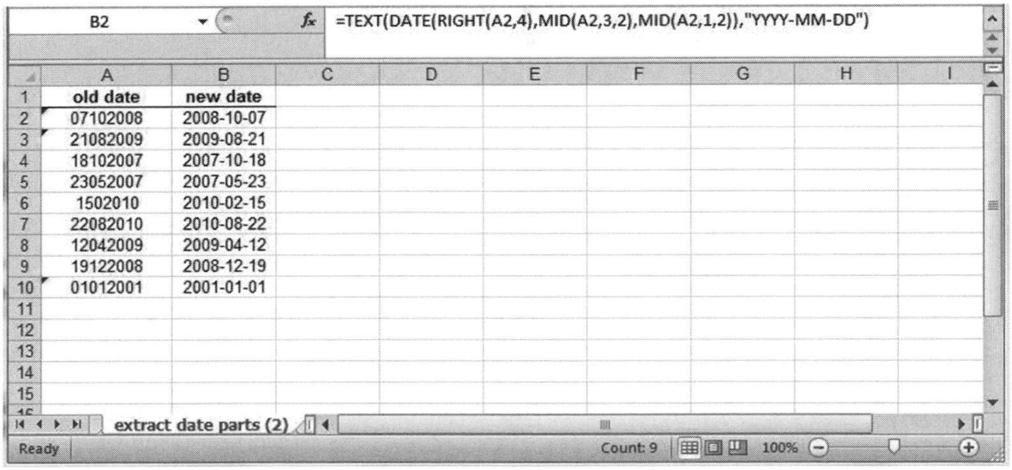
B2 =TEXT(DATE(RIGHT(A2,4),MID(A2,3,2),MID(A2,1,2)),"YYYY-MM-DD")

	A	B
1	old date	new date
2	07102008	2008-10-07
3	21082009	2009-08-21
4	18102007	2007-10-18
5	23052007	2007-05-23
6	1502010	2010-02-15
7	22082010	2010-08-22
8	12042009	2009-04-12
9	19122008	2008-12-19
10	01012001	2001-01-01

extract date parts (2)
Ready Count: 9 100%

FIGURE 4–9

NOTE *First, transfer the last four digits with the RIGHT function. Then use the MID function twice to get the two digits for month and day. With the TEXT function the date can be formatted individually.*

USE THE DATEVALUE FUNCTION TO RECALCULATE DATES FORMATTED AS TEXT

Figure 4–10 shows start and end dates in columns A and B. Excel cannot interpret the columns as dates because they are formatted as text. To convert and calculate these types of dates, use the DATEVALUE function. This function returns the serial number of the date represented by the "text date."

Let's determine the difference between start and end dates.

▶ To Calculate the Difference between Text Dates:

1. Select cells C2:C10.
2. Type the following formula: **=DATEVALUE(B2)-DATEVALUE(A2)**.
3. Press **<Ctrl+Enter>**.

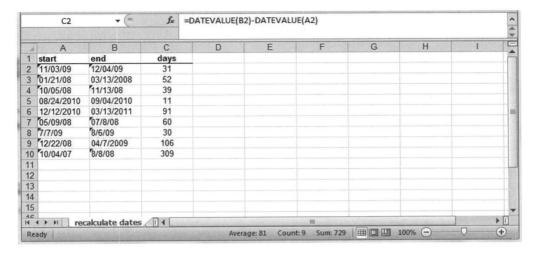

	C2		▼		●		*fx*	=DATEVALUE(B2)-DATEVALUE(A2)					

	A	B	C	D	E	F	G	H	I
1	start	end	days						
2	11/03/09	12/04/09	31						
3	01/21/08	03/13/2008	52						
4	10/05/08	11/13/08	39						
5	08/24/2010	09/04/2010	11						
6	12/12/2010	03/13/2011	91						
7	05/09/08	07/8/08	60						
8	7/7/09	8/6/09	30						
9	12/22/08	04/7/2009	106						
10	10/04/07	8/8/08	309						
11									
12									
13									
14									
15									

recalculate dates

Ready   Average: 81   Count: 9   Sum: 729   100%

FIGURE 4–10

USE THE YEAR FUNCTION TO EXTRACT THE YEAR PART OF A DATE

As shown in Figure 4–11, column A of a worksheet contains a list of dates formatted in different ways. To determine the year corresponding to a date, use the YEAR function. This function returns the year as an integer in the range 1900 to 9999. If the year is not specified, as in cell A9, the year is assumed to be the current year.

▶ **To Extract the Year as Part of a Date:**

1. In cells A2:A10, generate a list of dates using different formats.
2. Select cells B2:B10 and type the following formula: **=YEAR(A2)**.
3. Press **<Ctrl+Enter>**.

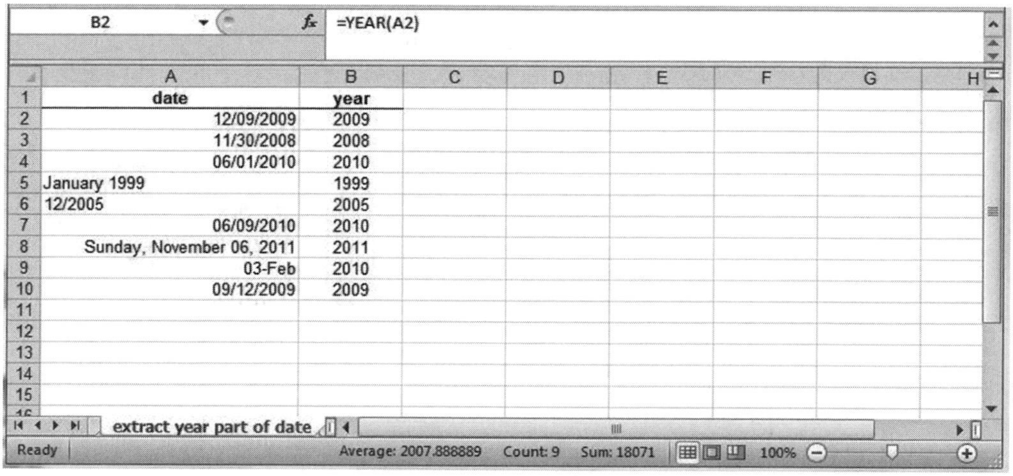

B2	fx =YEAR(A2)

	A	B	C	D	E	F	G	H
1	date	year						
2	12/09/2009	2009						
3	11/30/2008	2008						
4	06/01/2010	2010						
5	January 1999	1999						
6	12/2005	2005						
7	06/09/2010	2010						
8	Sunday, November 06, 2011	2011						
9	03-Feb	2010						
10	09/12/2009	2009						
11								
12								
13								
14								
15								

extract year part of date

Ready   Average: 2007.888889   Count: 9   Sum: 18071   100%

FIGURE 4–11

USE THE MONTH FUNCTION TO EXTRACT THE MONTH PART OF A DATE

For this tip use the worksheet from the previous example. Column A contains dates formatted in different ways. To determine the month part of a date, use the MONTH function. This function returns the month corresponding to a date as an integer in the range 1 to 12.

▶ **To Extract the Month Part of a Date:**

1. In cells A2:A10 generate a list of dates using different formats.
2. Select cells B2:B10 and type the following formula: **=MONTH(A2)**.
3. Press **<Ctrl+Enter>**.

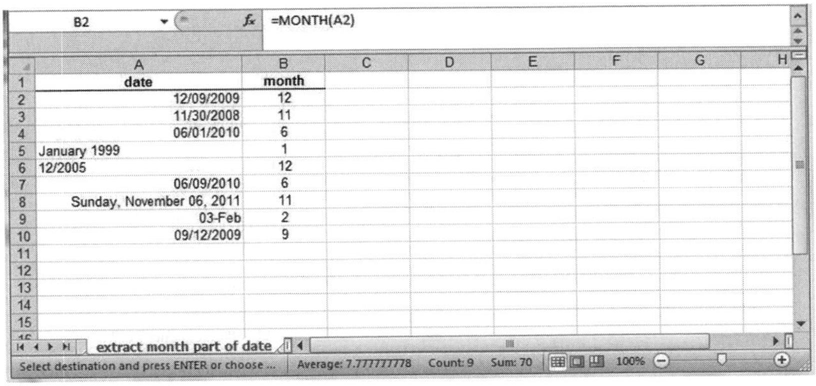

FIGURE 4–12

USE THE DAY FUNCTION TO EXTRACT THE DAY PART OF A DATE

Once again, use the worksheet from the previous two examples. Column A contains dates in different formats. To determine the day part of a date, use the DAY function. This function returns the day corresponding to a date as an integer in the range 1 to 31.

▶ **To Extract the Day as Part of a Date:**

1. In cells A2:A10 generate a list of dates using different formats.
2. Select cells B2:B10 and type the following formula: **=DAY(A2)**.
3. Press **<Ctrl+Enter>**.

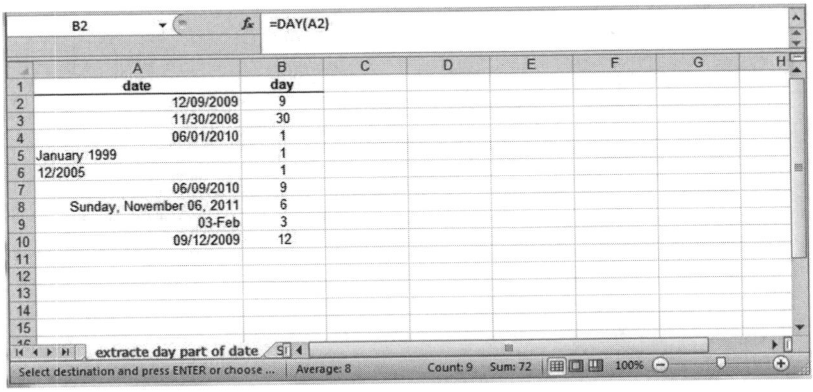

FIGURE 4–13

NOTE   *If the day part is missing (see rows 5 and 6), the function returns the value 1.*

USE THE MONTH AND DAY FUNCTIONS TO SORT BIRTHDAYS BY MONTH

The worksheet in Figure 4–14 contains a list of employees and their birth-days. This list has to be sorted by month, which is not possible with Excel's usual sort function. Use this tip to insert a supporting column to convert the month and day dates to serial values.

▶ **To Sort Birthdays by Month:**

1. In cells A2:B10 generate a list of employees and their birthdays.
2. Select cells C2:C10 and type the following formula: **=MONTH(B2)*100+DAY(B2)**.
3. Press **<Ctrl+Enter>**.
4. Select cell C1.
5. From the **Home** tab choose the **Editing** bar.
6. Click on **Sort & Filter** and choose **Sort smallest to largest**.
7. Format the column as General to display serial values rather than dates.

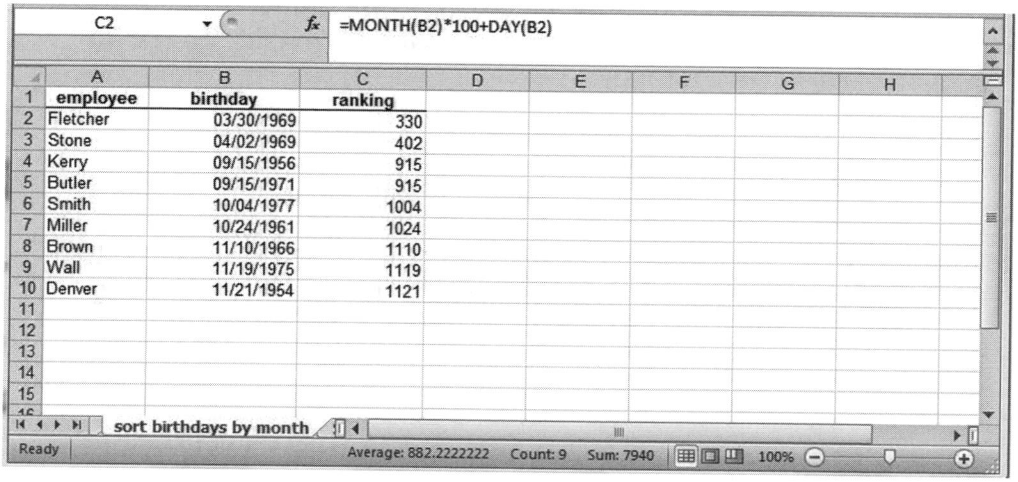

	C2	▾	f_x	=MONTH(B2)*100+DAY(B2)					
	A	B	C	D	E	F	G	H	
1	employee	birthday	ranking						
2	Fletcher	03/30/1969	330						
3	Stone	04/02/1969	402						
4	Kerry	09/15/1956	915						
5	Butler	09/15/1971	915						
6	Smith	10/04/1977	1004						
7	Miller	10/24/1961	1024						
8	Brown	11/10/1966	1110						
9	Wall	11/19/1975	1119						
10	Denver	11/21/1954	1121						
11									
12									
13									
14									
15									

sort birthdays by month

Ready   Average: 882.2222222   Count: 9   Sum: 7940   100%

FIGURE 4–14

USE THE DATE FUNCTION TO ADD MONTHS TO A DATE

Let's say we want to add a number of months to a given start date. In a new worksheet, list different start dates in column A. In column B, enter the number of months to be added to or subtracted from the start date. Based on that data, the end date can be calculated.

▶ **To Add Months to or Subtract Months from Dates:**

1. In cells A2:A10 list some start dates as shown in Figure 4–15.
2. In cells B2:B10 list the number of months to add or subtract.
3. Select cells C2:C10 and type the following formula:
   =DATE(YEAR(A2),MONTH(A2)+B2,DAY(A2)).
4. Press **<Ctrl+Enter>**.

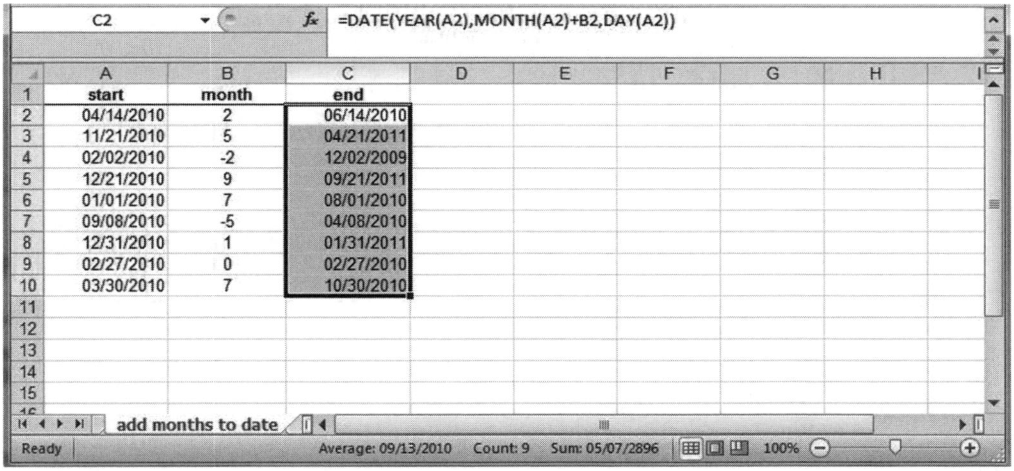

	C2		f_x	=DATE(YEAR(A2),MONTH(A2)+B2,DAY(A2))					
	A	B	C	D	E	F	G	H	
1	start	month	end						
2	04/14/2010	2	06/14/2010						
3	11/21/2010	5	04/21/2011						
4	02/02/2010	-2	12/02/2009						
5	12/21/2010	9	09/21/2011						
6	01/01/2010	7	08/01/2010						
7	09/08/2010	-5	04/08/2010						
8	12/31/2010	1	01/31/2011						
9	02/27/2010	0	02/27/2010						
10	03/30/2010	7	10/30/2010						

FIGURE 4–15

NOTE *To determine an end date in the past, put a minus sign in front of the number of months.*

USE THE EOMONTH FUNCTION TO DETERMINE THE LAST DAY OF A MONTH

To find the last day of a month, use the EOMONTH function (EOMONTH(*start_date*, *offset_months*)). This function returns the date of the last day of the month, offset_months from start_date. If the function is not available, load the Analysis ToolPak add-in. From the **File** tab choose **Options**. Select Add-Ins. From dropdown **Manage** select **Excel Add-Ins** and click **GO**. In the dialog **Add-Ins** tick the **Analysis ToolPak** box and click **OK**.

▶ **To Determine the Last Day of a Month:**

1. In cells A2:A10 enter some dates.
2. In cells B2:B10 enter the desired offset from the start date (positive or negative values).
3. Select cells C2:C10 and type the following formula:
   =EOMONTH(A2,B2).
4. Press **<Ctrl+Enter>**.

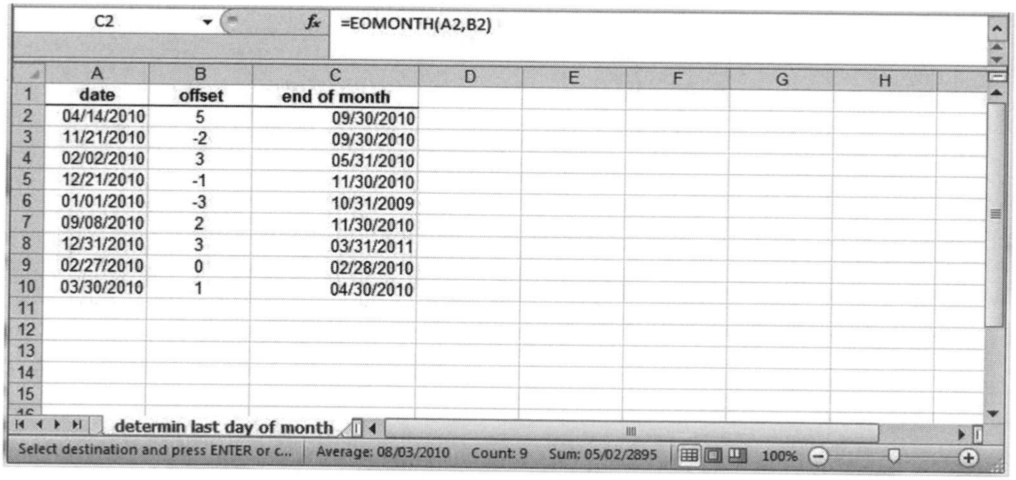

	C2		f_x	=EOMONTH(A2,B2)					
	A	B	C	D	E	F	G	H	
1	date	offset	end of month						
2	04/14/2010	5	09/30/2010						
3	11/21/2010	-2	09/30/2010						
4	02/02/2010	3	05/31/2010						
5	12/21/2010	-1	11/30/2010						
6	01/01/2010	-3	10/31/2009						
7	09/08/2010	2	11/30/2010						
8	12/31/2010	3	03/31/2011						
9	02/27/2010	0	02/28/2010						
10	03/30/2010	1	04/30/2010						
11									
12									
13									
14									
15									

determin last day of month

Select destination and press ENTER or c...   Average: 08/03/2010   Count: 9   Sum: 05/02/2895   100%

FIGURE 4–16

USE THE DAYS360 FUNCTION TO CALCULATE WITH A 360-DAY YEAR

If there is an accounting system installed that is based on 12 30-day months, the DAYS360 function can be used. This function returns the number of days between two dates based on a 360-day year.

Here is the syntax:

DAYS360(*start_date*, *end_date*, *method*)

start_date: The start date.

end_date: The end date.

method: A logical value that specifies which method to use (U.S. or European).

U.S. (NASD) method: Used if method is FALSE. If the starting date is the 31st of a month, it is considered to be the 30th of the same month. If the ending date is the 31st of a month and the starting date is earlier than the 30th of the month, the ending date is considered to be the first of the next month; otherwise, the ending date is considered to be the 30th of the same month.

European method: Used if method is TRUE. Starting or ending dates on the 31st of a month are considered to be the 30th of the same month.

▶ **To Calculate with 360-Day Years:**

1. In a worksheet, copy the data in columns A and B from Figure 4–17.
2. Select cells C2:C10 and type the following formula: **=DAYS360(A2,B2,FALSE)**.
3. Press **<Ctrl+Enter>**.

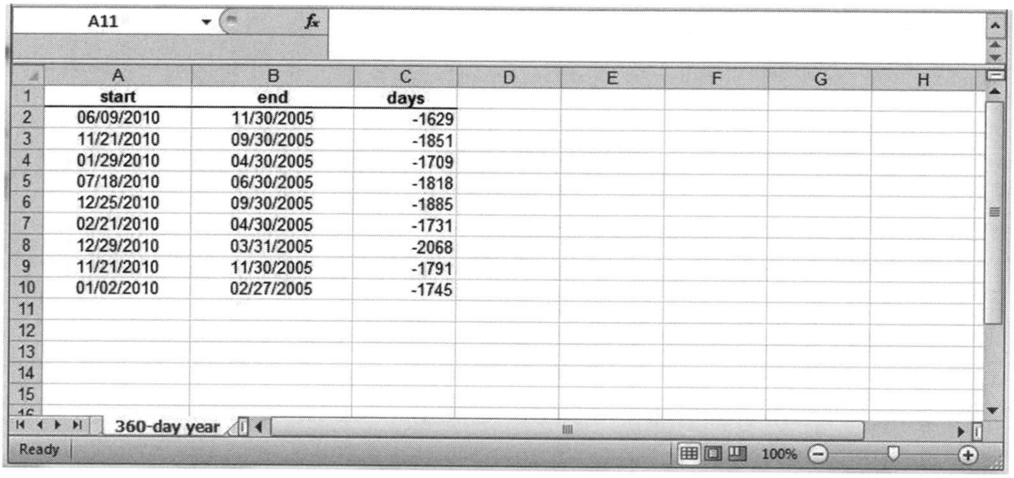

	start	end	days
2	06/09/2010	11/30/2005	-1629
3	11/21/2010	09/30/2005	-1851
4	01/29/2010	04/30/2005	-1709
5	07/18/2010	06/30/2005	-1818
6	12/25/2010	09/30/2005	-1885
7	02/21/2010	04/30/2005	-1731
8	12/29/2010	03/31/2005	-2068
9	11/21/2010	11/30/2005	-1791
10	01/02/2010	02/27/2005	-1745

FIGURE 4–17

USE THE WEEKDAY FUNCTION TO CALCULATE WITH DIFFERENT HOURLY PAY RATES

Many companies calculate payroll using hourly rates for each employee. The hourly rates depend on which days are worked, as work performed on the weekend is often paid at a higher rate than work performed Monday through Friday.

In this example, different hourly rates are defined based on which days are worked. Column A lists the dates, column B has the custom format DDD to show the day of the week, and column C lists the number of hours worked.

▶ To Calculate with Different Hourly Pay Rates:

1. In a worksheet, enter the data shown in columns A, B, and C in Figure 4–18.
2. Select cell F2 and enter **12.50** (hourly rate for Monday through Friday).
3. Select cell F5 and enter **18.50** (hourly rate for Saturday and Sunday).
4. Select cells D2:D10 and type the following formula: **=IF(OR(WEEKDAY(A2)=1,WEEKDAY(A2)=7), C2*$F$5,C2*$F$2)**.
5. Press **<Ctrl+Enter>**.

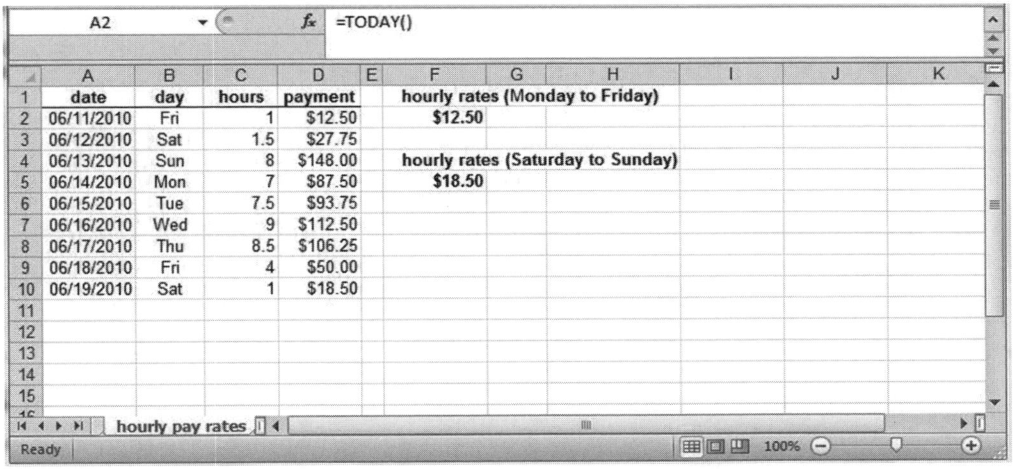

A2 | =TODAY()

	A	B	C	D	E	F	G	H
1	date	day	hours	payment		hourly rates (Monday to Friday)		
2	06/11/2010	Fri	1	$12.50		$12.50		
3	06/12/2010	Sat	1.5	$27.75				
4	06/13/2010	Sun	8	$148.00		hourly rates (Saturday to Sunday)		
5	06/14/2010	Mon	7	$87.50		$18.50		
6	06/15/2010	Tue	7.5	$93.75				
7	06/16/2010	Wed	9	$112.50				
8	06/17/2010	Thu	8.5	$106.25				
9	06/18/2010	Fri	4	$50.00				
10	06/19/2010	Sat	1	$18.50				

FIGURE 4–18

USE THE WEEKNUM FUNCTION TO DETERMINE THE WEEK NUMBER

To determine the week number of a particular date (a very common practice in Europe), load the Analysis ToolPak add-in. From the **File** tab choose **Options**. Select **Add-Ins**. From dropdown **Manage** select **Excel Add-Ins** and click **GO**. In the dialog **Add-Ins** tick the **Analysis ToolPak** box and click **OK**.

Now the WEEKNUM function is available. This function returns a number that indicates where the week falls numerically within a year.

▶ To Determine the Week Number:

1. Type different dates of the year in cells A2:A10.
2. Select cells B2:B10 and type the following formula: **=WEEKNUM(A2)**.
3. Press **<Ctrl+Enter>**.

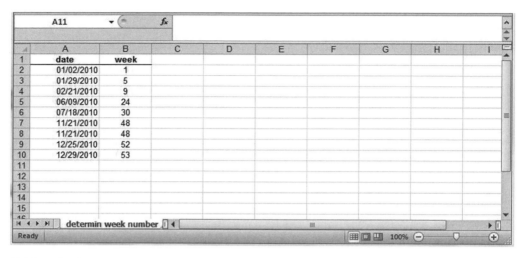

USE THE EDATE FUNCTION TO CALCULATE MONTHS

If a few months have to be added to or subtracted from a date, the EDATE function is very useful. This function returns a serial number that represents the date that is the indicated number of months before or after a specified date (offset).

In this example, column A of a worksheet contains the start dates. In column B, enter the offset in months to be added or subtracted. The result should show up in column C.

▶ **To Use EDATE and Add or Subtract a Number of Months to Start Dates:**

1. Enter different start dates in column A.
2. Enter offset months in column B.
3. Select cells C2:C10 and type the following formula: **=EDATE(A2,B2)**.
4. Press **<Ctrl+Enter>**.

	A	B	C	D	E	F	G	H
1	start	offset	end					
2	09/23/2010	1	10/23/2010					
3	12/11/2010	3	03/11/2011					
4	01/01/2010	6	07/01/2010					
5	08/08/2010	-5	03/08/2010					
6	10/21/2010	12	10/21/2011					
7	11/17/2010	1	12/17/2010					
8	05/09/2010	-3	02/09/2010					
9	10/30/2010	2	12/30/2010					
10	01/09/2010	10	11/09/2010					

FIGURE 4–20

NOTE *To use the EDATE function, the Analysis ToolPak add-in has to be installed as described in the previous example.*

USE THE WORKDAY FUNCTION TO CALCULATE WORKDAYS

A worksheet is used to schedule a project. The project contains the start date and five major steps. Each step takes an estimated number of days to accomplish. To determine the correct end date, weekends and additional days off have to be taken into consideration. To perform this task, use the WORKDAY function from the Analysis ToolPak add-in. This function returns a date that is the indicated number of workdays before or after a date. Workdays exclude weekends and any dates identified as holidays. The syntax is as follows:

WORKDAY(*start_date*, *days*, *holidays*)

start_date: The start date.

days: The total number of available days, not counting weekends and holidays, before or after start_date. Both positive and negative values are acceptable.

holidays: (optional) One or more dates that are to be excluded from the work schedule.

▶ **To Determine the End Date of a Project:**

1. In cell C2, enter the start date of the project.
2. In column B, enter the estimated days to finish each step.
3. In cell D2, type the following formula:
   =WORKDAY(C3,B3,$F$2:$F$8).
4. In cells F1:F8, additional holidays can be listed individually.
5. In cell C3, type the formula **=D2+1**.
6. Fill cells C3 and D2 down to C6 and D6.

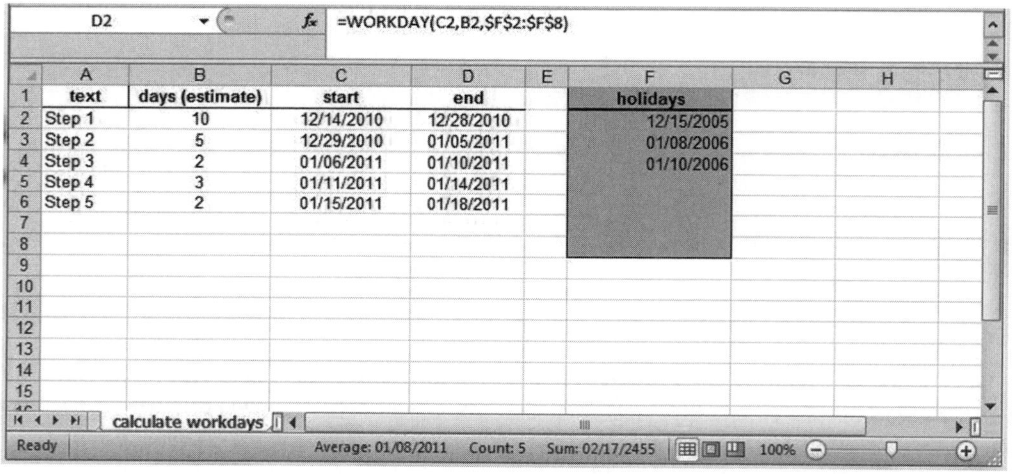

	A	B	C	D	E	F	G	H
			fx	=WORKDAY(C2,B2,$F$2:$F$8)				
1	text	days (estimate)	start	end		holidays		
2	Step 1	10	12/14/2010	12/28/2010		12/15/2005		
3	Step 2	5	12/29/2010	01/05/2011		01/08/2006		
4	Step 3	2	01/06/2011	01/10/2011		01/10/2006		
5	Step 4	3	01/11/2011	01/14/2011				
6	Step 5	2	01/15/2011	01/18/2011				

D2 cell selected. calculate workdays tab. Ready. Average: 01/08/2011　Count: 5　Sum: 02/17/2455　100%

FIGURE 4–21

USE THE NETWORKDAYS FUNCTION TO DETERMINE THE NUMBER OF WORKDAYS

In this example a project has to be scheduled. Each of the five steps has a fixed start and end date. To determine the number of complete workdays between the start and end dates, the NETWORKDAYS function from the Analysis ToolPak add-in can be used. This function excludes weekends and any dates identified as non-workdays and holidays. The syntax is as follows:

NETWORKDAYS(*start_date*, *end_date*, *holidays*)

start_date: The start date.

end_date: The end date.

holidays: (optional) One or more dates that are to be excluded from the work schedule.

▶ **To Determine the Number of Workdays:**

1. In column B, type the start date of each step.
2. In column C, type the end date of each step.
3. List additional holidays in cells F2:F6.
4. Select cells D2:D6 and type the following formula:
   =NETWORKDAYS(B2,C2,$F$2:$F$6).
5. Press **<Ctrl+Enter>**.

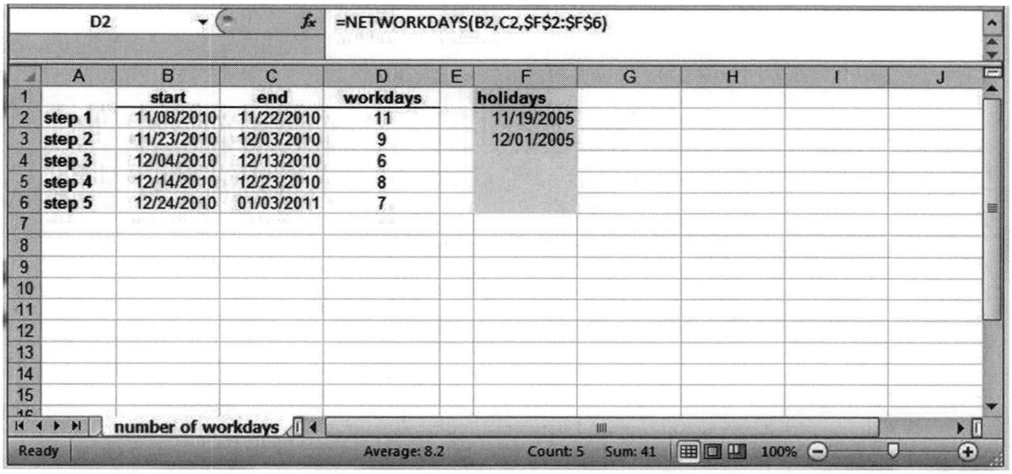

	A	B	C	D	E	F	G	H	I	J
1		start	end	workdays		holidays				
2	step 1	11/08/2010	11/22/2010	11		11/19/2005				
3	step 2	11/23/2010	12/03/2010	9		12/01/2005				
4	step 3	12/04/2010	12/13/2010	6						
5	step 4	12/14/2010	12/23/2010	8						
6	step 5	12/24/2010	01/03/2011	7						

FIGURE 4–22

USE THE YEARFRAC FUNCTION TO CALCULATE AGES OF EMPLOYEES

To calculate the difference between two dates, use the YEARFRAC function from the Analysis ToolPak add-in. This function calculates the fraction of the year represented by the number of whole days between start_date and end_date. The syntax is:

YEARFRAC(*start_date*, *end_date*, *basis*)

start_date: The start date.

end_date: The end date.

basis: Count basis to use. 0 or omitted = U.S. (NASD) 30/360, 1 = actual/actual, 2 = actual/360, 3 = actual/365, or 4 = European 30/360.

▶ **To Calculate the Age of Employees Based on the Current Date:**

1. In column A list the names of employees.
2. In column B enter their birthdays.
3. Select cells C2:C10 and type the formula **TODAY()**.
4. Press **<Ctrl+Enter>**.
5. Select cells D2:D10 and type the following formula: **=YEARFRAC(B2,C2,0)**.
6. Press **<Ctrl+Enter>**.

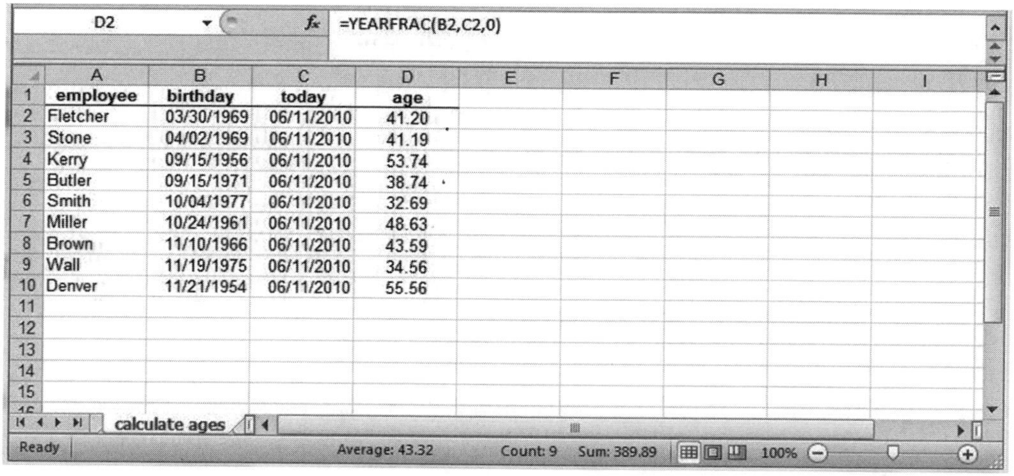

	A	B	C	D
	employee	birthday	today	age
1				
2	Fletcher	03/30/1969	06/11/2010	41.20
3	Stone	04/02/1969	06/11/2010	41.19
4	Kerry	09/15/1956	06/11/2010	53.74
5	Butler	09/15/1971	06/11/2010	38.74
6	Smith	10/04/1977	06/11/2010	32.69
7	Miller	10/24/1961	06/11/2010	48.63
8	Brown	11/10/1966	06/11/2010	43.59
9	Wall	11/19/1975	06/11/2010	34.56
10	Denver	11/21/1954	06/11/2010	55.56

D2 = YEARFRAC(B2,C2,0)

calculate ages

Ready   Average: 43.32   Count: 9   Sum: 389.89   100%

FIGURE 4–23

USE THE DATEDIF FUNCTION TO CALCULATE AGES OF EMPLOYEES

To calculate the exact age of employees, use the undocumented DATEDIF function from the Analysis ToolPak add-in. This function calculates the exact number of years, months, and days between two dates. The syntax is:

DATEDIF(*start_date*, *end_date*, *format*)

start_date: The start date.

end_date: The end date.

format: Indicates the format to use. "y" gives the difference in years; "m" in months; "d" in days; "ym" the difference in months, ignoring the year; "yd" in days, ignoring the year; and "md" in days, ignoring the month and year.

▶ **To Calculate the Ages of Employees:**

1. In column A list the names of employees.
2. In column B enter their birthdays.
3. Select cells C2:C10 and type the formula **TODAY()**.
4. Press **<Ctrl+Enter>**.
5. Select cells D2:D10 and type the following formula: **=DATEDIF(B2,C2,"Y") & " years and " & DATEDIF(B2,C2,"YM") & " months "**.
6. Press **<Ctrl+Enter>**.

	A	B	C	D	E	F	G
				D2 ▾ *fx* =DATEDIF(B2,C2,"Y") & " years and " & DATEDIF(B2,C2,"YM") & " months"			
1	employee	birthday	today	age in years and month			
2	Fletcher	03/30/1969	06/11/2010	41 years and 2 months			
3	Stone	04/02/1969	06/11/2010	41 years and 2 months			
4	Kerry	09/15/1956	06/11/2010	53 years and 8 months			
5	Butler	09/15/1971	06/11/2010	38 years and 8 months			
6	Smith	10/04/1977	06/11/2010	32 years and 8 months			
7	Miller	10/24/1961	06/11/2010	48 years and 7 months			
8	Brown	11/10/1966	06/11/2010	43 years and 7 months			
9	Wall	11/19/1975	06/11/2010	34 years and 6 months			
10	Denver	11/21/1954	06/11/2010	55 years and 6 months			
11							
12							
13							
14							
15							

FIGURE 4–24

USE THE WEEKDAY FUNCTION TO CALCULATE THE WEEKS OF ADVENT

As a practical task using previously learned functions, the start date of each week of Advent can be calculated easily. Consider that Advent begins on the fourth Sunday before Christmas. Enter in a cell the date of Christmas and use the WEEKDAY function to calculate when each week of Advent begins.

▶ **To Calculate When the Weeks of Advent Begin for 2006:**

1. In cell B2 enter **12/25/2006**.
2. In cell B4 enter this formula to find the first week of Advent: **=B2-(WEEKDAY(B2,2))-21**.
3. Enter this formula in cell B5: **=B2-(WEEKDAY(B2,2))-14**.
4. Enter this formula in cell B6: **=B2-(WEEKDAY(B2,2))-7**.
5. Enter this formula in cell B7: **=B2-(WEEKDAY(B2,2))**.

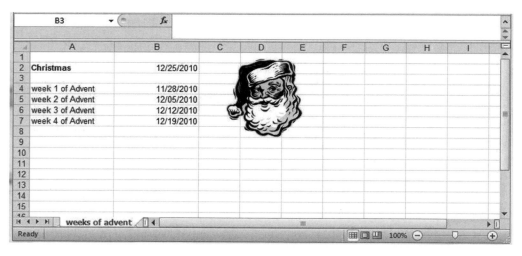

FIGURE 4–25

USE THE TIMEVALUE FUNCTION TO CONVERT TEXT TO TIME

In this example, a text string has to be converted to a valid time. Columns A and C contain different start and end times as part of a standardized text string. It is possible to extract the times and convert them to valid time values that can be used as the basis for calculations. To convert text into a valid time, use the TIMEVALUE function. This function returns the decimal number of the time represented by a text string. The decimal number is a value ranging from 0 to 0.99999999, representing the time from 0:00:00 (12:00:00 AM) to 23:59:59 (11:59:59 P.M.).

▶ **To Extract and Convert Text to Time:**

1. Select cells B2:B10 and type the following formula: **=TIMEVALUE(MID(A2,8,5))**.
2. Press **<Ctrl+Enter>**.
3. Select cells D2:D10 and type the following formula: **=TIMEVALUE(MID(C2,6,5))**.
4. Press **<Ctrl+Enter>**.
5. Select cells B2:B10 and D2:D10.
6. Press **Ctrl + 1** and select the **Number** tab, click **Time** under Category, then select the **1:30:55 PM** option in the **Type** box.
7. Click **OK**.

	D2	▾	f_x	=TIMEVALUE(MID(C2,6,5))					
	A	B	C	D	E	F	G	H	I
1	text	start-time	text	end-time					
2	start: 14:05	2:05:00 PM	end: 16:10	4:10:00 PM					
3	start: 16:59	4:59:00 PM	end: 18:11	6:11:00 PM					
4	start: 09:12	9:12:00 AM	end: 13:12	1:12:00 PM					
5	start: 14:08	2:08:00 PM	end: 17:59	5:59:00 PM					
6	start: 21:55	9:55:00 PM	end: 23:14	11:14:00 PM					
7	start: 23:10	11:10:00 PM	end: 23:45	11:45:00 PM					
8	start: 14:54	2:54:00 PM	end: 17:16	5:16:00 PM					
9	start: 11:12	11:12:00 AM	end: 13:17	1:17:00 PM					
10	start: 02:13	2:13:00 AM	end: 04:15	4:15:00 AM					
11									
12									
13									
14									
15									

convert text to time

Ready   Average: 15:17:03   Count: 18   Sum: 275:07:00   100%

FIGURE 4–26

USE A CUSTOM FORMAT TO CREATE A TIME FORMAT

When you enter time values in cells, you have to type the colon between the hours and minutes. However, this is unnecessary if you use a custom format.

▶ **To Create a Customized Time Format:**

1. Enter time values without colons and select the cells.
2. Press Ctrl + 1, select the **Number** tab, and click on **Custom** under Category.
3. Type **00":"00** as the custom format.
4. Click **OK**.

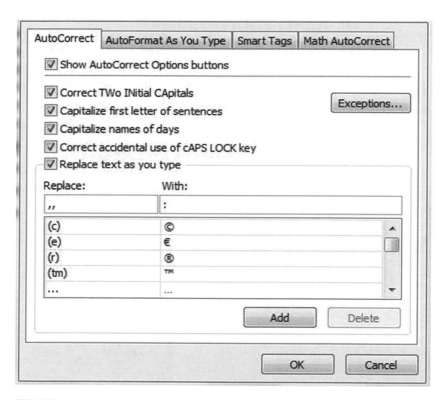

FIGURE 4–27

NOTE	*You can also use the AutoCorrect options. Click the **File** tab and then, under **Help**, click **Options**. Then click **Proofing** and afterwards click **AutoCorrect Options**. Type two commas in the Replace field and type the colon in the With field. Click **Add** to insert this option. Test this by typing 1200 in a cell. Excel corrects the input to 12:00.*

USE THE HOUR **FUNCTION TO CALCULATE**
WITH 100-MINUTE HOURS

Some companies record working time in 100-minute hours. For example, the time 6:45 is converted to 6:75, which sometimes makes further calculations easier. To convert to this format, extract the minutes from the time and divide them by 60 using the MINUTE function. This function returns the minutes of a time value. The minute is given as an integer, ranging from 0 to 59. The hours can be extracted with the HOUR function. This function returns the hour of a time value as an integer ranging from 0 (12:00 a.m.) to 23 (11:00 p.m.).

▶ **To Convert Normal Time to 100-Minute Hours:**

1. In cells A2:A10 list work dates.
2. In cells B2:B10 enter the start time for each day.
3. In cells C2:C10 record the end times.
4. Select cells D2:D10 and type the following formula:
   =HOUR(C2-B2)+MINUTE(C2-B2)/60.
5. Press **<Ctrl+Enter>**.

	A	B	C	D
1	date	start	end	time
2	11/08/2004	8:30	16:45	8.25
3	11/09/2004	7:15	15:30	8.25
4	11/10/2004	7:59	17:06	9.12
5	11/11/2004	9:11	18:34	9.38
6	11/12/2004	8:00	17:00	9.00
7	11/15/2004	8:05	19:01	10.93
8	11/18/2004	8:55	17:01	8.10
9	11/19/2004	9:12	15:02	5.83
10	11/20/2004	8:34	14:55	6.35

FIGURE 4–28

USE THE TIME FUNCTION TO COMBINE SINGLE TIME PARTS

The worksheet in Figure 4–29 shows single time parts in each column. Column B contains hours, column C contains minutes, and column D contains seconds. All three columns have to be combined into one time as shown in column E. To do this, use the TIME function. This function returns the decimal number for a particular time. The syntax is:

TIME(*hour, minute, second*)

>   *hour*: A number from 0 to 23 that represents the hour. Any value greater than 23 will be divided by 24, and the remainder will be treated as the hour value.

>   *minute*: A number from 0 to 59 that represents minutes. Any value greater than 59 will be converted to hours and minutes.

>   *second*: A number from 0 to 59 that represents seconds. Any value greater than 59 will be converted to hours, minutes, and seconds.

▶ **To Combine Single Time Parts into a Valid Time:**

1. Select cells E2:E10 and type the formula **=TIME(B2,C2,D2)**.
2. Press **<Ctrl+Enter>**.
3. From the **Format** menu, select **Cells**.
4. Select the **Number** tab and click **Custom** under Category.
5. Enter **hh:mm:ss** as the custom format.
6. Click **OK**.

	A	B	C	D	E
					fx =TIME(B2,C2,D2)
1	Name	Hour	Minute	Second	Result
2	Brian	2	12	45	2:12:45
3	Sue	2	14	10	2:14:10
4	Walter	3	1	5	3:01:05
5	Joseph	3	1	45	3:01:45
6	David	3	2	0	3:02:00
7	Wayne	3	24	59	3:24:59
8	Donald	4	0	0	4:00:00
9	Leon	4	0	37	4:00:37
10	Mark	4	2	2	4:02:02

FIGURE 4–29

Chapter 5 Basic Statistical Functions

USE THE MAX FUNCTION TO DETERMINE THE LARGEST VALUE IN A RANGE

This example finds the largest value in the range A3:D11 by using the MAX function. The function's return value is the largest value in a set.

MAX(*number1, number2, ...*)

> *number1, number2, ...*: From 1 to 30 numbers for which you want to find the largest value. It is possible to use a cell reference; however, the cells must contain numbers or values that can be converted to numbers.

▶ **To Determine the Largest Value:**

1. In cells A3:D11 type any values.
2. In cell B1 type the formula **=MAX(A3:D11)**.
3. Press **<Enter>**.

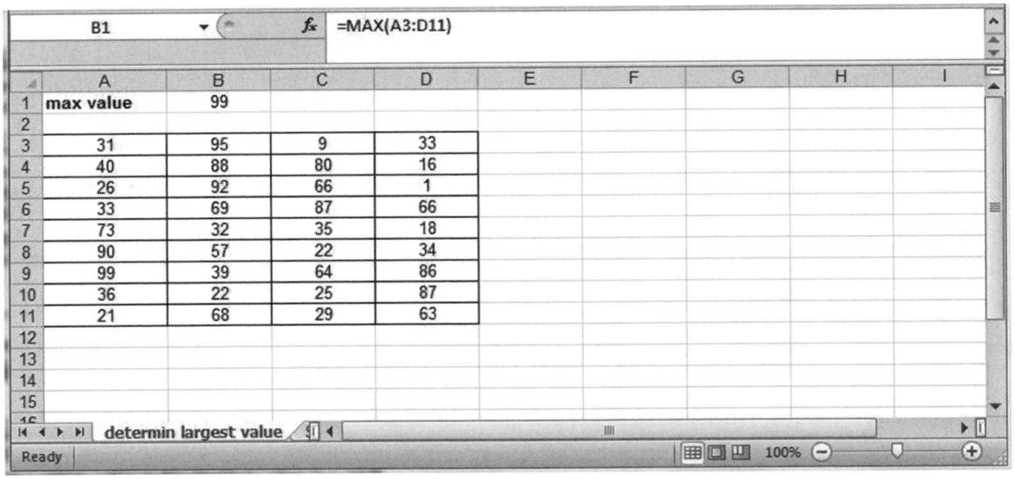

FIGURE 5–1

> **NOTE** *In Chapter 10 you will learn how to automatically mark and shade the largest value in a range.*

USE THE MIN FUNCTION TO FIND THE EMPLOYEE WITH THE LOWEST SALES

In a company, employee sales are monitored. Columns B to E contain the sales for the first four months of the year. To determine which employee has the lowest monthly sales, use the MIN function. The function's return value is the smallest value in a set.

MIN(*number1, number2, ...*)

> *number1, number2, ...*: From 1 to 30 numbers for which you want to find the smallest value. It is possible to use a cell reference; however, the cells must contain numbers or values that can be converted to numbers.

▶ **To Determine the Lowest Monthly Sales:**

1. In a worksheet, copy the range A1:E10 shown in Figure 5–2.
2. Select cells B12:E12 and type the following formula: **=MIN(B2:B10)**.
3. Press **<Ctrl+Enter>**.

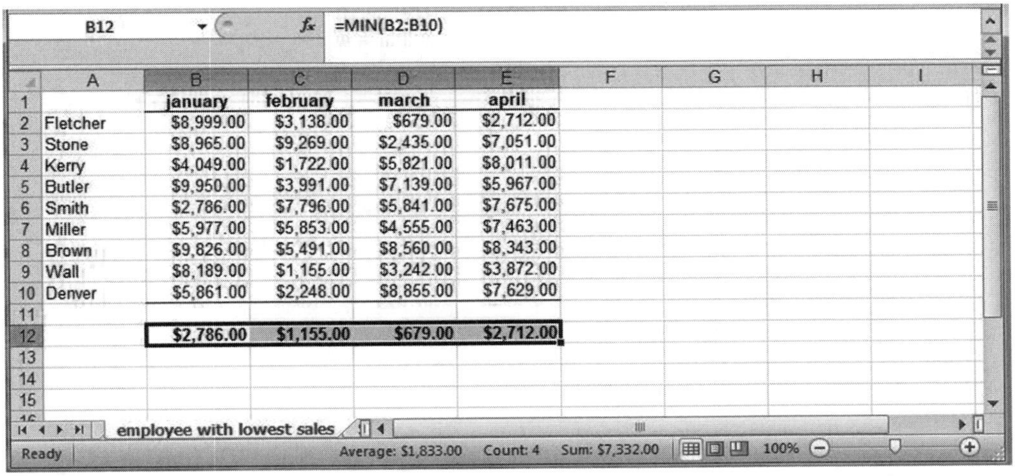

	B12		f_x	=MIN(B2:B10)					
	A	B	C	D	E	F	G	H	I
1		january	february	march	april				
2	Fletcher	$8,999.00	$3,138.00	$679.00	$2,712.00				
3	Stone	$8,965.00	$9,269.00	$2,435.00	$7,051.00				
4	Kerry	$4,049.00	$1,722.00	$5,821.00	$8,011.00				
5	Butler	$9,950.00	$3,991.00	$7,139.00	$5,967.00				
6	Smith	$2,786.00	$7,796.00	$5,841.00	$7,675.00				
7	Miller	$5,977.00	$5,853.00	$4,555.00	$7,463.00				
8	Brown	$9,826.00	$5,491.00	$8,560.00	$8,343.00				
9	Wall	$8,189.00	$1,155.00	$3,242.00	$3,872.00				
10	Denver	$5,861.00	$2,248.00	$8,855.00	$7,629.00				
11									
12		$2,786.00	$1,155.00	$679.00	$2,712.00				
13									
14									
15									

employee with lowest sales

Ready   Average: $1,833.00   Count: 4   Sum: $7,332.00   100%

FIGURE 5–2

NOTE   *In Chapter 10 you will learn how to automatically shade the smallest value in each column.*

USE THE MIN FUNCTION TO DETECT THE SMALLEST VALUE IN A COLUMN

To determine the smallest value in a single column, the MIN function is used. This function returns the smallest value in a set of values. The syntax is described in the previous tip.

▶ **To Determine the Smallest Value in a Column:**

1. In column A, type any values down to cell A10.
2. Select cell B1 and type the following formula: **=MIN(A:A)**.
3. Press **<Enter>**.

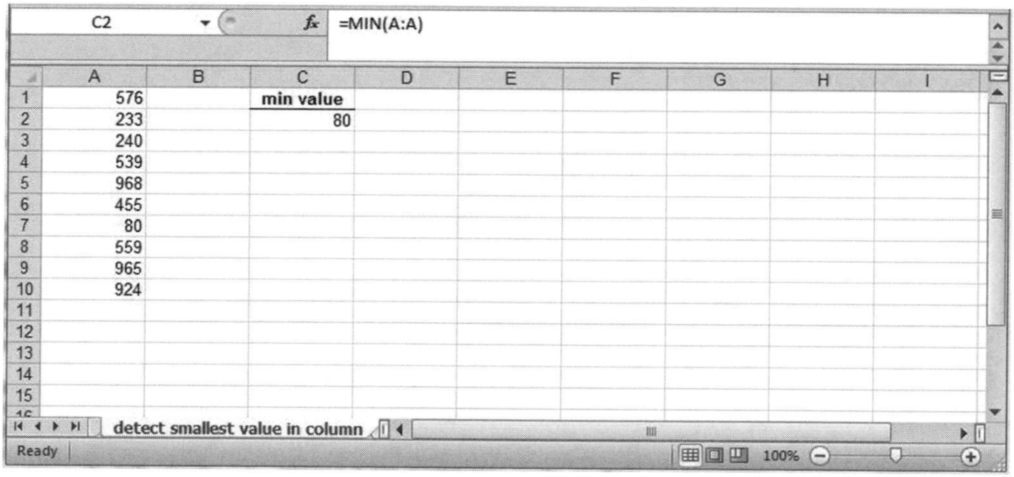

	C2	▼	ƒx	=MIN(A:A)						
	A	B	C	D	E	F	G	H	I	
1	576		min value							
2	233		80							
3	240									
4	539									
5	968									
6	455									
7	80									
8	559									
9	965									
10	924									
11										
12										
13										
14										
15										

detect smallest value in column

Ready   100%

FIGURE 5–3

NOTE *To determine the smallest value in a row, such as the smallest value in the first row, use the formula =MIN(1:1). To get the smallest value of the first three rows, use the following function: =MIN(1:3).*

USE THE SMALL FUNCTION TO FIND THE SMALLEST VALUES IN A LIST

To determine the smallest value in a list, we can use the MIN function. However, the easiest way to find multiple small values of a range is by using the SMALL function. This function returns the nth smallest value in a set of data.

SMALL(*array, n*)

array: An array or range of numerical data in which you want to find the nth smallest value.

n: The position from the smallest in the array or range of data to return.

▶ **To Determine the Three Smallest Values of a Range:**

1. In cells A1:A10 enter any values from 100 to 999.
2. Select cell C1 and type the following formula **=SMALL($A$1:$A$10,1)** to get the smallest value.
3. In cell C2 type the formula **=SMALL($A$1:$A$10,2)** to get the second smallest value.
4. In cell C3 type the formula **=SMALL($A$1:$A$10,3)** to get the third smallest value.

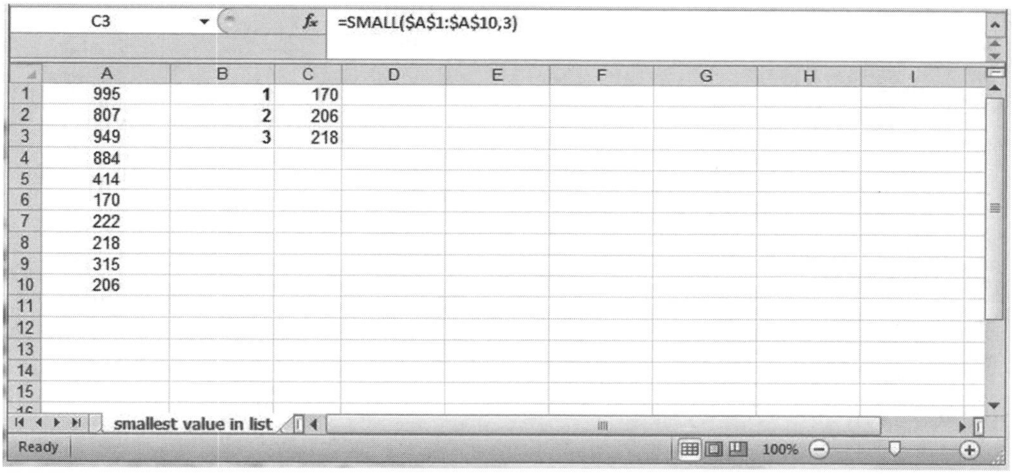

FIGURE 5–4

USE THE LARGE FUNCTION TO FIND THE HIGHEST VALUES

To determine the highest value in a list, we used the MAX function. To find out multiple high values of a range, the LARGE function can be used. This function returns the nth highest value in a set of data.

LARGE(*array, n*)

array: Array or range of numerical data in which we want to find the nth highest value.

n: The position from the highest in the array or range of data to return.

▶ **To Determine the Three Highest Values of a Range:**

1. In cells A2:C10 type any values from 0 to 99.
2. Number cells A12, A13, and A14 with 1, 2, and 3.
3. Select cells B12:D14 and type the following formula:
   =LARGE(B$2:B$10,$A12).
4. Press **<Ctrl+Enter>**.

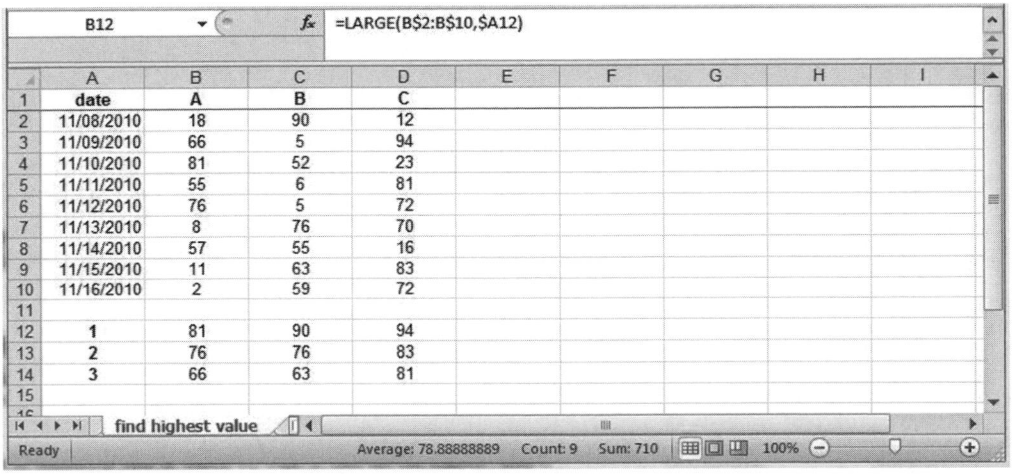

	A	B	C	D	E	F	G	H	I
	B12			fx	=LARGE(B$2:B$10,$A12)				
1	date	A	B	C					
2	11/08/2010	18	90	12					
3	11/09/2010	66	5	94					
4	11/10/2010	81	52	23					
5	11/11/2010	55	6	81					
6	11/12/2010	76	5	72					
7	11/13/2010	8	76	70					
8	11/14/2010	57	55	16					
9	11/15/2010	11	63	83					
10	11/16/2010	2	59	72					
11									
12	1	81	90	94					
13	2	76	76	83					
14	3	66	63	81					
15									

find highest value

Ready   Average: 78.88888889   Count: 9   Sum: 710   100%

FIGURE 5–5

USE THE INDEX, MATCH, AND LARGE FUNCTIONS TO DETERMINE AND LOCATE THE BEST SALESPERSON

As seen in the previous tips, it is easy to find out the highest value in a list. But how do you find the one person on a sales team who sold the most? And how do you find out how much ahead of the others he or she is?

Start with the LARGE function to determine the highest sale. Then use the INDEX and MATCH functions to retrieve the name of the employee.

▶ **To Determine and Locate the Best Employee:**

1. In cells B2:B10 type the daily sales of the employees.
2. Select cell D3 and type the following formula:
   **=INDEX($A$2:$A$10,MATCH(LARGE($B$2:$B$10,1),
   $B$2:$B$10,0))**.

3. Press **<Enter>**.
4. Select cell D6 and type the following formula:
   =LARGE($B$2:$B$10,1)-LARGE($B$2:$B$10,2).
5. Press **<Enter>**.

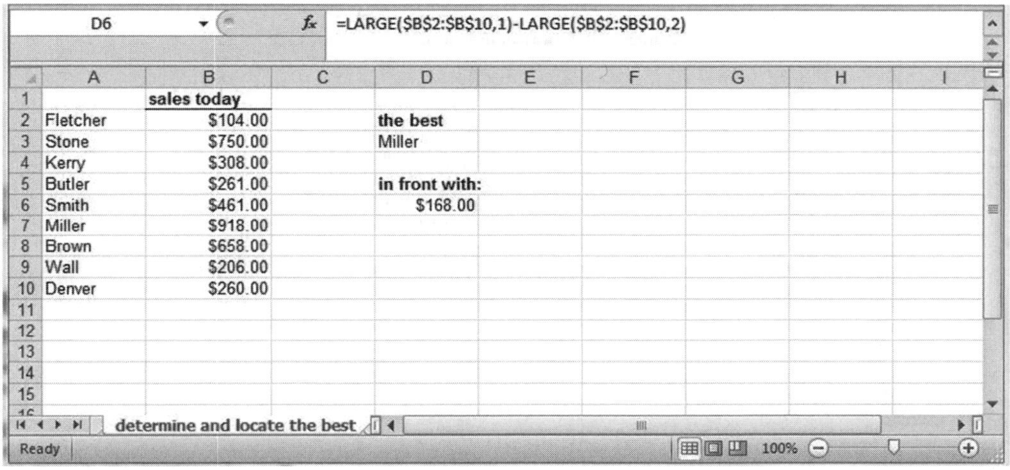

	A	B	C	D	E	F	G	H	I
	D6			fx =LARGE($B$2:$B$10,1)-LARGE($B$2:$B$10,2)					
1		sales today							
2	Fletcher	$104.00		the best					
3	Stone	$750.00		Miller					
4	Kerry	$308.00							
5	Butler	$261.00		in front with:					
6	Smith	$461.00		$168.00					
7	Miller	$918.00							
8	Brown	$658.00							
9	Wall	$206.00							
10	Denver	$260.00							
11									
12									
13									
14									
15									

determine and locate the best

FIGURE 5–6

USE THE SMALL FUNCTION TO COMPARE PRICES AND SELECT THE CHEAPEST OFFER

A worksheet lists offers from different suppliers. To make a decision as to which is the best offer, the SMALL function can be used to check for the lowest price. As in the previous tip, you can use the INDEX and MATCH functions to get the names of the companies.

▶ **To Find Out the Three Cheapest Offers and Their Supplier:**

1. In cells B2:B10 enter the offers.
2. Number the cells C2:C4 with 1, 2, and 3.
3. Select cells D2:D4 and type the following formula:
   =INDEX($A$2:$A$10,MATCH(SMALL($B$2:$B$10,C2), $B$2:$B$10,0)).
4. Press **<Ctrl+Enter>**.

5. Select cells E2:E4 and type the following formula:
   =SMALL($B$2:$B$10,C2).
6. Press **<Ctrl+Enter>**.

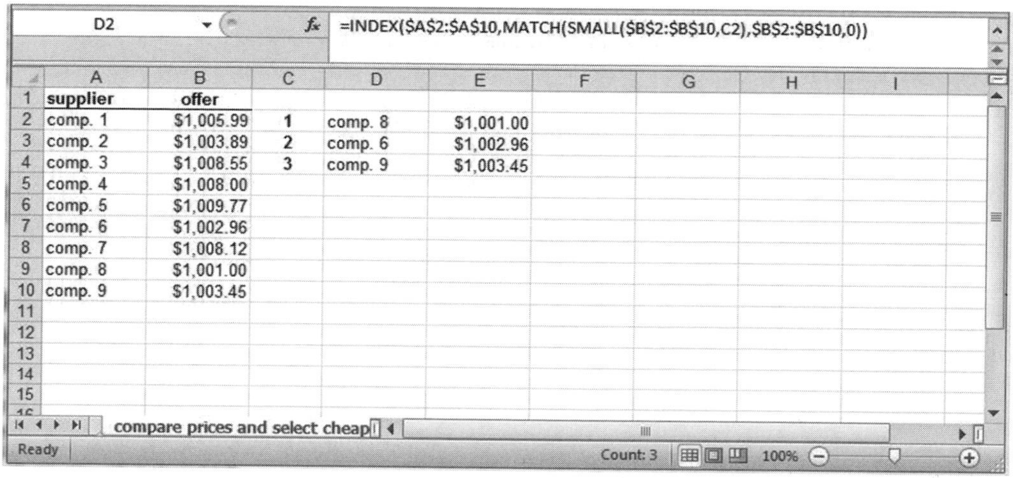

	D2	▼	f_x	=INDEX($A$2:$A$10,MATCH(SMALL($B$2:$B$10,C2),$B$2:$B$10,0))						
	A	B	C	D	E	F	G	H	I	
1	supplier	offer								
2	comp. 1	$1,005.99	1	comp. 8	$1,001.00					
3	comp. 2	$1,003.89	2	comp. 6	$1,002.96					
4	comp. 3	$1,008.55	3	comp. 9	$1,003.45					
5	comp. 4	$1,008.00								
6	comp. 5	$1,009.77								
7	comp. 6	$1,002.96								
8	comp. 7	$1,008.12								
9	comp. 8	$1,001.00								
10	comp. 9	$1,003.45								
11										
12										
13										
14										
15										

compare prices and select cheap

Ready   Count: 3   100%

FIGURE 5–7

USE THE AVERAGE FUNCTION TO CALCULATE THE AVERAGE OUTPUT

In this example, the output of three production lines has been recorded for several days. Now the average of the three highest outputs of each line has to be calculated. For this task, Excel provides the AVERAGE function, which returns the average, or arithmetic mean, of the arguments.

AVERAGE(*number1, number2, ...*)

number1, number2, ...: From 1 to 30 numeric arguments for which you want to determine the average. It is also possible to use a cell reference, as shown in this example.

▶ **To Calculate the Average of the Three Highest Capacities of Each Production Line:**

1. In cells B2:D10 type the output of each machine.
2. Select cells B13:D13 and type the following formula:
   **=AVERAGE(LARGE(B$2:B$10,1),LARGE(B$2:B$10,2),
   LARGE(B$2:B$10,3))**.
3. Press **<Ctrl+Enter>**.

	B13			fx	=AVERAGE(LARGE(B$2:B$10,1),LARGE(B$2:B$10,2),LARGE(B$2:B$10,3))					
	A	B	C	D	E	F	G	H	I	
1	date	A	B	C						
2	11/08/2010	62	79	52						
3	11/09/2010	62	47	33						
4	11/10/2010	24	1	44						
5	11/11/2010	18	42	12						
6	11/12/2010	84	19	5						
7	11/13/2010	58	19	89						
8	11/14/2010	95	73	48						
9	11/15/2010	56	70	44						
10	11/16/2010	53	47	75						
11										
12										
13	Top-3 avg	80.33	74.00	72.00						
14										
15										

calculate average output

Ready   Average: 75.44   Count: 3   Sum: 226.33   100%

FIGURE 5–8

USE THE SUBTOTAL FUNCTION TO SUM A FILTERED LIST

When using the Filter option in the Data menu, it is not advisable to use the SUM function to sum up filtered rows because it sums up all rows, including those that are hidden. Instead, use the SUBTOTAL function to get the subtotal of a list or database that is visible.

SUBTOTAL(*function_num*, *ref1*, *ref2*, ...)

function_num: A number from 1 to 11 that specifies a particular function to use for calculating subtotals. (1 = AVERAGE, 2 = COUNT, 3 = COUNTA , 4 = MAX, 5 = MIN, 6 = PRODUCT, 7 = STDEV, 8 = STDEVP, 9 = SUM, 10 = VAR, and 11 = VARP)

ref1, *ref2*, ...: From 1 to 29 ranges or references for which a subtotal is desired.

▶ **To Sum a Filtered List:**

1. In cells B2:B10 type group numbers from 1 to 3.
2. In cells C2:C10 type the daily sales for each group.
3. From the Data menu, select **Filter | AutoFilter**.
4. Select group 1 in the column B filter.
5. Select cell C12 and type the following formula:
    =SUBTOTAL(9,C2:C10).

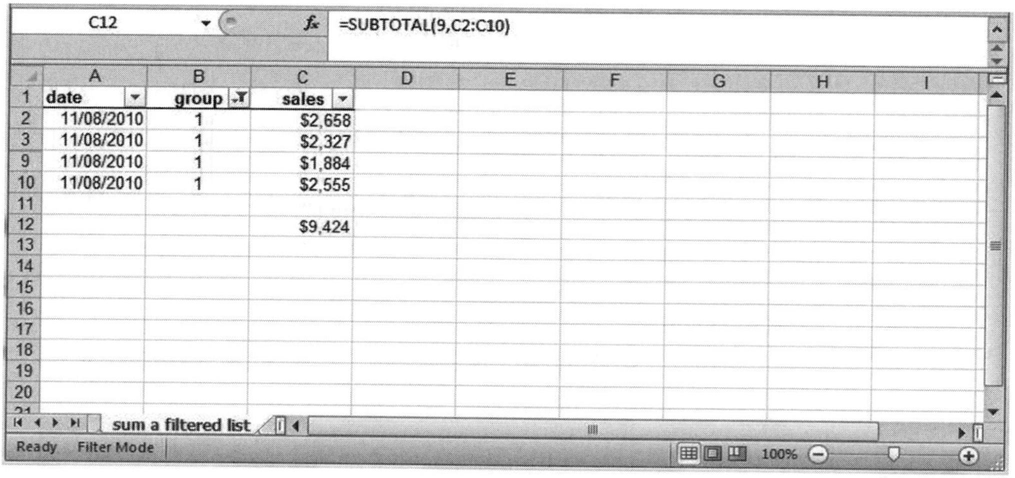

	C12		f_x	=SUBTOTAL(9,C2:C10)					

	A	B	C	D	E	F	G	H	I
1	date ▾	group ⏷	sales ▾						
2	11/08/2010	1	$2,658						
3	11/08/2010	1	$2,327						
9	11/08/2010	1	$1,884						
10	11/08/2010	1	$2,555						
11									
12			$9,424						
13									
14									
15									
16									
17									
18									
19									
20									

sum a filtered list

Ready   Filter Mode   100%

FIGURE 5–9

USE THE COUNT FUNCTION TO COUNT CELLS CONTAINING NUMERIC DATA

To count all cells that contain numbers, use the COUNT function. Empty cells, logical values, text, and error values are ignored.

COUNT(*value1*, *value2*, ...)

> *value1*, *value2*, ...: From 1 to 30 arguments of any type of data. However, all but numeric data is ignored.

▶ **To Count the Number of Cells that Contain Numbers:**

    1. In cells A1:A10 type data (numeric and text).
    2. Select cell C1 and type the following formula: **=COUNT(A1:A10)**.
    3. Press **<Enter>**.

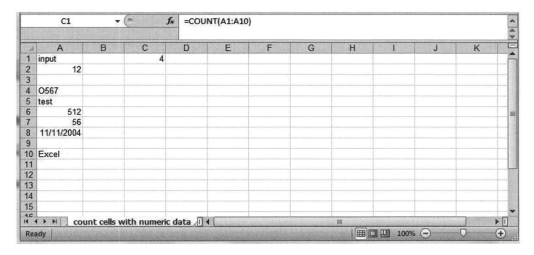

FIGURE 5–10

NOTE *Arguments that are date and time values are counted as numeric, too.*

USE THE COUNTA FUNCTION TO COUNT CELLS CONTAINING DATA

To count all cells that are not empty and contain data in a range or array, use the COUNTA function.

COUNTA(*value1, value2, ...*)

    value1, value2, ...: From 1 to 30 arguments representing the values to be counted.

▶ **To Count All Cells Containing Data:**

1. In cells A1:A10 type any kind of data (numeric and text).
2. Select cell C1 and type the following formula: **=COUNTA(A1:A10)**.
3. Press **<Enter>**.

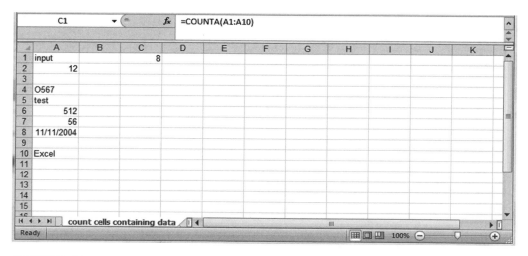

FIGURE 5–11

NOTE   *The COUNTA function does not count empty cells.*

USE THE COUNTA FUNCTION TO COUNT CELLS CONTAINING TEXT

To count all cells that contain text data, use a combination of functions in one formula. The number of cells with any kind of data is counted with the COUNTA function. All numeric cells are counted with the COUNT function. Just subtract the results of the COUNT function from the results of the COUNTA function, using the same range, to get all cells containing text.

▶ To Count Only Cells with Text:

1. In cells A1:A10 type any kind of data (numeric and text).
2. Select cell C1 and type the following formula:
   =COUNTA(A1:A10)-COUNT(A1:A10).
3. Press **<Enter>**.

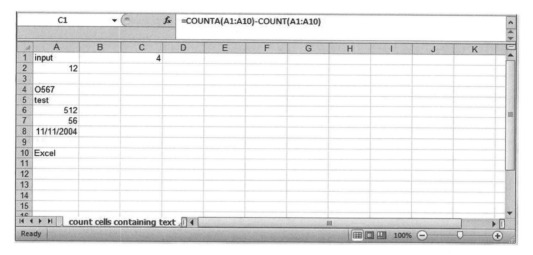

FIGURE 5–12

USE THE COUNTBLANK FUNCTION TO COUNT EMPTY CELLS

Occasionally it is may be useful to determine how many cells in a range are empty. You can use the COUNTBLANK function to count all empty cells in a range of cells.

COUNTBLANK(*range*)

range: The range in which to count blank cells.

▶ To Count All Empty Cells in a Specified Range:

1. In cells A1:A10 type data (numeric and text). Be sure to leave a few cells empty.
2. Select cell C1 and type the following formula:
   =COUNTBLANK(A1:A10).
3. Press **<Enter>**.

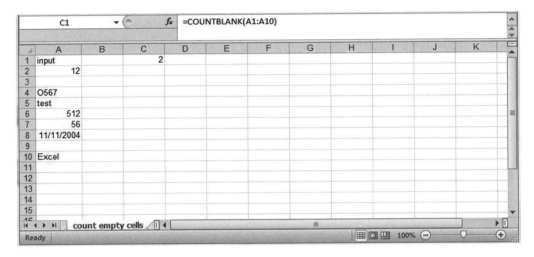

FIGURE 5–13

USE THE COUNTA FUNCTION TO DETERMINE THE LAST FILLED ROW

In this example, the last row that was filled in on a worksheet needs to be determined. If all cells of a column contain data and are not empty, the COUNTA function can be used. Define as the range the entire column in order to count all filled cells.

▶ **To Determine the Last Filled Row:**

1. In cells A1:A10 type data (numeric and text).
2. Select cell B1 and type the following formula: **=COUNTA(A:A)**.
3. Press **<Enter>**.

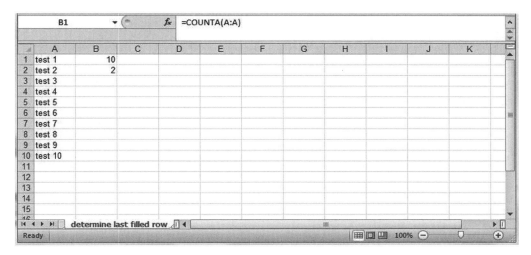

FIGURE 5–14

NOTE *To determine the last column of a worksheet that was filled, use the function =COUNTA(1:1) as shown in cell B2.*

USE THE SUBTOTAL FUNCTION TO COUNT ROWS IN FILTERED LISTS

When using the Filter option in the Data menu, it is recommended that the COUNT and COUNTA functions not be used because in a filtered worksheet they count both visible and hidden rows. Instead, use the SUBTOTAL function to get the subtotal of a list or database that is visible. The syntax for the SUBTOTAL function was presented earlier in this chapter.

▶ **To Count Rows in a Filtered List:**

1. In cells B2:B10 type group numbers from 1 to 3.
2. In cells C2:C10 type the daily sales of each group.
3. From the Data menu, select **Filter | AutoFilter**.
4. Select group 1 in the column B filter.
5. Select cell C12 and type the following formula:
   =SUBTOTAL(2,C2:C10) & "rows in filter".

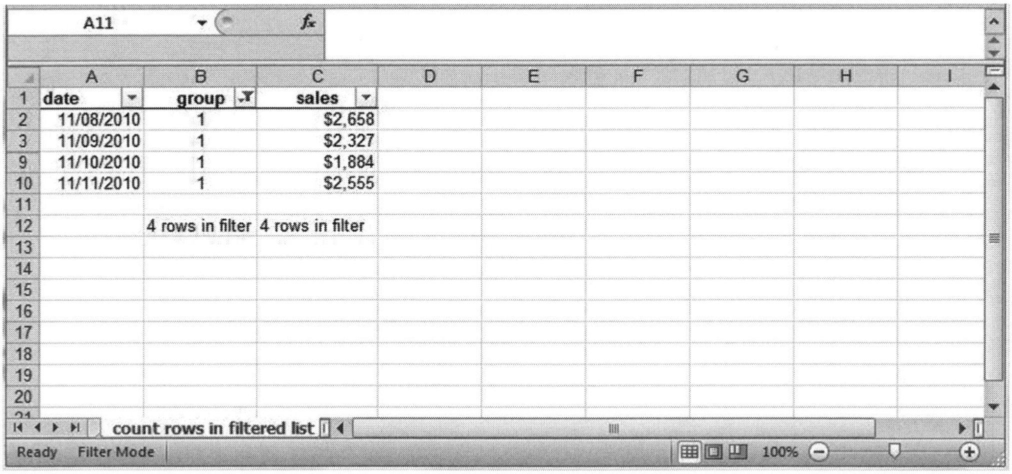

FIGURE 5–15

NOTE *Use the function =SUBTOTAL(3,B2:B10) & "rows in filter" in cell B12 to count the filtered cells as seen in Figure 5–15.*

USE THE RANK **FUNCTION TO DETERMINE THE RANK OF SALES**

To compare sales of several days and rank them, use the RANK function. This function returns a number that is the rank of a value. In this example, the list can be sorted to display sales in rank order.

RANK(*number, ref, order*)

> *number*: The number for which we want to find the rank.

> *ref*: A reference to a list of numbers. Only numeric values are considered.

> *order*: A number that specifies the ranking method. If order is 0 or omitted, the numbers are ranked in descending order. If order is a non-zero value, the numbers are ranked in ascending order.

▶ To Rank a List in Descending Order:

1. In cells A2:A10 enter dates.
2. In cells B2:B10 enter the sales for each date.
3. Select cells C2:C10 and type the following formula: **=RANK(B2,$B$2:$B$10)**.
4. Press **<Ctrl+Enter>**.

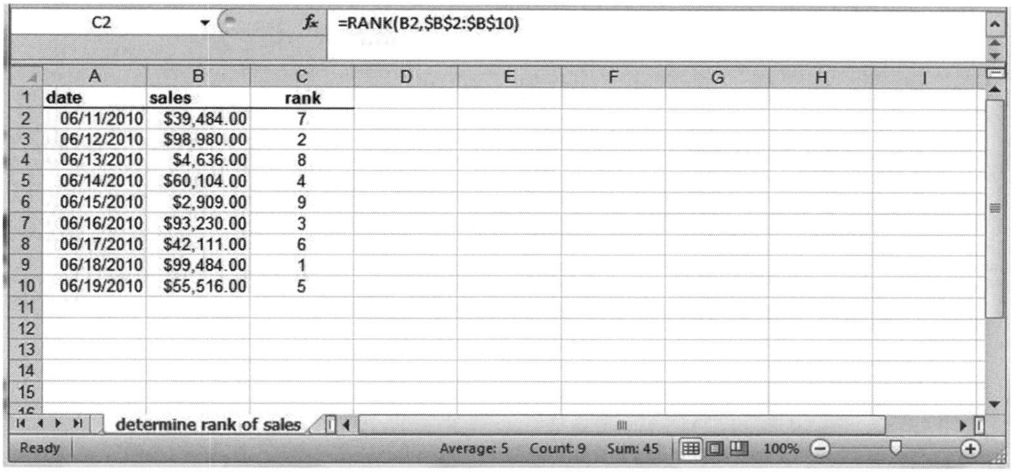

	A	B	C
1	date	sales	rank
2	06/11/2010	$39,484.00	7
3	06/12/2010	$98,980.00	2
4	06/13/2010	$4,636.00	8
5	06/14/2010	$60,104.00	4
6	06/15/2010	$2,909.00	9
7	06/16/2010	$93,230.00	3
8	06/17/2010	$42,111.00	6
9	06/18/2010	$99,484.00	1
10	06/19/2010	$55,516.00	5

FIGURE 5–16

NOTE *If you want to rank in ascending order, use this formula: =RANK (B2,$B$2:$B$10,1).*

USE THE MEDIAN FUNCTION TO CALCULATE THE MEDIAN SALES

In this example the average and median sales for a month have to be determined. Use the data shown in Figure 5–17 and calculate the average sales in cell E2. To calculate the median of the sales, use the MEDIAN function. The median is a value in the middle of a set of values; i.e., half the values are above the median and half the values are below.

MEDIAN(*number1, number2, ...*)

number1, number2,...: From 1 to 30 numbers for which you want to find the median.

▶ **To Calculate the Median Sales:**

1. In cells A2:A13 type the month.
2. In cells B2:B13 type the monthly sales.
3. Select cells E1 and type the following formula: **=MEDIAN(B2:B13)**.
4. Press **<Enter>**.

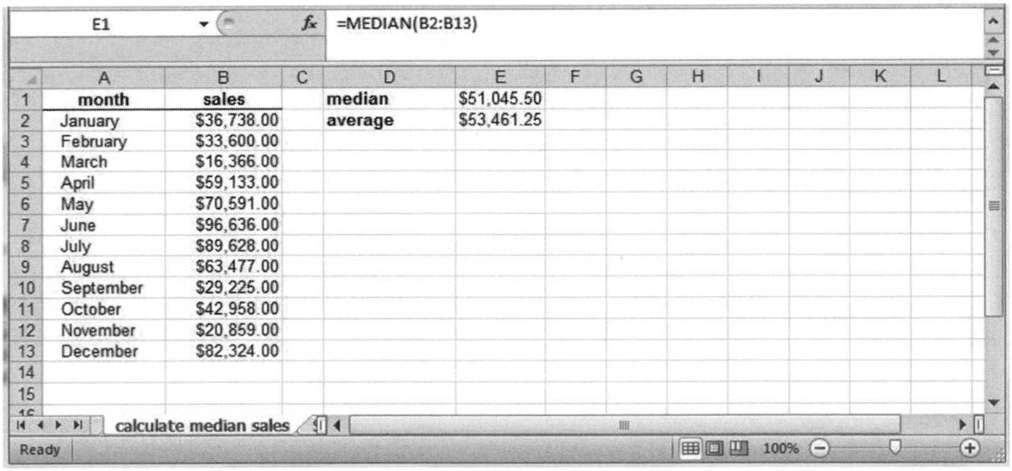

	A	B	C	D	E	F	G	H	I	J	K	L
	E1		*fx*	=MEDIAN(B2:B13)								
1	month	sales		median	$51,045.50							
2	January	$36,738.00		average	$53,461.25							
3	February	$33,600.00										
4	March	$16,366.00										
5	April	$59,133.00										
6	May	$70,591.00										
7	June	$96,636.00										
8	July	$89,628.00										
9	August	$63,477.00										
10	September	$29,225.00										
11	October	$42,958.00										
12	November	$20,859.00										
13	December	$82,324.00										
14												
15												

calculate median sales

Ready   100%

FIGURE 5–17

NOTE *You can find the average, as shown in cell E2, by using the formula =AVERAGE(B2:B13).*

USE THE QUARTILE **FUNCTION TO CALCULATE THE QUARTILES**

In this example, the quartile of a list has to be determined. The QUARTILE function returns the quartile of a data set. Quartiles are used to divide populations into four classes with each containing one-fourth of the total population.

QUARTILE(*array*, *quart*)

> *array*: An array or cell range of numeric values for which you want to find the quartile value.

> *quart*: A number from 0 to 4 that specifies the value to return. (0 = Minimum value, 1 = First quartile (25th percentile), 2 = Median value (50th percentile), 3 = Third quartile (75th percentile), 4 = Maximum value).

▶ **To Determine the Quartiles into which Employee Telephone Use Falls:**

1. In cells A2:A10 type the names of your employees.
2. In cells B2:B10 type the number of phone calls the employees make per month.
3. Select cells D2 and type the following formula: **=QUARTILE($B$2:$B$10,0)**.
4. Select cells D3 and type the following formula: **=QUARTILE($B$2:$B$10,1)**.

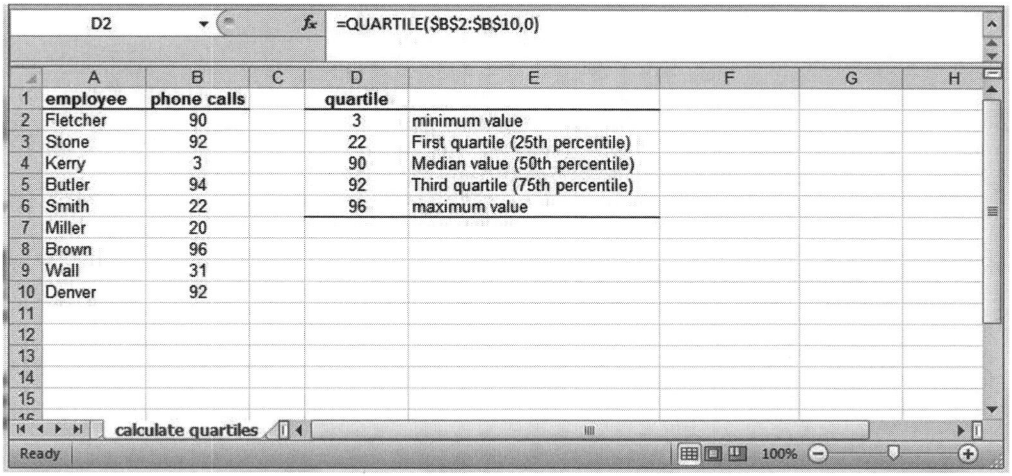

	A	B	C	D	E	F	G	H
1	employee	phone calls		quartile				
2	Fletcher	90		3	minimum value			
3	Stone	92		22	First quartile (25th percentile)			
4	Kerry	3		90	Median value (50th percentile)			
5	Butler	94		92	Third quartile (75th percentile)			
6	Smith	22		96	maximum value			
7	Miller	20						
8	Brown	96						
9	Wall	31						
10	Denver	92						
11								
12								
13								
14								
15								

FIGURE 5–18

USE THE STDEV FUNCTION TO DETERMINE THE STANDARD DEVIATION

In this example, the standard deviation of the number of phone calls has to be determined. Use the STDEV function for this purpose. This function measures how widely values in a set differ from the average, or mean, value.

STDEV(*number1, number2, ...*)

> *number1, number2, ...*: From 1 to 30 numerical arguments that represent a population sample.

▶ **To Determine the Standard Deviation for Employee Phone Calls:**

1. In cells A2:A10 type the names of your employees.
2. In cells B2:B10 type the number of phone calls the employees make per month.
3. Select cells E2 and type the following formula: **=STDEV(B2:B10)**.
4. Press **<Enter>**.

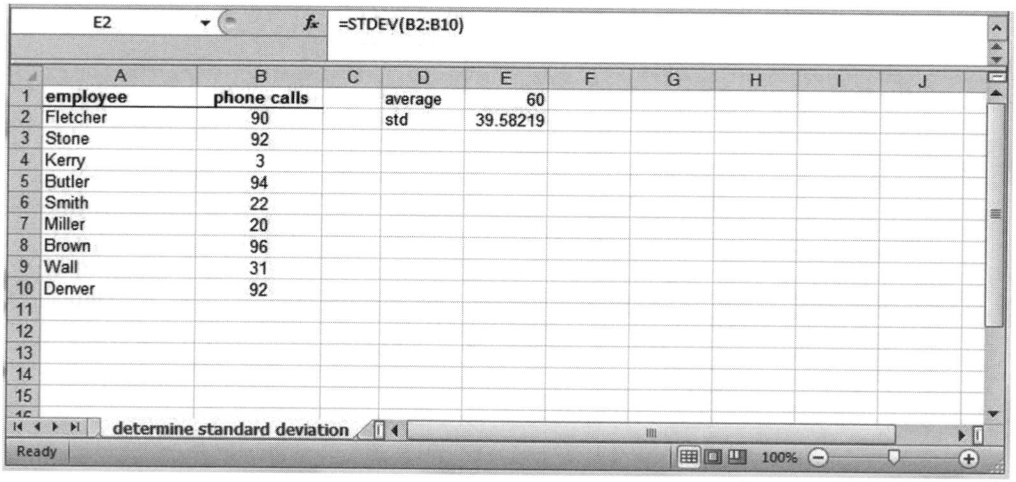

	E2		*fx*	=STDEV(B2:B10)						
	A	B	C	D	E	F	G	H	I	J
1	employee	phone calls		average	60					
2	Fletcher	90		std	39.58219					
3	Stone	92								
4	Kerry	3								
5	Butler	94								
6	Smith	22								
7	Miller	20								
8	Brown	96								
9	Wall	31								
10	Denver	92								
11										
12										
13										
14										
15										

determine standard deviation

Ready   100%

FIGURE 5–19

6 MATHEMATICAL FUNCTIONS

Chapter

USE THE SUM FUNCTION TO SUM A RANGE

In this example, each value of a range in a worksheet has to be added, with the sum appearing in cell A11. To do this, use the SUM function, which returns the sum of all numbers in a range of cells.

SUM(*number1*, *number2*, ...)

> *number1*, *number2*, ...: From 1 to 30 arguments to be summed up. Cell references are also valid.

▶ **To Sum a Range:**

1. In cells A2:A10 enter any values from 1 to 100. Figure 6–1 shows that we used dollar amounts.
2. In cell A11 type the following formula: **=SUM(A1:A10)**.
3. Press **<Enter>**.

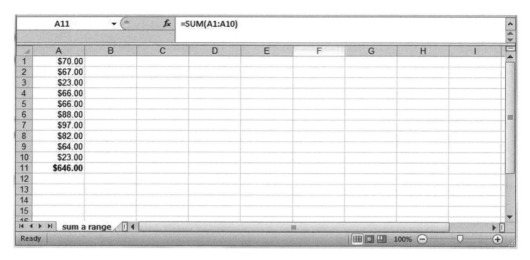

FIGURE 6–1

NOTE *To perform this task a little faster, just select cell A11 and click on the icon
(AutoSum) in the Editing bar under the Home tab. Then press <Enter> to
display the result of the calculation.*

USE THE SUM FUNCTION TO SUM SEVERAL RANGES

To sum several ranges, simply refer to each of them, separated by a comma,
using the SUM function from the previous tip.

▶ **To Sum Several Ranges:**

1. In cells A2:A10 enter prices from $1 to $100.
2. Select cells B2:B10 and type the formula **=A2*8%** to calculate the tax
   amount.
3. Press **<Ctrl+Enter>**.
4. In cells D2:D10 type some discount values from –1 to –3.
5. In cell B12 sum all three columns with the following function:
   =SUM(A2:A10,B2:B10,D2:D10).
6. Press **<Enter>**.

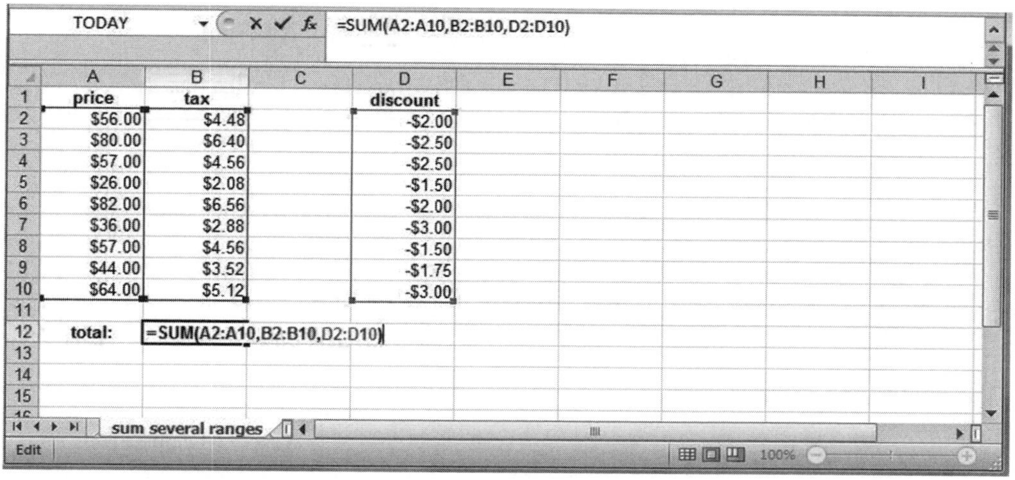

	A	B	C	D	E	F	G	H	I
1	price	tax		discount					
2	$56.00	$4.48		-$2.00					
3	$80.00	$6.40		-$2.50					
4	$57.00	$4.56		-$2.50					
5	$26.00	$2.08		-$1.50					
6	$82.00	$6.56		-$2.00					
7	$36.00	$2.88		-$3.00					
8	$57.00	$4.56		-$1.50					
9	$44.00	$3.52		-$1.75					
10	$64.00	$5.12		-$3.00					
11									
12	total:	=SUM(A2:A10,B2:B10,D2:D10)							
13									
14									
15									

TODAY ▼ × ✓ *fx* =SUM(A2:A10,B2:B10,D2:D10)

sum several ranges

FIGURE 6–2

NOTE *To place a border around all cells used in the function, select cell B12 and press <F2>. The function will be displayed as well.*

USE THE SUMIF FUNCTION TO DETERMINE SALES OF A TEAM

In this example, all the sales of different teams have to be summed up. You can use the SUMIF function to add all cells in a range, specified by a given criteria.

SUMIF(*range*, *criteria*, *sum_range*)

range: A range of cells to be evaluated.

criteria: The criteria that specifies which cells to add. This can be a number, expression, or text.

sum_range: The actual cells to be summed.

▶ **To Sum Specified Data:**

1. In cells A2:A10 enter a team number from 1 to 3.
2. List all team members in cells B2:B10.
3. In cells C2:C10 enter the daily sales of each employee.

4. List the numbers 1, 2, 3 for each team in cells E2:E4.
5. Select cells F2:F4 and type the following formula:
   =SUMIF($A$2:$A$10,E2,$C$2:$C$10).
6. Press **<Ctrl+Enter>**.

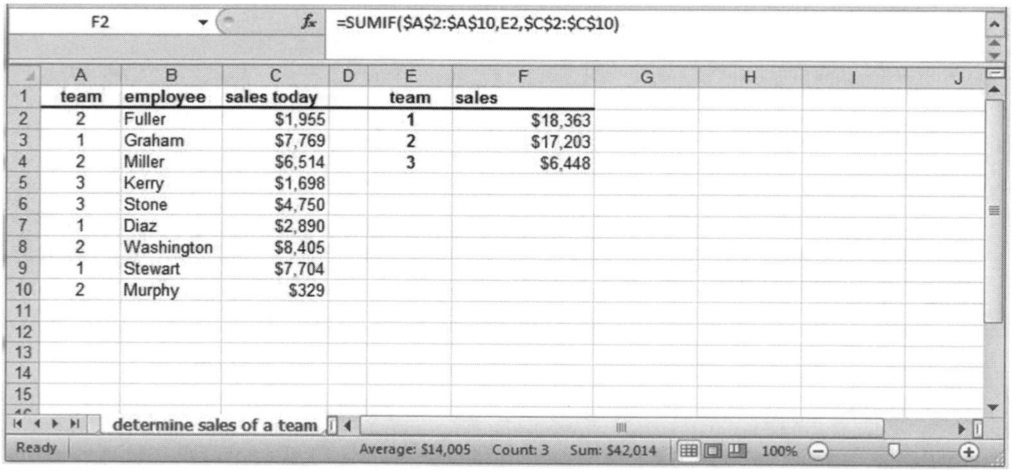

	F2			f_x	=SUMIF($A$2:$A$10,E2,$C$2:$C$10)					
	A	B	C	D	E	F	G	H	I	J
1	team	employee	sales today		team	sales				
2	2	Fuller	$1,955		1	$18,363				
3	1	Graham	$7,769		2	$17,203				
4	2	Miller	$6,514		3	$6,448				
5	3	Kerry	$1,698							
6	3	Stone	$4,750							
7	1	Diaz	$2,890							
8	2	Washington	$8,405							
9	1	Stewart	$7,704							
10	2	Murphy	$329							
11										
12										
13										
14										
15										

determine sales of a team

Ready   Average: $14,005   Count: 3   Sum: $42,014   100%

FIGURE 6–3

NOTE *At the end of Chapter 6 you will find a further example called sumifs, which has been available since Excel 2007.*

USE THE SUMIF FUNCTION TO SUM COSTS HIGHER THAN $1000

This tip can be used to determine the sum of all phases for which costs are higher than $1000. To sum just those cells, use the SUMIF function. It adds the cells that are specified by a given criteria.

▶ **To Sum Specified Costs:**

1. In cells A2:A11 enter the different phases.
2. Enter the costs of each phase in cells B2:B11.
3. In cell D1 enter **1000** as the given criteria.

4. Select cell D2 and type the following formula:
    =SUMIF(B2:B11,">" & D1).
5. Press **<Enter>**.

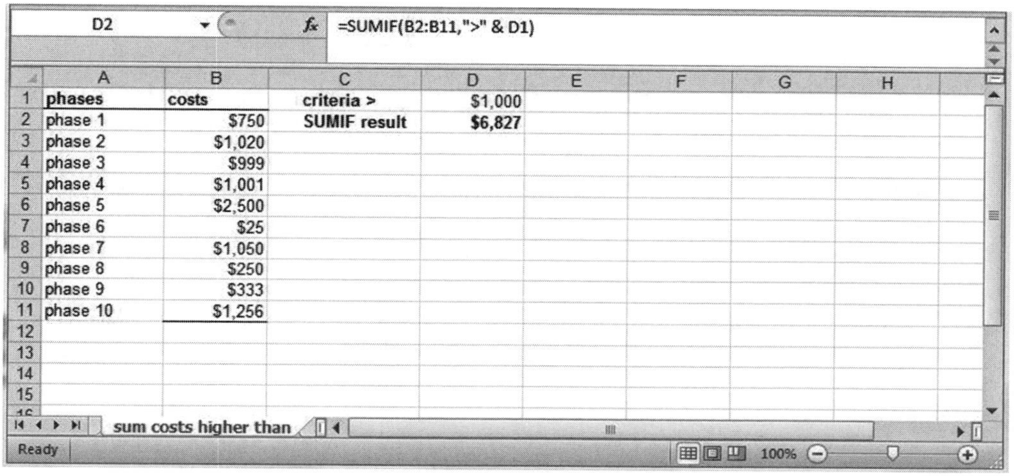

	D2	▾		f_x	=SUMIF(B2:B11,">" & D1)				
	A	B	C	D	E	F	G	H	
1	phases	costs	criteria >	$1,000					
2	phase 1	$750	SUMIF result	$6,827					
3	phase 2	$1,020							
4	phase 3	$999							
5	phase 4	$1,001							
6	phase 5	$2,500							
7	phase 6	$25							
8	phase 7	$1,050							
9	phase 8	$250							
10	phase 9	$333							
11	phase 10	$1,256							
12									
13									
14									
15									

sum costs higher than

Ready   100%

FIGURE 6–4

NOTE   *If the criteria should not be linked to a cell reference, use this formula:
=SUMIF(B2:B11,">1000").*

USE THE SUMIF FUNCTION TO SUM COSTS UP TO A CERTAIN DATE

Figure 6–5 contains a dynamic worksheet with daily costs. To sum all costs in a specified timeframe, use the SUMIF function.

▶ **To Sum Costs Up to a Certain Date:**

1. In cells A2:A11 list dates from 11/09/05 to 11/18/05.
2. In cells B2:B11 enter the corresponding costs for each day.
3. In cell E1 enter the date **11/16/05**.

4. Select cell E2 and type the following formula:
   =SUMIF(A2:A11,"<=" & E1,B2:B11).
5. Press **<Enter>**.

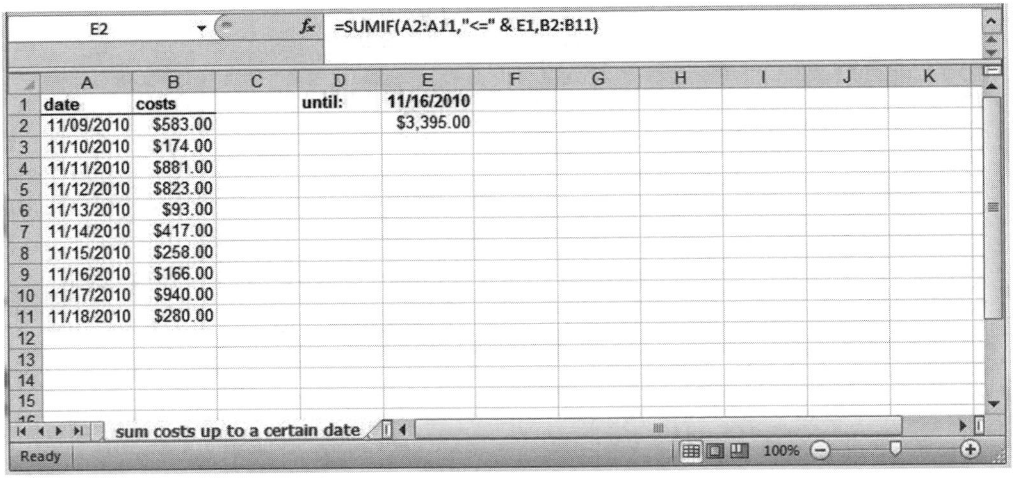

	E2	▼		*fx*	=SUMIF(A2:A11,"<=" & E1,B2:B11)						
	A	B	C	D	E	F	G	H	I	J	K
1	date	costs		until:	11/16/2010						
2	11/09/2010	$583.00			$3,395.00						
3	11/10/2010	$174.00									
4	11/11/2010	$881.00									
5	11/12/2010	$823.00									
6	11/13/2010	$93.00									
7	11/14/2010	$417.00									
8	11/15/2010	$258.00									
9	11/16/2010	$166.00									
10	11/17/2010	$940.00									
11	11/18/2010	$280.00									
12											
13											
14											
15											

sum costs up to a certain date

Ready   100%

FIGURE 6–5

NOTE *To check the calculated result, select cells B2:B9 and watch the displayed sum in the Excel status bar.*

USE THE COUNTIF FUNCTION TO COUNT PHASES THAT COST MORE THAN $1000

In this example, some project phases are listed in a worksheet. To determine how many phases cost more than $1000, use the COUNTIF function. This function counts the number of cells in a range that meet the specified criteria.

COUNTIF(*range, criteria*)

range: The range of cells.

criteria: The criteria that specifies which cells to count. This can be a number, expression, or text.

▶ **To Count Specified Phases:**

1. In cells A2:A11 enter the different phases.
2. Enter the costs of each phase in cells B2:B11.
3. In cell D1 enter **1000** as the given criteria.
4. Select cell D2 and type the following formula:
   =COUNTIF(B2:B11,">" & D1).
5. Press **<Enter>**.

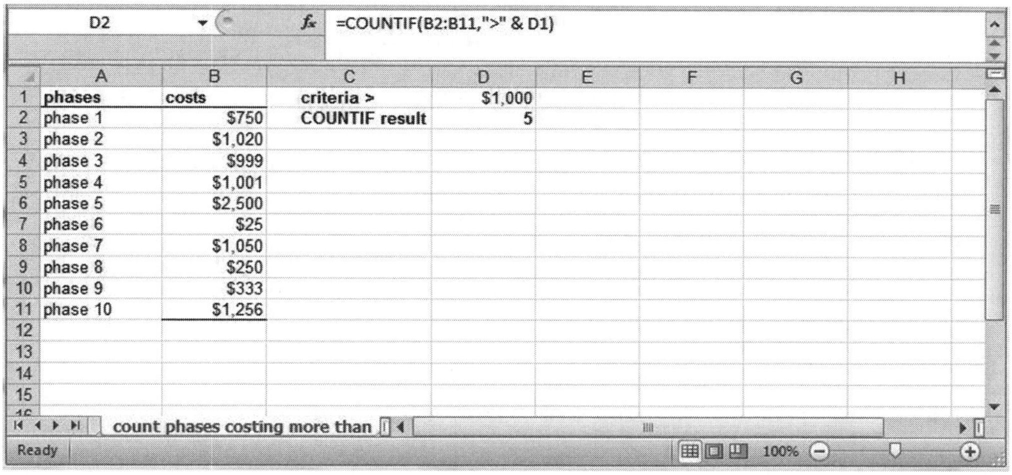

	D2	▾	f_x	=COUNTIF(B2:B11,">" & D1)					
	A	B	C	D	E	F	G	H	
1	phases	costs	criteria >	$1,000					
2	phase 1	$750	COUNTIF result	5					
3	phase 2	$1,020							
4	phase 3	$999							
5	phase 4	$1,001							
6	phase 5	$2,500							
7	phase 6	$25							
8	phase 7	$1,050							
9	phase 8	$250							
10	phase 9	$333							
11	phase 10	$1,256							
12									
13									
14									
15									

count phases costing more than

Ready   100%

FIGURE 6–6

NOTE *If the criteria should not be linked to a cell reference, use this formula:* *=COUNTIF(B2:B11,">1000").*

NOTE *At the end of Chapter 6 you will find a further example called countifs, which has been available since Excel 2007.*

USE THE COUNTIF FUNCTION TO CALCULATE AN ATTENDANCE LIST

For this task an attendance list has to be generated and the number of those who are present each day determined. Generate the list shown in Figure 6–7. Column A contains the dates and column B uses the user-defined format DDD to determine the day of the week. In columns C to G the letter "X" is entered for each person in attendance.

▶ **To Calculate the Attendance for Each Day:**

1. Select cells H2:H11 and type the formula **=COUNTIF(C2:G2,"X")** to get the attendance for each day.
2. Press **<Ctrl+Enter>**.
3. Select cells C13:G13 and type the formula **=COUNTIF(C2:C11,"X")** to count the attendance of each employee.
4. Press **<Ctrl+Enter>**.

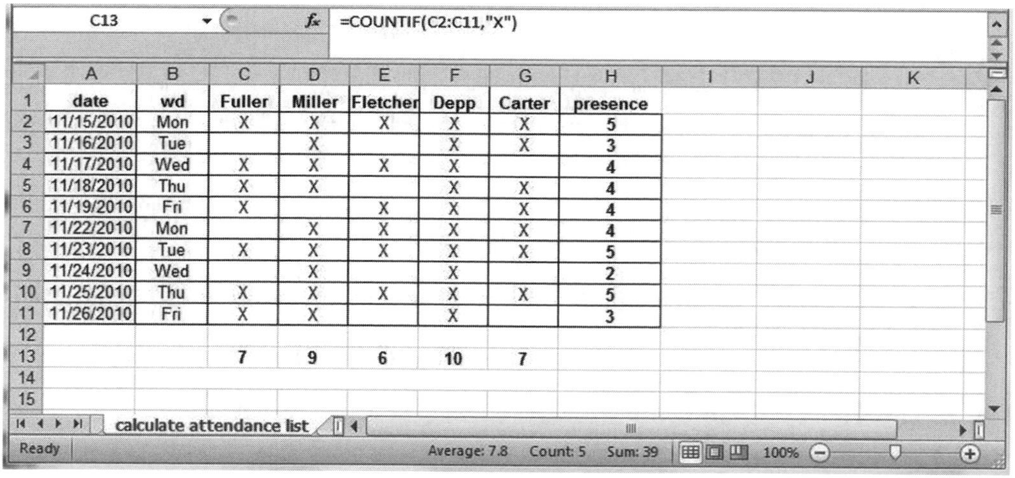

	C13		▼	f_x	=COUNTIF(C2:C11,"X")						
	A	B	C	D	E	F	G	H	I	J	K
1	date	wd	Fuller	Miller	Fletcher	Depp	Carter	presence			
2	11/15/2010	Mon	X	X	X	X	X	5			
3	11/16/2010	Tue		X		X	X	3			
4	11/17/2010	Wed	X	X	X	X		4			
5	11/18/2010	Thu	X	X		X	X	4			
6	11/19/2010	Fri	X		X	X	X	4			
7	11/22/2010	Mon		X	X	X	X	4			
8	11/23/2010	Tue	X	X	X	X	X	5			
9	11/24/2010	Wed		X		X		2			
10	11/25/2010	Thu	X	X	X	X	X	5			
11	11/26/2010	Fri	X	X		X		3			
12											
13			7	9	6	10	7				
14											
15											

calculate attendance list

Ready   Average: 7.8   Count: 5   Sum: 39   100%

FIGURE 6–7

USE THE SUMPRODUCT FUNCTION TO CALCULATE THE VALUE OF THE INVENTORY

In this example, the costs of all products in a warehouse have to be summed up to obtain the value of the entire inventory. To do so, use the SUMPRODUCT function. This function multiplies corresponding components in the given arrays and returns the sum of those products.

SUMPRODUCT(*array1, array2, array3, …*)

array1, array2, array3, …: From 2 to 30 arrays whose components are to be multiplied and then added.

▶ **To Calculate the Inventory Value:**

1. Enter the data shown in columns A and B in Figure 6–8. The quantity of each product is listed along with the cost of each unit.
2. Select cell B12 and type the following formula: **=SUMPRODUCT(B2:B10,A2:A10)**.
3. Check the result by selecting cells D2:D10 and typing the following formula: **=A2*B2**.
4. Press **<Ctrl+Enter>**.
5. Sum this range in cell D12.

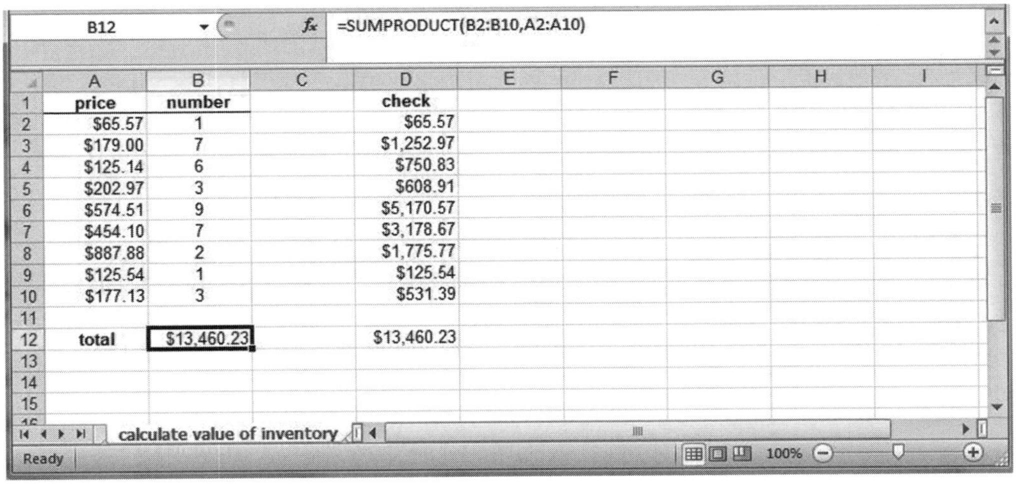

	A	B	C	D	E	F	G	H	I
B12			fx	=SUMPRODUCT(B2:B10,A2:A10)					
1	price	number		check					
2	$65.57	1		$65.57					
3	$179.00	7		$1,252.97					
4	$125.14	6		$750.83					
5	$202.97	3		$608.91					
6	$574.51	9		$5,170.57					
7	$454.10	7		$3,178.67					
8	$887.88	2		$1,775.77					
9	$125.54	1		$125.54					
10	$177.13	3		$531.39					
11									
12	total	$13,460.23		$13,460.23					
13									
14									
15									

calculate value of inventory

Ready   100%

FIGURE 6–8

USE THE SUMPRODUCT FUNCTION TO SUM SALES OF A PARTICULAR TEAM

The worksheet below contains the sales of different teams. As discussed earlier, summing up the sales of each team can be done with the SUMIF function. Another way to get a result is by using the SUMPRODUCT function.

▶ **To Sum the Sales of Team 1:**

1. Use the values in Figure 6–9 to fill in columns A and B.
2. Select cell B12 and type the following formula:
   =SUMPRODUCT((A2:A10=1)*(B2:B10)).
3. To check the result, select cells D2:D10 and type the following formula:
   =IF(A2=1,B2,"").
4. Press **<Ctrl+Enter>** to enter the formula in the selected range of cells.
5. Select cell D12 and enter the following formula: **=SUM(D2:D10).**

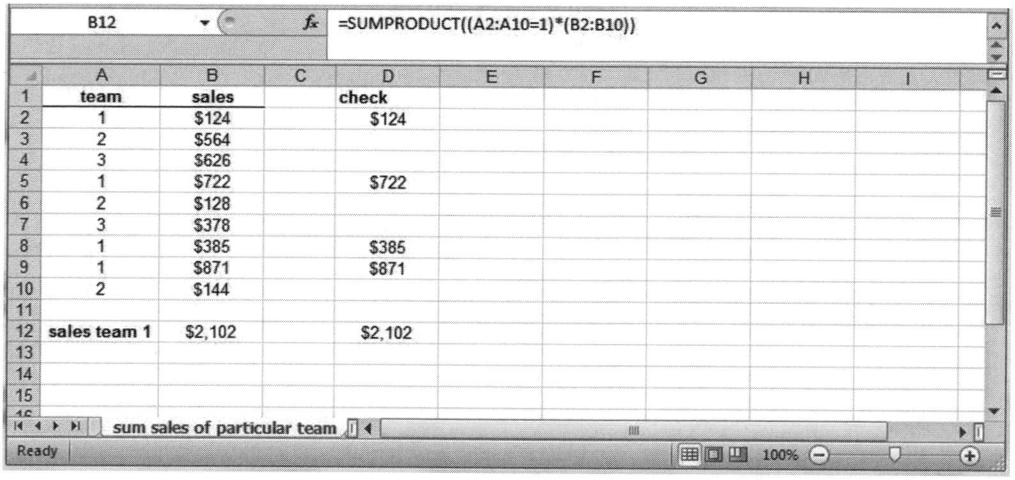

	B12		▼	f_x	=SUMPRODUCT((A2:A10=1)*(B2:B10))					
	A	B	C	D	E	F	G	H	I	
1	team	sales		check						
2	1	$124		$124						
3	2	$564								
4	3	$626								
5	1	$722		$722						
6	2	$128								
7	3	$378								
8	1	$385		$385						
9	1	$871		$871						
10	2	$144								
11										
12	sales team 1	$2,102		$2,102						
13										
14										
15										

sum sales of particular team

Ready   100%

FIGURE 6–9

USE THE SUMPRODUCT FUNCTION TO MULTIPLY AND SUM AT ONCE

The salary of each team has to be calculated. The teams' numbers, the daily working hours, and daily payment is recorded in a table. To calculate the total salary for each team, the working hours have to be multiplied by the payment and summed up for each day worked. Use the SUMPRODUCT function to get the result.

▶ **To Multiply and Sum in One Operation for Each Team:**

1. In a worksheet, copy the range A1:E11 shown in Figure 6–10.
2. Select cells C13:C15 and type the following formula:
   =SUMPRODUCT(((\$C\$2:\$C\$11=B13)*(\$E\$2:\$E\$11))).
3. Press **<Ctrl+Enter>**.

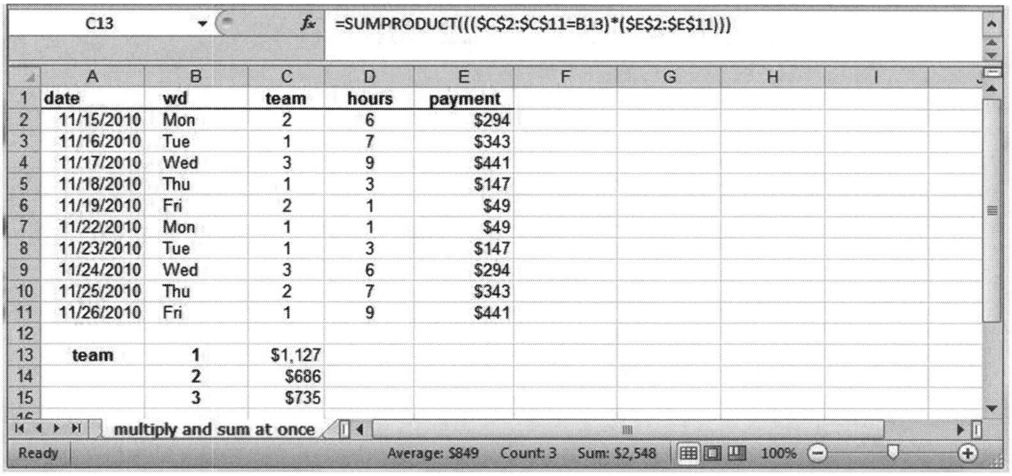

	C13			ƒx	=SUMPRODUCT(((\$C\$2:\$C\$11=B13)*(\$E\$2:\$E\$11)))					
	A	B	C	D	E	F	G	H	I	
1	date	wd	team	hours	payment					
2	11/15/2010	Mon	2	6	$294					
3	11/16/2010	Tue	1	7	$343					
4	11/17/2010	Wed	3	9	$441					
5	11/18/2010	Thu	1	3	$147					
6	11/19/2010	Fri	2	1	$49					
7	11/22/2010	Mon	1	1	$49					
8	11/23/2010	Tue	1	3	$147					
9	11/24/2010	Wed	3	6	$294					
10	11/25/2010	Thu	2	7	$343					
11	11/26/2010	Fri	1	9	$441					
12										
13	team	1	$1,127							
14		2	$686							
15		3	$735							

multiply and sum at once

Ready   Average: $849   Count: 3   Sum: $2,548   100%

FIGURE 6–10

USE THE ROUND FUNCTION TO ROUND NUMBERS

In this example, all numbers have to be rounded. Use the Excel built-in ROUND function to round a number to a specified number of digits.

ROUND(*number, num_digits*)

number: The number to be rounded.

num_digits: The number of digits the number will be rounded to. If greater than 0, the number is rounded to num_digits decimal places. If 0, the number is rounded to the nearest integer. If less than 0, the number is rounded to the left of the decimal point.

▶ **To Round Numbers:**

1. In cells A2:A10 enter numbers with a decimal point.
2. In cells B2:B10 enter the number of decimal places the number should be rounded to.
3. Select cells C2:C10 and type the following formula:
   =ROUND($A2,$B2).
4. Press **<Ctrl+Enter>**.

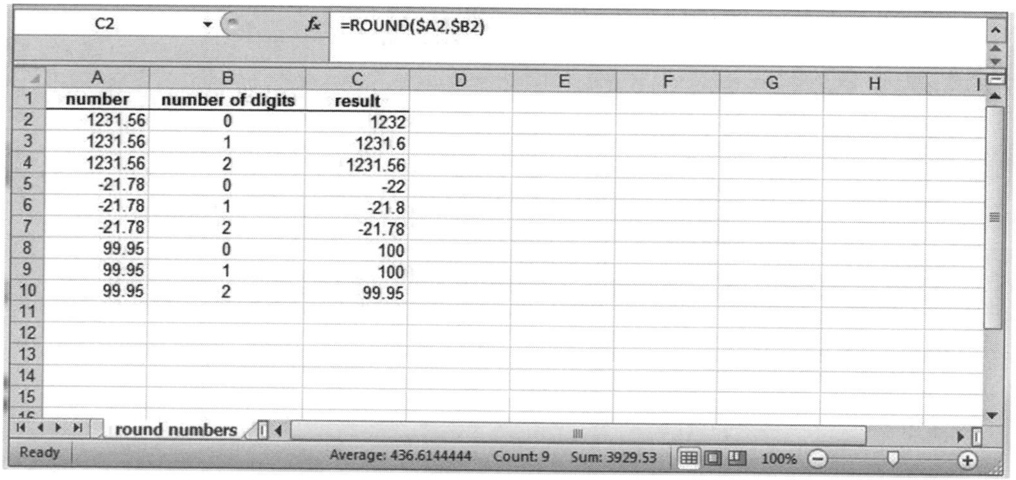

	A	B	C	D	E	F	G	H
	C2		f_x =ROUND($A2,$B2)					
1	number	number of digits	result					
2	1231.56	0	1232					
3	1231.56	1	1231.6					
4	1231.56	2	1231.56					
5	-21.78	0	-22					
6	-21.78	1	-21.8					
7	-21.78	2	-21.78					
8	99.95	0	100					
9	99.95	1	100					
10	99.95	2	99.95					
11								
12								
13								
14								
15								

round numbers

Ready   Average: 436.6144444   Count: 9   Sum: 3929.53   100%

FIGURE 6–11

USE THE ROUNDDOWN FUNCTION TO ROUND NUMBERS DOWN

To cut off numbers to a specific decimal place or round numbers down in a worksheet, use the ROUNDDOWN function. This function rounds a number down, toward zero.

ROUNDDOWN(*number, num_digits*)

number: Any real number to be rounded down.

num_digits: The number of digits the number will be rounded down to. If greater than 0, the number is rounded to num_digits decimal places. If 0, the number is rounded to the nearest integer. If less than 0, the number is rounded to the left of the decimal point.

▶ **To Round Down Numbers:**

1. In cells A2:A10 enter numbers with a decimal point.
2. Enter in cells B2:B10 the number of decimal places the number should be rounded down to.
3. Select cells C2:C10 and type the following formula: **=ROUNDDOWN($A2,$B2)**.
4. Press **<Ctrl+Enter>**.

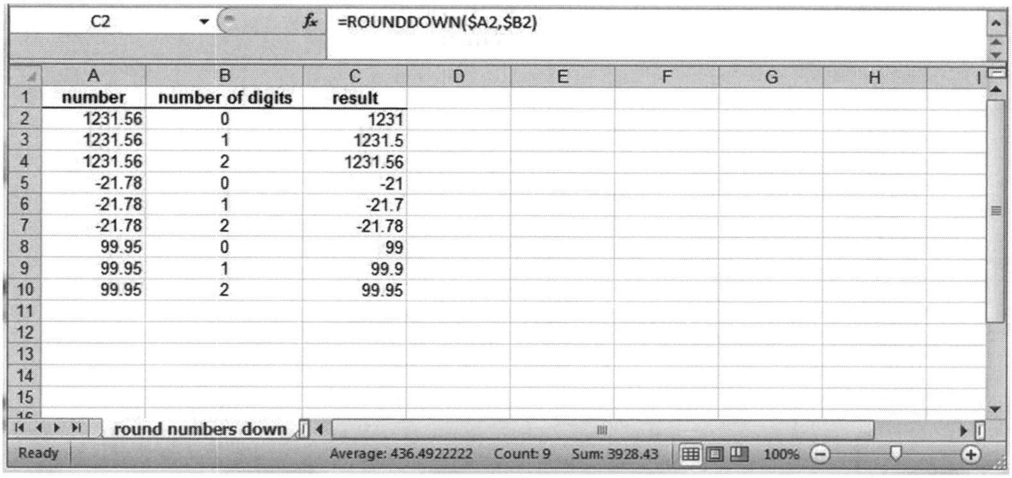

	A	B	C	D	E	F	G	H
	number	number of digits	result					
2	1231.56	0	1231					
3	1231.56	1	1231.5					
4	1231.56	2	1231.56					
5	-21.78	0	-21					
6	-21.78	1	-21.7					
7	-21.78	2	-21.78					
8	99.95	0	99					
9	99.95	1	99.9					
10	99.95	2	99.95					

C2   *fx* =ROUNDDOWN($A2,$B2)

round numbers down

Ready   Average: 436.4922222   Count: 9   Sum: 3928.43   100%

FIGURE 6–12

USE THE ROUNDUP FUNCTION TO ROUND NUMBERS UP

Similar to the ROUNDDOWN function as explained in the previous tip, the ROUNDUP function can be used to round up numbers in a worksheet.
ROUNDUP(*number, num_digits*)

number: Any real number to be rounded up.

num_digits: The number of digits the number will be rounded up to. If greater than 0, the number is rounded to num_digits decimal places. If 0, the number is rounded to the nearest integer. If less than 0, the number is rounded to the left of the decimal point.

▶ **To Round Up Numbers:**

1. In cells A2:A10 enter the numbers with a decimal point.
2. In cells B2:B10 enter the number of decimal places the number should be rounded up to.
3. Select cells C2:C10 type the following formula:
   =ROUNDUP($A2,$B2).
4. Press **<Ctrl+Enter>**.

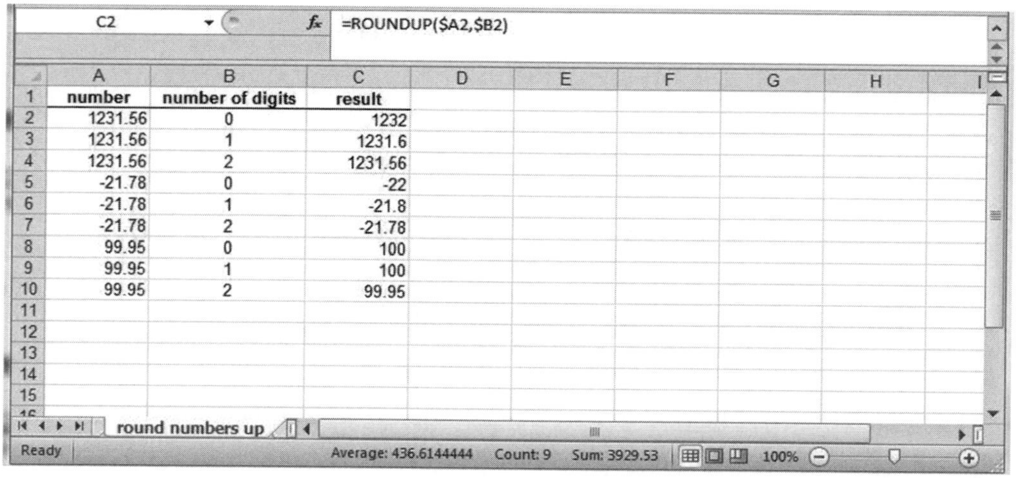

	A	B	C	D	E	F	G	H	I
			fx	=ROUNDUP($A2,$B2)					
1	number	number of digits	result						
2	1231.56	0	1232						
3	1231.56	1	1231.6						
4	1231.56	2	1231.56						
5	-21.78	0	-22						
6	-21.78	1	-21.8						
7	-21.78	2	-21.78						
8	99.95	0	100						
9	99.95	1	100						
10	99.95	2	99.95						

C2 … =ROUNDUP($A2,$B2)

round numbers up

Ready   Average: 436.6144444   Count: 9   Sum: 3929.53   100%

FIGURE 6–13

USE THE ROUND FUNCTION TO ROUND TIME VALUES TO WHOLE MINUTES

A worksheet contains time values including hours, minutes, and seconds as shown in Figure 6–14. The task is to round the minutes to whole minutes by using the standard ROUND function. Note that a day has 24 hours, which is 1440 minutes.

▶ **To Round Different Time Values to Whole Minutes:**

1. In cells A2:A10 list some time values in this format: 12:02:59 AM.
2. Select cells B2:B10 and type the following formula:
   =ROUND(A2*1440,0)/1440.
3. Press **<Ctrl+Enter>**.

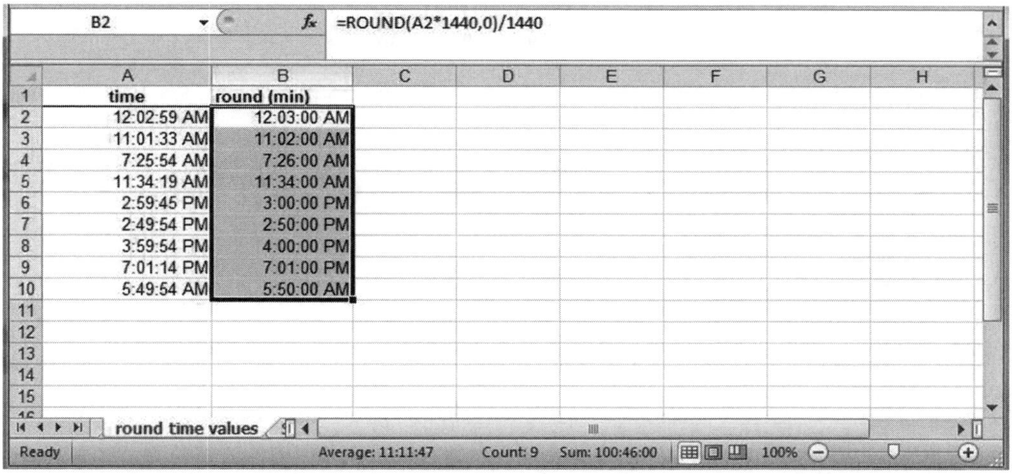

	B2	▾	*fx*	=ROUND(A2*1440,0)/1440				
	A	B	C	D	E	F	G	H
1	time	round (min)						
2	12:02:59 AM	12:03:00 AM						
3	11:01:33 AM	11:02:00 AM						
4	7:25:54 AM	7:26:00 AM						
5	11:34:19 AM	11:34:00 AM						
6	2:59:45 PM	3:00:00 PM						
7	2:49:54 PM	2:50:00 PM						
8	3:59:54 PM	4:00:00 PM						
9	7:01:14 PM	7:01:00 PM						
10	5:49:54 AM	5:50:00 AM						
11								
12								
13								
14								
15								

round time values

Ready   Average: 11:11:47   Count: 9   Sum: 100:46:00   100%

FIGURE 6–14

USE THE ROUND FUNCTION TO ROUND TIME VALUES TO WHOLE HOURS

As in the previous tip, a worksheet contains time values including hours, minutes, and seconds as shown in Figure 6–15. To round these time values to whole hours, use the standard ROUND function. Recall that a day has 24 hours.

▶ **To Round Time Values to Whole Hours:**

1. In cells A2:A10 list some time values in this format: 12:02:59 AM.
2. Select cells B2:B10 and type the following formula:
   =ROUND(A2*24,0)/24.
3. Press **<Ctrl+Enter>**.

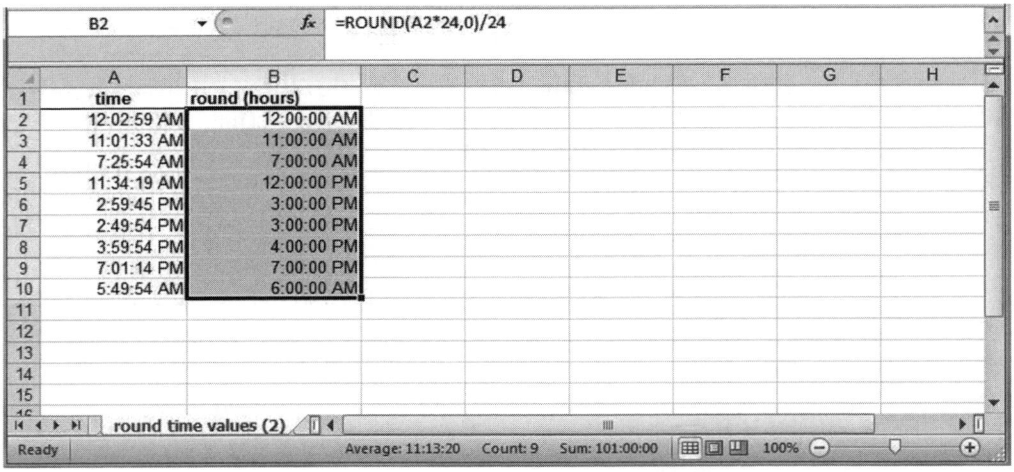

FIGURE 6–15

USE THE MROUND FUNCTION TO ROUND PRICES TO 5 OR 25 CENTS

In this example, prices have to be rounded to the nearest 5 or 25 cents. Use the MROUND function, which returns a number rounded to the desired multiple.
    MROUND(*number, multiple*)

number: The value to be rounded.

multiple: The multiple to which the number will be rounded.

▶ **To Round Prices to a Multiple of 5 or 25 Cents:**

1. In cells A2:A10 list some prices with a decimal point.
2. Select cells B2:B10 and type the following formula:
   =MROUND(A2,0.05).
3. Press **<Ctrl+Enter>**.
4. Select cells C2:C10 and type the following formula:
   =MROUND(A2,0.25).
5. Press **<Ctrl+Enter>**.

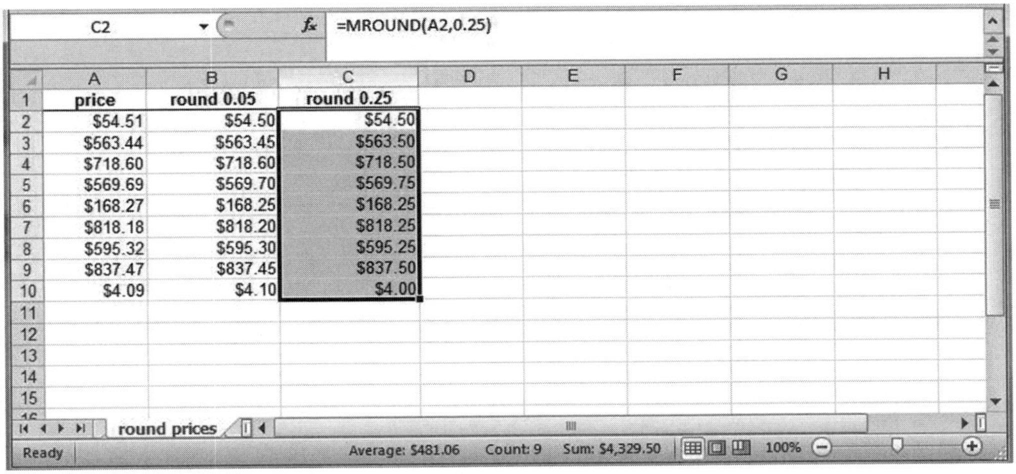

	C2			f_x	=MROUND(A2,0.25)				
	A	B	C	D	E	F	G	H
1	price	round 0.05	round 0.25					
2	$54.51	$54.50	$54.50					
3	$563.44	$563.45	$563.50					
4	$718.60	$718.60	$718.50					
5	$569.69	$569.70	$569.75					
6	$168.27	$168.25	$168.25					
7	$818.18	$818.20	$818.25					
8	$595.32	$595.30	$595.25					
9	$837.47	$837.45	$837.50					
10	$4.09	$4.10	$4.00					
11								
12								
13								
14								
15								

round prices

Ready   Average: $481.06   Count: 9   Sum: $4,329.50   100%

FIGURE 6–16

NOTE *To use this function you need to have the Analysis ToolPak installed and loaded. From the Tools menu, select the Add-Ins… option. Select the desired add-in and click OK.*

USE THE MROUND FUNCTION TO ROUND VALUES TO THE NEAREST MULTIPLE OF 10 OR 50

Sometimes it is necessary to round up values to the nearest multiple of 10 or 50. To perform this task, use the MROUND function from the Analysis ToolPak add-in. MROUND returns a number rounded to the desired specified multiple.

▶ **To Round Values to the Nearest Multiple of 10 or 50:**

1. In cells A2:A10 list any kind of values.
2. Select cells B2:B10 and type the following formula:
   =MROUND(A2,10).
3. Press **<Ctrl+Enter>**.
4. Select cells C2:C10 and type the following formula:
   =MROUND(A2,50).
5. Press **<Ctrl+Enter>**.

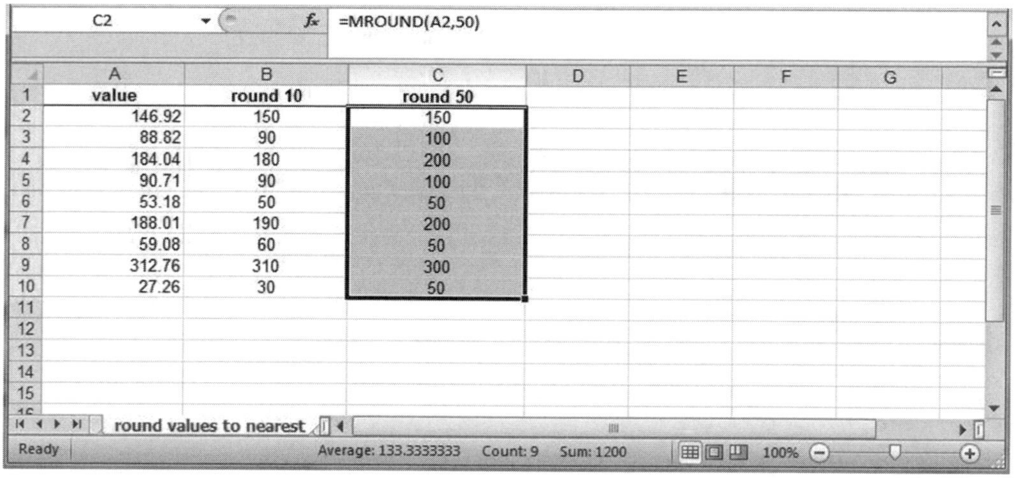

	A	B	C	D	E	F	G
1	value	round 10	round 50				
2	146.92	150	150				
3	88.82	90	100				
4	184.04	180	200				
5	90.71	90	100				
6	53.18	50	50				
7	188.01	190	200				
8	59.08	60	50				
9	312.76	310	300				
10	27.26	30	50				

C2 = MROUND(A2,50)

round values to nearest

Ready   Average: 133.3333333   Count: 9   Sum: 1200   100%

FIGURE 6–17

NOTE   *To use this function, you need to have the Analysis ToolPak installed and loaded as described in the previous tip.*

USE THE CEILING FUNCTION TO ROUND UP VALUES TO THE NEAREST 100

For this example, all prices have to be rounded up to whole $100 units. To do this, you use the CEILING function. This function returns a number that is rounded up to the nearest multiple of significance.

CEILING(*number*, *significance*)

number: The value to be rounded.

significance: The multiple to which the number will be rounded up.

▶ **To Round Up Values to Multiples of 100:**

1. In cells A2:A10 list some prices.
2. Select cells B2:B10 and type the following formula:
   =CEILING(A2,100).
3. Press **<Ctrl+Enter>**.

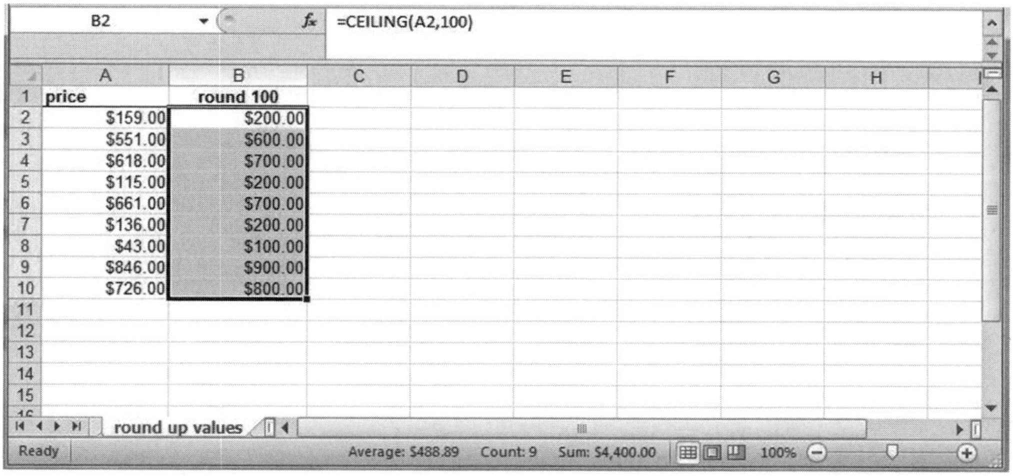

	A	B	C	D	E	F	G	H
	B2		*fx* =CEILING(A2,100)					
1	price	round 100						
2	$159.00	$200.00						
3	$551.00	$600.00						
4	$618.00	$700.00						
5	$115.00	$200.00						
6	$661.00	$700.00						
7	$136.00	$200.00						
8	$43.00	$100.00						
9	$846.00	$900.00						
10	$726.00	$800.00						
11								
12								
13								
14								
15								

round up values

Ready   Average: $488.89   Count: 9   Sum: $4,400.00   100%

FIGURE 6–18

USE THE FLOOR FUNCTION TO ROUND DOWN VALUES TO THE NEAREST 100

As seen in the previous example, it is easy to round up values to multiples of 100. To round numbers down to the nearest multiple of significance, use the FLOOR function.

FLOOR(*number, significance*)

number: The value to be rounded.

significance: The multiple to which the number will be rounded down.

▶ **To Round Down Values to Multiples of 100:**

1. In cells A2:A10 list some prices.
2. Select cells B2:B10 and type the following formula: **=FLOOR(A2,100)**.
3. Press **<Ctrl+Enter>**.

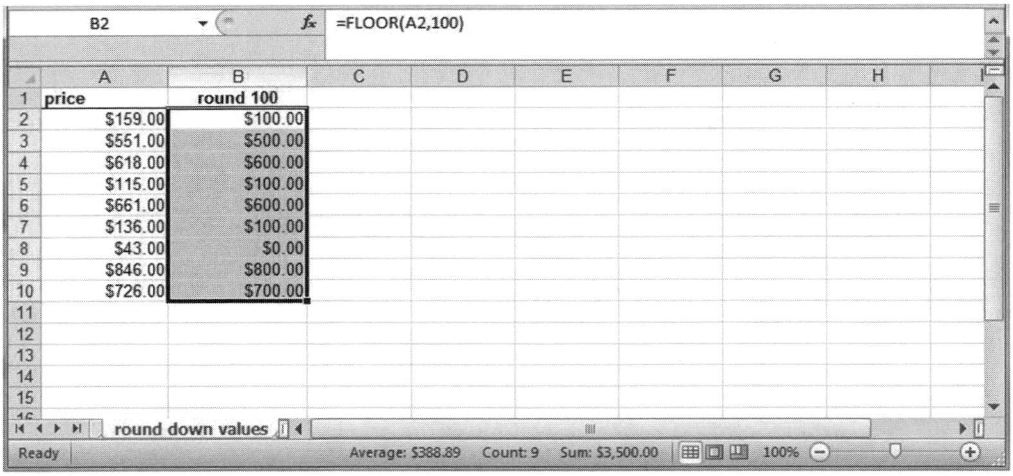

	A	B
1	price	round 100
2	$159.00	$100.00
3	$551.00	$500.00
4	$618.00	$600.00
5	$115.00	$100.00
6	$661.00	$600.00
7	$136.00	$100.00
8	$43.00	$0.00
9	$846.00	$800.00
10	$726.00	$700.00

B2 =FLOOR(A2,100)

Average: $388.89   Count: 9   Sum: $3,500.00   100%

round down values

FIGURE 6–19

USE THE PRODUCT FUNCTION TO MULTIPLY VALUES

Normally values in a worksheet are multiplied with the * operator in formulas like =A1*B1. However, Excel also provides a useful function to do the same calculation. Use the PRODUCT function to multiply all the given numbers and return the product.

PRODUCT(*number1*, *number2*, ...)

number1, *number2*, ...: From 1 to 30 numbers to be multiplied.

As an example, calculate a price reduction with the PRODUCT function using a standard factor in cell D1.

▶ **To Calculate the Price Reduction:**

1. In cells A2:A10 list some prices.
2. Enter in cell D1 the value **0.15** to calculate a 15% price reduction.
3. Select cells B2:B10 and type the following formula:
   =PRODUCT(A2,$D$1).
4. Press **<Ctrl+Enter>**.

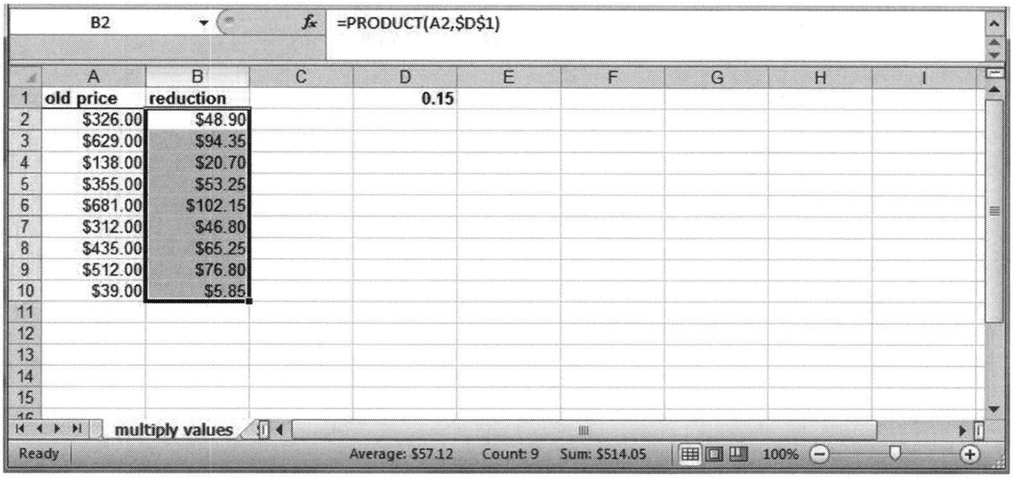

	A	B	C	D	E	F	G	H	I
1	old price	reduction		0.15					
2	$326.00	$48.90							
3	$629.00	$94.35							
4	$138.00	$20.70							
5	$355.00	$53.25							
6	$681.00	$102.15							
7	$312.00	$46.80							
8	$435.00	$65.25							
9	$512.00	$76.80							
10	$39.00	$5.85							

B2 = PRODUCT(A2,$D$1)

multiply values

Ready   Average: $57.12   Count: 9   Sum: $514.05   100%

FIGURE 6–20

USE THE PRODUCT **FUNCTION TO MULTIPLY CONDITIONAL VALUES**

In this example, values are listed in columns A and B. Excel should calculate the product of each value in a row but only if both values exist. If one value is missing, the result is an empty cell, as shown in column C. To get the desired results, use the PRODUCT function in combination with the IF and OR functions as described below.

▶ **To Multiply Conditional Values:**

1. In cells A2:A10 enter some numbers for value 1.
2. In cells B2:B10 enter some numbers for value 2.
3. Select cells C2:C10 and type the following formula:
   =IF(OR(A2="",B2=""),"",PRODUCT(A2,B2)).
4. Press **<Ctrl+Enter>**.

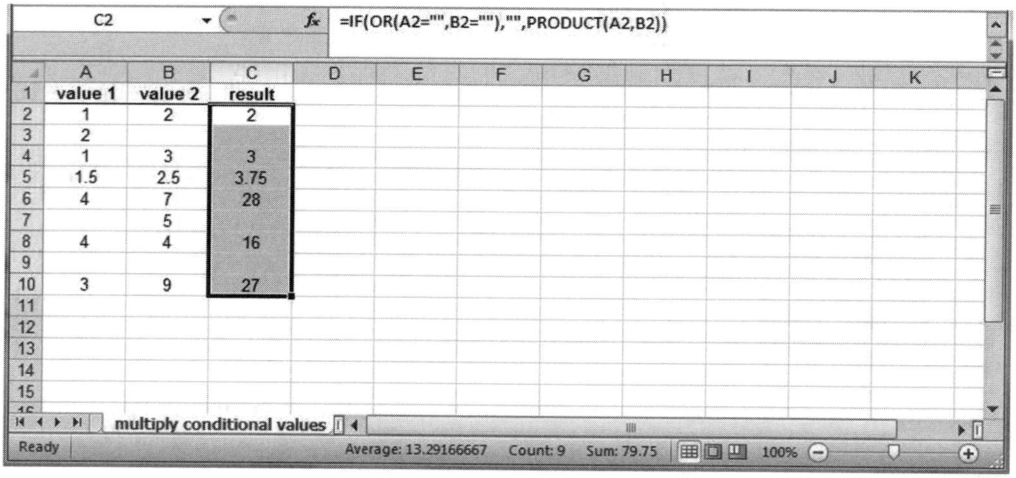

	C2			f_x	=IF(OR(A2="",B2=""),"",PRODUCT(A2,B2))						
	A	**B**	**C**	**D**	**E**	**F**	**G**	**H**	**I**	**J**	**K**
1	value 1	value 2	result								
2	1	2	2								
3	2										
4	1	3	3								
5	1.5	2.5	3.75								
6	4	7	28								
7		5									
8	4	4	16								
9											
10	3	9	27								
11											
12											
13											
14											
15											

multiply conditional values

Ready   Average: 13.29166667   Count: 9   Sum: 79.75   100%

FIGURE 6–21

NOTE *The following formula produces the same result: =IF(OR(A2="",B2=""),"", A2 * B2).*

USE THE QUOTIENT FUNCTION TO RETURN THE INTEGER PORTION OF A DIVISION

The opposite of PRODUCT, which was used in the previous tip, is QUO-TIENT. This function calculates the integer portion of a division operation and discards the remainder. To use this function, you must first install and load the Analysis ToolPak add-in.

QUOTIENT(*numerator, denominator*)

numerator: The dividend.

denominator: The divisor.

▶ **To Calculate the Integer Portion:**

1. Select cells A2:A10 and enter the number **100**.
2. Press **<Ctrl+Enter>**.
3. In cells B2:B10 enter any values as the divisor.
4. Select cells C2:C10 and type the following formula:
   =QUOTIENT(A2,B2).
5. Press **<Ctrl+Enter>**.

C2			*fx*	=QUOTIENT(A2,B2)				
	A	B	C	D	E	F	G	H
1	value	divisor	result					
2	100	5	20	20				
3	100	33	3	3				
4	100	41	2	2				
5	100	0	#DIV/0!					
6	100	50	2	2				
7	100	150	0	0				
8	100	25	4	4				
9	100	1.75	57	57				
10	100	?	#VALUE!					
11								
12								
13								
14								
15								

FIGURE 6–22

NOTE *To avoid incorrect calculations (division with zero) and the error value shown in cells C5 and C10, use the following formula:* **=IF(ISERROR (QUOTIENT(A10,B10)),"",QUOTIENT(A10,B10)).**

USE THE POWER FUNCTION TO CALCULATE THE SQUARE AND CUBE ROOTS

To raise numbers to the power of another number, the POWER function is used. It can also be used to calculate the root.

POWER(*number, power*)

number: The base number, which can be any real number.

power: The exponent.

NOTE *The operator ^ can be used instead of POWER, so =POWER(3,2) could be written like this: =3^2.*

▶ **To Calculate Roots Using the POWER Function:**

1. In cells A2:A10 list some values.
2. Select cells B2:B10 and type the formula **=POWER((A2),1/2)** to calculate the square root.
3. Press **<Ctrl+Enter>**.
4. Select cells C2:C10 and type the formula **=POWER((A2),1/3)** to calculate the cube root.
5. Press **<Ctrl+Enter>**.

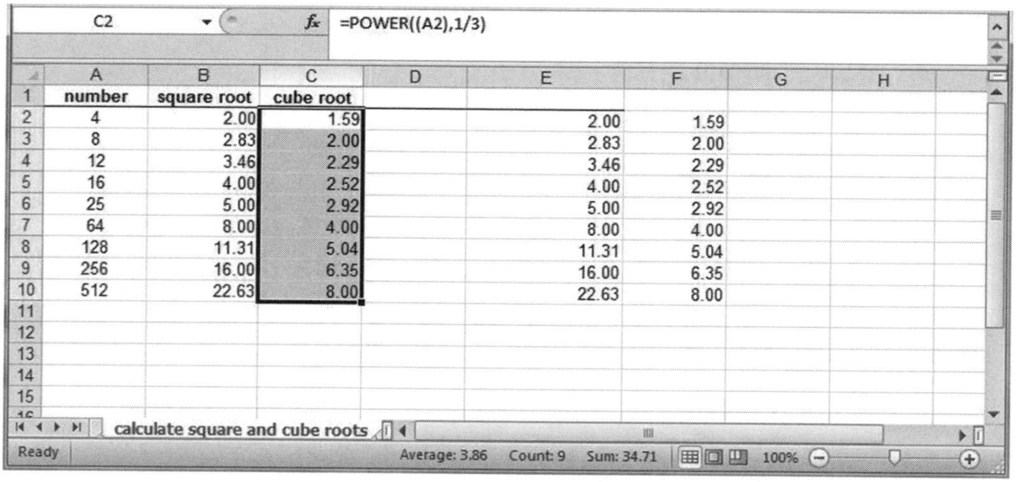

	C2	▼	*fx*	=POWER((A2),1/3)				
	A	B	C	D	E	F	G	H
1	number	square root	cube root					
2	4	2.00	1.59		2.00	1.59		
3	8	2.83	2.00		2.83	2.00		
4	12	3.46	2.29		3.46	2.29		
5	16	4.00	2.52		4.00	2.52		
6	25	5.00	2.92		5.00	2.92		
7	64	8.00	4.00		8.00	4.00		
8	128	11.31	5.04		11.31	5.04		
9	256	16.00	6.35		16.00	6.35		
10	512	22.63	8.00		22.63	8.00		
11								
12								
13								
14								
15								

calculate square and cube roots

Ready   Average: 3.86   Count: 9   Sum: 34.71   100%

FIGURE 6–23

NOTE *To use the ^ operator, type =A2^(1/2) to calculate the square root and =A2^(1/3) to determine the cube root.*

USE THE POWER FUNCTION TO CALCULATE INTEREST

Imagine you won $1,000 and wanted to save it in a bank account. Depending on the bank, the account could earn 2.5 to 5 percent in interest compounded annually. How many dollars would be in the bank account after several years if it was saved and not touched? Follow along with this example to find out.

▶ **To Calculate the Total Amount of Money Saved Depending on the Interest Rate:**

1. Select cells A2:A10 and enter **$1,000** as the starting amount.
2. Press **<Ctrl+Enter>**.
3. In cells B2:B10 enter different interest rates.
4. In cells C2:C10 enter the number of years the money will be saved.
5. Select cells D2:D10 and enter the following formula:
   =A2*POWER((1+B2/100),C2).
6. Press **<Ctrl+Enter>**.

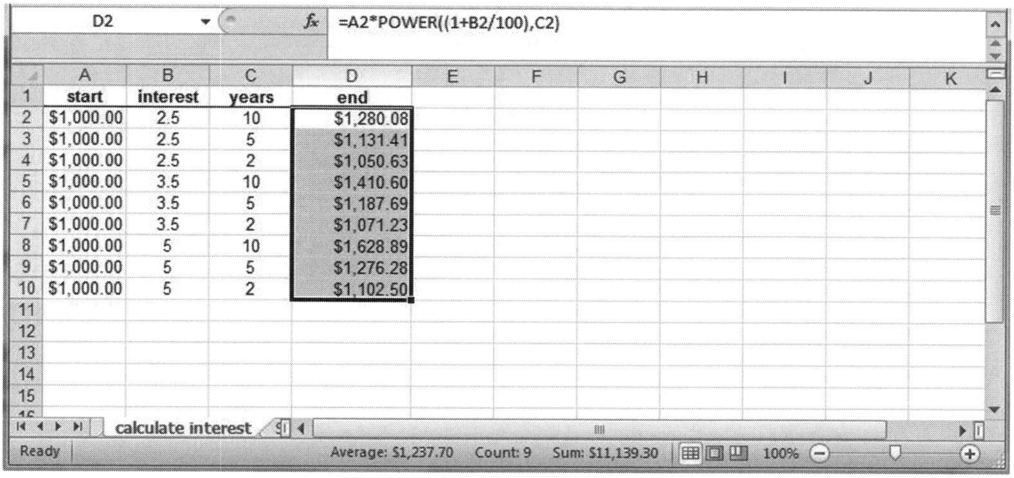

	A	B	C	D
1	start	interest	years	end
2	$1,000.00	2.5	10	$1,280.08
3	$1,000.00	2.5	5	$1,131.41
4	$1,000.00	2.5	2	$1,050.63
5	$1,000.00	3.5	10	$1,410.60
6	$1,000.00	3.5	5	$1,187.69
7	$1,000.00	3.5	2	$1,071.23
8	$1,000.00	5	10	$1,628.89
9	$1,000.00	5	5	$1,276.28
10	$1,000.00	5	2	$1,102.50

D2   fx =A2*POWER((1+B2/100),C2)

calculate interest

Ready   Average: $1,237.70   Count: 9   Sum: $11,139.30   100%

FIGURE 6–24

USE THE MOD FUNCTION TO EXTRACT THE REMAINDER OF A DIVISION

This example contains the value 100 in cells A2:A10 and divisors in column B. The MOD function is used here to find the remainder of a division operation. The result has the same sign as the divisor.

MOD(*number, divisor*)

number: The number to find the remainder for.

divisor: The number to divide number by.

▶ **To Extract the Remainder of a Division Operation:**

1. Select cells A2:A10 and enter **100**.
2. Press **<Ctrl+Enter>**.
3. In cells B2:B10 enter different divisors.
4. Select cells C2:C10 and type the formula **=A2/B2**.
5. Press **<Ctrl+Enter>**.
6. Select cells D2:D10 and type the formula **=MOD(A2,B2)**.
7. Press **<Ctrl+Enter>**.

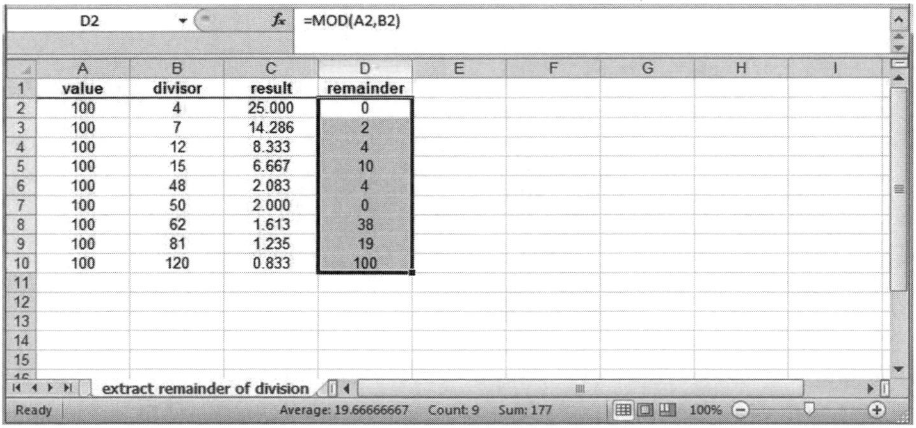

	A	B	C	D
1	value	divisor	result	remainder
2	100	4	25.000	0
3	100	7	14.286	2
4	100	12	8.333	4
5	100	15	6.667	10
6	100	48	2.083	4
7	100	50	2.000	0
8	100	62	1.613	38
9	100	81	1.235	19
10	100	120	0.833	100

D2 = =MOD(A2,B2)

FIGURE 6–25

NOTE *The function can also be expressed in terms of the mathematical INT function: $MOD(n,d) = n - d*INT(n/d)$. Notice that the value in cell D10 is incorrect. See the following tip for a way to avoid this.*

MODIFY THE MOD FUNCTION FOR DIVISORS LARGER THAN THE NUMBER

As seen in the previous tip, a problem occurs when the divisor is larger than the number for which you want to find the remainder. The result will always be the number itself. To handle this using the MOD function, follow these steps.

▶ **Handling Divisors that are Larger than the Number:**

1. Select cells A2:A10 and enter **100**.
2. Press **<Ctrl+Enter>**.
3. In cells B2:B10 enter different divisors.
4. Select cells C2:C10 and type this formula: **=A2/B2**.
5. Press **<Ctrl+Enter>**.
6. Select cells D2:D10 and type this formula: **=MOD(A2,B2)*(A2>B2)**.
7. Press **<Ctrl+Enter>**.

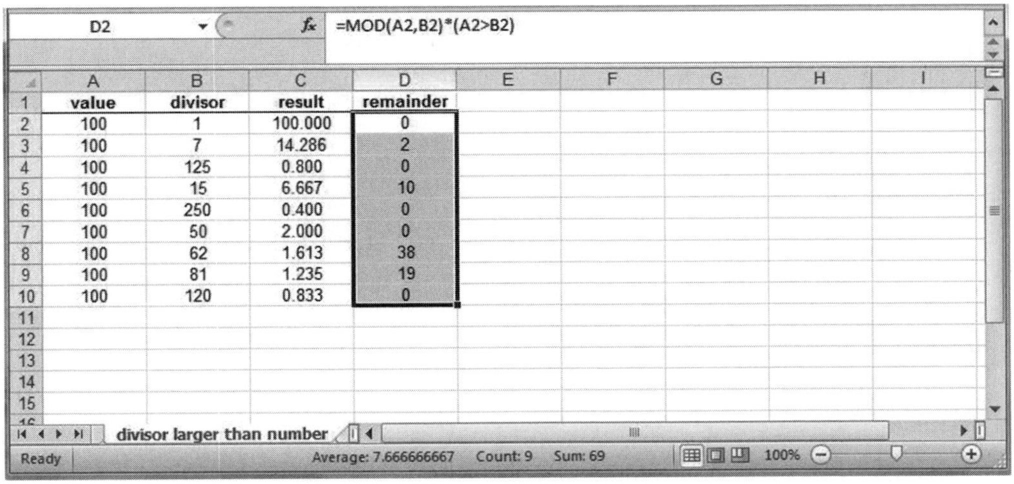

FIGURE 6–26

USE THE ROW FUNCTION TO MARK EVERY OTHER ROW

Sometimes it is necessary to mark every other row in a worksheet. Several functions can be used in combination to do this. Use the MOD, ROW, and IF functions together as described below.

▶ **To Mark Every Other Row:**

1. Select cells A1:A10 and type the following formula:
   =IF(MOD(ROW(),2),"XXX"," ").
2. Press **<Ctrl+Enter>**.

NOTE *If every other column has to be marked, use the following formula:*
=IF(MOD(COLUMN(),2),"XXX"," ").

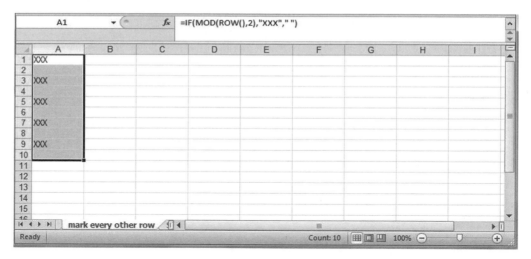

FIGURE 6–27

NOTE *See Chapter 10, "Conditional Formatting," for additional tips on using the MOD function.*

USE THE SUBTOTAL FUNCTION TO PERFORM SEVERAL OPERATIONS

The SUBTOTAL function can be used to calculate subtotals in a list or database. There are different subtotal operations available that are all covered by just one function. The syntax is provided in Chapter 5.

▶ To Use the SUBTOTAL Function for a Number of Calculations:

1. Copy the data shown in columns A and B in Figure 6–28.
2. Select cells C2:C10 and enter the daily sales of each team.
3. Calculate the average in cell F2 with the following formula: **=SUBTOTAL(1,$C$2:$C$10)**.
4. Calculate the sum in cell F3 with the following formula: **=SUBTOTAL(9,$C$2:$C$10)**.
5. Calculate the lowest sales value in cell F4 with the following formula: **=SUBTOTAL(5,$C$2:$C$10)**.
6. Calculate the maximum value in cell F5 with the following formula: **=SUBTOTAL(4,$C$2:$C$10)**.

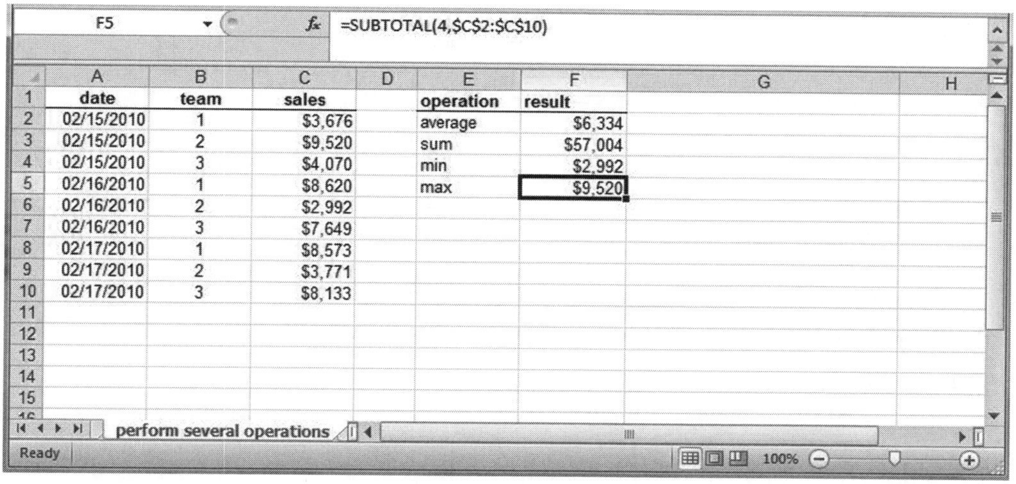
F5 =SUBTOTAL(4,$C$2:$C$10)

	A	B	C	D	E	F
1	date	team	sales		operation	result
2	02/15/2010	1	$3,676		average	$6,334
3	02/15/2010	2	$9,520		sum	$57,004
4	02/15/2010	3	$4,070		min	$2,992
5	02/16/2010	1	$8,620		max	$9,520
6	02/16/2010	2	$2,992			
7	02/16/2010	3	$7,649			
8	02/17/2010	1	$8,573			
9	02/17/2010	2	$3,771			
10	02/17/2010	3	$8,133			

FIGURE 6–28

USE THE SUBTOTAL FUNCTION TO COUNT ALL VISIBLE ROWS IN A FILTERED LIST

This example shows a filtered list. The task is to count all visible and used rows. Note that the COUNT and COUNTA functions can also be used in a non-filtered list. However, they also count hidden rows. To get the right result, use the SUBTOTAL function and use "3" as the function_num value (see this function's syntax in the previous tip).

▶ **To Count All Visible Rows in a Filtered List:**

1. Generate a filtered list like the one shown in Figure 6–29.
2. Select cell C13 and type the following formula:
   =SUBTOTAL(3,B2:B10).
3. Press **<Enter>**.

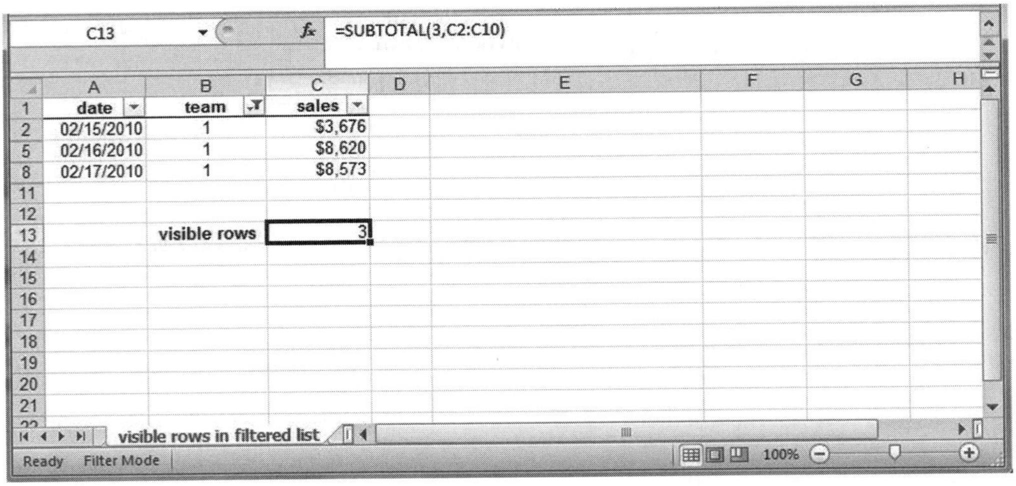

FIGURE 6–29

USE THE RAND FUNCTION TO GENERATE RANDOM VALUES

To generate randomized values Excel provides the RAND function. This function returns a random number greater than or equal to 0 and less than 1. Each time the worksheet is calculated, a new random number is generated.

This example generates randomized integer values from 1 to 999 in cells A2:D10 and then replaces the formulas with calculated values.

▶ **To Generate Integer Random Values:**

1. Select cells A2:D10 and type the following formula: **=INT(RAND()*1000)**.
2. Press **<Ctrl+Enter>**.
3. Press **<Ctrl+C>** to copy the filled cells.
4. In the **Home** tab choose the dropdown arrow underneath **Paste**.
5. From **Paste Values** choose **Values (V)**.

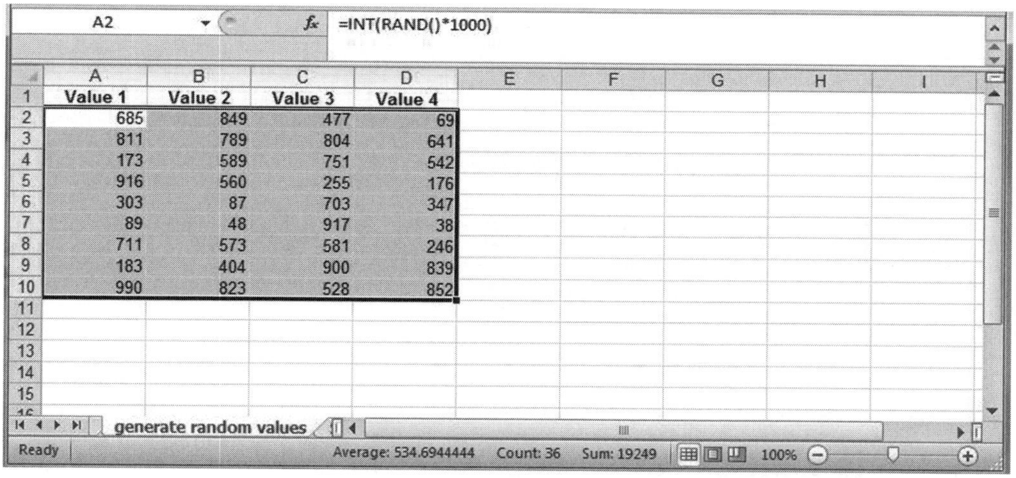

| | A2 | | | f_x | =INT(RAND()*1000) | | | | | |

	A	B	C	D	E	F	G	H	I
1	Value 1	Value 2	Value 3	Value 4					
2	685	849	477	69					
3	811	789	804	641					
4	173	589	751	542					
5	916	560	255	176					
6	303	87	703	347					
7	89	48	917	38					
8	711	573	581	246					
9	183	404	900	839					
10	990	823	528	852					
11									
12									
13									
14									
15									

generate random values

Ready   Average: 534.6944444   Count: 36   Sum: 19249   100%

FIGURE 6–30

USE THE RANDBETWEEN FUNCTION TO GENERATE RANDOM VALUES IN A SPECIFIED RANGE

To generate randomized values in a specified range, such as from 1 to 49, use the RANDBETWEEN function. This function returns a random number in the range you specify, returning a new random number every time the worksheet is calculated. If this function is not available and returns the #NAME? error, install and load the Analysis ToolPak add-in.

RANDBETWEEN(*bottom, top*)

> *bottom*: The lowest integer in the range.

> *top*: The highest integer in the range.

▶ **To Create Random Values from 1 to 49:**

1. Select cells A2:D10 and type the following formula:
   =RANDBETWEEN(1,49).
2. Press **<Ctrl+Enter>**.
3. Press **<Ctrl+C>** to copy the filled cells.
4. In the **Home** tab choose the dropdown arrow underneath Paste.
5. From Paste **Values** choose Values (V).

	A	B	C	D
1	Value 1	Value 2	Value 3	Value 4
2	27	13	20	32
3	35	7	10	30
4	38	16	27	45
5	13	32	13	47
6	1	32	4	11
7	18	32	26	39
8	48	2	8	40
9	25	44	21	21
10	42	21	46	4
11	48	1	40	39

FIGURE 6–31

USE THE EVEN AND ODD FUNCTIONS TO DETERMINE THE NEAREST EVEN/ODD VALUE

In addition to the standard functions for rounding up a number, there are other functions available like EVEN and ODD. For example, to round up a number to the nearest even integer, use the EVEN function.

EVEN(*number*)

> *number*: The value to be rounded.

To round up a number to the nearest odd value, use the ODD function. ODD(*number*)

number: The value to be rounded.

▶ **To Determine the Nearest Even/Odd Value:**

1. In cells A2:A10 list some valid numbers with decimal points.
2. Select cells B2:B10 and enter the following function: **=EVEN(A2)**.
3. Press **<Ctrl+Enter>**.
4. Select cells C2:C10 and enter the following function: **=ODD(A2)**.
5. Press **<Ctrl+Enter>**.

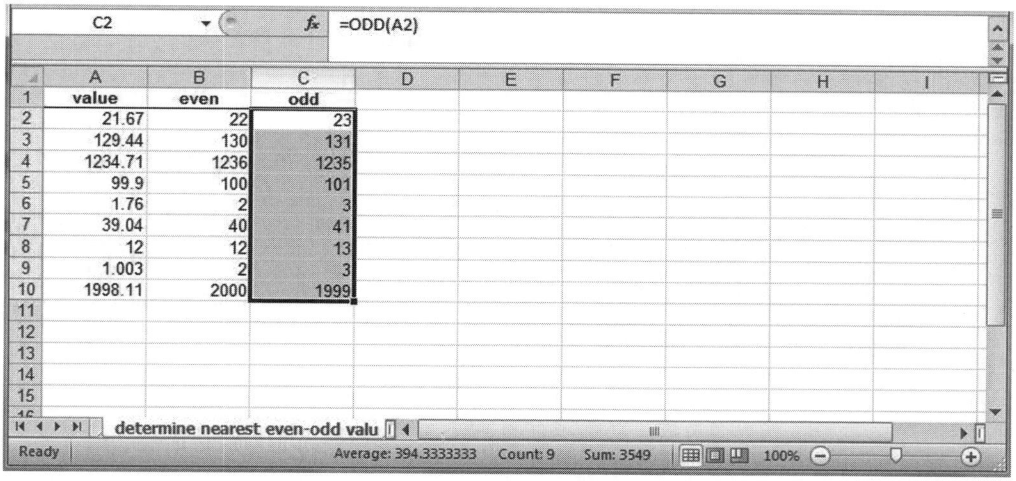

	C2			*fx*	=ODD(A2)					
	A	B	C	D	E	F	G	H	I	
1	value	even	odd							
2	21.67	22	23							
3	129.44	130	131							
4	1234.71	1236	1235							
5	99.9	100	101							
6	1.76	2	3							
7	39.04	40	41							
8	12	12	13							
9	1.003	2	3							
10	1998.11	2000	1999							
11										
12										
13										
14										
15										

determine nearest even-odd valu

Ready   Average: 394.3333333   Count: 9   Sum: 3549   100%

FIGURE 6–32

USE THE ISEVEN AND ISODD FUNCTIONS TO CHECK IF A NUMBER IS EVEN OR ODD

To find out whether numbers are even or odd, use the ISEVEN or ISODD functions. ISEVEN returns TRUE if the number is even and FALSE if the number is odd, while ISODD returns TRUE if the number is odd and FALSE if the number is even.

ISEVEN(*number*)
ISODD(*number*)

number: The value to be tested. Non-integer values are truncated.

▶ **To Check if a Number is Even or Odd:**

1. In cells A2:A10 enter some numbers.
2. Select cells B2:B10 and type the following formula:
   =IF(ISEVEN(A2),"X","").
3. Press **<Ctrl+Enter>**.
4. Select cell C2:C10 and type the following formula:
   =IF(ISODD(A2),"X","").
5. Press **<Ctrl+Enter>**.

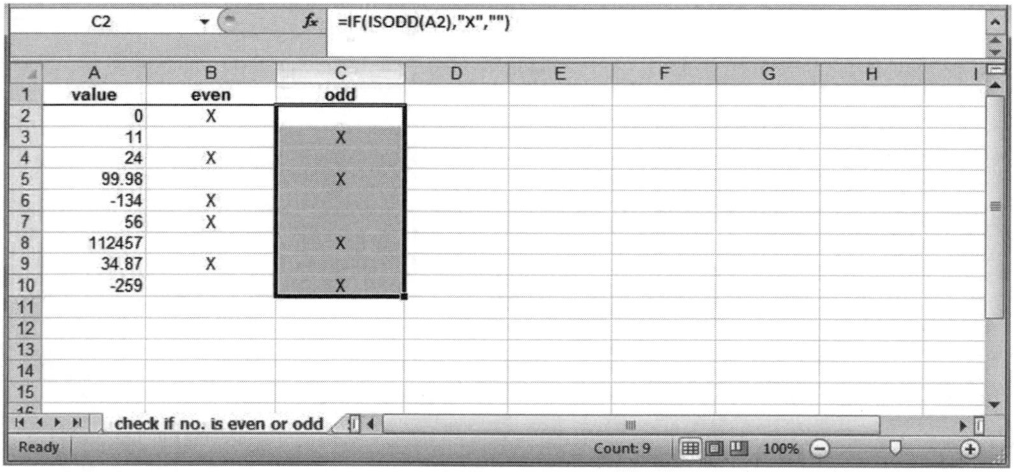

	A	B	C	D	E	F	G	H	I
	C2		fx	=IF(ISODD(A2),"X","")					
1	value	even	odd						
2	0	X							
3	11		X						
4	24	X							
5	99.98		X						
6	-134	X							
7	56	X							
8	112457		X						
9	34.87	X							
10	-259		X						

check if no. is even or odd

Ready   Count: 9   100%

FIGURE 6–33

NOTE   *To use these functions, you will need to install and load the Analysis ToolPak add-in as described earlier.*

USE THE ISODD AND ROW FUNCTIONS TO DETERMINE ODD ROWS

In this example, we need to determine whether a row number in a range is even or odd, and then fill each odd row with the character "X". Use the ISODD function in combination with IF and ROW() to get the result shown in Figure 6–34.

If this function is not available and returns an error, install and load the Analysis ToolPak add-in.

▶ **To Determine Odd Rows and Mark Them:**

1. Select cells A1:E11 and type the following formula:
   =IF(ISODD(ROW()),"X","").
2. Press **<Ctrl+Enter>**.

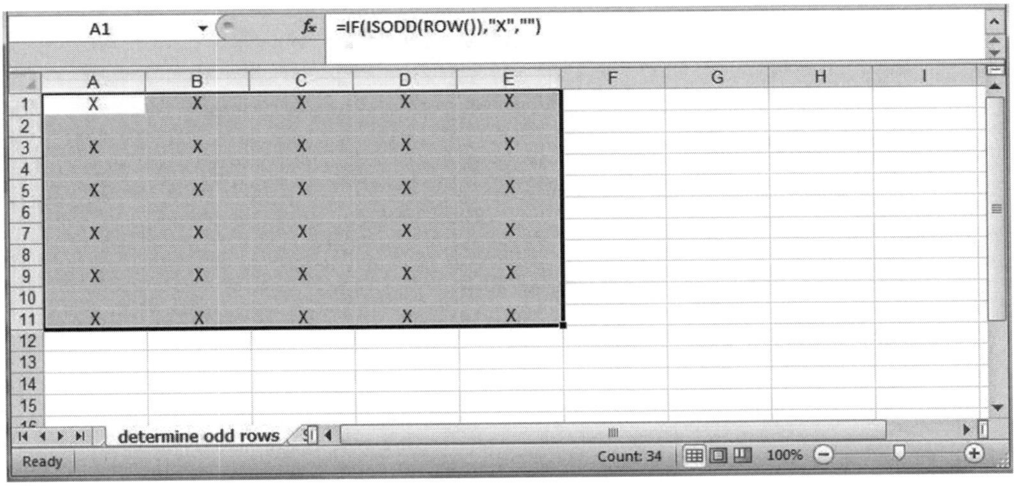

FIGURE 6–34

NOTE   *To mark all even rows, use the following formula:*
=IF(ISEVEN(ROW()),"X","").

USE THE ISODD AND COLUMN FUNCTIONS TO DETERMINE ODD COLUMNS

In this example, we want to determine whether a column's index in a range is even or odd, and then fill each odd row with the character "X". Use the ISODD function in combination with IF and COLUMN() to get the result shown in Figure 6–35. If this function is not available and returns an error, install and load the Analysis ToolPak add-in.

▶ **To Determine Odd Columns:**

1. Select cells A1:E11 and type the following formula:
   =IF(ISODD(COLUMN()),"X","").
2. Press **<Ctrl+Enter>**.

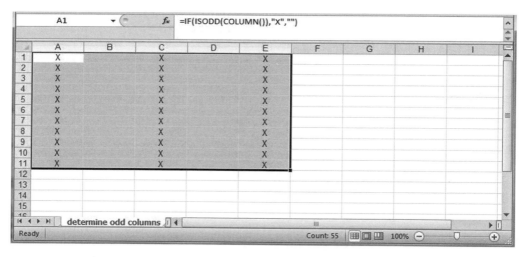

FIGURE 6–35

| NOTE | *To mark even columns, type the following formula: =IF(ISEVEN(COLUMN()), "X","").* |

USE THE ROMAN FUNCTION TO CONVERT ARABIC NUMERALS TO ROMAN NUMERALS

This tip explains how to convert an Arabic numeral to a Roman numeral. To get this result, use the ROMAN function, which returns the Roman value as text.

ROMAN(*number, form*)

number: The Arabic numeral to be converted.

form: (optional) A number from 0 to 4 that specifies the type of Roman numeral. Styles range from Classic to Simplified and become more concise (using fewer characters) as the value of form increases. If omitted, the Classic type is used.

▶ **To Convert Arabic Numerals to Roman Numerals:**

1. In cells A2:A10 enter valid numbers from 1 to 3999.
2. Select cells B2:B10 and type the following formula: **=ROMAN(A2,0)**.
3. Press **<Ctrl+Enter>**.

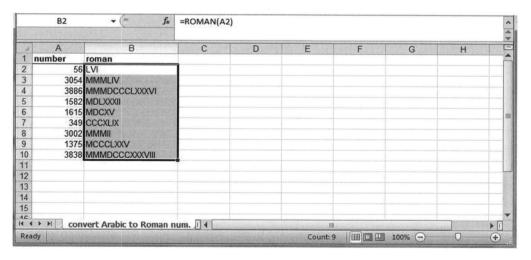

FIGURE 6–36

USE THE SIGN FUNCTION TO CHECK FOR THE SIGN OF A NUMBER

Excel provides the SIGN function to check the sign of a number. This function returns 1 if the number is positive, 0 if the number is 0, and -1 if the number is negative. If the user enters text instead of a number, the SIGN function returns the error code #VALUE!.

SIGN(*number*).

number: Any real number.

▶ **To Check for the Sign of a Number:**

1. In cells A2:A10 list numbers or text.
2. Select cells B2:B10 and type the following formula:
   =IF(ISERROR(SIGN(A2)),"",SIGN(A2)).
3. Press **<Ctrl+Enter>**.

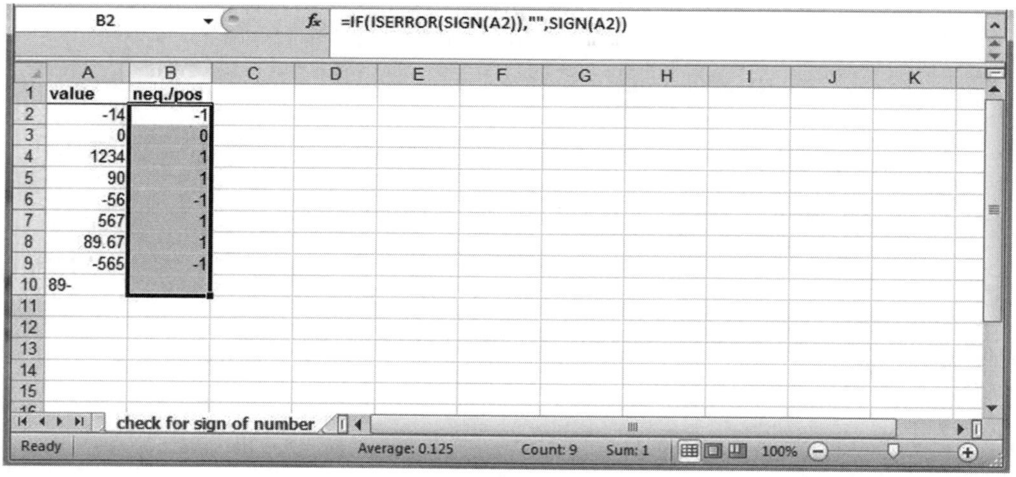

FIGURE 6–37

NOTE *The same result for numeric values can also be generated by combining IF functions. Use this formula: =IF(A1>0;1;IF(A2<0;-1;0)).*

USE THE SUMSQ FUNCTION TO DETERMINE THE SQUARE SUM

Excel provides the SUMSQ function to sum the squares of the arguments.
SUMSQ(*number1, number2, ...*)

number1, number2, ...: From 1 to 30 arguments that will have their
squares summed up. Instead of values, you can use a single array or a
reference to an array separated by commas.

▶ **To Determine the Square Sum:**

1. In cells A2:A10 list valid numbers.
2. In cells B2:B10 list valid numbers.
3. Select cells C2:C10 and type the following formula: **=SUMSQ(A2,B2)**.
4. Press **<Ctrl+Enter>**.

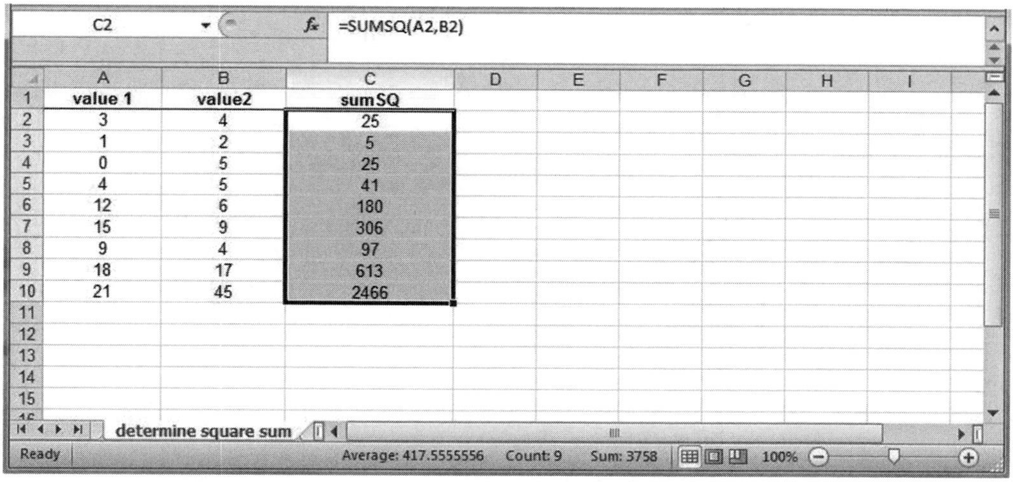

	C2			*fx*	=SUMSQ(A2,B2)						
	A	B	C	D	E	F	G	H	I	
1	value 1	value2	sum SQ							
2	3	4	25							
3	1	2	5							
4	0	5	25							
5	4	5	41							
6	12	6	180							
7	15	9	306							
8	9	4	97							
9	18	17	613							
10	21	45	2466							
11										
12										
13										
14										
15										

determine square sum

Ready   Average: 417.5555556   Count: 9   Sum: 3758   100%

FIGURE 6–38

USE THE GCD FUNCTION TO DETERMINE THE GREATEST COMMON DIVISOR

In this example, the greatest common divisor of two integers has to be determined. To do so, use the GCD function. This function is only available if you have the Analysis ToolPak add-in installed.

GCD(*number1*, *number2*, ...)

> *number1*, *number2*, ...: From 1 to 29 values for which you want to find the greatest common divisor. Non-integer values are truncated.

▶ **To Determine the Greatest Common Divisor:**

1. In cells A2:A10 list any valid numbers.
2. In cells B2:B10 list any valid numbers.
3. Select cells C2:C10.
4. Type the following formula: **=GCD(A2,B2)**.
5. Press **<Ctrl+Enter>**.

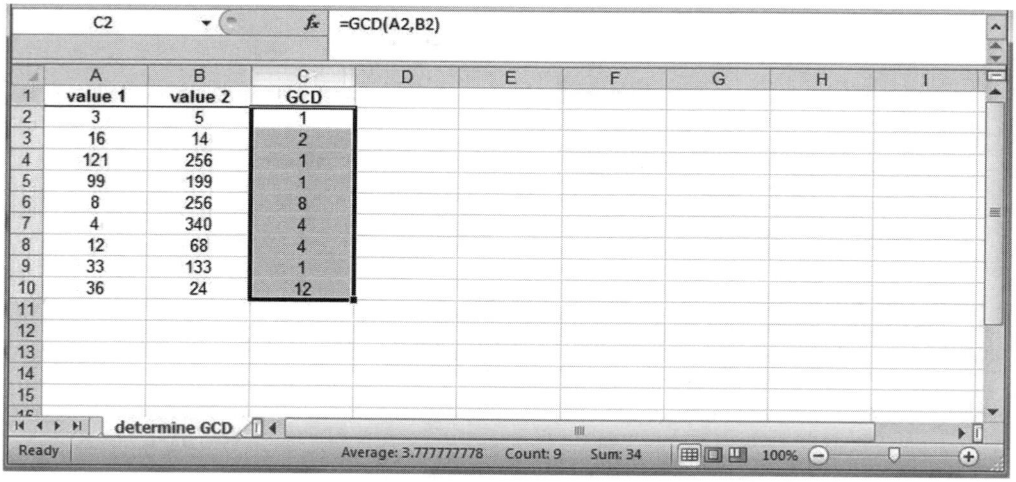

	A	B	C	D	E	F	G	H	I
1	value 1	value 2	GCD						
2	3	5	1						
3	16	14	2						
4	121	256	1						
5	99	199	1						
6	8	256	8						
7	4	340	4						
8	12	68	4						
9	33	133	1						
10	36	24	12						

C2   *fx* =GCD(A2,B2)

determine GCD

Ready   Average: 3.777777778   Count: 9   Sum: 34   100%

FIGURE 6–39

USE THE LCM FUNCTION TO DETERMINE THE LEAST COMMON MULTIPLE

This example shows how to determine the least common multiple of two integers. Excel provides the LCM function through the Analysis ToolPak add-in. You will need to install and load the add-in to perform these steps.
LCM(*number1, number2, ...*)

> *number1, number2, ...*: From 1 to 29 values for which you want to find the least common multiple. Non-integer values are truncated.

▶ **To Determine the Least Common Multiple:**

1. In cells A2:A10 list any valid numbers.
2. In cells B2:B10 list any valid numbers.
3. Select cells C2:C10 and type the following formula:
   =LCM(A2,B2).
4. Press **<Ctrl+Enter>**.

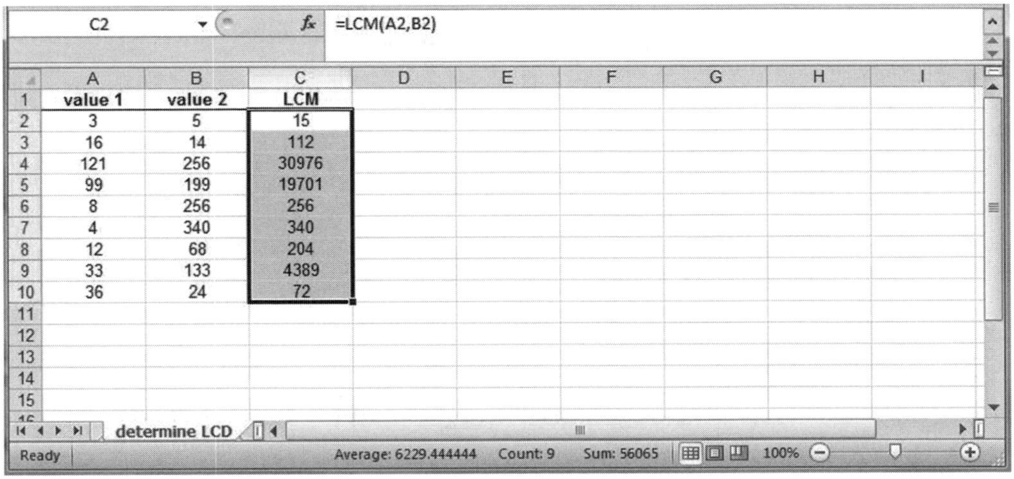

	A	B	C	D	E	F	G	H	I
1	value 1	value 2	LCM						
2	3	5	15						
3	16	14	112						
4	121	256	30976						
5	99	199	19701						
6	8	256	256						
7	4	340	340						
8	12	68	204						
9	33	133	4389						
10	36	24	72						

C2 fx =LCM(A2,B2)

determine LCD

Average: 6229.444444   Count: 9   Sum: 56065   100%

FIGURE 6–40

USE THE SUMIFS FUNCTION TO DETERMINE SALES OF A TEAM AND SEX

This example refers to Figure 6–3, however, the table is not only summed up to the sales of different teams but is also enlarged to the sex of the sales persons. You can use the SUMIFS function to add all cells in a range, specified by given several criteria.

The SUMIFS function syntax has the following arguments:

SUMIFS(sum_range, criteria_range1, criteria1, [criteria_range2, criteria2], ...)

sum_range: Required. One or more cells to sum, including numbers or names, ranges, or cell.

criteria_range1: Required. The first range in which to evaluate the associated criteria.

criteria: Required. The criteria in the form of a number, expression, cell reference, or text that define which cells in the *criteria_range1* argument will be added.

criteria_range2, criteria2:   Optional. Additional ranges and their associated criteria.

▶ **To Sum Specified Data:**

1. In cells A2:A10 enter a team number from 1 to 3.
2. List all team members in cells B2:B10.
3. In column C enter sex of sales persons.
4. In cells D2:D10 enter the daily sales of each employee.
5. List the numbers 1, 2, 3, and sex for each team in cells F2:F7 as shown in Figure 6–41.
6. Select cells H2:H7 and type the following formula:
   =SUMIFS($D$2:$D$10,$A$2:$A$10,F2,$C$2:$C$10,G2)
7. Press **<Ctrl+Enter>**.

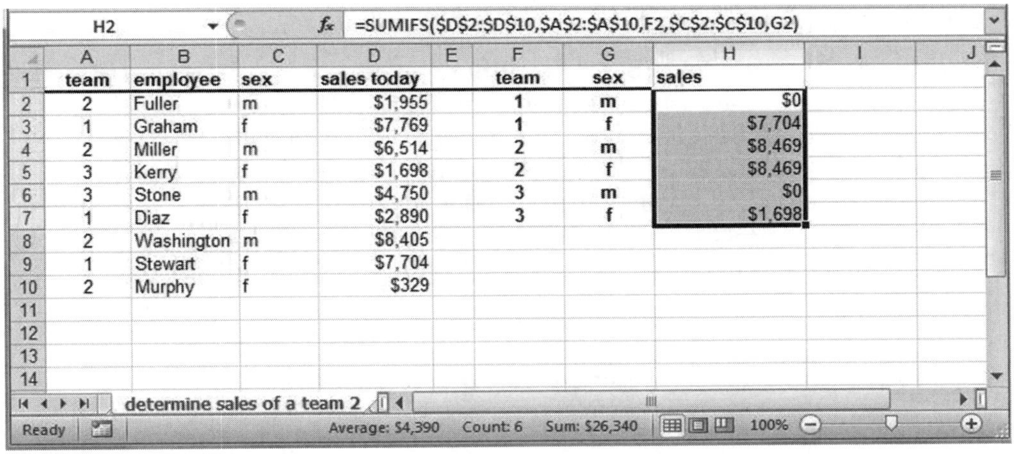

	H2	▼		f_x	=SUMIFS($D$2:$D$10,$A$2:$A$10,F2,$C$2:$C$10,G2)					
⊿	A	B	C	D	E	F	G	H	I	J
1	team	employee	sex	sales today		team	sex	sales		
2	2	Fuller	m	$1,955		1	m	$0		
3	1	Graham	f	$7,769		1	f	$7,704		
4	2	Miller	m	$6,514		2	m	$8,469		
5	3	Kerry	f	$1,698		2	f	$8,469		
6	3	Stone	m	$4,750		3	m	$0		
7	1	Diaz	f	$2,890		3	f	$1,698		
8	2	Washington	m	$8,405						
9	1	Stewart	f	$7,704						
10	2	Murphy	f	$329						
11										
12										
13										
14										

determine sales of a team 2

Ready   Average: $4,390   Count: 6   Sum: $26,340   100%

FIGURE 6–41

NOTE   *Up to 127 range/criteria pairs are allowed.*

USE THE COUNTIF FUNCTION TO COUNT PHASES THAT COST MORE THAN $1000 IN A CERTAIN DURATION

This example refers to Figure 6–6, however, not only project phases but also duration of the project are listed. To determine how many phases cost more than $1000 and take less or even 2 days, use the COUNTIFS function. This function counts the number of cells in a range that meet the specified criteria.

COUNTIFS(*criteria_range1, criteria1, [criteria_range2, criteria2]…*)

criteria_range1. Required. The first range in which to evaluate the associated criteria.

criteria1. Required. The criteria in the form of a number, expression, cell reference, or text that define which cells will be counted.

criteria_range2, criteria2, … Optional. Additional ranges and their associated criteria.

▶ To Count Specified Phases:

1. In cells A3:A12 enter the different phases.
2. Enter the costs of each phase in cells B3:B12.
3. Enter the duration of each phase in cells C3:C12.
4. In cell E2 enter **1000,** and in cell F2 enter **2** as the given criteria.
5. Select cell E4 and type the following formula:
   =COUNTIFS(B3:B12,">" & E2,C3:C12,"<=" & F2).
6. Press **<Enter>**.

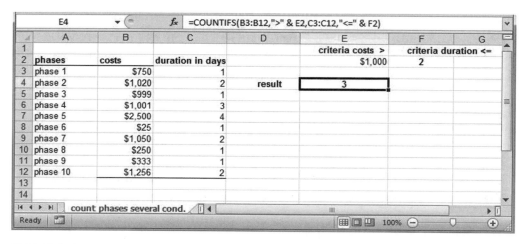

FIGURE 6–42

| NOTE | *Up to 127 range/criteria pairs are allowed.* |

7 Basic Financial Functions

Chapter

USE THE SYD FUNCTION TO CALCULATE DEPRECIATION

In this tip, we calculate the depreciation of an investment. To do so, use the SYD function, which returns the sum-of-years' digits depreciation of an asset for a specified period.

SYD(*cost, salvage, life, per*)

> *cost*: The asset's initial cost.
>
> *salvage*: The value of the asset at the end of the deprecation.
>
> *life*: The number of periods over which the asset is depreciated.
>
> *per*: The period. *per* must use the same units as *life*.

▶ **To Calculate Depreciation:**

1. In cell B1 enter the cost of purchase.
2. In cell B2 enter in years the number of periods over which the purchase will be depreciated.
3. Enter the salvage value in cell B3.
4. Calculate the depreciation in the fifth year in cell B5 with the following formula: **=SYD($B$1,$B$3,$B$2,5)**.
5. Press **<Enter>**.

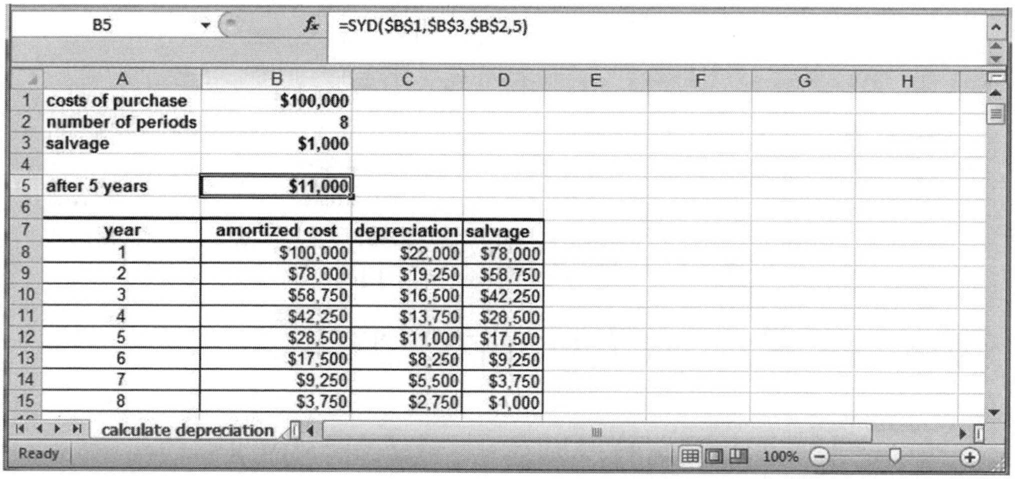

FIGURE 7–1

NOTE *SYD is calculated as follows:* = **((cost–salvage)* (life–per+1)*2)** / **(life*(life+1)).**

USE THE SLN FUNCTION TO CALCULATE STRAIGHT-LINE DEPRECIATION

Here we want to calculate the straight-line depreciation of an investment. Use the SLN function, which returns the straight-line depreciation of an asset for one period.

SLN(*cost, salvage, life*)

> *cost*: The asset's initial cost.

> *salvage*: The value of the asset at the end of the depreciation.

> *life*: The number of periods over which the asset is depreciated.

▶ **To Calculate Depreciation:**

1. In cell B1 enter the initial cost.
2. In cell B2 enter the number of periods as years.
3. Enter the salvage in cell B3.

4. Calculate the depreciation in the fifth year in cell B5 with the following formula: **=SLN($B$1,$B$3,$B$2)**.
5. Press **<Enter>**.

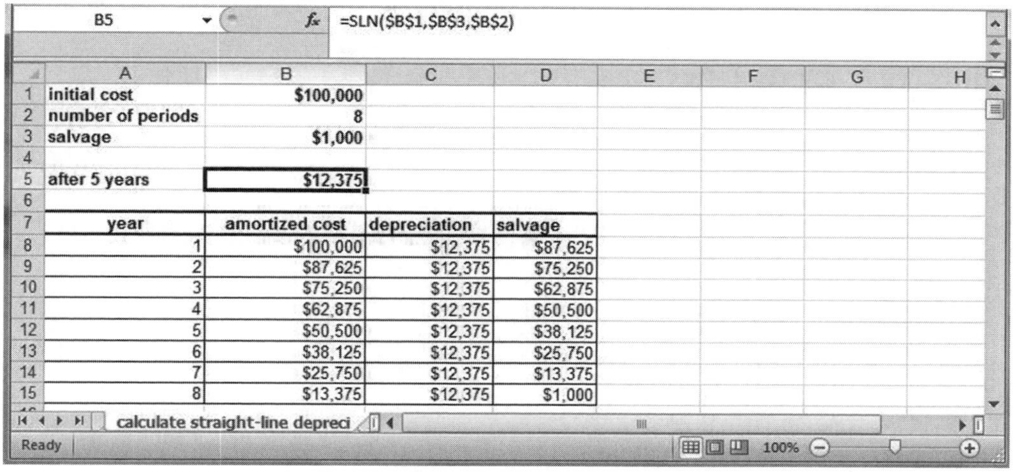

	B5		f_x	=SLN($B$1,$B$3,$B$2)				
	A	B	C	D	E	F	G	H
1	initial cost	$100,000						
2	number of periods	8						
3	salvage	$1,000						
4								
5	after 5 years	$12,375						
6								
7	year	amortized cost	depreciation	salvage				
8	1	$100,000	$12,375	$87,625				
9	2	$87,625	$12,375	$75,250				
10	3	$75,250	$12,375	$62,875				
11	4	$62,875	$12,375	$50,500				
12	5	$50,500	$12,375	$38,125				
13	6	$38,125	$12,375	$25,750				
14	7	$25,750	$12,375	$13,375				
15	8	$13,375	$12,375	$1,000				

calculate straight-line depreci

Ready   100%

FIGURE 7–2

USE THE PV FUNCTION TO DECIDE THE AMOUNT TO INVEST

In this example you have to decide on the amount of money you want to invest. To solve this problem, you use the PV function, which returns the present value of an investment. This is the total amount that a series of future payments is worth now.

PV(*rate, nper, pmt, fv, type*)

rate: The interest rate per period.

nper: The total number of payment periods in an annuity.

pmt: The payment made each period, which is a constant value.

fv: The future value. This is the amount you want after the last payment is made.

type: A number that indicates when payments are due. 0 or omitted indicates the end of the period, and 1 indicates the beginning of the period.

▶ **To Decide How Much to Invest:**

1. In cell C1 enter the estimated return per year.
2. In cell C2 enter the number of periods in years.
3. Enter the interest rate in cell C3.
4. Calculate the maximum investment amount in cell C4 with the following formula: **=PV(C3,C2,C1)**.
5. Press **<Enter>**.

	C4	▾	f_x	=PV(C3,C2,C1)							
	A	B	C	D	E	F	G	H	I	J	
1		return per year	$55,000								
2		number of periods	5								
3		interest rate	5.00%								
4		invest (max)	-$238,121								
5											
6		investment amount	interest	profit	salvage						
7	1	$238,121	$11,906	$55,000	$195,027						
8	2	$195,027	$9,751	$55,000	$149,779						
9	3	$149,779	$7,489	$55,000	$102,268						
10	4	$102,268	$5,113	$55,000	$52,381						
11	5	$52,381	$2,619	$55,000	$0						
12											
13											
14											
15											
16											

decide amount to invest

Ready   100%

FIGURE 7–3

USE THE PV FUNCTION TO COMPARE INVESTMENTS

Two investments have to be compared. The amount of each investment, the number of periods, the interest, and the estimated return are given. To calculate and compare, use the PV function as described below.

▶ **To Compare Investments:**

1. In cells B2 and C2 enter the investment amounts.
2. In cells B3 and C3 enter the interest rates.
3. In cells B4 and C4 enter the number of periods.
4. In cells B5 and C5 enter the estimated return of each investment.
5. Select cells B7:C7 and type the following formula: **=-PV(B3,B4,B5)**.

6. Press **<Ctrl+Enter>**.
7. Select cells B8:C8 and type the formula **=B7-B2**.
8. Press **<Ctrl+Enter>**.

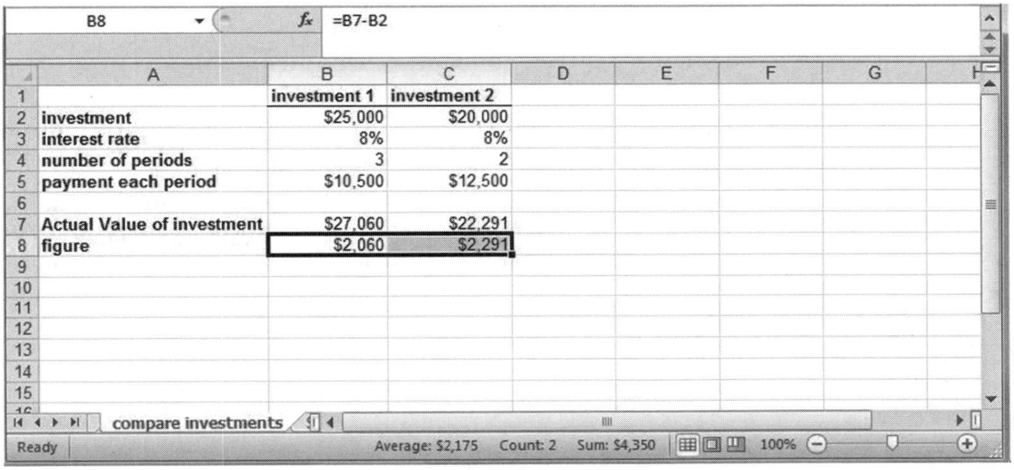

B8		fx	=B7-B2				

	A	B	C	D	E	F	G
1		investment 1	investment 2				
2	investment	$25,000	$20,000				
3	interest rate	8%	8%				
4	number of periods	3	2				
5	payment each period	$10,500	$12,500				
6							
7	Actual Value of investment	$27,060	$22,291				
8	figure	$2,060	$2,291				
9							
10							
11							
12							
13							
14							
15							

compare investments

Ready   Average: $2,175   Count: 2   Sum: $4,350   100%

FIGURE 7–4

NOTE   *Investment 2 is more expensive than Investment 1.*

USE THE DDB FUNCTION TO CALCULATE USING THE DOUBLE-DECLINING BALANCE METHOD

The DDB function returns the depreciation of an asset for a specified period, using the double-declining balance method or some other method that can be specified.

DDB(*cost, salvage, life, period, factor*)

cost: The asset's initial cost.

salvage: The value of the asset at the end of the depreciation.

life: The number of periods over which the asset is being depreciated.

period: The period for which the depreciation is being calculated.

factor: The rate at which the balance declines. If *factor* is omitted, it is assumed to be 2, which specifies the double-declining balance method.

▶ To Use the Double-Declining Balance Method:

1. Enter the initial cost in cell B1, the number of periods in cell B2, and the salvage in cell B3.
2. Calculate the depreciation in the fifth year in cell B4 with the following formula: **=DDB($B$1,$B$3,$B$2,5)**.
3. To calculate the depreciation after one day, type this formula in cell B5: **=DDB($B$1,$B$3,$B$2*365,1)**.
4. To calculate the depreciation after the first month, use this formula in cell B6: **=DDB($B$1,$B$3,$B$2*12,1)**.

	B6	▾	f_x	=DDB($B$1,$B$3,$B$2*12,1)				
	A	B	C	D	E	F	G	H
1	initial cost	$100,000						
2	number of periods	5						
3	salvage	$12,500						
4	after 5 years	$460						
5	after the first day	$110						
6	after the first month	$3,333						
7	year	amortized cost	depreciation	salvage				
8	1	$100,000	$40,000	$60,000				
9	2	$60,000	$24,000	$36,000				
10	3	$36,000	$14,400	$21,600				
11	4	$21,600	$8,640	$12,960				
12	5	$12,960	$460	$12,500				
13								
14								
15								

double-declining balance method

Ready   100%

FIGURE 7–5

USE THE PMT FUNCTION TO DETERMINE THE PAYMENT OF A LOAN

To determine the payment amount for a loan based on constant payments and a constant interest rate, use the PMT function.

PMT(*rate, nper, pv, fv, type*)

     rate: The interest rate of the loan.

     nper: The total number of payments for the loan.

     pv: The present value. This is also referred to as the principal.

fv: The future value. This is the amount you want after the last payment is made. If *fv* is omitted, it is assumed to be 0.

type: A number that indicates when payments are due. 0 or omitted indicates the end of the period, and 1 indicates the beginning of the period.

▶ **To Determine the Payment for a Loan:**

1. In cell B1 enter the interest rate.
2. In cell B2 enter the number of periods in months.
3. In cell B3 enter the amount of the loan.
4. In cell B5 calculate the payment after one month with the following formula: **=-PMT($B$1/12,$B$2,$B$3)**.
5. Press **<Enter>**.

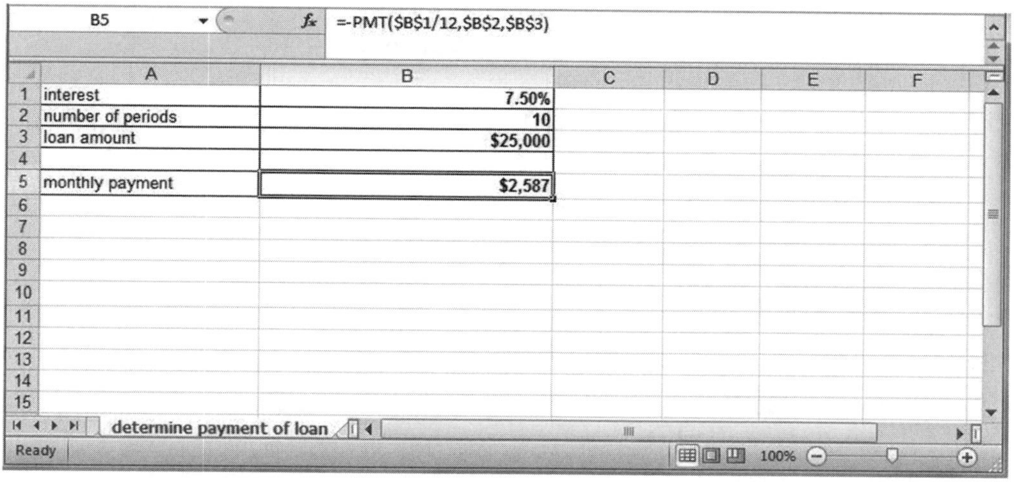

	B5	▼	*fx*	=-PMT($B$1/12,$B$2,$B$3)					
	A		B		C	D	E	F	
1	interest		7.50%						
2	number of periods		10						
3	loan amount		$25,000						
4									
5	monthly payment		$2,587						
6									
7									
8									
9									
10									
11									
12									
13									
14									
15									

determine payment of loan

Ready   100%

FIGURE 7–6

USE THE FV FUNCTION TO CALCULATE TOTAL SAVINGS ACCOUNT BALANCE

In this example you want to save money for five months. The interest rate is 3.5%. Every month you deposit $500 at the bank. How much money is in your bank account after five months? This question can be answered by using the FV function. It returns the future value of an investment based on periodic, constant payments, and a constant interest rate.

FV(*rate, nper, pmt, pv, type*)

rate: The interest rate per period.

nper: The total number of payment periods in an annuity.

pmt: The payment made each period, which is a constant value.

pv: The present value. This is the amount that a series of future payments is worth right now.

type: A number that indicates when payments are due. 0 indicates the end of the period, and 1 indicates the beginning of the period.

▶ **To Calculate the Total of an Account with Regular Deposits and a Constant Interest Rate:**

1. Enter the current interest rate in cell B1 and the number of periods in cell B2.
2. In cell B3 enter the monthly amount to be put in the savings account.
3. In cell B4 type the formula **=-FV(B1/12,B2,B3)**.
4. Press **<Enter>**.

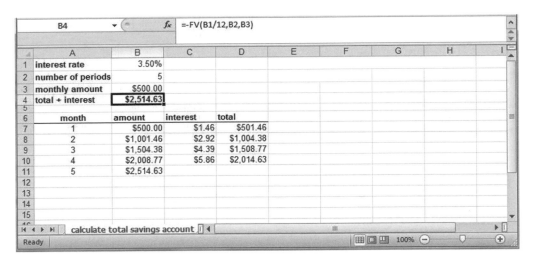

FIGURE 7–7

USE THE *RATE* FUNCTION TO CALCULATE INTEREST RATE

Let's say a bank advertises that if you deposit $500 each month for 12 years, you will have $100,000 at the end of the period. What is the interest rate the bank is paying? To answer this question, use the RATE function, which returns the interest rate per period of an annuity.

RATE(*nper, pmt, pv, fv, type, guess*)

> *nper*: The total number of payment periods in an annuity.

> *pmt*: The payment made each period, which is a constant value.

> *pv*: The present value. This is the amount that a series of future payments is worth right now.

> *fv*: The future value. This is the amount you want after the last payment is made.

> *type*: A number that indicates when payments are due. 0 or omitted indicates the end of the period, and 1 indicates the beginning of the period.

> *guess*: A guess for what the interest rate will be. If omitted, Excel uses 10%.

▶ **To Calculate the Interest Rate:**

1. In cell B1 enter the number of periods in years.
2. In cell B2 enter the monthly amount to deposit.
3. In cell B3 enter the final value the bank has advertised.
4. In cell B5 type the following formula: **=RATE(B1*12,-B2,0,B3,0)*12**.
5. Press **<Enter>**.

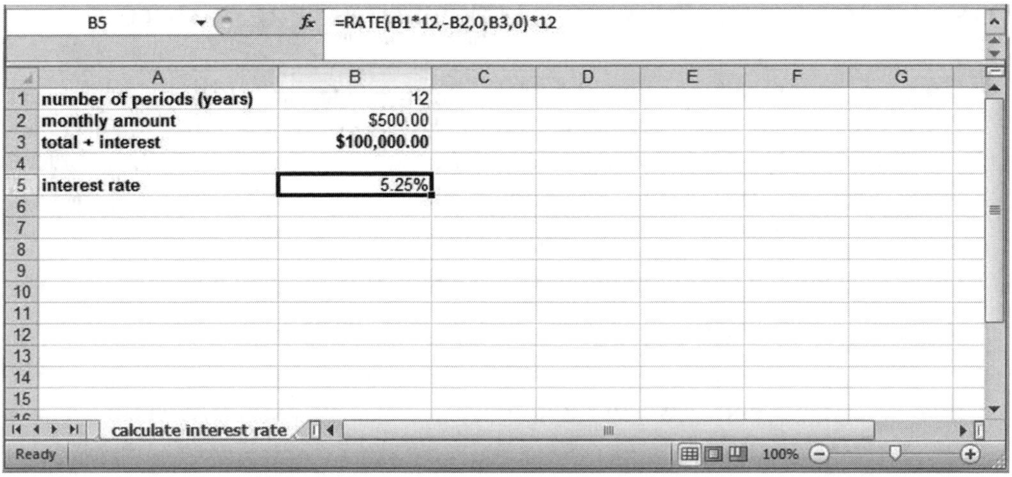

	A	B	C	D	E	F	G
	B5	fx =RATE(B1*12,-B2,0,B3,0)*12					
1	number of periods (years)	12					
2	monthly amount	$500.00					
3	total + interest	$100,000.00					
4							
5	interest rate	5.25%					
6							
7							
8							
9							
10							
11							
12							
13							
14							
15							

calculate interest rate

Ready   100%

FIGURE 7–8

8 DATABASE FUNCTIONS

USE THE DCOUNT **FUNCTION TO COUNT SPECIAL CELLS**

Using this tip, cells in a list can be counted by specific criteria. Use the DCOUNT function to count all cells that contain numbers in a column of a list or database that match specified conditions.

DCOUNT(*database, field, criteria*)

database: The range of cells in the list or database. The first row of the list contains column headings.

field: Indicates the column to use in the function. *field* can be provided as text with the column heading enclosed in double quotation marks or as a number representing the position of the column within the list: 1 for the first column, 2 for the second column, and so on.

criteria: The range of cells containing the specified conditions. Any range can be used for the *criteria* argument, as long as it includes at least one column heading and at least one cell below the column heading to specify a condition.

Use the following data for this tip.

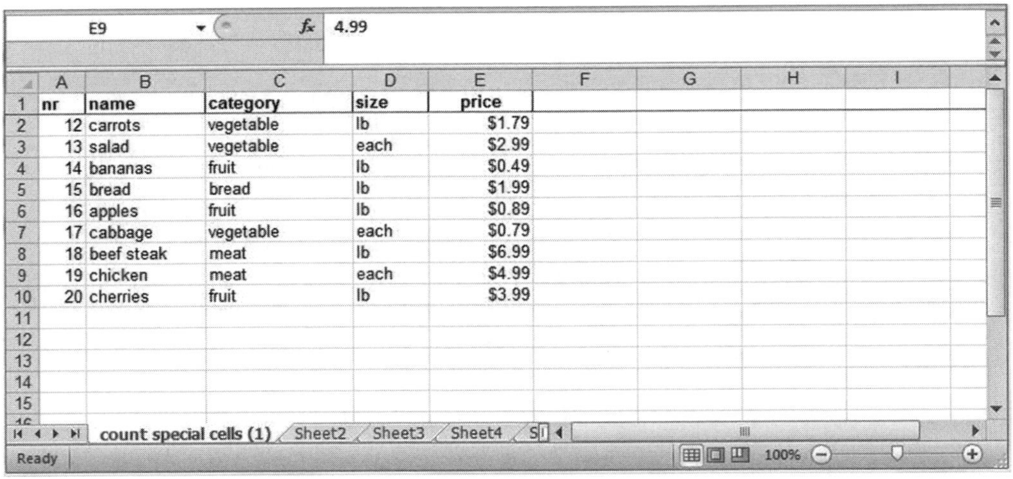

FIGURE 8–1

You can manually count all products in the vegetable category with a price less than or equal to $2.50, or you can let Excel do the counting as described next:

▶ **To Count Special Cells:**

1. Copy the range A1:E1 as shown in the preceding figure.
2. Select cell A14 and press **<Ctrl+V>**.
3. Select cell C15 and type **vegetable**.
4. In cell E15 type **<=2.50** to define the search criteria.
5. In cell C17 type the following formula:
   =DCOUNT(A1:E11,E14,A14:E15).
6. Press **<Enter>**.

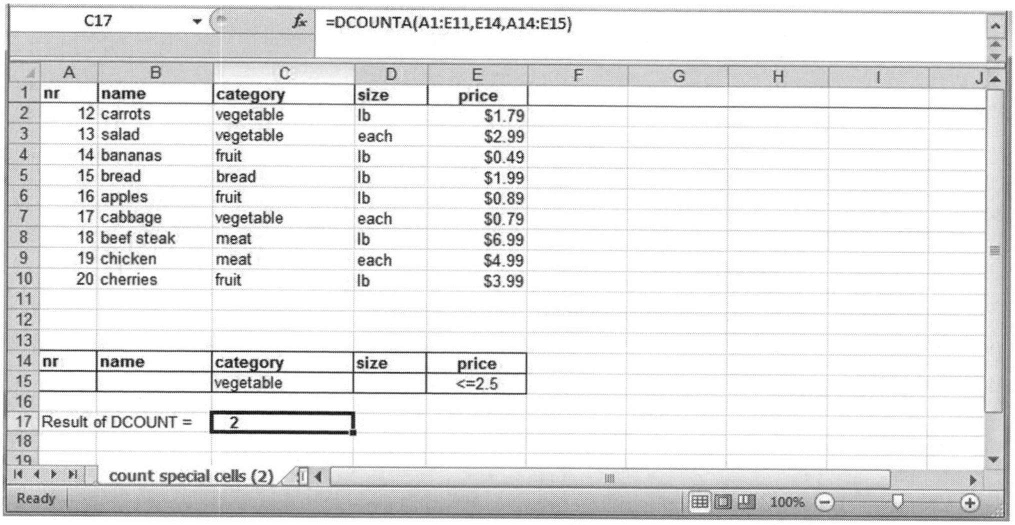

FIGURE 8–2

NOTE *The category in cell C15 can be changed. To count several categories, just type meat in cell C16 and change the formula in cell A17 to this:* **=DCOUNT(A1:E11,E14,A14:E16)**.

USE THE DCOUNT FUNCTION TO COUNT CELLS IN A RANGE BETWEEN X AND Y

Use the data in the previous example to continue working with the DCOUNT function. Here we want to count all products of the vegetable category that cost more than $1.75 but less than or equal to $2.50.

▶ **To Count Cells in a Specific Range Between x and y:**

1. Copy range A1:E1.
2. Select cell A14 and paste the copied cells with **<Ctrl+V>**.
3. Select cell C15 and type **vegetable**.
4. In cell E15 type **>1.75**.
5. In cell F15 type **<=2.50**.

6. In cell C17 type the following formula:
   =DCOUNT(A1:E11,E14,A14:F15).
7. Press **<Enter>**.

	C17	▾	fx	=DCOUNT(A1:E11,E14,A14:F15)					
	A	B	C	D	E	F	G	H	I	J
1	nr	name	category	size	price					
2	12	carrots	vegetable	lb	$1.79					
3	13	salad	vegetable	each	$2.99					
4	14	bananas	fruit	lb	$0.49					
5	15	bread	bread	lb	$1.99					
6	16	apples	fruit	lb	$0.89					
7	17	cabbage	vegetable	each	$0.79					
8	18	beef steak	meat	lb	$6.99					
9	19	chicken	meat	each	$4.99					
10	20	cherries	fruit	lb	$3.99					
11										
12										
13										
14	nr	name	category	size	price	price				
15			vegetable		>1.75	<=2.50				
16										
17	Result of CDCOUNT =		1							
18										
19										

count cells in range between

Ready   100%

FIGURE 8–3

USE THE DCOUNTA FUNCTION TO COUNT ALL CELLS BEGINNING WITH THE SAME CHARACTER

Continuing with the previous example, now we want to count all cells that begin with the letter "b," like bread, beef steak, and bananas. To do this, use the DCOUNTA function, which counts the non-blank cells in a column of a list or database that match the specified conditions.

The arguments are the same as used with the DCOUNT function.

▶ **To Count Cells Beginning with the Letter "b":**

1. Copy range A1:E1.
2. Select cell A14 and press **<Ctrl+V>**.
3. In cell B15 type **b***.
4. In cell C17 type the following formula:
   =DCOUNTA(A1:E11,E14,A14:E15).
5. Press **<Enter>**.

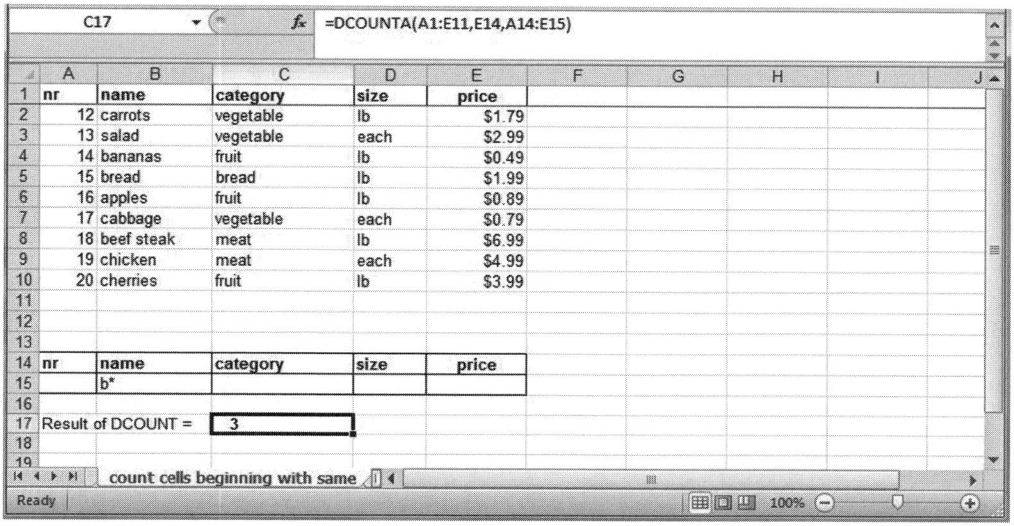

FIGURE 8–4

USE THE DGET FUNCTION TO SEARCH FOR A PRODUCT NUMBER

In this example, enter a product number to let Excel search a list for the corresponding product. To do so, use the DGET function, which selects a value from a column of a list or database that matches specified conditions.

DGET(*database*, *field*, *criteria*)

database: The range of cells in the list or database. The first row of the list contains column headings.

field: Indicates the column to use in the function. *field* can be provided as text with the column heading enclosed in double quotation marks or as a number representing the position of the column within the list.

criteria: The range of cells containing the specified conditions.

▶ **To Search for a Product Number:**

1. Copy the range A1:B1.
2. Select cell D1 and press **<Ctrl+V>**.
3. In cell D2 enter the number **13**.

4. In cell E2 type the following formula: **=DGET(A1:B10,E1,D1:D2)**.
5. Press **<Enter>**.

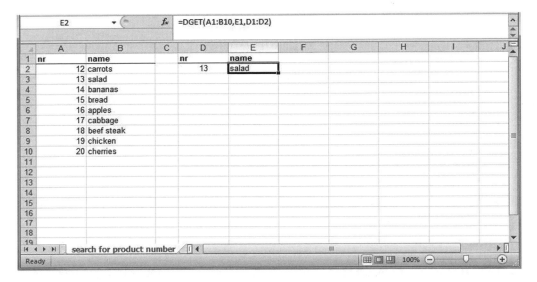

FIGURE 8–5

USE THE DMAX FUNCTION TO FIND THE MOST EXPENSIVE PRODUCT IN A CATEGORY

This tip shows how to determine the most expensive product in a list specified by a category using the DMAX function. This function returns the largest number in a column of a list or database that matches specified conditions.

DMAX(*database*, *field*, *criteria*)

database: The range of cells in the list or database. The first row of the list contains column headings.

field: Indicates the column to use in the function.

criteria: The range of cells containing the specified conditions.

▶ **To Find the Most Expensive Vegetable:**

1. Copy the range A1:E1.
2. Select cell A14 and press **<Ctrl+V>**.

3. In cell C15 enter **vegetable** as the search criteria.
4. In cell E17 type the following formula:
   =DMAX(A1:E11,E14,A14:E15).
5. Press **<Enter>**.

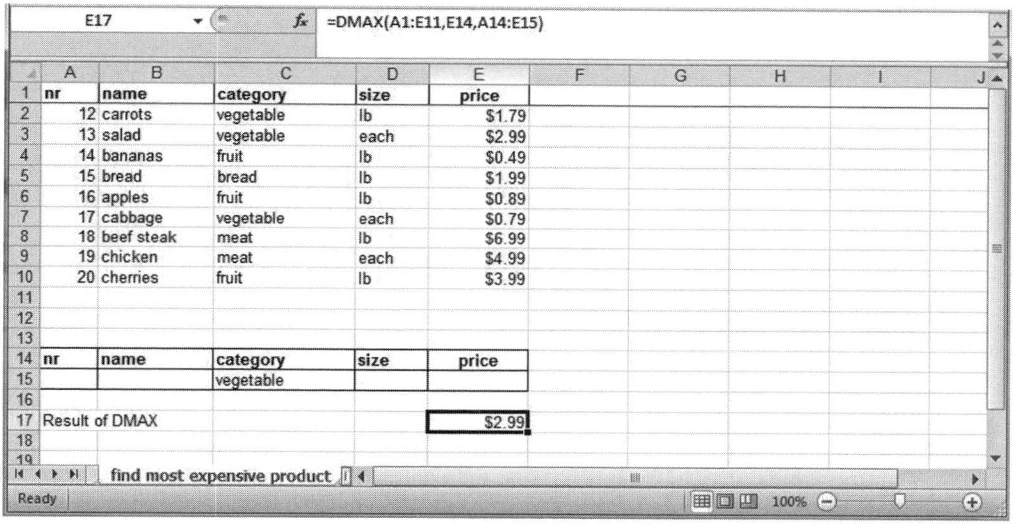

	E17	▼		*fx*	=DMAX(A1:E11,E14,A14:E15)					
	A	B	C	D	E	F	G	H	I	J
1	nr	name	category	size	price					
2	12	carrots	vegetable	lb	$1.79					
3	13	salad	vegetable	each	$2.99					
4	14	bananas	fruit	lb	$0.49					
5	15	bread	bread	lb	$1.99					
6	16	apples	fruit	lb	$0.89					
7	17	cabbage	vegetable	each	$0.79					
8	18	beef steak	meat	lb	$6.99					
9	19	chicken	meat	each	$4.99					
10	20	cherries	fruit	lb	$3.99					
11										
12										
13										
14	nr	name	category	size	price					
15			vegetable							
16										
17	Result of DMAX				$2.99					
18										
19										

find most expensive product

Ready   100%

FIGURE 8–6

USE THE DMIN FUNCTION TO FIND THE LEAST EXPENSIVE PRODUCT

For this example, use the same list of food products to determine the least expensive fruit. To do so, use the DMIN function to return the smallest number in a column of a list or database that matches specified conditions.
DMIN(*database, field, criteria*)

database: The range of cells in the list or database. The first row of the list contains column headings.

field: Indicates the column to use in the function.

criteria: The range of cells containing the specified conditions.

▶ **To Find the Least Expensive Fruit:**

1. Copy range A1:E1.
2. Select cell A14 and press **<Ctrl+V>**.
3. In cell C15 enter **fruit** as the search criteria.
4. In cell E17 type the following formula:
   =DMIN(A1:E11,E14,A14:E15).
5. Press **<Enter>**.

	E17	▼	*fx*	=DMIN(A1:E11,E14,A14:E15)						
	A	B	C	D	E	F	G	H	I	J
1	nr	name	category	size	price					
2	12	carrots	vegetable	lb	$1.79					
3	13	salad	vegetable	each	$2.99					
4	14	bananas	fruit	lb	$0.49					
5	15	bread	bread	lb	$1.99					
6	16	apples	fruit	lb	$0.89					
7	17	cabbage	vegetable	each	$0.79					
8	18	beef steak	meat	lb	$6.99					
9	19	chicken	meat	each	$4.99					
10	20	cherries	fruit	lb	$3.99					
11										
12										
13										
14	nr	name	category	size	price					
15			fruit							
16										
17	Result of DMIN				$0.49					
18										
19										

find least expensive product

Ready

FIGURE 8–7

USE THE DMIN FUNCTION TO FIND THE OLDEST PERSON ON A TEAM

The oldest member of a team can be found by using the DMIN function. (To find the youngest person, use DMAX.) Dates are stored in Excel as integer values beginning with 1 for January 1, 1900, and incrementing by 1 for each subsequent day. For example, the date 11/16/2004 has the value 38307. The syntax for DMIN is described in the previous tip.

▶ **To Find the Oldest Person on a Team:**

1. Copy to a worksheet cells A1:C10 as shown in Figure 8–8.
2. Copy the range A1:C1.

3. Select cell A12 and press **<Ctrl+V>**.
4. In cell B13 enter **1** to search just inside team 1.
5. In cell C15 type the following formula:
   =DMIN(A1:C10,B1,A12:C13).

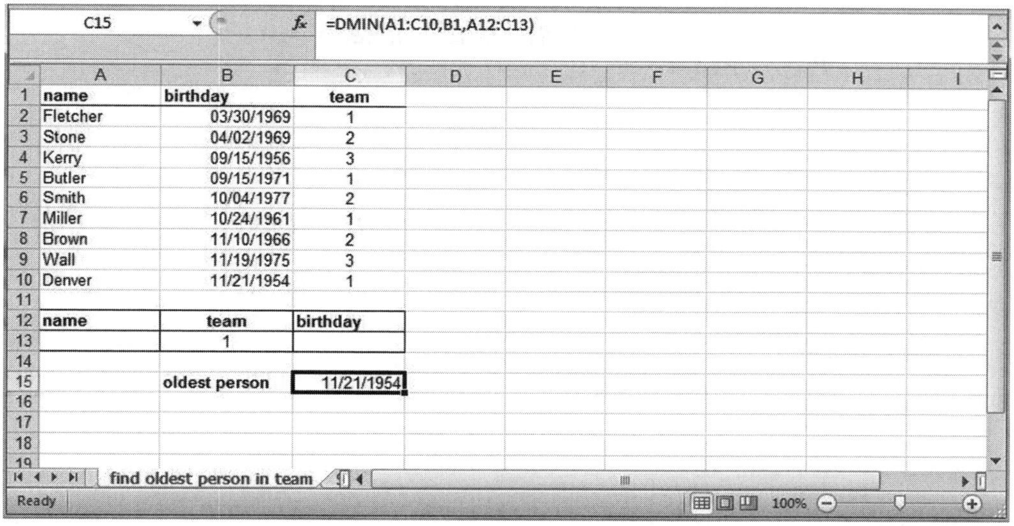

	C15	▾ (	*fx*	=DMIN(A1:C10,B1,A12:C13)					
	A	B	C	D	E	F	G	H	I
1	name	birthday	team						
2	Fletcher	03/30/1969	1						
3	Stone	04/02/1969	2						
4	Kerry	09/15/1956	3						
5	Butler	09/15/1971	1						
6	Smith	10/04/1977	2						
7	Miller	10/24/1961	1						
8	Brown	11/10/1966	2						
9	Wall	11/19/1975	3						
10	Denver	11/21/1954	1						
11									
12	name	team	birthday						
13		1							
14									
15		oldest person	11/21/1954						
16									
17									
18									
19									

find oldest person in team

Ready   100%

FIGURE 8–8

USE THE DSUM FUNCTION TO SUM SALES OF A PERIOD

Sometimes a list has to be summed up if it matches particular conditions. For example, you might want to sum sales in a certain category or for a specified time period. Use the DSUM function, which adds the numbers in a column of a list or database that matches specified conditions.

DSUM(*database, field, criteria*)

database: The range of cells in the list or database. The first row of the list contains column headings.

field: Indicates the column to use in the function.

criteria: The range of cells containing the specified conditions.

▶ **To Sum Sales for a Particular Time Period:**

1. Copy to a worksheet cells A2:C10 as shown in Figure 8–9.
2. Copy the range A1:C1.
3. Select cell A12 and press **<Ctrl+V>**.
4. In cell D12 type **date**.
5. Fill in the criteria range as shown in cells A13:D13.
6. In cell D15 type the following formula:
   =DSUM(A1:C10,C1,A12:D13).
7. Press **<Enter>**.

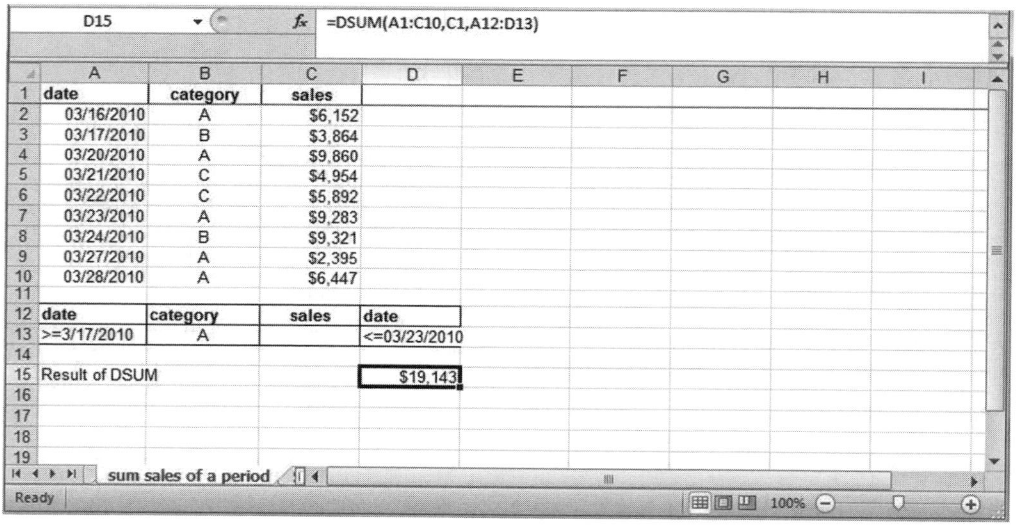

	A	B	C	D	E	F	G	H	I
	D15		fx	=DSUM(A1:C10,C1,A12:D13)					
1	date	category	sales						
2	03/16/2010	A	$6,152						
3	03/17/2010	B	$3,864						
4	03/20/2010	A	$9,860						
5	03/21/2010	C	$4,954						
6	03/22/2010	C	$5,892						
7	03/23/2010	A	$9,283						
8	03/24/2010	B	$9,321						
9	03/27/2010	A	$2,395						
10	03/28/2010	A	$6,447						
11									
12	date	category	sales	date					
13	>=3/17/2010	A		<=03/23/2010					
14									
15	Result of DSUM			$19,143					
16									
17									
18									
19									

sum sales of a period

Ready   100%

FIGURE 8–9

USE THE DSUM FUNCTION TO SUM ALL PRICES OF A CATEGORY THAT ARE ABOVE A PARTICULAR LEVEL

The list in the following figure shows the prices of a number of goods in different categories. To sum up all prices in one category that are above a particular price, use the DSUM function. Here we will sum up all prices of category A that are above $100.

▶ **To Sum all Prices of Category A above $100:**

1. Copy to a worksheet cells A1:C10 as shown in Figure 8–10.
2. Copy range A1:C1.
3. Select cell A12 and press **<Ctrl+V>**.
4. In cell B13 enter **A** to search inside category A.
5. In cell C13 type the argument **>100**.
6. In cell D15 type the following formula:
   =DSUM(A1:C10,C1,A12:C13).
7. Press **<Enter>**.

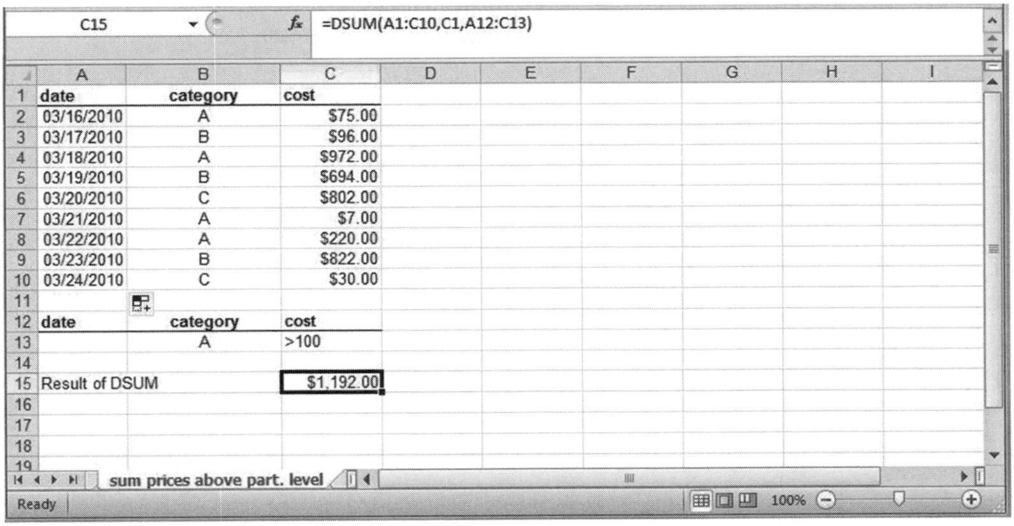

	C15			*fx*	=DSUM(A1:C10,C1,A12:C13)						
	A	B	C	D	E	F	G	H	I	
1	date	category	cost							
2	03/16/2010	A	$75.00							
3	03/17/2010	B	$96.00							
4	03/18/2010	A	$972.00							
5	03/19/2010	B	$694.00							
6	03/20/2010	C	$802.00							
7	03/21/2010	A	$7.00							
8	03/22/2010	A	$220.00							
9	03/23/2010	B	$822.00							
10	03/24/2010	C	$30.00							
11										
12	date	category	cost							
13		A	>100							
14										
15	Result of DSUM		$1,192.00							
16										
17										
18										
19										

sum prices above part. level

Ready   100%

FIGURE 8–10

USE THE DAVERAGE FUNCTION TO DETERMINE THE AVERAGE PRICE OF A CATEGORY

To determine the average price of a category, use the DAVERAGE function. This function averages the values in a column of a list or database that match specified conditions.

DAVERAGE(*database, field, criteria*)

database: The range of cells in the list or database. The first row of the list contains column headings.

field: Indicates the column to use in the function.

criteria: The range of cells containing the specified conditions.

▶ **To Determine the Average Price of a Category:**

1. Copy to a worksheet cells A1:C10 as shown in Figure 8–10.
2. Copy range A1:C1.
3. Select cell A12 and press **<Ctrl+V>**.
4. In cell B13 enter **A** to search inside category A.
5. In cell D15 type the following formula:
   =DAVERAGE(A1:C10,C1,A12:C13).
6. Press **<Enter>**.

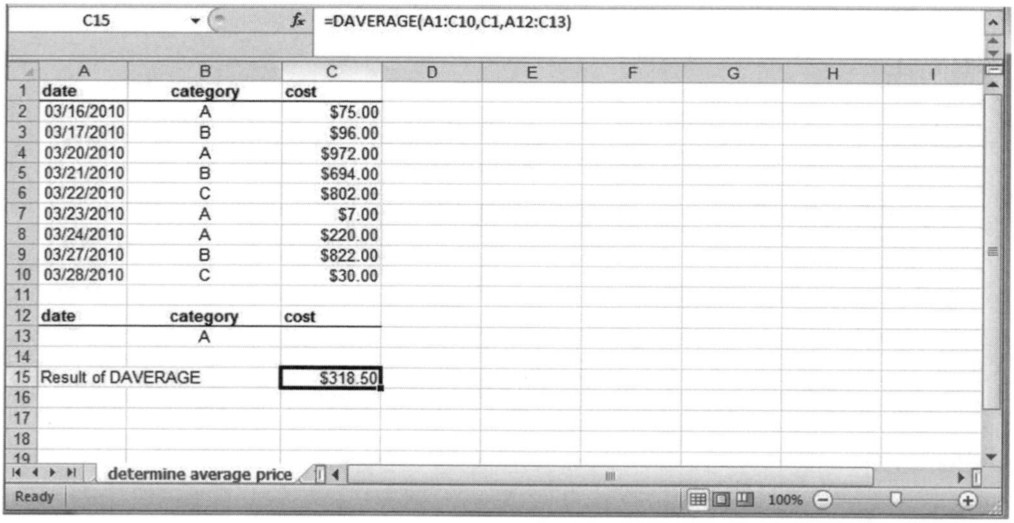

	C15			fx	=DAVERAGE(A1:C10,C1,A12:C13)					
	A	B	C	D	E	F	G	H	I
1	date	category	cost						
2	03/16/2010	A	$75.00						
3	03/17/2010	B	$96.00						
4	03/20/2010	A	$972.00						
5	03/21/2010	B	$694.00						
6	03/22/2010	C	$802.00						
7	03/23/2010	A	$7.00						
8	03/24/2010	A	$220.00						
9	03/27/2010	B	$822.00						
10	03/28/2010	C	$30.00						
11									
12	date	category	cost						
13		A							
14									
15	Result of DAVERAGE		$318.50						
16									
17									
18									
19									

determine average price

Ready   100%

FIGURE 8–11

Chapter 9

9

LOOKUP AND REFERENCE FUNCTIONS

USE THE ADDRESS, MATCH, AND MAX FUNCTIONS TO FIND THE LARGEST NUMBER

We learned in previous tips how to look up a single value in a list. Now we want to determine the position of the largest value in a list by combining three Excel functions. First, we use the MAX function to get the largest value, then we use the MATCH function to find its relative position, and finally, we use the ADDRESS function to determine the exact cell address.

> **NOTE** *The MAX function was described in Chapter 5.*
> MATCH(*lookup_value, lookup_array, match_type*)

lookup_value: The value that corresponds to the entry to be found in a table.

lookup_array: A contiguous range of cells that contains possible lookup values.

match_type: Specifies how Excel matches *lookup_value* with values in *lookup_array*. 1 specifies that MATCH is to find the largest value that is less than or equal to *lookup_value*; 0 specifies that MATCH is to find the first value equal to *lookup_value*; and −1 specifies that MATCH is to find the smallest value that is greater than or equal to *lookup_value*.

The ADDRESS function returns the exact cell address as text.
ADDRESS(*row_num*, *column_num*, *abs_num*, *sheet_text*)

row_num: The row number to be used in the cell reference.

column_num: The column number to be used in the cell reference.

abs_num: The type of reference to return. 1 or omitted indicates absolute, 2 indicates absolute row and relative column, 3 indicates relative row and absolute column, and 4 indicates relative.

sheet_text: The name of the worksheet to be used as the external reference. If omitted, no sheet name is used.

For example:

=ADDRESS(5,2) is an absolute reference to cell $B$5.

=ADDRESS(4,4,2) is an absolute row reference and relative column reference to cell D$4.

=ADDRESS(1,1,3) is a relative row reference and an absolute column reference to cell $A1.

Take a look at the following example.

▶ **To Search for the Cell Reference of the Greatest Number:**

1. In cells A2:A10 enter some numbers.
2. Select cell C2 and type the following formula:
   =ADDRESS(MATCH(MAX(A1:A10),A1:A10),1,4).
3. Press **<Enter>**.

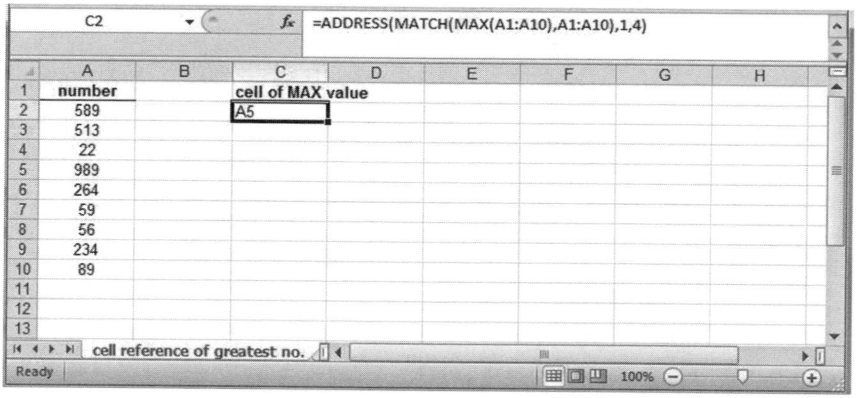

FIGURE 9–1

USE THE ADDRESS, MATCH, AND MIN FUNCTIONS TO FIND THE SMALLEST NUMBER

Similar to the previous tip, we can find the cell address for the smallest value in a list. We will again use the ADDRESS and MATCH functions but this time in combination with MIN.

The MIN function finds the smallest value in a list. MATCH returns the relative position of 2, which will be transferred to the ADDRESS function to determine the cell address as shown in the following figure.

▶ **To Search for the Smallest Number:**

1. In cells A2:A10 list some numbers.
2. Select cell C2 and type the following formula:
   =ADDRESS(MATCH(MIN(A1:A10),A1:A10,0),1).
3. Press **<Enter>**.

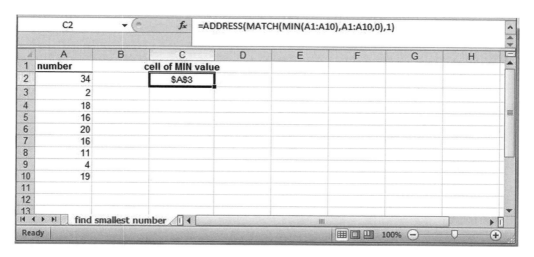

FIGURE 9–2

USE THE ADDRESS, MATCH, AND TODAY FUNCTIONS TO SUM SALES UP TO TODAY'S DATE

In a worksheet daily sales are recorded. To sum up all listed sales until today's date, use the functions learned from previous tips including the TODAY function, which returns the actual date. MATCH returns the relative position of TODAY, which will be transferred to the ADDRESS function to determine the cell address as seen in cell E2 of the following figure. With the SUM and INDIRECT functions, you can sum up all sales up to today and get the desired result.

▶ To Sum Sales Up to Today:

1. In cells A2:A10 list dates in ascending order.
2. In cells B2:B10 enter the daily sales amounts.
3. Select cell E1 and type the formula **=TODAY()** to get the actual date.
4. In cell E2 type the following formula: **=ADDRESS(MATCH(TODAY(),$A$1:$A$10,1),2)**.
5. Determine the sum in cell E3 with the following formula: **=SUM(B2:INDIRECT(E2))**.

NOTE *INDIRECT(ref_text) returns the reference specified by a text string.*

6. Press **<Enter>**.

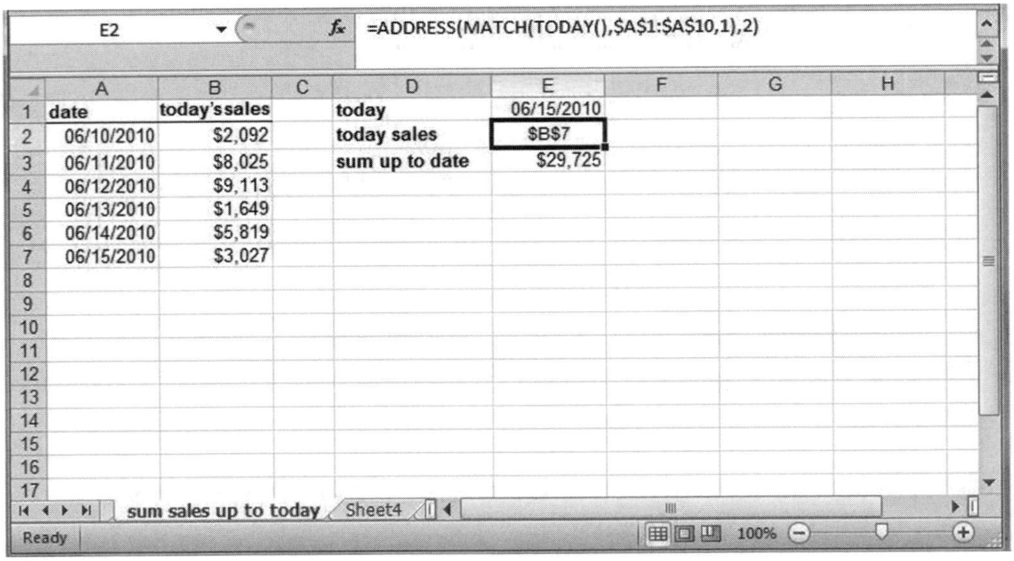
E2
=ADDRESS(MATCH(TODAY(),$A$1:$A$10,1),2)
A B C D E F G H
1 date today's sales today 06/15/2010
2 06/10/2010 $2,092 today sales $B$7
3 06/11/2010 $8,025 sum up to date $29,725
4 06/12/2010 $9,113
5 06/13/2010 $1,649
6 06/14/2010 $5,819
7 06/15/2010 $3,027
8 9 10 11 12 13 14 15 16 17
sum sales up to today
Sheet4
Ready
100%

FIGURE 9–3

USE THE VLOOKUP FUNCTION TO LOOK UP AND EXTRACT DATA FROM A DATABASE

This tip explains how to search for a certain product in a list. First, take a look at the data in the following figure:

	A	B	C	D	E	F	G	H
			fx	T3				
1	number	T3						
2	name							
3	price							
4	amount							
5								
6	number	name	price	amount				
7	T1	product 1	$3.00	7				
8	T2	product 2	$42.00	1				
9	T3	product 3	$75.00	5				
10	T4	product 4	$87.00	9				
11	T5	product 5	$44.00	14				
12	T6	product 6	$35.00	5				
13	T7	product 7	$81.00	1				
14	T8	product 8	$42.00	34				
15	T9	product 9	$34.00	2				
16	T10	product 10	$74.00	5				
17								

extract data from database (1)

Ready   100%

FIGURE 9–4

Typing a valid product number in cell B1 fills cells B2 to B4 with the corresponding data from the list. To do this, use the VLOOKUP function, which searches for a value in the left-hand column of a table and returns a value in the same row from a column specified in the table.

VLOOKUP(*lookup_value*, *table_array*, *col_index_num*, *range_lookup*)

lookup_value: The value to be found in the left-hand column of the array.

table_array: The table in which data is looked up.

col_index_num: The column number in *table_array* from which the matching value must be returned. 1 returns the value in the first column in *table_array*, 2 returns the value in the second column in *table_array*, and so on.

range_lookup: A logical value that indicates whether VLOOKUP is to find an exact match or an approximate match. If TRUE or omitted, an approximate match is returned.

▶ **To Look Up and Extract Data from a List:**

1. In cell B2 type the following formula:
   =VLOOKUP($B$1,$A$7:$D$16,2,FALSE).
2. In cell B3 type the following formula:
   =VLOOKUP($B$1,$A$7:$D$16,3,FALSE).
3. In cell B4 type the following formula:
   =VLOOKUP($B$1,$A$7:$D$16,4,FALSE).
4. Press **<Enter>**.

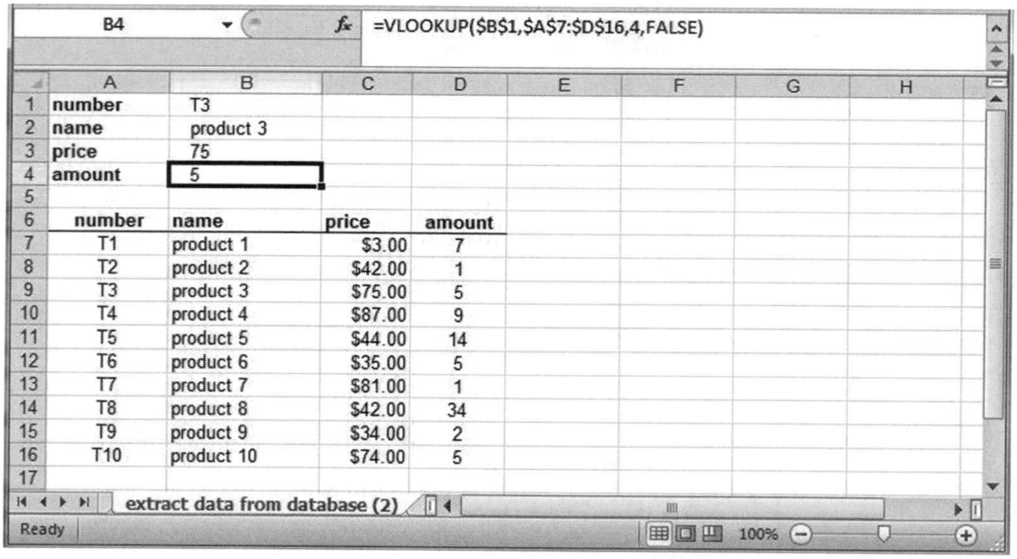

	B4			f_x	=VLOOKUP($B$1,$A$7:$D$16,4,FALSE)				
	A	B	C	D	E	F	G	H
1	number	T3						
2	name	product 3						
3	price	75						
4	amount	5						
5								
6	number	name	price	amount				
7	T1	product 1	$3.00	7				
8	T2	product 2	$42.00	1				
9	T3	product 3	$75.00	5				
10	T4	product 4	$87.00	9				
11	T5	product 5	$44.00	14				
12	T6	product 6	$35.00	5				
13	T7	product 7	$81.00	1				
14	T8	product 8	$42.00	34				
15	T9	product 9	$34.00	2				
16	T10	product 10	$74.00	5				
17								

extract data from database (2)

Ready   100%

FIGURE 9–5

USE THE VLOOKUP FUNCTION TO COMPARE OFFERS FROM DIFFERENT SUPPLIERS

This example contains a table with offers from different suppliers for a product listed vertically. To search for the best offer, use the built-in MIN function in combination with VLOOKUP to display the supplier with the lowest price.

▶ To Find the Supplier with the Lowest Price:

1. In cells A2:A10 enter the offers.
2. In cells B2:B10 enter the name of each supplier.
3. Select cell D2 and type the following formula:
   =VLOOKUP(MIN(A2:A10),A2:B10,2,FALSE).
4. Press **<Enter>**.

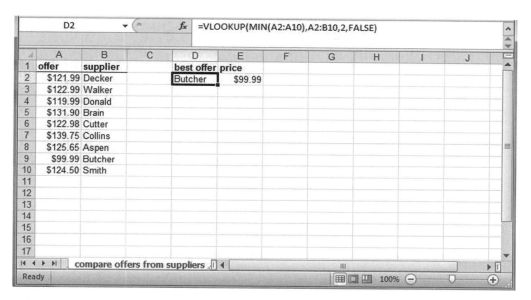

	A	B	C	D	E	F	G	H	I	J
1	offer	supplier		best offer	price					
2	$121.99	Decker		Butcher	$99.99					
3	$122.99	Walker								
4	$119.99	Donald								
5	$131.90	Brain								
6	$122.98	Cutter								
7	$139.75	Collins								
8	$125.65	Aspen								
9	$99.99	Butcher								
10	$124.50	Smith								

D2 | =VLOOKUP(MIN(A2:A10),A2:B10,2,FALSE)

compare offers from suppliers

FIGURE 9–6

NOTE *To determine the lowest offer, use the function MIN(A2:A10), the result of which is shown in cell E2.*

USE THE HLOOKUP FUNCTION TO DETERMINE SALES AND COSTS OF A TEAM

The costs and sales of a team have to be looked up in a table. Each team is listed by column with its costs and sales. To get the desired information, use the HLOOKUP function, which searches for a value in the top row of a table or an array of values, and then returns a value in the same column from a row that is specified in the table or array.

HLOOKUP(*lookup_value, table_array, row_index_num, range_lookup*)

lookup_value: The value to be found in the top row of the table.

table_array: A table in which data is looked up.

row_index_num: The row number in *table_array* from which the matching value will be returned.

range_lookup: A logical value that indicates whether HLOOKUP is to find an exact match or an approximate match.

▶ **To Determine Sales and Cost for a Team:**

1. In a worksheet, copy the information in cells A1:E3, as shown in Figure 9–7.
2. In cell A7 enter a valid team name.
3. In cell B7 type the following formula:
   =HLOOKUP($A$7,$B$1:$E$3,2,FALSE).
4. Press **<Enter>**.
5. Select cell C7 and type the following formula:
   =HLOOKUP($A$7,$B$1:$E$3,3,FALSE).
6. Press **<Enter>**.

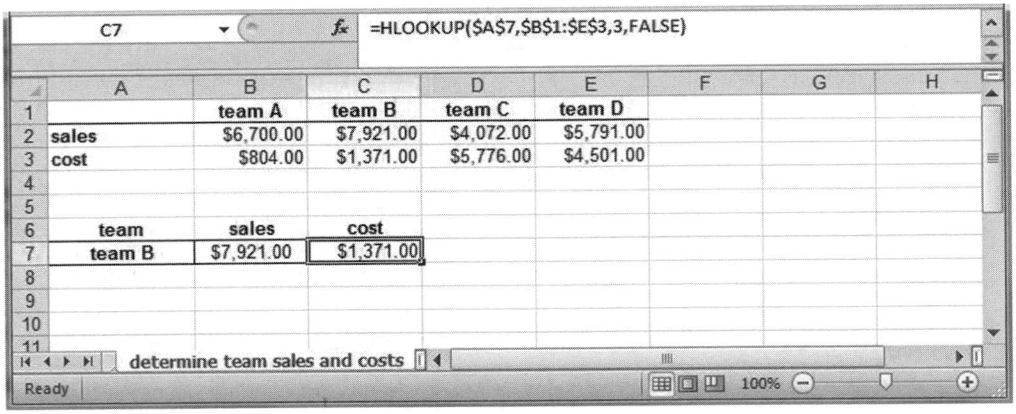

	C7			ƒ*x* =HLOOKUP($A$7,$B$1:$E$3,3,FALSE)					
	A	B	C	D	E	F	G	H	
1		team A	team B	team C	team D				
2	sales	$6,700.00	$7,921.00	$4,072.00	$5,791.00				
3	cost	$804.00	$1,371.00	$5,776.00	$4,501.00				
4									
5									
6	team	sales	cost						
7	team B	$7,921.00	$1,371.00						
8									
9									
10									
11		determine team sales and costs							

FIGURE 9–7

USE THE HLOOKUP FUNCTION TO DETERMINE SALES FOR A PARTICULAR DAY

In this example, all sales for a certain day have to be listed in the first column of a table. In addition, all sales have to be summed up in cell A7 to show the total amount of sales for this day.

▶ **To Determine the Total Amount of Sales for One Day:**

1. In a worksheet, copy the information in cells C1:G5, as shown in Figure 9–8.
2. Enter in cell A1 the desired day for which the sales of each team have to be listed.
3. Select cells A2:A5 and type the following formula:
   =HLOOKUP($A$1,$D$1:$G$5,(ROW())).
4. Press **<Ctrl+Enter>**.
5. Select cell A7 and type the following formula:
   ="SUM = " & TEXT(SUM(A2:A5),"$#,000.00").
6. Press **<Enter>**.

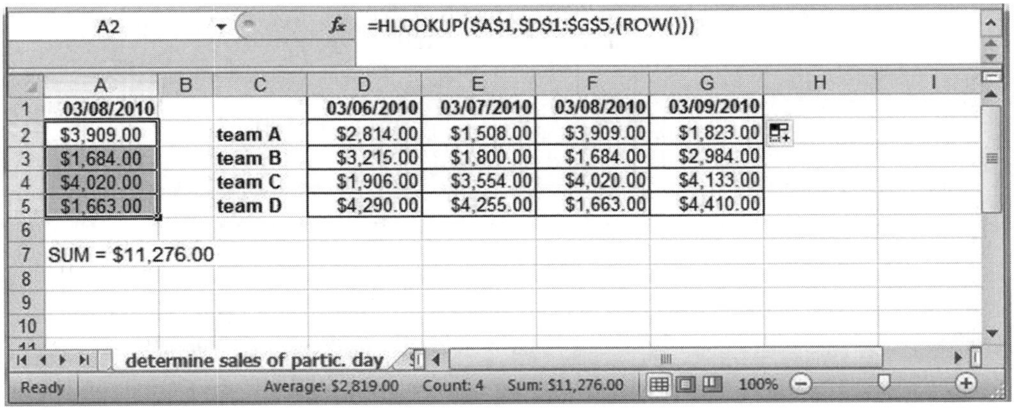

	A	B	C	D	E	F	G	H	I
A2			fx	=HLOOKUP($A$1,$D$1:$G$5,(ROW()))					
1	03/08/2010			03/06/2010	03/07/2010	03/08/2010	03/09/2010		
2	$3,909.00		team A	$2,814.00	$1,508.00	$3,909.00	$1,823.00		
3	$1,684.00		team B	$3,215.00	$1,800.00	$1,684.00	$2,984.00		
4	$4,020.00		team C	$1,906.00	$3,554.00	$4,020.00	$4,133.00		
5	$1,663.00		team D	$4,290.00	$4,255.00	$1,663.00	$4,410.00		
6									
7	SUM = $11,276.00								
8									
9									
10									

determine sales of partic. day

Ready   Average: $2,819.00   Count: 4   Sum: $11,276.00   100%

FIGURE 9–8

NOTE *The ROW function returns the active row number.*

USE THE HLOOKUP FUNCTION TO GENERATE A LIST FOR A SPECIFIC MONTH

The dates on which errors occur in a system are recorded each month in an Excel table as shown in the following figure. The first column lists the dates of all errors that occurred in a certain month. Enter in cell A1 the month and use a combination of functions based on HLOOKUP to return all recorded dates.

▶ **To Generate a List for a Specific Month:**

1. In a worksheet, copy cells C2:F5, as shown in Figure 9–9.
2. In cell A1 type the month **11**.
3. Select cells A3:A8 and type the following formula:
   =IF(HLOOKUP($A$1,$C$2:$F$11,ROW()-1,FALSE)=0,"",
   HLOOKUP($A$1,$C$2:$F$11,ROW()-1,FALSE)).
4. Press **<Ctrl+Enter>**.

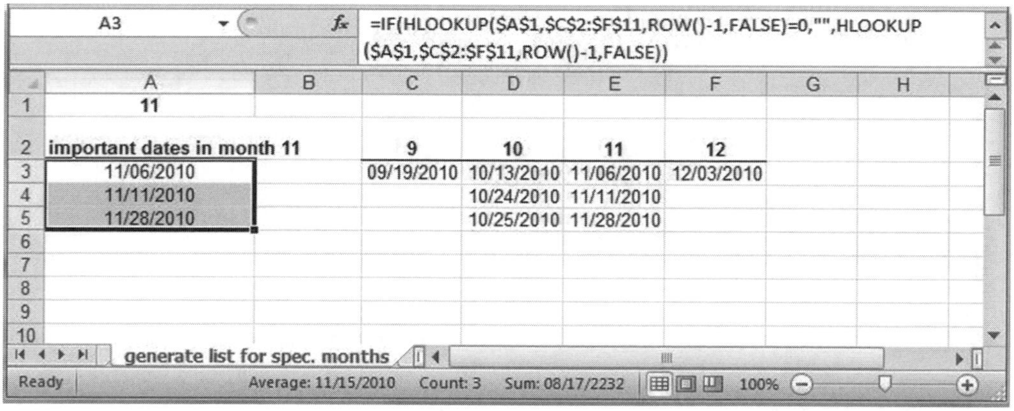

A3			f_x	=IF(HLOOKUP($A$1,$C$2:$F$11,ROW()-1,FALSE)=0,"",HLOOKUP ($A$1,$C$2:$F$11,ROW()-1,FALSE))				
	A	B	C	D	E	F	G	H
1	11							
2	important dates in month 11		9	10	11	12		
3	11/06/2010		09/19/2010	10/13/2010	11/06/2010	12/03/2010		
4	11/11/2010			10/24/2010	11/11/2010			
5	11/28/2010			10/25/2010	11/28/2010			
6								
7								
8								
9								
10								

generate list for spec. months

Ready   Average: 11/15/2010   Count: 3   Sum: 08/17/2232   100%

FIGURE 9–9

NOTE *You may need to format cells A3:A8 with a date format.*

USE THE LOOKUP FUNCTION TO GET THE DIRECTORY OF A STORE

A store sells different products in a big warehouse. Each floor contains different categories of products. For example, the customer can find software on the first floor and hardware on the second floor. Each category is assigned a combination of two letters, such as software = SO, hardware = HA, food = FO, indoor = IN, and outdoor = OU. The task now is to find which products are sold on which floor by entering the category abbreviation in cell A9. Do this by using the array form of the LOOKUP function to return a value from a one-row or one-column range or from an array.

LOOKUP(*lookup_value*, *array*)

> *lookup_value*: A value that will be looked up in an array.

> *array*: A range of cells containing text, numbers, or logical values that are to be compared with *lookup_value*.

NOTE   *The array form of the LOOKUP function is provided for compatibility with other spreadsheet programs. Additionally, VLOOKUP can be used in this situation, provided that the values in the first column are sorted in ascending order.*

▶ **To Display the Correct Floor:**

1. In a worksheet, copy cells A1:C6, as shown in Figure 9–10.
2. In cell A9 enter the abbreviation of the product category.
3. Select cell B9 and type the following formula:
   =LOOKUP($A$9,$A$1:$B$8).
4. Press **<Enter>**.
5. Select cell C9 and type the following formula:
   =LOOKUP($A$9,$A$1:$C$8).
6. Press **<Enter>**.

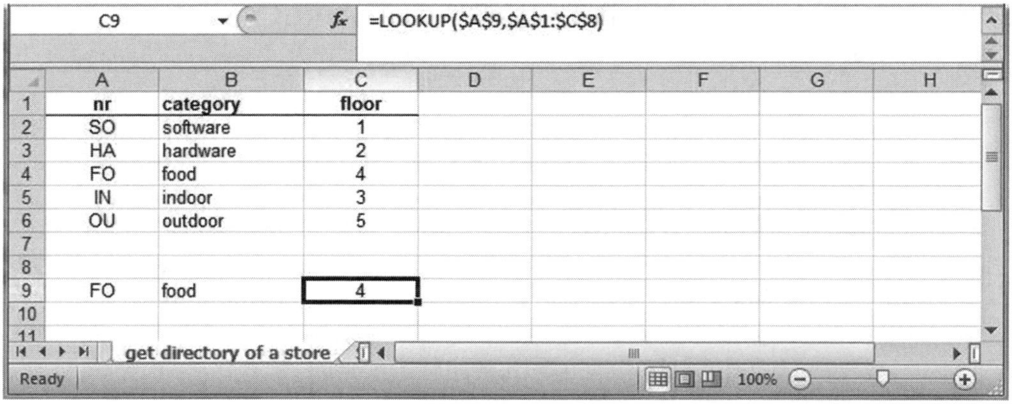

	A	B	C	D	E	F	G	H

C9 =LOOKUP($A$9,$A$1:$C$8)

	A	B	C	D	E	F	G	H
1	nr	category	floor					
2	SO	software	1					
3	HA	hardware	2					
4	FO	food	4					
5	IN	indoor	3					
6	OU	outdoor	5					
7								
8								
9	FO	food	4					
10								
11								

get directory of a store

Ready   100%

FIGURE 9–10

USE THE LOOKUP FUNCTION TO GET THE INDICATOR FOR THE CURRENT TEMPERATURE

The following list contains indicators like icy, cold, warm, or hot for different temperature ranges. Enter the current temperature in one cell and let Excel determine the corresponding indicator with the vector form of the LOOKUP function.

LOOKUP(*lookup_value, lookup_vector, result_vector*)

lookup_value: A value that will be searched for in the first vector.

lookup_vector: A range containing only one row or one column.

result_vector: A range containing only one row or one column. *result_vector* and *lookup_vector* must be the same size.

If LOOKUP can't find the *lookup_value*, it matches the largest value in *lookup_vector* that is less than or equal to, which is quite useful for our task because we have just four indicators.

They are defined as follows:

- From –50°F to 31°F = icy
- From 32°F to 49°F = cold
- From 50°F to 76°F = warm
- 77°F and above = hot

▶ **To Add an Indicator for the Temperature:**

1. In a worksheet, copy the information in cells A1:B5, as shown in Figure 9–11.
2. In cell D2 enter the actual temperature.
3. Select cell E2 and type the following formula: =**LOOKUP($D$2,B2:B5,A2:A5)**.
4. Press **<Enter>**.

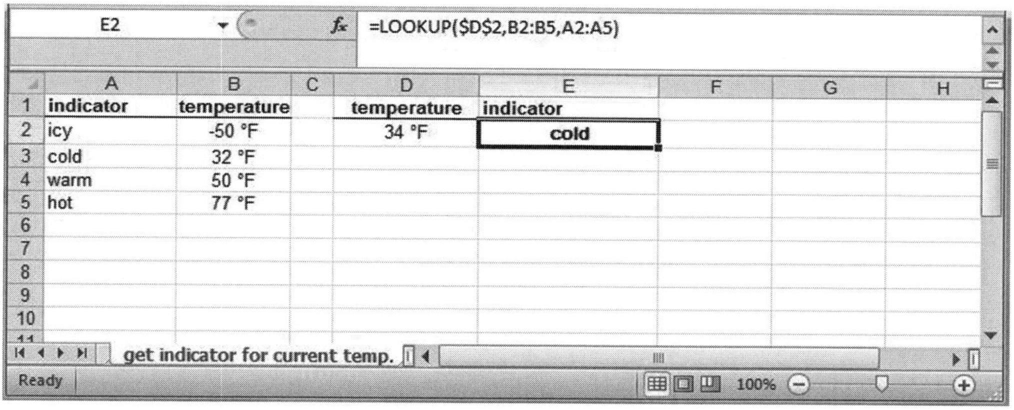

	A	B	C	D	E	F	G	H
1	indicator	temperature		temperature	indicator			
2	icy	-50 °F		34 °F	cold			
3	cold	32 °F						
4	warm	50 °F						
5	hot	77 °F						

E2   fx   =LOOKUP($D$2,B2:B5,A2:A5)

get indicator for current temp.

Ready   100%

FIGURE 9–11

USE THE INDEX FUNCTION TO SEARCH FOR DATA IN A SORTED LIST

In addition to VLOOKUP, the INDEX function can be used to search for data in a sorted list. Copy the table below to a new worksheet and enter in cell A2 the team number for which you want to search. Let Excel search for the team name and corresponding costs with the INDEX or VLOOKUP functions as described in the next steps.

▶ **To Search for Data in a List:**

1. In cell A2 enter a valid number from 1 to 7.
2. Select cell B2 and type the following formula: =**INDEX($A$6:$C$12,MATCH($A$2,$A$6:$A$12,0),2)**.

3. In cell B3 type the following formula:
    =VLOOKUP($A$2,$A$5:$C$12,2,FALSE).
4. Select cell C2 and type the following formula:
    =INDEX($A$6:$C$12,MATCH($A$3,$A$6:$A$12,0),3).
5. In cell C3 type the following formula:
    =VLOOKUP($A$3,$A$5:$C$12,3,FALSE).
6. Press **<Enter>**.

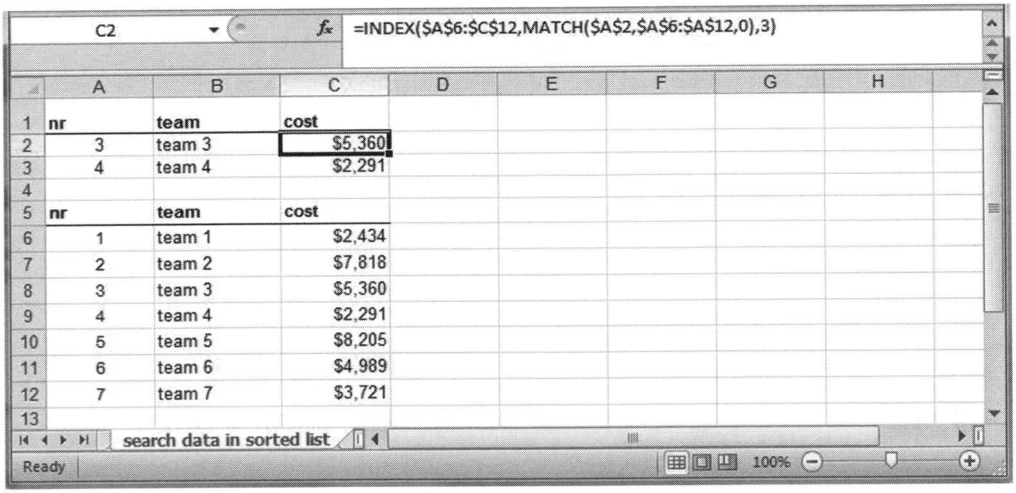

C2		fx	=INDEX($A$6:$C$12,MATCH($A$2,$A$6:$A$12,0),3)					
	A	B	C	D	E	F	G	H
1	nr	team	cost					
2	3	team 3	$5,360					
3	4	team 4	$2,291					
4								
5	nr	team	cost					
6	1	team 1	$2,434					
7	2	team 2	$7,818					
8	3	team 3	$5,360					
9	4	team 4	$2,291					
10	5	team 5	$8,205					
11	6	team 6	$4,989					
12	7	team 7	$3,721					
13								

search data in sorted list

Ready   100%

FIGURE 9–12

USE THE INDIRECT **FUNCTION TO PLAY "BATTLESHIP"**

Why not take a break and play "Battleship"? It's easy to create, and when you're finished reading this tip, you can enjoy playing.

Define in a new worksheet the range C1:E10 as the battlefield and border it as desired. Place some Xs to define the location of the ships and enter in cells B1 and B2 the coordinates of the cell to be fired. Use the INDIRECT function to get the functionality that returns the reference, specified by a text string (e.g., "HIT").

INDIRECT(*ref_text, a1*)

ref_text: A reference to a cell containing an A1-style reference, an R1C1-style reference, a name defined as a reference, or a reference to a cell as a text string.

a1: A logical value specifying the type of reference that is contained in the cell *ref_text*. If *a1* is TRUE or omitted, *ref_text* will be an A1-style reference. If *a1* is FALSE, *ref_text* will be an R1C1-style reference.

▶ **To Set Up and Play "Battleship":**

1. In cell B1 enter a valid row number from 1 to 10.
2. In cell B2 enter a valid column from C to E.
3. Select cell B3 and type the following formula:
   =IF(INDIRECT(B2&B1)="X","Hit","").
4. Press **<Enter>**.

	A	B	C	D	E	F	G	H
	B3			*fx*	=IF(INDIRECT(B2&B1)="X","Hit","")			
1	row	7						
2	column	D	X					
3	value	Hit	X					
4								
5				X				
6				X				
7				X				
8								
9					X			
10					X			
11								

FIGURE 9–13

USE THE INDIRECT FUNCTION TO COPY CELL VALUES FROM DIFFERENT WORKSHEETS

The INDIRECT function can also be used to address cells in other worksheets and copy their values to the current sheet. Column A lists the names of worksheets, and column B lists cell references. With the INDIRECT function, the value of each cell reference can be copied to the current worksheet.

▶ **To Copy Cell Values of Different Worksheets:**

1. In a worksheet, copy cells A1:B10, as shown in Figure 9–14.
2. Select cells C2:C10 and type the following formula:
   =INDIRECT(A2&"!"&B2).
3. Press **<Ctrl+Enter>**.

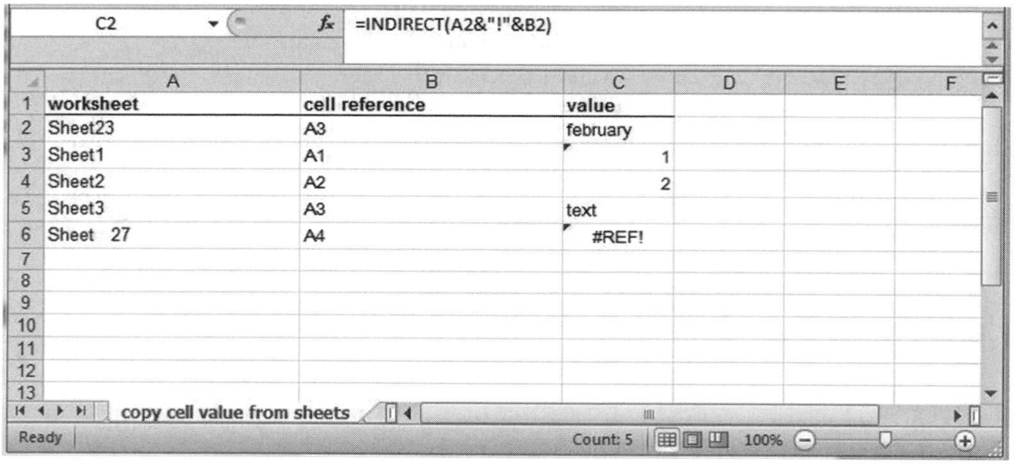

	A	B	C	D	E	F
1	worksheet	cell reference	value			
2	Sheet23	A3	february			
3	Sheet1	A1	1			
4	Sheet2	A2	2			
5	Sheet3	A3	text			
6	Sheet 27	A4	#REF!			
7						
8						
9						
10						
11						
12						
13						

C2   *fx* =INDIRECT(A2&"!"&B2)

copy cell value from sheets

Ready   Count: 5   100%

FIGURE 9–14

NOTE   *If you rename the worksheets make sure not to use blanks (see row 6 in the previous example).*

USE THE INDEX FUNCTION TO DETERMINE THE LAST NUMBER IN A COLUMN

Sometimes it is very useful to let Excel automatically determine the last value in a list. Use the INDEX function in combination with COUNTA and COUNTBLANK to determine the last number in a column. The INDEX function returns the value of an element in a table or an array that is selected by the row and column number indexes.

INDEX(*array, row_num, column_num*)

array: A range of cells or an array constant.

row_num: Indicates the row in an array from which a value will be returned. If omitted, *column_num* is required.

column_num: Indicates the column in an array from which a value will be returned. If omitted, *row_num* is required.

▶ **To Determine the Last Number in a Column:**

1. In cells A2:A11 list any kind of numbers.
2. Select cell C1 and type the following formula:
   =INDEX(A:A,COUNTA(A:A)+COUNTBLANK(A1:A11),1).
3. Press **<Enter>**.

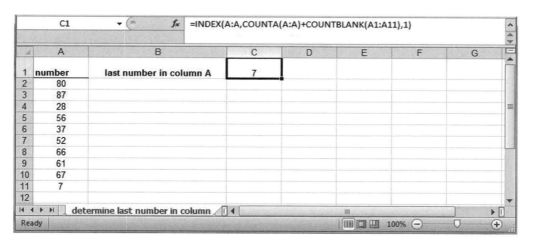

FIGURE 9–15

USE THE INDEX AND COUNTA FUNCTIONS TO DETERMINE THE LAST NUMBER IN A ROW

In the previous tip, we learned how to determine the last value for each column. Use the INDEX function in combination with COUNTA to determine the last number in a row. The INDEX function will return the value of an element in a table or an array, selected by the row and column number indexes.

▶ **To Determine the Last Number in a Row:**

1. In cells B2:G10 enter some numbers, leaving some cells empty.
2. Select cells A2:A10 and type the following formula:
   =INDEX(B2:G2,1,COUNTA(B2:G2)).
3. Press **<Ctrl+Enter>**.

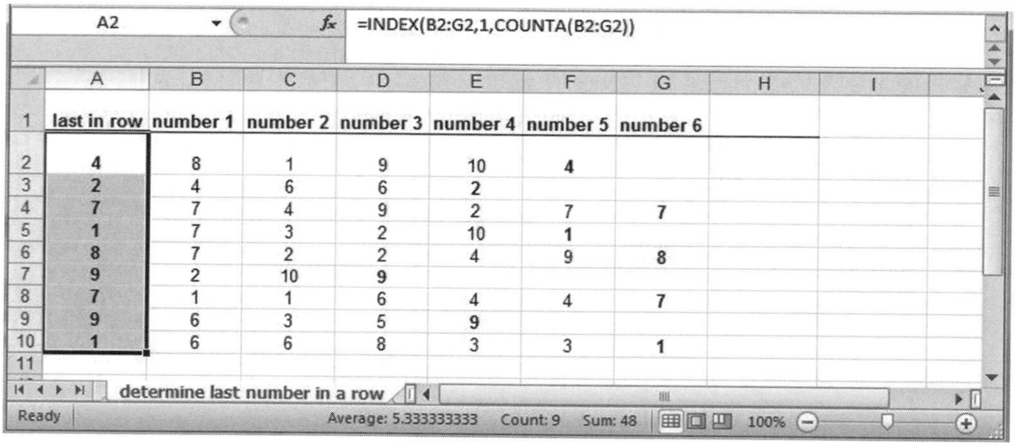

	A2		fx	=INDEX(B2:G2,1,COUNTA(B2:G2))				
	A	B	C	D	E	F	G	H	I
1	last in row	number 1	number 2	number 3	number 4	number 5	number 6		
2	4	8	1	9	10	4			
3	2	4	6	6	2				
4	7	7	4	9	2	7	7		
5	1	7	3	2	10	1			
6	8	7	2	2	4	9	8		
7	9	2	10	9					
8	7	1	1	6	4	4	7		
9	9	6	3	5	9				
10	1	6	6	8	3	3	1		
11									

determine last number in a row

Ready   Average: 5.333333333   Count: 9   Sum: 48   100%

FIGURE 9–16

USE THE OFFSET FUNCTION TO SUM SALES FOR A SPECIFIED PERIOD

Figure 9–17 gives an overview of the monthly sales figures from the previous year. Let's sum the sales from January to November. To do so, use the OFFSET function in combination with SUM. OFFSET returns a reference to a range that is a specific number of rows and columns from a cell or range of cells.

The syntax is:

OFFSET(*reference, rows, cols, height, width*)

    reference: The reference that is the base for the offset.

    rows: The number of rows to which the upper-left cell should refer.

    cols: The number of columns to which the upper-left cell should refer.

height: The height, in number of rows, that the returned reference should be. *height* must be a positive number.

width: The width, in number of columns, that the returned reference should be. *width* must be a positive number.

▶ **To Sum Sales for a Specified Period:**

1. In a worksheet, copy cells A1:B13, as shown in Figure 9–17.
2. In cell D1 enter a number from 1 to 12 for the desired month.
3. In cell E2 type the following formula:
   =SUM(OFFSET($B$2,0,0,$D$2,1)).
4. Press **<Enter>**.

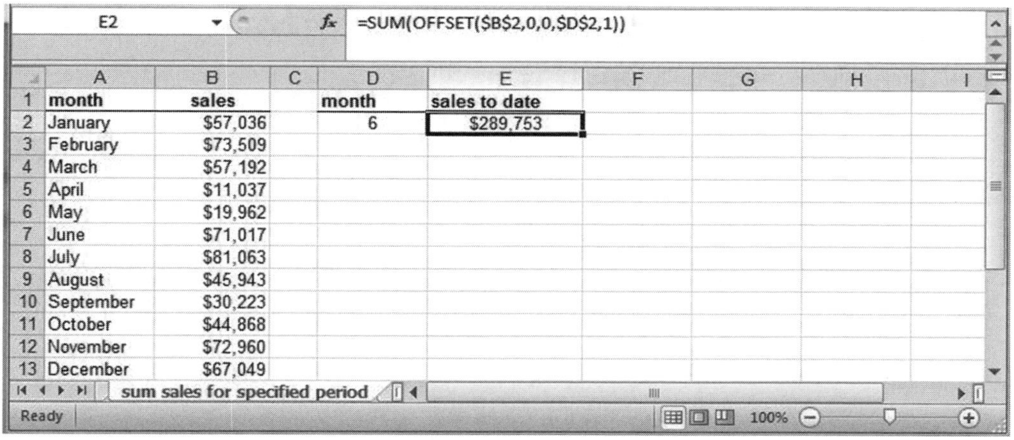

	E2			*f_x*	=SUM(OFFSET($B$2,0,0,$D$2,1))					
	A	B	C	D	E	F	G	H	I
1	month	sales		month	sales to date				
2	January	$57,036		6	$289,753				
3	February	$73,509							
4	March	$57,192							
5	April	$11,037							
6	May	$19,962							
7	June	$71,017							
8	July	$81,063							
9	August	$45,943							
10	September	$30,223							
11	October	$44,868							
12	November	$72,960							
13	December	$67,049							

sum sales for specified period

Ready   100%

FIGURE 9–17

USE THE OFFSET FUNCTION TO CONSOLIDATE SALES FOR A DAY

This tip shows an effective way of summing all the sales of each team for one specific day. The tricky part of the task is that the dates appear more than once. To calculate all sales for each team on one specific date, use the OFFSET function in combination with SUMIF.

▶ **To Consolidate Sales Per Day and Team:**

1. In a worksheet, copy cells A1:E12, as shown in Figure 9–18.
2. In cell H1 enter a desired date.
3. In cells G3:G6 type the team names.
4. Select cells H3:H6 and type the following formula:
   =SUMIF($A$2:$A$12,$H$1,OFFSET($A$2:$A$12,0,
   MATCH(G3,$1:$1,)-1)).
5. Press **<Ctrl+Enter>**.

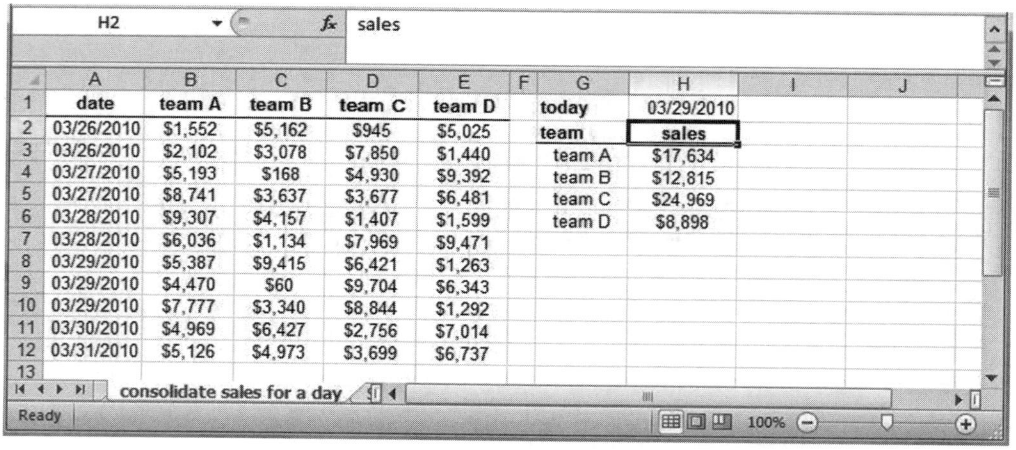

	H2			f_x	sales					
	A	B	C	D	E	F	G	H	I	J
1	date	team A	team B	team C	team D		today	03/29/2010		
2	03/26/2010	$1,552	$5,162	$945	$5,025		team	sales		
3	03/26/2010	$2,102	$3,078	$7,850	$1,440		team A	$17,634		
4	03/27/2010	$5,193	$168	$4,930	$9,392		team B	$12,815		
5	03/27/2010	$8,741	$3,637	$3,677	$6,481		team C	$24,969		
6	03/28/2010	$9,307	$4,157	$1,407	$1,599		team D	$8,898		
7	03/28/2010	$6,036	$1,134	$7,969	$9,471					
8	03/29/2010	$5,387	$9,415	$6,421	$1,263					
9	03/29/2010	$4,470	$60	$9,704	$6,343					
10	03/29/2010	$7,777	$3,340	$8,844	$1,292					
11	03/30/2010	$4,969	$6,427	$2,756	$7,014					
12	03/31/2010	$5,126	$4,973	$3,699	$6,737					
13										

consolidate sales for a day

Ready   100%

FIGURE 9–18

USE THE OFFSET FUNCTION TO FILTER EVERY OTHER COLUMN

This example shows a table where every other column has to be filtered. Use the COLUMN function to get the actual column and combine it with the OFFSET function to reach the goal.

▶ **To Extract Every Other Column:**

1. In cells A2:G6 type numbers from 1 to 6.
2. Select cells A9:D13 and type the following formula:
   =OFFSET($A2,0,(COLUMN()-1)*2).
3. Press **<Ctrl+Enter>**.

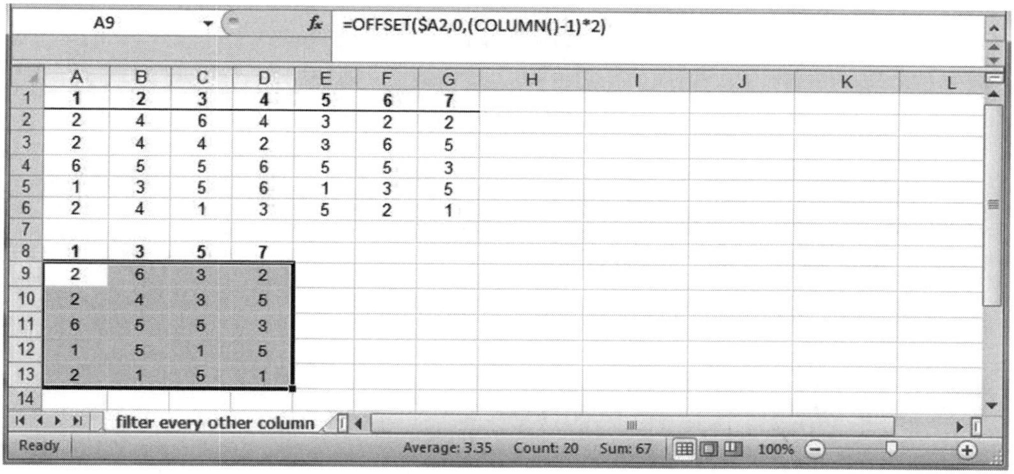

FIGURE 9–19

USE THE OFFSET FUNCTION TO FILTER EVERY OTHER ROW

In the previous example, we filtered every other column. To do the same with rows, use the ROW function to get the actual row and combine it with the OFFSET function to get the result shown below.

▶ **To Extract Every Other Row:**

1. In cells A2:A16 type any numbers.
2. Select cells B2:D9 and type the following formula:
   =OFFSET($A$2,(ROW()-2)*COLUMN(),0).
3. Press **<Ctrl+Enter>**.

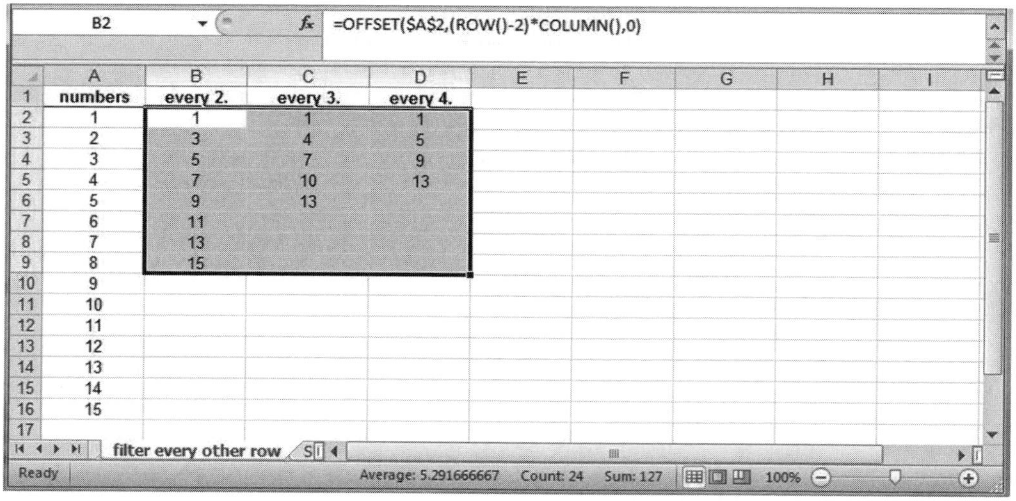

FIGURE 9–20

NOTE *To hide all cells containing zero, select Options from the Tools menu, click the View tab, and deactivate Zero values.*

USE THE HYPERLINK **FUNCTION TO JUMP DIRECTLY TO A CELL INSIDE THE CURRENT WORKSHEET**

Hyperlinks are usually used to navigate through the Internet or link different Office documents. You can also use the HYPERLINK function to jump directly to a specific cell in your worksheet with one mouse click. This function normally creates a shortcut to a document stored on a network server or located in the intranet or the Internet. When a user clicks on a cell that contains the HYPERLINK function, Excel opens the file stored at *link_location*.

HYPERLINK(*link_location, friendly_name*)

link_location: The path and file name of the document to be opened.

friendly_name: The text or numeric value that is displayed in the cell and that the user must select.

In this example, we insert a hyperlink that jumps to the already opened file and its cell containing the actual month.

▶ **To Jump with One Mouse Click to the Actual Month:**

1. In cell A1 enter **January**.
2. Drag the right corner of this cell down to A12.
3. In cell C1 type the following formula:
   =HYPERLINK("[Lookup.xls]sheet19!A"&MONTH (TODAY()),"jump to actual month").
4. Press **<Enter>**.
5. Click with the mouse on the displayed hyperlink in cell C1.

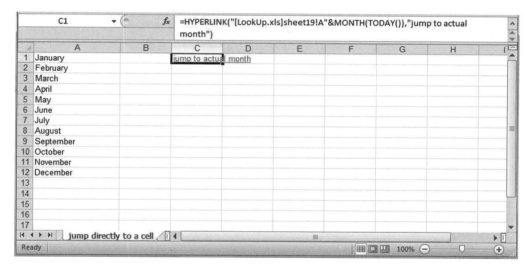

FIGURE 9–21

NOTE   *"Lookup.xls" is included in the companion files available on the CD-ROM*

USE THE HYPERLINK FUNCTION TO LINK TO THE INTERNET

This final tip in Chapter 9 shows how the HYPERLINK function is normally used to create links to the Internet. You can jump directly from your Excel application to predefined web sites using the HYPERLINK function.

▶ To Link to the Internet:

1. In column A type the URLs of the web sites to which you want to link.
2. In column B type the caption of the hyperlinks.
3. Select cells C2:C5 and type the following formula:
   =HYPERLINK("http://" & A2,"Click to " & B2).
4. Press **<Ctrl+Enter>**.

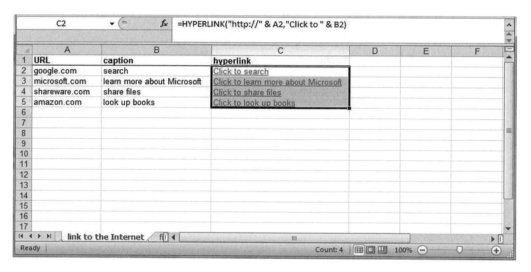

FIGURE 9–22

Chapter 10
CONDITIONAL FORMATTING WITH FORMULAS

USE THE WEEKDAY **FUNCTION TO DETERMINE WEEKENDS AND SHADE THEM**

With the help of the WEEKDAY function we can find out the day of the week for a particular date. This function returns the days as an integer ranging from 1 (Sunday) to 7 (Saturday) by default. You can also use this function in conditional formatting. In this example, some dates are listed in column A and the weekends are then marked as shown.

▶ **To Detect and Shade Weekends:**

1. Copy cells A1 and B1 into a new worksheet, as shown in Figure 10–1.
2. Enter **=TODAY()** in cell A2 and **=A2+1** in cell A3. For the remaining cells A4:A12, enter **=A*x*+1**, using the previous cell number for A*x*.
3. Select cells B2:B12 and enter the function **=WEEKDAY(A2)**.
4. Press **<Ctrl+Enter>**.
5. Select cells A2:B12.
6. From the **Home** tab, go to the **Styles** bar and click on **Conditional Formatting**.
7. Choose **New Rule**.
8. In the **Select a Rule Type** dialog select **Use a formula to determine which cells to format**.
9. In the **Edit** box type the following formula to mark Saturday: **=WEEKDAY($A2)=7**.

10. Click **Format** to select the desired formatting to apply when the cell value meets the condition.
11. Select a color from the **Fill** tab and click **OK**.
12. Click **OK**.
13. Repeat step 2 and choose **Manage Rule**.
14. Click **New Rule** and insert the following formula (to mark Sunday): **=WEEKDAY($A2)=1**.
15. Repeat step 10.
16. Click **OK**.

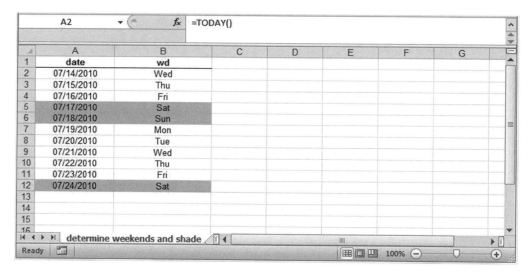

FIGURE 10–1

> **NOTE** *To display the short versions of the day of the week rather than the integer returned by the function, highlight cells B2:B12, select Cells from the Format menu, and enter ddd in the Type box. Click OK.*

USE THE TODAY FUNCTION TO SHOW ACTUAL SALES

All daily sales are listed in an Excel table. The list contains estimated sales as well, which are assigned this status as shown in column C. We need to mark all completed sales by using conditional formatting, being sure to exclude the estimated sales.

▶ To Show Completed Sales:

1. In a worksheet, copy cells A1:C13, as shown in Figure 10–2.
2. In cell E1 enter the function **TODAY()**.
3. Select cells A2:C13.
4. From the **Home** tab, go to the **Styles** bar and click on **Conditional Formatting**.
5. Choose **New Rule**.
6. In the **Select a Rule Type** dialog select **Use a formula to determine which cells to format**.
7. In the **Edit** box type the following formula to mark Saturday: =**$A2<=$E$1**.
8. Click **Format** to select the desired formatting to apply when the cell value meets the condition.
9. Select a color from the **Fill** tab and click **OK**.
10. Go to the **Font** tab and select **Bold** in the **Font Style**.
11. Click **OK**.

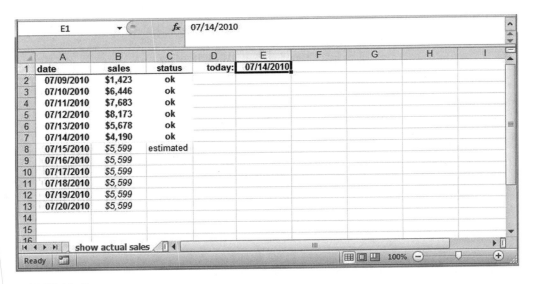

FIGURE 10–2

USE CONDITIONAL FORMATS TO INDICATE UNAVAILABLE PRODUCTS

When checking the existing inventory of a warehouse, it needs to be determined which products are out of stock so they can be ordered. To get a better overview of the inventory, all products that are unavailable need to be marked by using conditional formatting. The formatting criterion is taken from column D, which indicates whether or not a product is available.

▶ **To Mark All Products that are Out of Stock:**

1. Copy the table shown in Figure 10–3 into a worksheet and select cells A2:D13.
2. From the **Home** tab, go to the **Styles** bar and click on **Conditional Formatting**.
3. Choose **New Rule**.
4. In the **Select a Rule Type** dialog select **Use a formula to determine which cells to format**.
5. In the **Edit** box type the following formula: **=$D2="no"**.
6. Click **Format** to select the desired formatting to apply when the cell value meets the condition.
7. Select a color from the **Fill** tab and click **OK**.
8. Click **OK**.

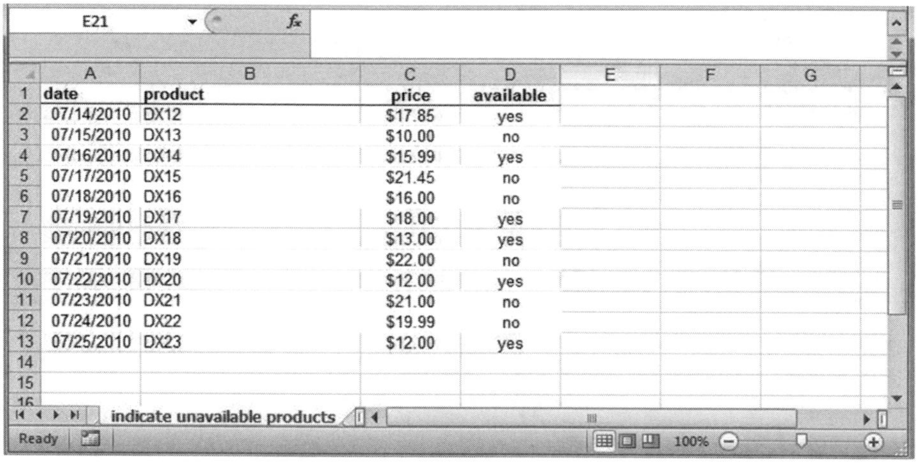

	A	B	C	D	E	F	G
1	date	product	price	available			
2	07/14/2010	DX12	$17.85	yes			
3	07/15/2010	DX13	$10.00	no			
4	07/16/2010	DX14	$15.99	yes			
5	07/17/2010	DX15	$21.45	no			
6	07/18/2010	DX16	$16.00	no			
7	07/19/2010	DX17	$18.00	yes			
8	07/20/2010	DX18	$13.00	yes			
9	07/21/2010	DX19	$22.00	no			
10	07/22/2010	DX20	$12.00	yes			
11	07/23/2010	DX21	$21.00	no			
12	07/24/2010	DX22	$19.99	no			
13	07/25/2010	DX23	$12.00	yes			
14							
15							
16							

indicate unavailable products

FIGURE 10–3

USE THE TODAY FUNCTION TO SHADE A SPECIAL COLUMN

A project schedule can be generated quite easily through Excel. To make it easier to read at a glance, the current day can be colored automatically. Use the TODAY function to determine the actual date and define it as the criterion for conditional formatting.

▶ **To Shade the Column for the Current Day:**

1. In cell H1 enter the function **TODAY()**.
2. Select cells A3:H12.
3. From the **Home** tab, go to the **Styles** bar and click on **Conditional Formatting**.
4. Choose **New Rule**.
5. In the **Select a Rule Type** dialog select **Use a formula to determine which cells to format**.
6. In the **Edit** box type the following formula: **=A$3=TODAY()**.
7. Click **Format** to select the desired formatting to apply when the cell value meets the condition.
8. Select a color from the **Fill** tab and click **OK**.
9. Click **OK**.

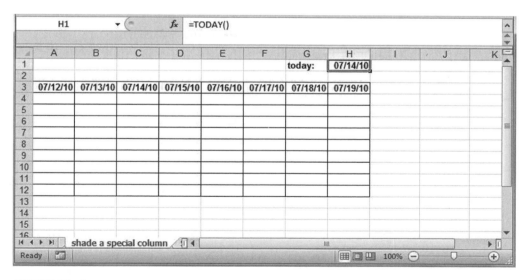

FIGURE 10–4

NOTE *To remove all conditional formats as well as all other cell formats for selected cells do as mentioned in step 3 and choose Clear Rules.*

USE THE WEEKNUM AND MOD FUNCTIONS TO SHADE EVERY OTHER TUESDAY

The table shown in Figure 10–5 is part of a schedule for the purchasing department. Purchases are made every other Tuesday. Create a schedule and color every other Tuesday as a reminder. Use the WEEKNUM function (introduced in Chapter 4) from the Analysis ToolPak add-in. This function returns a number that indicates where the week falls numerically within a year. In combination with the MOD function, it can be determined if the week number is even or odd.

▶ **To Mark Every Second Tuesday:**

1. Select cells A2:C20.
2. From the **Home** tab, go to the **Styles** bar and click on **Conditional Formatting**.
3. Choose **New Rule**.
4. In the **Select a Rule Type** dialog select **Use a formula to determine which cells to format**.
5. In the **Edit** box type the following formula:
   =AND(WEEKNUM($A3)=4,MOD($C3,2)<>0).
6. Click **Format** to select the desired formatting to apply when the cell value meets the condition.
7. Select a color from the **Fill** tab and click **OK**.
8. Click **OK**.

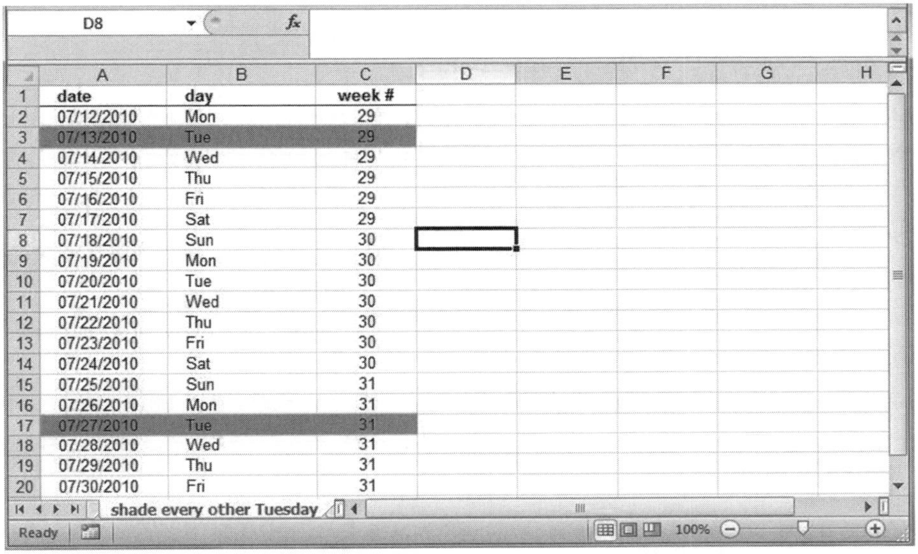

	A	B	C
1	date	day	week #
2	07/12/2010	Mon	29
3	07/13/2010	Tue	29
4	07/14/2010	Wed	29
5	07/15/2010	Thu	29
6	07/16/2010	Fri	29
7	07/17/2010	Sat	29
8	07/18/2010	Sun	30
9	07/19/2010	Mon	30
10	07/20/2010	Tue	30
11	07/21/2010	Wed	30
12	07/22/2010	Thu	30
13	07/23/2010	Fri	30
14	07/24/2010	Sat	30
15	07/25/2010	Sun	31
16	07/26/2010	Mon	31
17	07/27/2010	Tue	31
18	07/28/2010	Wed	31
19	07/29/2010	Thu	31
20	07/30/2010	Fri	31

FIGURE 10–5

USE THE MOD AND ROW FUNCTIONS TO SHADE EVERY THIRD ROW

In this example, every third row of a table has to be marked. To do this automatically, use the ROW function in combination with MOD. The ROW function returns the row number of the active cell and then uses the MOD function to divide it by 3. If the remainder is zero, the row can be shaded using conditional formatting.

▶ To Shade Every Third Row:

1. Select rows 1 to 20.
2. From the **Home** tab, go to the **Styles** bar and click on **Conditional Formatting**.
3. Choose **New Rule**.
4. In the **Select a Rule Type** dialog select **Use a formula to determine which cells to format**.
5. In the **Edit** box type the following formula: **=MOD(ROW(),3)=0**.
6. Click **Format** to select the desired formatting to apply when the cell value meets the condition.

7. Select a color from the **Fill** tab and click **OK**.
8. Click **OK**.

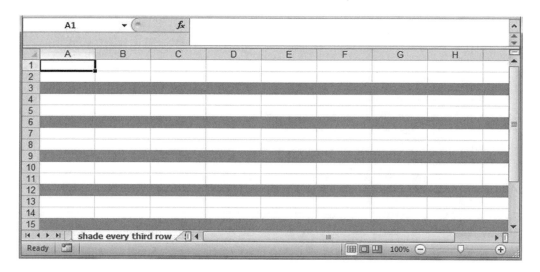

FIGURE 10–6

> **NOTE**   *Up to three conditions can be specified as conditional formats. If none of the specified conditions are true, the cells keep their existing formats.*

USE THE MOD **AND** COLUMN **FUNCTIONS TO SHADE EVERY THIRD COLUMN**

The previous tip showed how to mark every third row. Now let's find out how to automatically mark every third column in a range. Use the COLUMN function in combination with MOD. The COLUMN function returns the column number of the active cell and divides it by 3 with the MOD function. If the remainder is zero, the column can be shaded through conditional formatting.

▶ **To Shade Every Third Column:**

1. Select range A1:P14.
2. From the **Home** tab, go to the **Styles** bar and click on **Conditional Formatting**.
3. Choose **New Rule**.

4. In the **Select a Rule Type** dialog select **Use a formula to determine which cells to format**.
5. In the **Edit** box type the following formula:
=MOD(COLUMN(),3)=0.
6. Click **Format** to select the desired formatting to apply when the cell value meets the condition.
7. Select a color from the **Fill** tab and click **OK**.
8. Click **OK**.

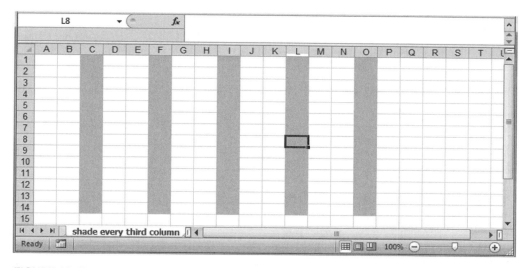

FIGURE 10–7

 NOTE   *Because conditional formatting causes the document file size to grow very quickly, you should format only the ranges where it is really needed.*

USE THE MAX FUNCTION TO FIND THE LARGEST VALUE

This example shows how to find and automatically mark the largest value in a range. All occurrences of the largest value will be shaded. Use the MAX function to determine the largest value in a range and then use that value as the formatting criterion for conditional formatting.

▶ **To Search for and Shade the Largest Value:**

1. In a worksheet, enter numbers in cells A1:E10 (or copy the values in Figure 10–8) and select the range.
2. From the **Home** tab, go to the **Styles** bar and click on **Conditional Formatting**.
3. Choose **New Rule**.
4. In the **Select a Rule Type** dialog select **Use a formula to determine which cells to format**.
5. In the **Edit** box type the following formula: **=A1=MAX($A$1:$E$10)**.
6. Click **Format** to select the desired formatting to apply when the cell value meets the condition.
7. Select a color from the **Fill** tab and click **OK**.
8. Click **OK**.

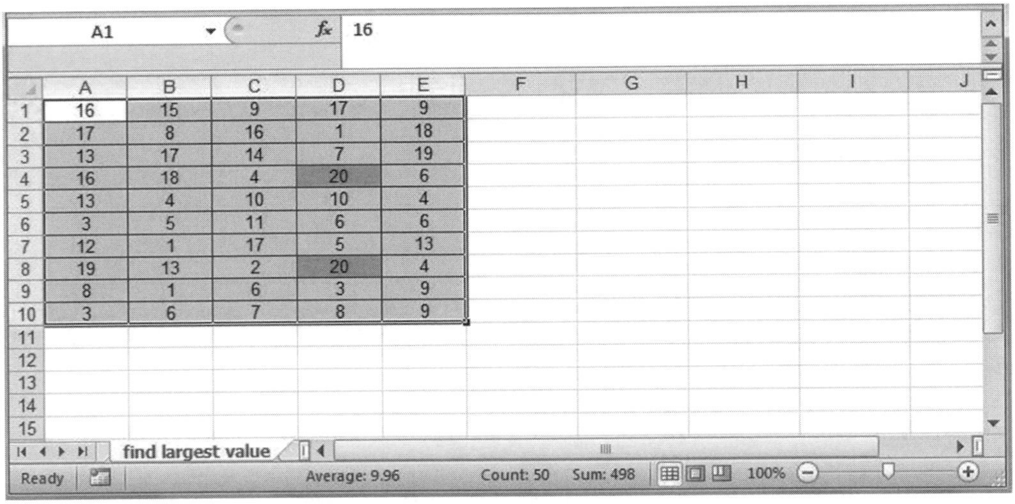

FIGURE 10–8

USE THE LARGE FUNCTION TO FIND THE THREE LARGEST VALUES

The three largest values in a range need to be found and shaded, regardless of how many times they appear. Use the LARGE function to determine the three largest values in a range and specify those three conditions as criteria for conditional formatting.

▶ **To Search for and Shade the Three Largest Values:**

1. In a worksheet, enter numbers in cells A1:E10 (or copy the values in Figure 10–9) and select the range.
2. From the **Home** tab, go to the **Styles** bar and click on **Conditional Formatting**.
3. Choose **Top/Bottom Rules** and then **Top 10 items**.
4. In the dialog box choose 3 and the required cell format.
5. Click **OK**.

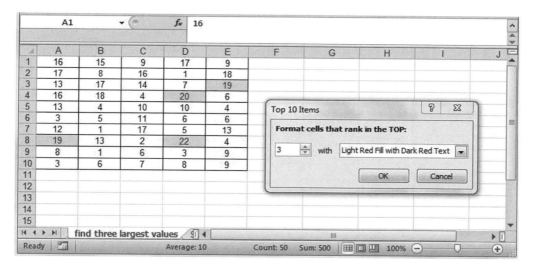

FIGURE 10–9

USE THE MIN FUNCTION TO FIND THE MONTH WITH THE WORST PERFORMANCE

Salespeople usually do some market analysis to find their current share of the market. Before you can investigate the reasons for a bad fiscal year, you need to find the worst month of sales and then shade it. Use the MIN function to get the lowest value in a range and use it as the formatting criteria for conditional formatting.

▶ **To Search for the Worst Month:**

1. In a worksheet, enter the months in cells A2:A13 and the sales amounts in cells B2:B13 (or copy the values in Figure 10–10) and select the range.
2. From the **Home** tab, go to the **Styles** bar and click on **Conditional Formatting**.
3. Choose **New Rule**.
4. In the **Select a Rule Type** dialog select **Use a formula to determine which cells to format**.
5. In the **Edit** box type the following formula:
   =$B2=MIN($B$2:$B$13).
6. Click **Format** to select the desired formatting to apply when the cell value meets the condition.
7. Select a color from the **Fill** tab and click **OK**.
8. Click **OK**.

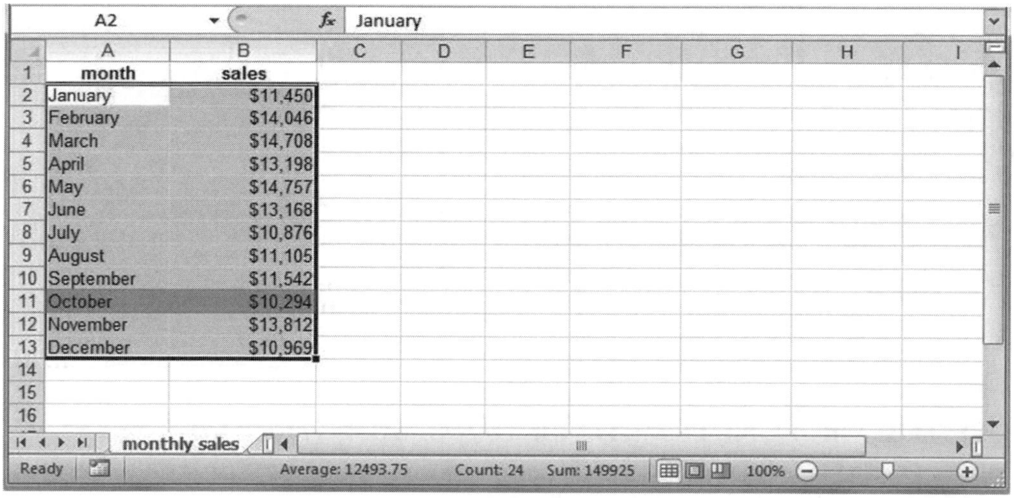

	A	B
	month	**sales**
2	January	$11,450
3	February	$14,046
4	March	$14,708
5	April	$13,198
6	May	$14,757
7	June	$13,168
8	July	$10,876
9	August	$11,105
10	September	$11,542
11	October	$10,294
12	November	$13,812
13	December	$10,969

Average: 12493.75   Count: 24   Sum: 149925   100%

FIGURE 10–10

USE THE MIN FUNCTION TO SEARCH FOR THE LOWEST NON-ZERO NUMBER

In this example, the smallest non-zero number in a range has to be found and marked automatically. Use the MIN function to get the lowest value in a range, then use the IF function to check whether the number is not zero. Insert this formula as the formatting criterion for conditional formatting, and the lowest numbers will be colored as desired. This function finds the lowest number, whether it is positive or negative.

▶ **To Search for the Lowest Non-Zero Number:**

1. In a worksheet, enter numbers in cells A1:D10 (or copy the values in Figure 10–11) and select the range.
2. From the **Home** tab, go to the **Styles** bar and click on **Conditional Formatting**.
3. Choose **New Rule**.
4. In the **Select a Rule Type** dialog select **Use a formula to determine which cells to format**.
5. In the **Edit** box type the following formula
   =A1=MIN(IF($A$1:$D$10<>0,$A$1:$D$10)).
6. Click **Format** to select the desired formatting to apply when the cell value meets the condition.
7. Select a color from the **Fill** tab and click **OK**.
8. Click **OK**.

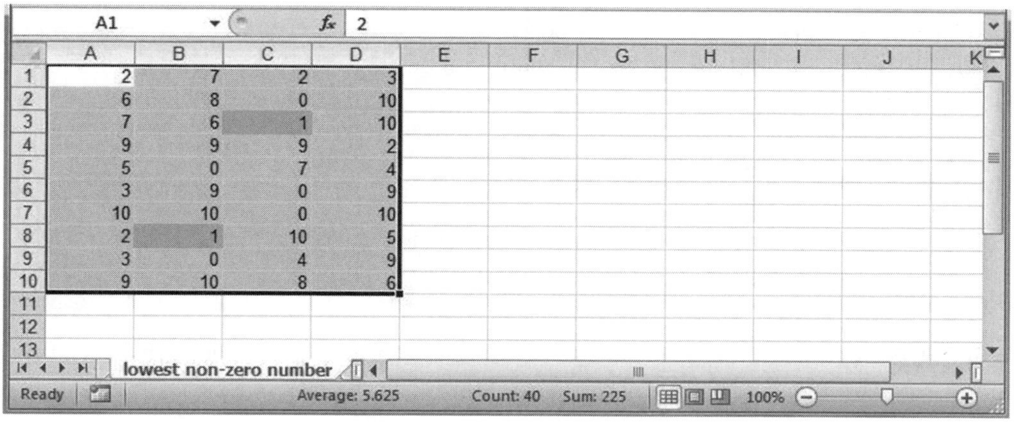

FIGURE 10–11

USE THE COUNTIF FUNCTION TO MARK DUPLICATE INPUT AUTOMATICALLY

Sometimes a list has to be checked for duplicate entries. This example creates a randomized list, and then finds all duplicate values and marks them. Use the COUNTIF function to count numbers that are repeated in a range, and then use this function with conditional formatting to shade all duplicate values as desired.

▶ **To Mark Duplicate Entries Automatically:**

    1. Select the range A1:D10.
    2. Type the following formula to generate randomized numbers from 1 to 300: **=RANDBETWEEN(1,300)**.
    3. Press **<Ctrl+Enter>**.
    4. In the **Format** menu, click **Conditional Formatting**.
    5. Select **Formula Is** and type the following formula: **=COUNTIF($A$1:$D$12,A1)>1**.
    6. Click **Format**.
    7. From the **Patterns** tab, choose a color and click **OK**.
    8. Click **OK**.

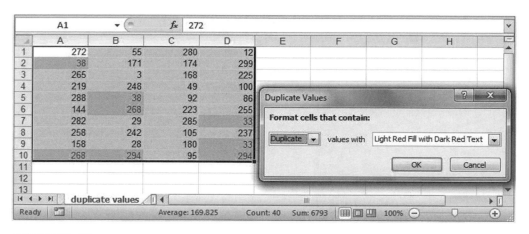

FIGURE 10–12

NOTE *Press <F9> to recalculate and generate new randomized numbers for the range.*

USE THE COUNTIF FUNCTION TO CHECK WHETHER A NUMBER EXISTS IN A RANGE

With this example you can learn how to check whether a specific number is found in a range and have Excel automatically mark each cell of the range that contains the number. Use the COUNTIF function to check whether the range contains the number in cell B1 and combine it with conditional formatting to shade the specific value as desired.

▶ **To Check Whether a Number Exists in a Range:**

1. Copy cells A1:D10 as shown in Figure 10–13, or use your own data.
2. Select cell B1.
3. From the **Home** tab, go to the **Styles** bar and click on **Conditional Formatting**.
4. Choose **New Rule**.
5. In the **Select a Rule Type** dialog select **Use a formula to determine which cells to format**.
6. In the **Edit** box type the following formula: **=COUNTIF($A$3:$D$10,$B$1)>0**.
7. Click **Format** to select the desired formatting to apply when the cell value meets the condition.
8. Select a color from the **Fill** tab and click **OK**.
9. Click **OK**.
10. Select cells A3:D10.
11. Repeat step 3 and choose **Manage Rule**.
12. Click **New Rule** and insert the following formula: **=$B$1=A3**.
13. Repeat steps 7–8.
14. Click **OK**.

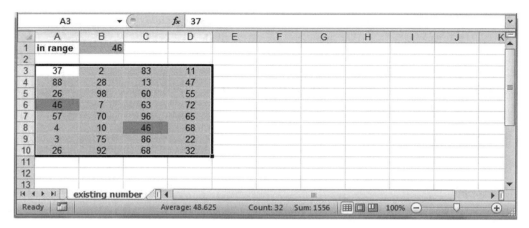

FIGURE 10–13

USE CONDITIONAL FORMATTING TO CONTROL FONT STYLES IN A SPECIFIC RANGE

Conditional formatting can also be used to control font styles in a specified range. Use cell E1 to enter letters like "i" for italic, "b" for bold, and "s" for strikethrough. Use conditional formatting to format the range as desired based on the input in cell E1.

▶ **To Control Font Styles in a Specified Range:**

1. In a worksheet, enter numbers in cells A1:D10 (or copy the values in Figure 10–14), and select the range A1:D10.
2. From the **Home** tab, go to the **Styles** bar and click on **Conditional Formatting**.
3. Choose **New Rule**.
4. In the **Select a Rule Type** dialog select **Use a formula to determine which cells to format**.
5. In the **Edit** box type the following formula: **=$E$1="i"**.
6. Click **Format** to select the desired formatting to apply when the cell value meets the condition.
7. On the **Font** tab, select **Italic** from the **Font style** box.
8. Click **OK**.
9. In cell E1, enter the character **i** to indicate that you want to italicize all the items in the range.

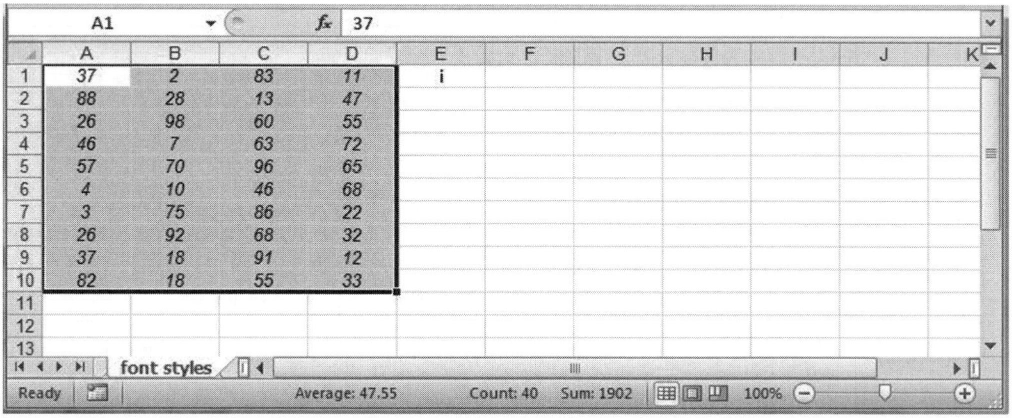

FIGURE 10–14

NOTE *You can add further font styles to the Conditional Formatting dialog using different conditions.*

USE A USER-DEFINED FUNCTION TO DETECT CELLS WITH FORMULAS

This example requires you to be familiar with the VBA Editor. Here we want to mark all cells in a specific range that contain a formula. First, you need to write a user-defined function:

1. Press **<Alt+F11>** to open up the VBA window.
2. On the **Insert** menu, click **Module** and enter the following function:

```
Function HF(rng)As Boolean
HF = rng.HasFormula
'returns TRUE if rng contains
'a formula
End Function
```

(The lines above that begin with an apostrophe indicate the information that follows is a comment.)

3. Press **<Alt+Q>** to return to the Excel worksheet.

Now you can use this user-defined function in conditional formatting.

▶ **To Shade All Cells that Contain Formulas:**

1. In a worksheet, enter numbers in cells A1:D10, being sure to enter formulas in some of the cells, and select cells A1:D10.
2. From the **Home** tab, go to the **Styles** bar and click on **Conditional Formatting**.
3. Choose **New Rule**.
4. In the **Select a Rule Type** dialog select **Use a formula to determine which cells to format**.
5. In the **Edit** box type the following formula: **=HF(A1)**.
6. Click **Format** to select the desired formatting to apply when the cell value meets the condition.
7. Select a color from the **Fill** tab and click **OK**.
8. Click **OK**.

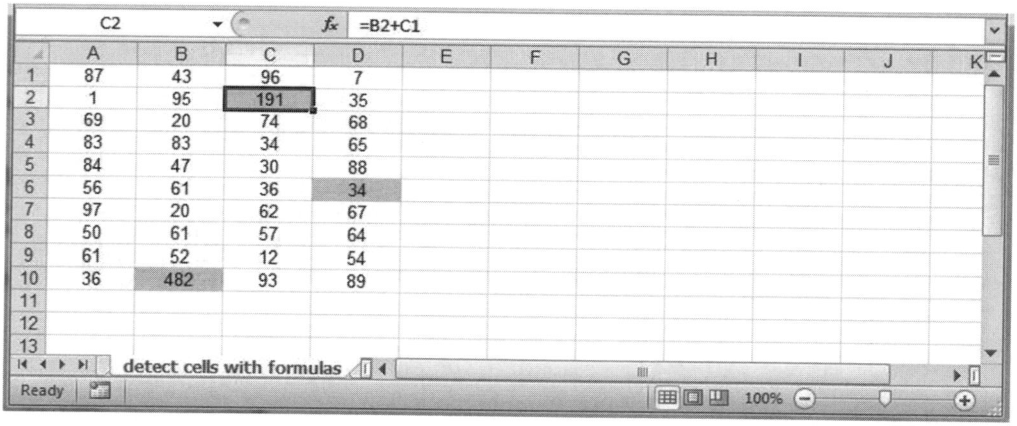

FIGURE 10–15

USE A USER-DEFINED FUNCTION TO DETECT CELLS WITH NUMERIC VALUES

Continuing with the previous tip, let's now mark all cells in a range that contain valid numeric values. First, you need to write a user-defined function:

1. Press **<Alt+F11>** to open up the VBA window.

2. On the **Insert** menu, click **Module** and enter the following function:

```
Function ISNUM(rng) As Boolean
If rng.Value <> "" Then
ISNUM = IsNumeric(rng.Value)
End If
'returns TRUE if rng contains
'numeric values
End Function
```

3. Press **<Alt+Q>** to return to the Excel worksheet.

Now you can use this user-defined function in conditional formatting.

▶ **To Shade Cells with Valid Numeric Values:**

1. In a worksheet, enter data in cells A1:C10, being sure to use numeric values in some of the cells (or copy the values in Figure 10–16), and select cells A1:C10.
2. From the **Home** tab, go to the **Styles** bar and click on **Conditional Formatting**.
3. Choose **New Rule**.
4. In the **Select a Rule Type** dialog select **Use a formula to determine which cells to format**.
5. In the **Edit** box type the following formula: **=isnum(A1)**.
6. Click **Format** to select the desired formatting to apply when the cell value meets the condition.
7. Select a color from the **Fill** tab and click **OK**.
8. Click **OK**.

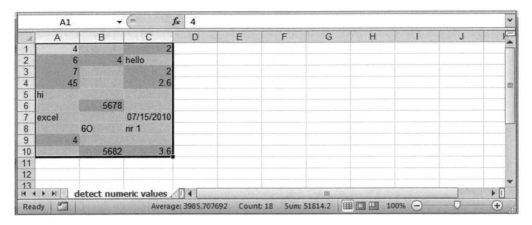

FIGURE 10–16

USE THE EXACT FUNCTION TO PERFORM A CASE-SENSITIVE SEARCH

Usually Excel doesn't differentiate between uppercase and lowercase letters. To search for a string that has the same case, use the EXACT function. The search string is entered in cell B1. With the support of conditional formatting, all cells within a specified range will be formatted if they contain the exact search string.

▶ **To Perform a Case-Sensitive Search on Text:**

1. In a worksheet, enter a variety of values in cells A3:E13, being sure to use "Excel" in several cells (or copy the values in Figure 10–17).
2. In cell B1 enter **Excel**.
3. Select cells A3:E13.
4. From the **Home** tab, go to the **Styles** bar and click on **Conditional Formatting**.
5. Choose **New Rule**.
6. In the **Select a Rule Type** dialog select **Use a formula to determine which cells to format**.
7. In the **Edit** box type the following formula: **=EXACT(A3,$B$1)**.
8. Click **Format** to select the desired formatting to apply when the cell value meets the condition.
9. Select a color from the **Fill** tab and click **OK**.

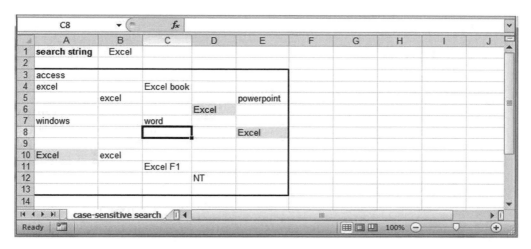

FIGURE 10–17

USE THE SUBSTITUTE **FUNCTION TO SEARCH FOR TEXT**

This tip can help you look for specific text in a list and mark each occurrence. The search text is specified in cell B13. Specify the SUBSTITUTE function as a condition to search for, and shade each cell where the text string is found.

▶ **To Search for Text:**

1. Copy the data shown in Figure 10–18 to a new worksheet and select cells B2:B11.
2. From the **Home** tab, go to the **Styles** bar and click on **Conditional Formatting**.
3. Choose **New Rule**.
4. In the **Select a Rule Type** dialog select **Use a formula to determine which cells to format**.
5. In the **Edit** box type the following formula:
   =LEN(B2)<>LEN(SUBSTITUTE(B2,B13,"")).
6. Click **Format** to select the desired formatting to apply when the cell value meets the condition.
7. Select a color from the **Fill** tab and click **OK**.
8. Click **OK**.

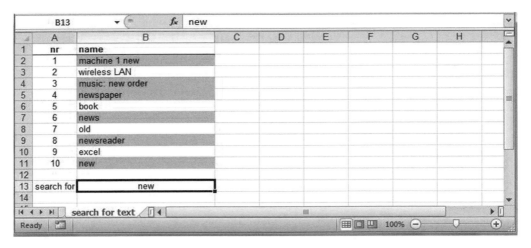

FIGURE 10–18

USE CONDITIONAL FORMATTING TO SHADE PROJECT STEPS WITH MISSED DEADLINES

The project schedule shown in Figure 10–19 contains different steps and their starting and projected ending dates. The actual end dates are listed in column E. Use conditional formatting to search for all steps that ended late by comparing the dates in columns D and E. As usual, select the desired formatting to apply when the cell value meets the condition.

▶ **To Shade Project Steps with Missed Deadlines:**

1. In a worksheet, copy the values shown in Figure 10–19, and select cells A2:E11.
2. From the **Home** tab, go to the **Styles** bar and click on **Conditional Formatting**.
3. Choose **New Rule**.
4. In the **Select a Rule Type** dialog select **Use a formula to determine which cells to format**.
5. In the **Edit** box type the following formula: **=$E2>$D2**.
6. Click **Format** to select the desired formatting to apply when the cell value meets the condition.
7. Select a color from the **Fill** tab and click **OK**.
8. Click **OK**.

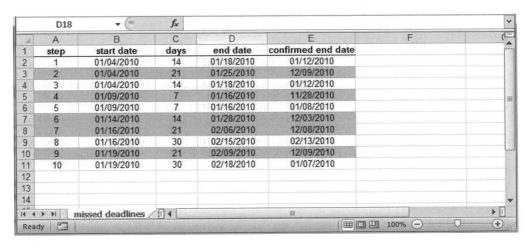

	A	B	C	D	E	F
1	step	start date	days	end date	confirmed end date	
2	1	01/04/2010	14	01/18/2010	01/12/2010	
3	2	01/04/2010	21	01/25/2010	12/09/2010	
4	3	01/04/2010	14	01/18/2010	01/12/2010	
5	4	01/09/2010	7	01/16/2010	11/28/2010	
6	5	01/09/2010	7	01/16/2010	01/08/2010	
7	6	01/14/2010	14	01/28/2010	12/03/2010	
8	7	01/16/2010	21	02/06/2010	12/08/2010	
9	8	01/16/2010	30	02/15/2010	02/13/2010	
10	9	01/19/2010	21	02/09/2010	12/09/2010	
11	10	01/19/2010	30	02/18/2010	01/07/2010	
12						
13						
14						

FIGURE 10–19

USE CONDITIONAL FORMATTING TO CREATE A GANTT CHART IN EXCEL

With the help of this tip, you can easily create a project plan that includes a Gantt chart in Excel. Begin by inserting a new worksheet, and then copy the header row as shown in Figure 10–20.

▶ **To Create a Project Plan and Gantt Chart Step by Step:**

1. Copy the data in cells A2:C11, as shown in Figure 10–20.
2. Select cells D2:D11 and type the formula **=C2-D2**.
3. Press **<Ctrl+Enter>**.
4. Select cell E1 and type the formula **=B2**.
5. Select cells F1:AB1 and type the formula **=E1+1**.
6. Press **<Ctrl+Enter>**.
7. Select cells E2:AB11.
8. From the **Home** tab, go to the **Styles** bar and click on **Conditional Formatting**.
9. Choose **New Rule**.
10. In the **Select a Rule Type** dialog select **Use a formula to determine which cells to format**.
11. In the **Edit** box type the following formula:
    =AND(E$1>=$B2,E$1<$C2).

12. Click **Format** to select the desired formatting to apply when the cell value meets the condition.
13. Select a color from the **Fill** tab and click **OK**.
14. Click **OK**.

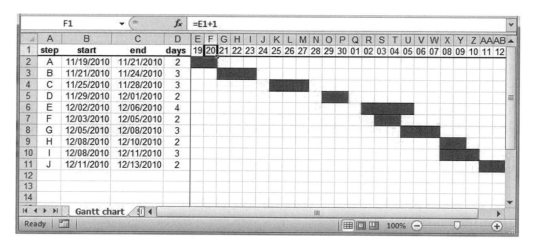

FIGURE 10–20

USE THE OR FUNCTION TO INDICATE DIFFERENCES HIGHER THAN 5% AND LOWER THAN -5%

At the end of a fiscal year a company compares the monthly sales of the last two years. Take a look at the following sales report for 2008 and 2009. Monthly sales of fiscal year 2008 are listed in column B, and column C contains the sales for 2009. Check the difference in column D by inserting the formula =(C2/B2)-1 and format it to percentages with one decimal place. The following steps show how to use conditional formatting to shade each cell that meets the desired condition.

▶ **To Shade Differences Higher than 5% and Lower than -5%:**

1. Select cells C2:C13.
2. From the **Home** tab, go to the **Styles** bar and click on **Conditional Formatting**.
3. Choose **New Rule**.

4. In the **Select a Rule Type** dialog select **Use a formula to determine which cells to format**.
5. In the **Edit** box type the following formula:
   =OR((C2/B2)-1>5%,(C2/B2)-1<-5%).
6. Click **Format** to select the desired formatting to apply when the cell value meets the condition.
7. Select a color from the **Fill** tab and click **OK**.
8. Click **OK**.

	A	B	C	D	E	F	G
		C2		fx	11068		
1	sales	2008	2009	check			
2	January	$10,121	$11,068	9.4%			
3	February	$10,729	$10,972	2.3%			
4	March	$10,845	$11,301	4.2%			
5	April	$11,209	$10,772	-3.9%			
6	May	$11,467	$11,935	4.1%			
7	June	$11,072	$10,081	-9.0%			
8	July	$11,614	$10,534	-9.3%			
9	August	$11,962	$10,268	-14.2%			
10	September	$11,115	$11,409	2.6%			
11	October	$10,093	$11,751	16.4%			
12	November	$11,788	$11,880	0.8%			
13	December	$10,522	$10,562	0.4%			
14							

indicate differences

Ready   Average: $11,044   Count: 12   Sum: $132,533   100%

FIGURE 10–21

USE THE CELL FUNCTION TO DETECT UNLOCKED CELLS

If a worksheet has been protected, all cells are locked by default. The protection for each cell has to be unlocked before activating sheet protection. If a sheet is protected, usually it is not possible to see at one glance which cells are locked and unlocked. Use conditional formatting to shade all unlocked cells in a range.

▶ **To Shade Unlocked Cells:**

1. Create the worksheet shown in Figure 10–22 and unlock cells B2, B4, B6, and B8.
2. Select cells A1:D10.
3. From the **Home** tab, go to the **Styles** bar and click on **Conditional Formatting**.

3. Choose **New Rule**.
4. In the **Select a Rule Type** dialog select **Use a formula to determine which cells to format**.
5. In the **Edit** box type the following formula:
   =CELL("protect",A1)=0.
6. Click **Format** to select the desired formatting to apply when the cell value meets the condition.
7. Select a color from the **Fill** tab and click **OK**.
8. Click **OK**.

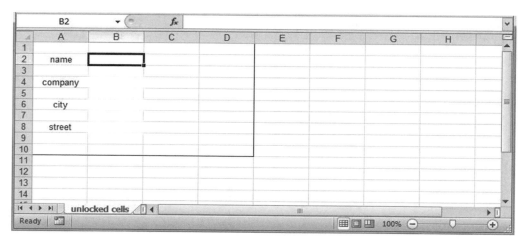

FIGURE 10–22

USE THE COUNTIF FUNCTION TO SHADE MATCHING NUMBERS IN COLUMN B

Cells A2:A4 in Figure 10–23 contain numbers that have to be found in column B. If values in column B match values in column A, the cell should be marked. Use the COUNTIF function in combination with conditional formatting to shade each cell that meets the desired condition.

▶ **To Shade Values in Column B that Correspond to Values in Column A:**

1. Create the worksheet shown in Figure 10–23 and select cells B1:B10.
2. From the **Home** tab, go to the **Styles** bar and click on **Conditional Formatting**.

3. Choose **New Rule**.
4. In the **Select a Rule Type** dialog select **Use a formula to determine which cells to format**.
5. In the **Edit** box type the following formula:
   =COUNTIF($A$2:$A$4,B2)>=1.
6. Click **Format** to select the desired formatting to apply when the cell value meets the condition.
7. Select a color from the **Fill** tab and click **OK**.
8. Click **OK**.

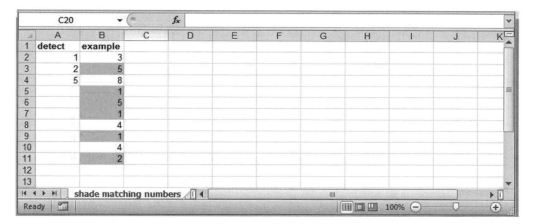

FIGURE 10–23

USE THE ISERROR **FUNCTION TO MARK ERRORS**

In this example, the value in column B is divided by the value in column A, and the result is displayed in column C. If the result of this operation is invalid, an error appears in column C. Use the ISERROR function in combination with conditional formatting to shade each cell that contains an error.

▶ **To Detect and Shade Errors:**

1. In a worksheet, enter numbers in cells A2:B11, as shown in Figure 10–24.
2. Select cells C2:C11 and type the formula **=B2/A2**.
3. Press **<Ctrl+Enter>**.

4. Select cells C2:C11.
5. From the **Home** tab, go to the **Styles** bar and click on **Conditional Formatting**.
6. Choose **New Rule**.
7. In the **Select a Rule Type** dialog select **Use a formula to determine which cells to format**.
8. In the **Edit** box type the following formula: **=ISERROR(B2/A2)**.
9. Click **Format** to select the desired formatting to apply when the cell value meets the condition.
10. Select a color from the **Fill** tab and click **OK**.
11. Click **OK**.

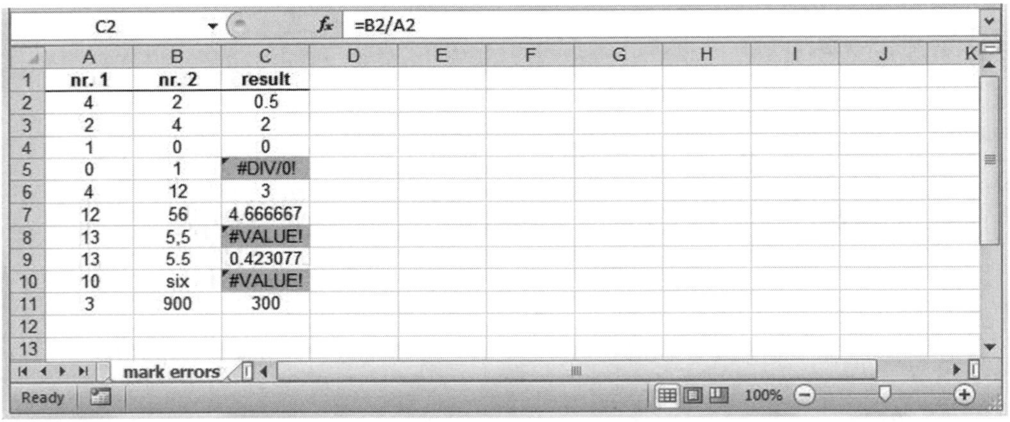

	A	B	C
C2			fx =B2/A2
1	nr. 1	nr. 2	result
2	4	2	0.5
3	2	4	2
4	1	0	0
5	0	1	#DIV/0!
6	4	12	3
7	12	56	4.666667
8	13	5,5	#VALUE!
9	13	5.5	0.423077
10	10	six	#VALUE!
11	3	900	300

FIGURE 10–24

USE THE DATEDIF FUNCTION TO DETERMINE ALL FRIENDS YOUNGER THAN 30

You have the birth dates of your friends listed in a worksheet and want to shade those who are currently younger than 30 years old. Use the TODAY function to determine the actual date and the DATEDIF function to calculate the exact age, then combine those functions with conditional formatting.

▶ **To Determine All Friends Younger than 30:**

1. In a worksheet, enter data in cells A2:B10, as shown in Figure 10–25.
2. Select cells A2:B10.

3. From the **Home** tab, go to the **Styles** bar and click on **Conditional Formatting**.
4. Choose **New Rule**.
5. In the **Select a Rule Type** dialog select **Use a formula to determine which cells to format**.
6. In the **Edit** box type the following formula:
   =DATEDIF($B2,TODAY(),"Y")<30.
7. Click **Format** to select the desired formatting to apply when the cell value meets the condition.
8. Select a color from the **Fill** tab and click **OK**.
9. Click **OK**.

	A	B	C	D	E	F	G	H
	E1			fx	=TODAY()			
1	name	birthday		Today	07/15/2010			
2	james	12/03/1956						
3	curtis	05/03/1980						
4	sarah	11/18/1966						
5	sue	02/23/1970						
6	steve	04/21/1979						
7	bob	05/07/1981						
8	donna	12/30/1993						
9	alex	01/22/2002						
10	walter	04/25/1945						
11								
12								
13								

FIGURE 10–25

USE THE MONTH AND TODAY FUNCTIONS TO FIND BIRTHDAYS IN THE CURRENT MONTH

Use the same list from the previous tip to determine whose birthday falls in the current month. Use the TODAY function to determine the actual date and the MONTH function to compare the month of everyone's birthday with the current month, then combine those functions with conditional formatting.

▶ **To Determine All Friends Whose Birthday is in the Current Month:**

1. In cell D1 enter the formula **TODAY()**.
2. Select cells A2:B10.

3. From the **Home** tab, go to the **Styles** bar and click on **Conditional Formatting**.
4. Choose **New Rule**.
5. In the **Select a Rule Type** dialog select **Use a formula to determine which cells to format**.
6. In the **Edit** box type the following formula:
   =(MONTH(TODAY())=MONTH($B2)).
7. Click **Format** to select the desired formatting to apply when the cell value meets the condition.
8. Select a color from the **Fill** tab and click **OK**.
9. Click **OK**.

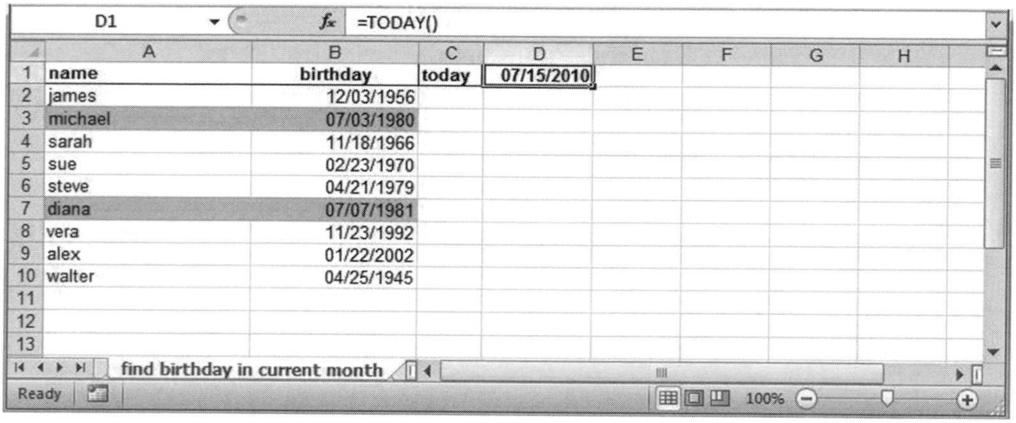

	A	B	C	D	E	F	G	H
1	name	birthday	today	07/15/2010				
2	james	12/03/1956						
3	michael	07/03/1980						
4	sarah	11/18/1966						
5	sue	02/23/1970						
6	steve	04/21/1979						
7	diana	07/07/1981						
8	vera	11/23/1992						
9	alex	01/22/2002						
10	walter	04/25/1945						
11								
12								
13								

find birthday in current month

FIGURE 10–26

USE CONDITIONAL FORMATTING TO BORDER SUMMED ROWS

Enhance worksheets with this tip for placing a border on special cells. The worksheet contains daily sales for different teams. Their sales are summed up after a certain period to get a current status. To enhance the visibility of each sum, we want to border it automatically through conditional formatting. Use a simple instruction as the condition for conditional formatting and border the row of each cell that meets the desired condition.

▶ **To Border All Rows Containing a Sum:**

1. In a worksheet, enter data in cells A1:C11, as shown in Figure 10–27, and select the range A2:C11.
2. From the **Home** tab, go to the **Styles** bar and click on **Conditional Formatting**.
3. Choose **New Rule**.
4. In the **Select a Rule Type** dialog select **Use a formula to determine which cells to format**.
5. In the **Edit** box type the following formula: **=$B2="sum"**.
6. Click **Format**.
7. On the **Border** tab, click the bottom line in the Border field.
8. Select the color **red** from the **Color** drop-down box.
9. Click **OK**.

	A	B	C
1	date	team	sales
2	07/13/2010	A	$10,984
3	07/14/2010	A	$17,107
4	07/15/2010	A	$16,216
5	07/16/2010	A	$11,701
6		sum	$56,008
7	07/13/2010	B	$16,124
8	07/14/2010	B	$15,819
9	07/15/2010	B	$12,859
10	07/16/2010	B	$21,035
11		sum	$65,837
12			
13			

FIGURE 10–27

USE THE LEFT FUNCTION IN A PRODUCT SEARCH

In this example, you need to find all the product numbers that contain the same first three characters. Enter in cell A2 the product number as the search criteria and let Excel find each product that corresponds to the same first three characters. The first three characters of the numbers can be extracted by the LEFT function. The name of the first product appears automatically in cell B2 with the following formula: =VLOOKUP($A$2,$A$5:$B$15,2,FALSE).

Use a combination of the LEFT function and conditional formatting to shade each cell that meets the desired condition.

▶ **To Shade Product Numbers that Meet the Criteria:**

1. In a worksheet, copy the data in cells A4:B15, as shown in Figure 10–28, and select cells A5:B15.
2. From the **Home** tab, go to the **Styles** bar and click on **Conditional Formatting**.
3. Choose **New Rule**.
4. In the **Select a Rule Type** dialog select **Use a formula to determine which cells to format**.
5. In the **Edit** box type the following formula:
   =LEFT($A5,3)=LEFT($A$2,3).
6. Click **Format** to select the desired formatting to apply when the cell value meets the condition.
7. Select a color from the **Fill** tab and click **OK**.
8. Click **OK**.

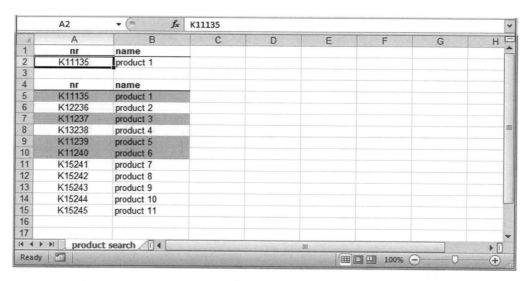

FIGURE 10–28

USE THE AND FUNCTION TO DETECT EMPTY ROWS IN A RANGE

The last tip in this chapter marks all empty cells in a range. Use a combination of the AND function and conditional formatting to shade each cell that meets the desired condition.

▶ **To Detect Empty Rows in a Range:**

1. In a worksheet, copy the data in cells A1:B12, as shown in Figure 10–29, and select the range A2:B12.
2. From the **Home** tab, go to the **Styles** bar and click on **Conditional Formatting**.
3. Choose **New Rule**.
4. In the **Select a Rule Type** dialog select **Use a formula to determine which cells to format**.
5. In the **Edit** box type the following formula:
   =AND($A3>($A2+1),$B3>($B2+1)).
6. Click **Format** to select the desired formatting to apply when the cell value meets the condition.
7. Select a color from the **Fill** tab and click **OK**.
8. Click **OK**.

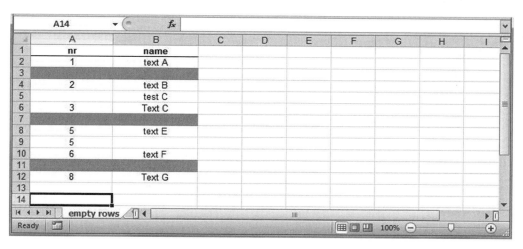

FIGURE 10–29

11 WORKING WITH ARRAY FORMULAS

Chapter

USE THE ADDRESS, MAX, AND ROW FUNCTIONS TO DETERMINE THE LAST USED CELL

With this tip, we learn the definition of an array formula. Here, we want to determine the last used cell in a range and shade it. Combine the ADDRESS, MAX, and ROW functions as described below to get the desired result.

▶ To Determine the Last Used Cell in a Range and Shade It:

1. In column A list any kind of numbers.
2. Select cell B2 and type the following array formula:
   =ADDRESS(MAX((A2:A100<>"")*ROW(A2:A100)),1).
3. Press **<Ctrl+Shift+Enter>**.
4. Select cells A2:A11.
5. From the **Home** tab, go to the **Styles** bar and click on **Conditional Formatting**.
6. Choose **New Rule**.
7. In the **Select a Rule Type** dialog select **Use a formula to determine which cells to format**.
8. In the **Edit** box type the following formula:
   =ADDRESS(ROW(),1)=$B$2.
9. Click **Format**, select a color from the **Fill** tab and click **OK**.
10. Click **OK**.

NOTE   *As shown in Figure 11–1, Excel automatically inserts the combined functions, which are defined as an array formula between the braces ({ and }).
Use an array formula to perform several calculations to generate a single
result or multiple results.*

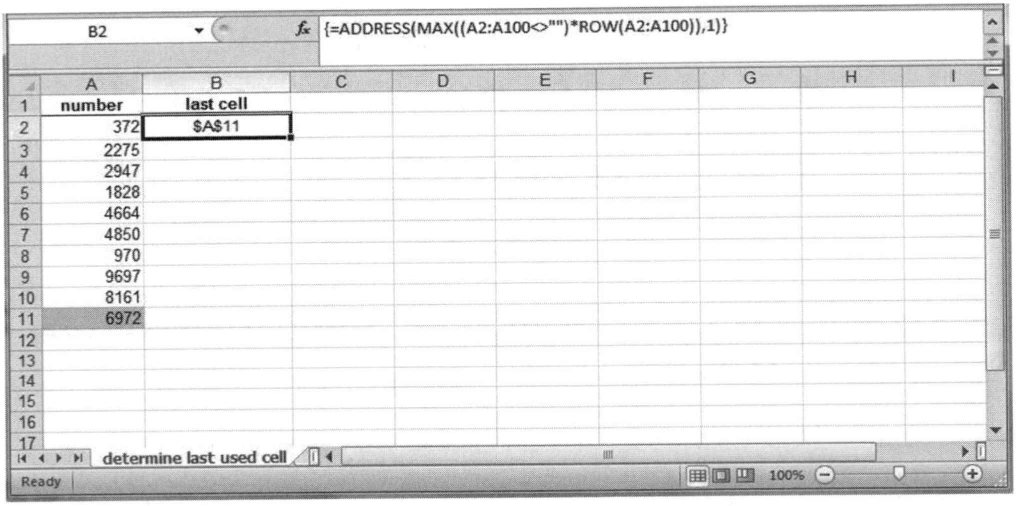

	B2		fx	{=ADDRESS(MAX((A2:A100<>"")*ROW(A2:A100)),1)}

	A	B	C	D	E	F	G	H	I
1	number	last cell							
2	372	$A$11							
3	2275								
4	2947								
5	1828								
6	4664								
7	4850								
8	970								
9	9697								
10	8161								
11	6972								
12									
13									
14									
15									
16									
17									

determine last used cell

Ready   100%

FIGURE 11–1

USE THE INDEX, MAX, ISNUMBER, AND ROW FUNCTIONS
TO FIND THE LAST NUMBER IN A COLUMN

Use the table from the previous tip and continue with array formulas. Now
we want to determine the last value in column A. Use a combination of the
INDEX, MAX, ISNUMBER, and ROW functions inside an array formula to
have the desired result displayed in cell B2.

Don't forget to enter the array formula by pressing <Ctrl+Shift+Enter>
to enclose it in braces.

▶ **To Determine the Last Number in a Column:**

   1. In column A list values or use the table from the previous tip.
   2. Select cell B2 and type the following array formula:
      =INDEX(A:A,MAX(ISNUMBER(A1:A1000)*
      ROW (A1:A1000))).
   3. Press **<Ctrl+Shift+Enter>**.

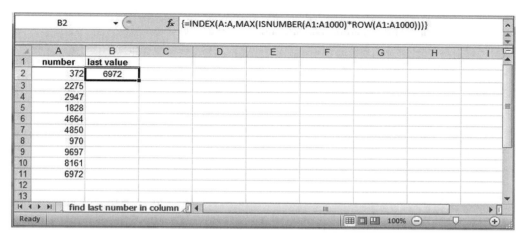

FIGURE 11–2

USE THE INDEX, MAX, ISNUMBER, AND COLUMN FUNCTIONS TO FIND THE LAST NUMBER IN A ROW

In this example, the last value in each row has to be determined and copied to another cell. To do this, combine the INDEX, MAX, ISNUMBER, and COLUMN functions in an array formula.

▶ **To Determine the Last Number in a Row:**

1. Generate a table like the one shown in Figure 11–3 using the range A1:F6.
2. In cells A9:A13 enter numbers from 2 to 6.
3. Select cell B9 and type the following array formula: **=INDEX(2:2,MAX(ISNUMBER(2:2)*COLUMN(2:2)))**.
4. Press **<Ctrl+Shift+Enter>**.
5. Select cells B9:B13.
6. In the **Home** tab go to the **Editing** bar and choose the **Fill** button.
7. Select **down** to retrieve the last value in each of the remaining rows.

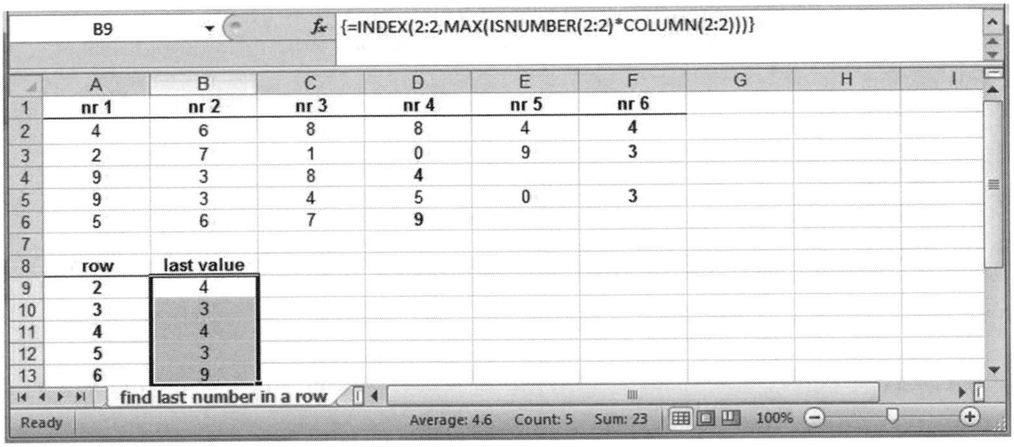

	A	B	C	D	E	F
1	nr 1	nr 2	nr 3	nr 4	nr 5	nr 6
2	4	6	8	8	4	4
3	2	7	1	0	9	3
4	9	3	8	4		
5	9	3	4	5	0	3
6	5	6	7	9		
7						
8	row	last value				
9	2	4				
10	3	3				
11	4	4				
12	5	3				
13	6	9				

FIGURE 11–3

USE THE MAX, IF, AND COLUMN FUNCTIONS TO DETERMINE THE LAST USED COLUMN IN A RANGE

Now let's determine the last used column in a defined range by using an array formula. All columns in the range A1:X10 have to be checked and the last used column is then shaded automatically. Here we use the MAX, IF, and COLUMN functions in an array formula and combine them with conditional formatting.

▶ To Determine the Last Used Column in a Range:

1. Select cells A1:D10 and enter any numbers.
2. Select cell B12 and type the following array formula: **=MAX(IF(A1:X10<>"",COLUMN(A1:X10)))**.
3. Press **<Ctrl+Shift+Enter>**.
4. Select cells A1:X10.
5. From the **Home** tab, go to the **Styles** bar and click on **Conditional Formatting**.
6. Choose **New Rule**.
7. In the **Select a Rule Type** dialog select **Use a formula to determine which cells to format**.
8. In the **Edit** box type the following formula: **=$B$12=COLUMN(A1)**.
9. Click **Format,** select a color from the **Fill** tab, and click **OK**.
10. Click **OK**.

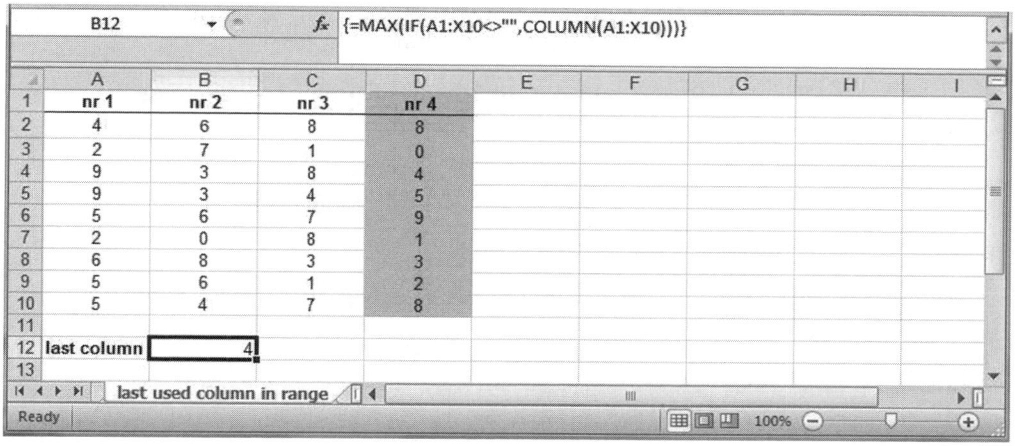

	B12		▼ ⊙		f_x	{=MAX(IF(A1:X10<>"",COLUMN(A1:X10)))}				

	A	B	C	D	E	F	G	H	I
1	nr 1	nr 2	nr 3	nr 4					
2	4	6	8	8					
3	2	7	1	0					
4	9	3	8	4					
5	9	3	4	5					
6	5	6	7	9					
7	2	0	8	1					
8	6	8	3	3					
9	5	6	1	2					
10	5	4	7	8					
11									
12	last column	4							
13									

last used column in range

Ready   100%

FIGURE 11–4

USE THE MIN AND IF FUNCTIONS TO FIND THE LOWEST NON-ZERO VALUE IN A RANGE

The sales for a fiscal year are recorded by month. The month with the lowest sales during the year has to be determined. If the list contains all sales from the year, we simply use the MIN function to get the lowest value. However, if we want to find the lowest sales sometime during the year and we don't have sales figures available for some of the months, we have to use the IF function to take care of the zero values. Combine the MIN and IF functions in an array formula and use conditional formatting to shade the lowest value.

▶ **To Detect the Lowest Non-Zero Value in a Range:**

1. In cells A2:A13 list the months January through December.
2. In column B list some sales values down to row 7.
3. Select cell F2 and type the following array formula:
   =MIN(IF(B1:B13>0,B1:B13)).
4. Press **<Ctrl+Shift+Enter>**.
5. Select cells B2:B13.
6. From the **Home** tab, go to the **Styles** bar and click on **Conditional Formatting**.
7. Choose **New Rule**.

8. In the **Select a Rule Type** dialog select **Use a formula to determine which cells to format**.
9. In the **Edit** box type the following formula: **=$F$2=B2**.
10. Click **Format,** select a color from the **Fill** tab, and click **OK**.
11. Click **OK**.

	F2			fx	{=MIN(IF(B1:B13>0,B1:B13))}					
	A	B	C	D	E	F	G	H	I	
1	month	sales			today	06/17/2010				
2	January	469,299			lowest sales	201,945				
3	February	201,945								
4	March	520,776								
5	April	755,867								
6	May	585,591								
7	June	307,584								
8	July	0								
9	August	0								
10	September	0								
11	October	0								
12	November	0								
13	December	0								

find lowest non-zero value

Ready   100%

FIGURE 11–5

USE THE AVERAGE AND IF FUNCTIONS TO CALCULATE THE AVERAGE OF A RANGE, TAKING ZERO VALUES INTO CONSIDERATION

Normally, Excel calculates the average of a range without considering empty cells. Use this tip to calculate the correct average when some values in a range are missing. As in the previous example, we use the IF function to take care of the zero values. Combine the AVERAGE and IF functions in an array formula to obtain the correct average of all listed costs.

▶ **To Calculate the Average of a Range, Taking Zero Values into Consideration:**

1. In cells A2:A13 list the months January through December.
2. In column B list monthly costs down to row 7.
3. Select cell E1 and type the following array formula:
   =AVERAGE(IF($B$2:$B$13<>0,$B$2:$B$13)).
4. Press **<Ctrl+Shift+Enter>**.

	E1			ƒx	{=AVERAGE(IF($B$2:$B$13<>0,$B$2:$B$13))}				

	A	B	C	D	E	F	G	H	I
1		costs		average	473,510				
2	January	469,299							
3	February	201,945							
4	March	520,776							
5	April	755,867							
6	May	585,591							
7	June	307,584							
8	July	0							
9	August	0							
10	September	0							
11	October	0							
12	November	0							
13	December	0							
14									

calc. range average cons. zero

FIGURE 11-6

NOTE *The result can be checked by selecting cells B2:B7. Right-click in the Excel status bar and select the built-in Average function instead of the usually displayed Sum.*

USE THE SUM AND IF FUNCTIONS TO SUM VALUES WITH SEVERAL CRITERIA

To sum values in a list, the SUMIF function is normally used. Unfortunately, it is not that easy to sum values with different criteria. Using a combination of different functions in an array formula is once again the solution. Use the SUM and IF functions together to take several criteria into consideration. In this example, we want to sum all values of a list that match both the word "wood" in column A and a value larger than 500 in column B. The result is displayed in cell E2.

▶ **To Sum Special Values with Several Criteria:**

1. In cells A2:A11 enter materials like wood, aluminum, and metal.
2. In cells B2:B11 list sizes from 100 to 1000.
3. In cells C2:C11 enter the corresponding costs.
4. Select cell E2 and type the following array formula:
   =(SUM(IF(A2:A11="wood",IF(B2:B11>500,C2:C11)))).
5. Press **<Ctrl+Shift+Enter>**.

	A	B	C	D	E	F	G	H	I
	E2		f_x	{=(SUM(IF(A2:A11="wood",IF(B2:B11>500,C2:C11)))))}					
1	material	size	sales		wood, > 500				
2	wood	457	$4,169		$10,126				
3	metal	562	$1,013						
4	metal	425	$3,723						
5	wood	388	$5,914						
6	wood	527	$1,885						
7	metal	1000	$2,861						
8	aluminum	597	$9,029						
9	metal	374	$3,229						
10	wood	566	$8,241						
11	aluminum	896	$4,219						
12									
13									
14									

FIGURE 11–7

USE THE INDEX AND MATCH FUNCTIONS TO SEARCH FOR A VALUE THAT MATCHES TWO CRITERIA

To search for a value that takes one or more criteria into consideration, use the INDEX and MATCH functions together. In this example, the search criteria can be entered in cells E1 and F1. Generate a search function using those two search criteria for the range A2:C11 and return the result in cell E2.

▶ **To Search for a Special Value Considering Two Criteria:**

1. In a worksheet, copy the data in cells A1:C11, as shown in Figure 11–8.
2. Enter **W46** as the first criterion in cell E1, and enter **1235** as the second criterion in cell F1.
3. Select cell E2 and type the following array formula:
   =INDEX(C1:C11,MATCH(E1&F1,A1:A11&B1:B11,0)).
4. Press **<Ctrl+Shift+Enter>**.

	A	B	C	D	E	F	G	H	I
					fx {=INDEX(C1:C11,MATCH(E1&F1,A1:A11&B1:B11,0))}				
1	category	number	value		W46	1235			
2	W45	1234	81		89				
3	W46	1235	89						
4	W47	1236	45						
5	W48	1237	92						
6	W49	1238	69						
7	W50	1239	90						
8	W51	1240	76						
9	W52	1241	4						
10	W53	1242	4						
11	W54	1243	64						
12									
13									
14									

FIGURE 11–8

USE THE SUM FUNCTION TO COUNT VALUES THAT MATCH TWO CRITERIA

To count values in a list, normally the COUNTIF function is used. Unfortunately, COUNTIF cannot be used to count when several criteria must be taken into consideration. However, it is possible to get the desired result using an array formula. Use the SUM function to consider several criteria. In this example, we count the rows that contain the word "wood" in column A and have a size larger than 500 in column B.

▶ **To Count Special Values that Match Two Criteria:**

1. In cells A2:A11 list materials like wood, aluminum, and metal.
2. In cells B2:B11 enter sizes from 100 to 1000.
3. In cells C2:C11 list the cost of each product.
4. Select cell E2 and type the following array formula:
   =SUM((A2:A11="wood")*(B2:B11>500)).
5. Press **<Ctrl+Shift+Enter>**.

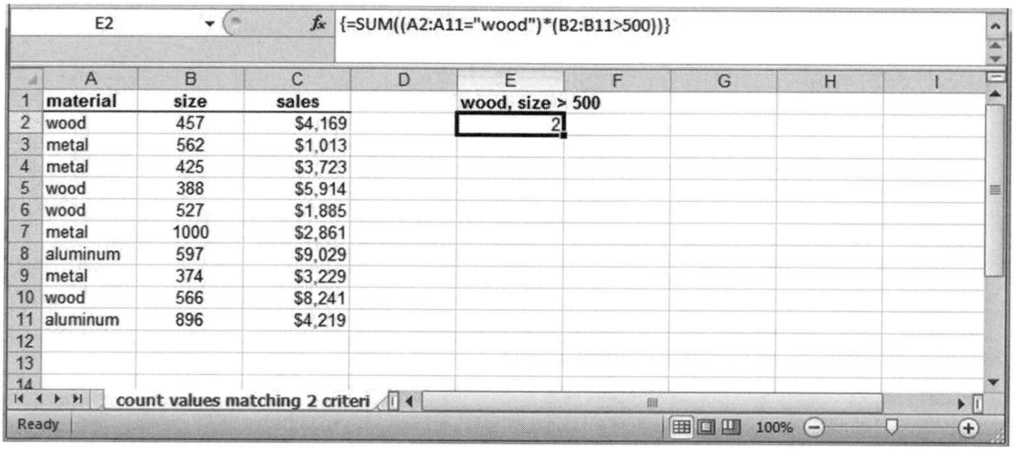

	E2		▾		f_x	{=SUM((A2:A11="wood")*(B2:B11>500))}				
	A	B	C	D	E	F	G	H	I
1	material	size	sales		wood, size > 500				
2	wood	457	$4,169		2				
3	metal	562	$1,013						
4	metal	425	$3,723						
5	wood	388	$5,914						
6	wood	527	$1,885						
7	metal	1000	$2,861						
8	aluminum	597	$9,029						
9	metal	374	$3,229						
10	wood	566	$8,241						
11	aluminum	896	$4,219						
12									
13									
14									

count values matching 2 criteri

Ready   100%

FIGURE 11–9

USE THE SUM FUNCTION TO COUNT VALUES THAT MATCH SEVERAL CRITERIA

In the previous example, we took two criteria into consideration. Now let's adapt that example for three criteria. Count all rows that meet these criteria: The material is "wood" (column A), the size is larger than 500 (column B), and the sales price is higher than $5,000 (column C). To get the desired result, use an array formula that takes care of all three criteria.

▶ **To Count Special Values that Match Several Criteria:**

1. In cells A2:A11 enter materials like wood, aluminum, and metal.
2. In cells B2:B11 list sizes from 100 to 1000.
3. In cells C2:C11 enter the sales price for each product.
4. Select cell E6 and type the following array formula:
   =SUM((A2:A11="wood")*(B2:B11>500)*(C2:C11>5000)).
5. Press **<Ctrl+Shift+Enter>**.

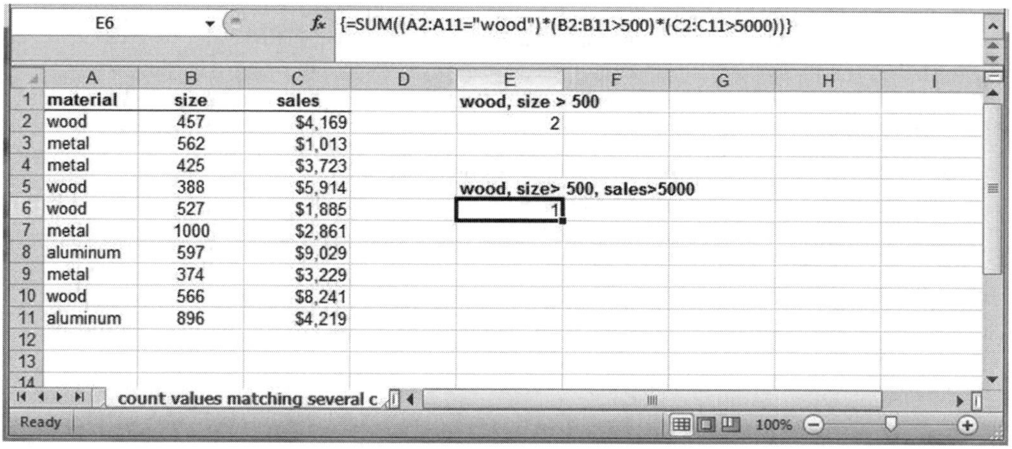

	A	B	C	D	E	F	G	H	I
1	material	size	sales		wood, size > 500				
2	wood	457	$4,169		2				
3	metal	562	$1,013						
4	metal	425	$3,723						
5	wood	388	$5,914		wood, size> 500, sales>5000				
6	wood	527	$1,885		1				
7	metal	1000	$2,861						
8	aluminum	597	$9,029						
9	metal	374	$3,229						
10	wood	566	$8,241						
11	aluminum	896	$4,219						
12									
13									
14									

E6 ▾ f_x {=SUM((A2:A11="wood")*(B2:B11>500)*(C2:C11>5000))}

count values matching several c

FIGURE 11–10

USE THE SUM FUNCTION TO COUNT NUMBERS FROM *X* TO *Y*

For this tip, we want to count all sales from $2500 to less than $5000. As previously described, COUNTIF handles only one condition. Use an array formula with the SUM function to get the correct result here.

▶ **To Count Sales from $2500 to Less Than $5000:**

1. In cells A2:B11 list the daily sales and dates.
2. Select cell D2 and type the following array formula:
   =SUM((A2:A11>=2500)*(A2:A11<5000)).
3. Press **<Ctrl+Shift+Enter>**.
4. Select cells A2:B11.
5. From the **Home** tab, go to the **Styles** bar and click on **Conditional Formatting**.
6. Choose **New Rule**.
7. In the **Select a Rule Type** dialog select **Use a formula to determine which cells to format**.
8. In the **Edit** box type the following formula:
   =AND($A2>=2500,$A2<5000).
9. Click **Format,** select a color from the **Fill** tab, and click **OK**.
10. Click **OK**.

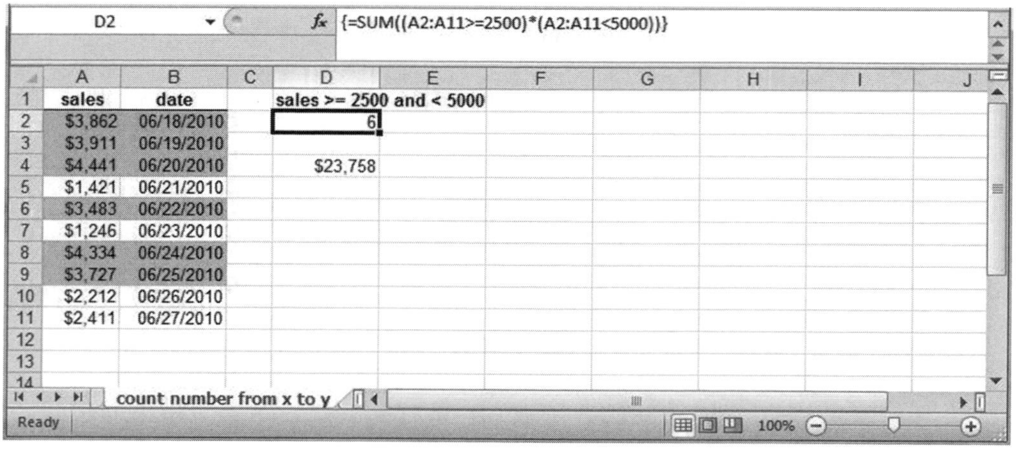

FIGURE 11–11

> **NOTE** *To sum all shaded sales, use the array formula*
> *=(SUM(IF(A2:A11>=2500,IF(A2:A11<5000,A2:A11))))*
> *and press <Ctrl+Shift+Enter>.*

USE THE SUM AND DATEVALUE FUNCTIONS TO COUNT TODAY'S SALES OF A SPECIFIC PRODUCT

The table in Figure 11–12 contains a number of products sold on different days. We want to count all sales of one specific product for just one day. To handle dates this way, use the DATEVALUE function, which converts a date represented by text to a serial number. Use an array formula to count all the sales of one product for the desired day.

▶ **To Count Today's Sales of a Specific Product:**

1. In cells A2:A15 list dates.
2. In cells B2:B15 enter product numbers.
3. In cell E1 enter **=TODAY()**.
4. Select cell E2 and type the following array formula:
   =SUM((DATEVALUE("11/25/10")=$A$2:$A$15)*
   ("K7896"=$B$2:$B$15)).
5. Press **<Ctrl+Shift+Enter>**.

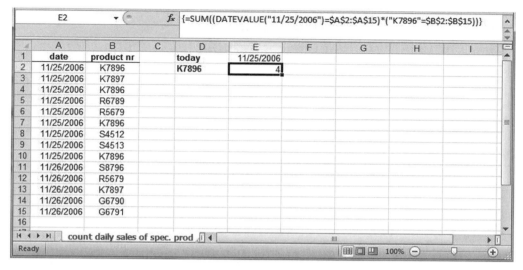

FIGURE 11–12

USE THE SUM FUNCTION TO COUNT TODAY'S SALES OF A SPECIFIC PRODUCT

This example is similar to the previous one, except the search criteria are variable. The array formula refers now to cells E1 and E2 and sums up all counted sales for one product on a specified date in cell E4.

▶ **To Count Sales of a Specific Product for One Day:**

1. In cells A2:A15 list dates.
2. In cells B2:B15 enter product numbers.
3. Select cell E1 and enter the desired date to be considered for counting.
4. Select cell E2 and select one product number.
5. Select cell E4 and type the following array formula:
   =SUM((E1=$A$2:$A$15)*(E2=$B$2:$B$15)).
6. Press **<Ctrl+Shift+Enter>.**

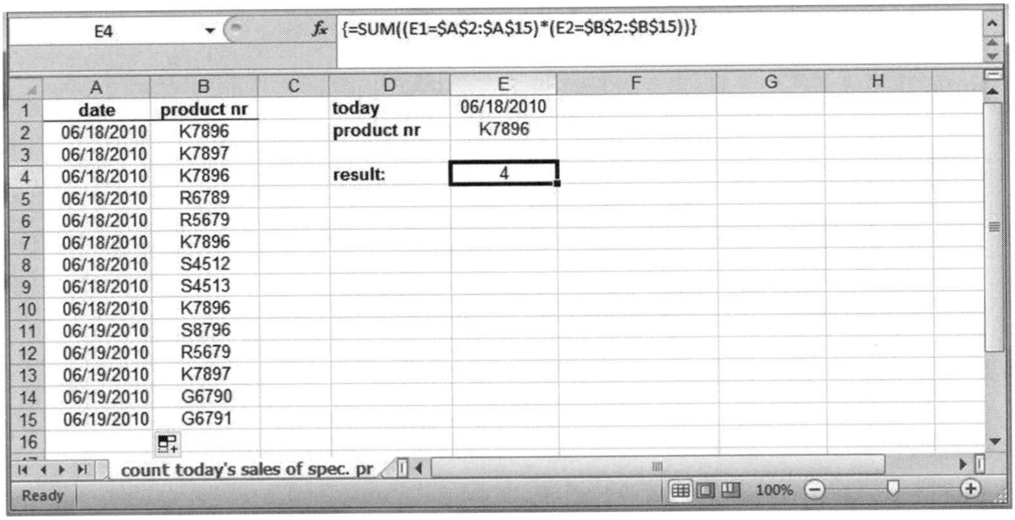

	E4	▾		*fx*	{=SUM((E1=$A$2:$A$15)*(E2=$B$2:$B$15))}		

	A	B	C	D	E	F	G	H
1	date	product nr		today	06/18/2010			
2	06/18/2010	K7896		product nr	K7896			
3	06/18/2010	K7897						
4	06/18/2010	K7896		result:	4			
5	06/18/2010	R6789						
6	06/18/2010	R5679						
7	06/18/2010	K7896						
8	06/18/2010	S4512						
9	06/18/2010	S4513						
10	06/18/2010	K7896						
11	06/19/2010	S8796						
12	06/19/2010	R5679						
13	06/19/2010	K7897						
14	06/19/2010	G6790						
15	06/19/2010	G6791						
16								

count today's sales of spec. pr

Ready   100%

FIGURE 11–13

USE THE SUM, OFFSET, MAX, IF, AND ROW FUNCTIONS TO SUM THE LAST ROW IN A DYNAMIC LIST

Figure 11–14 shows a list that is updated constantly. The task here is to determine the last row and sum its entries. Use the MAX and ROW functions to detect the last used row, then sum that row with help from the SUM and OFFSET functions. Combine all these functions in one array formula and assign the calculated result to cell H2.

▶ **To Sum the Last Row in a Dynamic List:**

1. In cells A2:A11 enter dates.
2. In cells B2:F11 list numbers for each team.
3. Select cell H2 and type the following array formula:
   =SUM(OFFSET(B1:F1,MAX(IF(B1:F100<>"",
   ROW(1:100)))-1,)).
4. Press **<Ctrl+Shift+Enter>**.

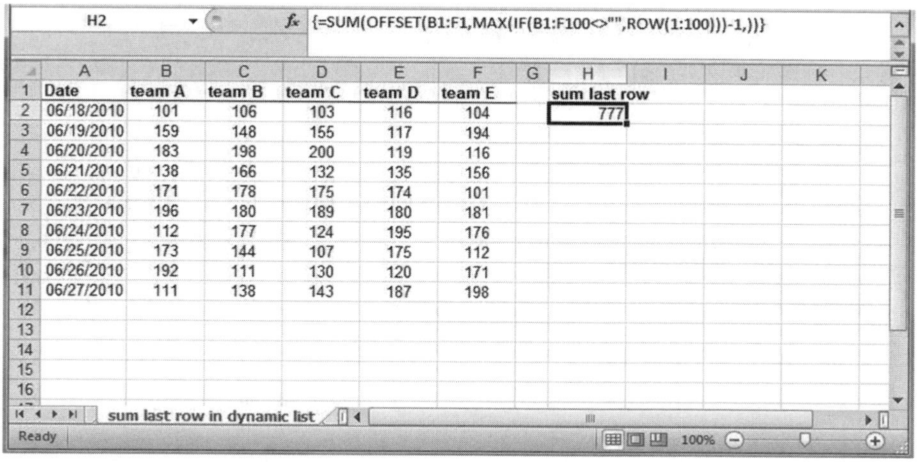

FIGURE 11–14

NOTE *Check the result by selecting cells B11:F11. With the right mouse button, click on the status bar at the bottom of the Excel window and select the Sum function.*

USE THE SUM, MID, AND COLUMN FUNCTIONS TO COUNT SPECIFIC CHARACTERS IN A RANGE

In this example, we want to count specific characters that appear in a range. Use the MID function to extract each character from the cells, then define the range to be searched using the COLUMN function. The SUM function counts the result. Combine all these functions into one array formula.

▶ **To Count Certain Characters in a Range:**

    1. In cells A2:A11 list IP addresses.

    2. Insert in any cells one or more characters like x or xxx.

    3. Select cell D2 and type the following array formula:
       =SUM((MID(A1:A11,COLUMN(1:1),3)="xxx")*1).

    4. Press **<Ctrl+Shift+Enter>**.

    5. Select cell D3 and type the following array formula:
       =SUM((MID(A1:A11,COLUMN(1:1),1)="x")*1).

    6. Press **<Ctrl+Shift+Enter>**.

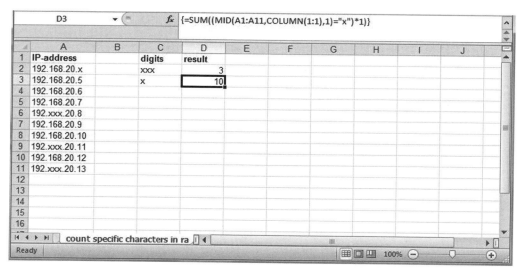

FIGURE 11–15

USE THE SUM, LEN, AND SUBSTITUTE FUNCTIONS TO COUNT THE OCCURRENCES OF A SPECIFIC WORD IN A RANGE

In this example, we want to count how many times a specific word appears in a range. Use the SUM, SUBSTITUTE, and LEN functions in one array formula to do this. Enter the criterion in cell C1 and let Excel display the result of counting in cell C2.

▶ **To Count the Occurrences of a Specific Word in a Range:**

1. In cells A2:A11 type any text but enter the word **test** at least once.
2. In cell C1 enter the word **test**.
3. Select cell C2 and type the following array formula: **=SUM((LEN(A1:A10)-LEN(SUBSTITUTE (A1:A10,C1,"")))/LEN(C1))**.
4. Press **<Ctrl+Shift+Enter>**.
5. Select cells A2:A10.
6. From the **Home** tab, go to the **Styles** bar and click on **Conditional Formatting**.
7. Choose **New Rule**.
8. In the **Select a Rule Type** dialog select **Use a formula to determine which cells to format**.

9. In the **Edit** box type the following formula: **=$C$1=A1.**
10. Click **Format,** select a color from the **Fill** tab, and click **OK.**
11. Click **OK.**

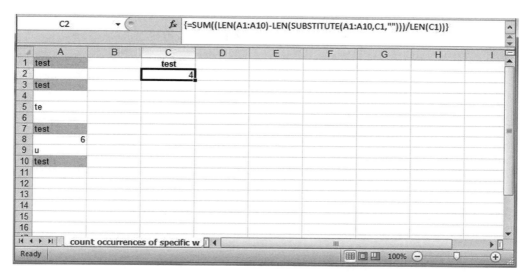

C2			*fx*	{=SUM((LEN(A1:A10)-LEN(SUBSTITUTE(A1:A10,C1,"")))/LEN(C1))}				
	A	B	C	D	E	F	G	H
1	test		test					
2			4					
3	test							
4								
5	te							
6								
7	test							
8		6						
9	u							
10	test							
11								
12								
13								
14								
15								
16								

count occurrences of specific w

Ready   100%

FIGURE 11–16

USE THE SUM AND LEN FUNCTIONS TO COUNT ALL DIGITS IN A RANGE

With what you have learned so far about array formulas, this task should be easy. Here we will count all digits in the range A1:A10 and display the result in cell C2. As you have probably already guessed, both the SUM and LEN functions can be combined in an array formula.

▶ **To Count All Digits in a Range:**

1. In cells A2:A10 type any text.
2. Select cell C2 and type the following array formula:
   =SUM(LEN(A1:A10)).
3. Press **<Ctrl+Shift+Enter>.**

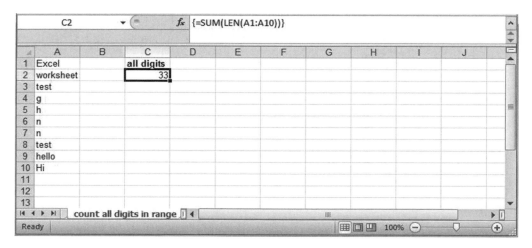

FIGURE 11–17

USE THE MAX, INDIRECT, AND COUNT FUNCTIONS TO DETERMINE THE LARGEST GAIN/LOSS OF SHARES

Let's say you record the daily share prices of a stock in an Excel worksheet. In this example, you want to monitor your stock to determine the largest gain and loss in dollars.

▶ **To Determine the Largest Gain and Loss:**

1. In cells A2:A11 enter the daily value of a stock.
2. In cells B2:B11 list dates.
3. Select cell D2 and type the array formula
   **=MAX(A3:INDIRECT("A"&COUNT(A:A))-
   A2:INDIRECT("A"& COUNT(A:A)-1))** to find the largest gain.
4. Press **<Ctrl+Shift+Enter>**.
5. Select cell E2 and type the array formula
   **=MIN(A3:INDIRECT("A"&COUNT(A:A))-
   A2:INDIRECT("A"& COUNT(A:A)-1))** to find the greatest loss.
6. Press **<Ctrl+Shift+Enter>**.

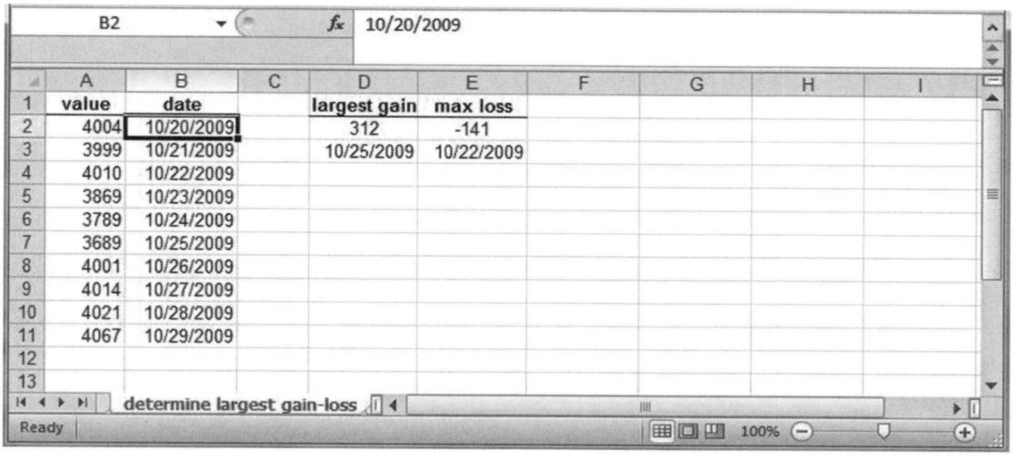

FIGURE 11–18

NOTE *To determine the dates of the largest gain and loss, use*
=INDEX(B:B,MATCH(D2,A$3:A$1002-A$2:A$1001,0)+1) *in cell D3 and*
=INDEX(B:B,MATCH(E2,A$3:A$1002-A$2:
A$1001,0)+1) *in cell E3.*

USE THE SUM AND COUNTIF FUNCTIONS TO COUNT UNIQUE RECORDS IN A LIST

Excel offers a feature to extract unique values from a list. This feature usually is used by filtering the list through the Data menu option Filter | Advanced Filter. But how do you count unique records in a list without filtering them? Use the SUM and COUNTIF functions together in an array formula.

▶ **To Count Unique Records in a List:**

1. In cells A2:A11 list numbers, repeating some.
2. Select cell C2 and type the following array formula:
    =SUM(1/COUNTIF($A$2:$A11,$A$2:$A11)).
3. Press **<Ctrl+Shift+Enter>**.

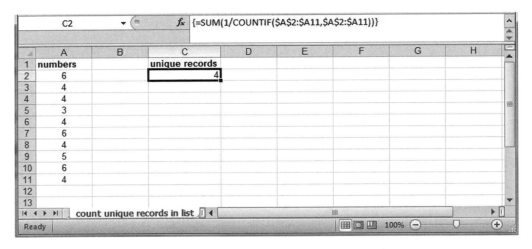

FIGURE 11–19

USE THE AVERAGE AND LARGE FUNCTIONS TO CALCULATE THE AVERAGE OF THE *X* LARGEST NUMBERS

With this tip you will learn how to calculate the average of the largest five numbers in a list. Combine the AVERAGE and LARGE functions in one array formula.

▶ **To Calculate the Average of the Five Largest Numbers:**

1. In cells A2:A11 list some numbers.
2. Select cell C2 and type the following array formula:
   =AVERAGE(LARGE(A:A,{1,2,3,4,5})).
3. Press **<Enter>**.

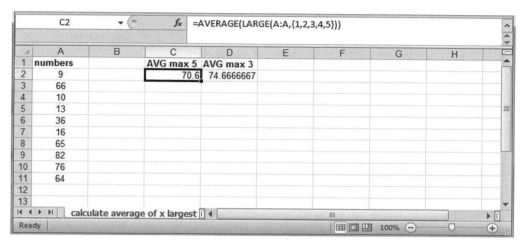

FIGURE 11–20

<table>
<tr><td>**NOTE**</td><td>*To calculate the average of the three largest numbers, enter the following formula in cell D2:* **=AVERAGE(LARGE(A:A,{1,2,3})).**</td></tr>
</table>

USE THE TRANSPOSE AND OR FUNCTIONS TO DETERMINE DUPLICATE NUMBERS IN A LIST

Imagine you have a long list of numbers, and your task is to identify all numbers that occur more than once. All of the values need to be checked to see if they appear more than once by using the TRANSPOSE and OR functions. Then all duplicated numbers have to be shaded with the help of the COUNTIF function, which is connected to conditional formatting.

▶ **To Determine Duplicate Numbers in a List:**

1. In columns A and B list numbers, some of which are repeated at least once.
2. Select cell D2 and type the following array formula:
   =OR(TRANSPOSE(A2:A11)=B2:B11).
3. Press **<Ctrl+Shift+Enter>**.
4. Select cells A2:B11.
5. From the **Home** tab, go to the **Styles** bar and click on **Conditional Formatting**.

6. Choose **New Rule**.
7. In the **Select a Rule Type** dialog select **Use a formula to determine which cells to format**.
8. In the **Edit** box type the following formula:
   =COUNTIF($A$2:$B$11,A2)>1.
9. Click **Format,** select a color from the **Fill** tab, and click **OK**.
10. Click **OK**.

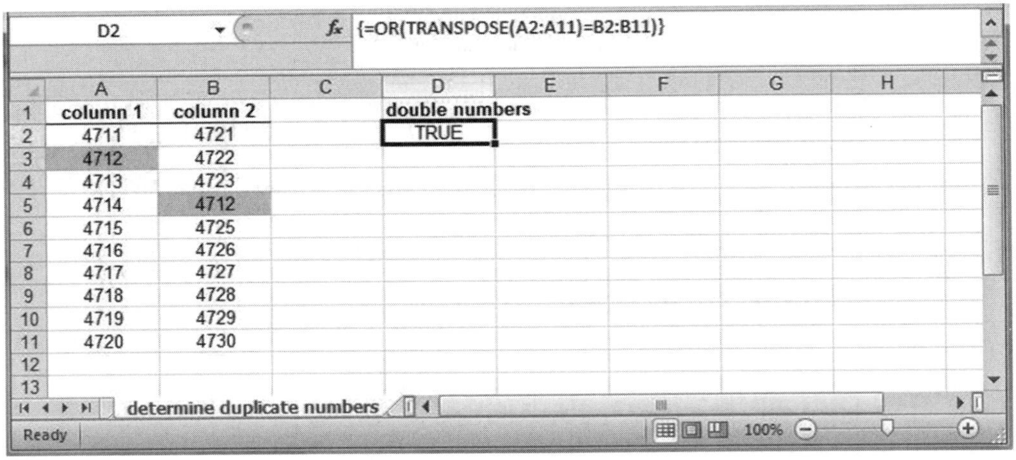

FIGURE 11–21

USE THE MID, MATCH, AND ROW FUNCTIONS TO EXTRACT NUMERIC VALUES FROM TEXT

This tip can help you extract numeric digits from text. Use the MID, MATCH, and ROW functions and combine them in an array formula.

▶ **To Extract Numeric Values from Text:**

1. In cells A2:A11 enter numbers with leading characters like YE2004 or FGS456.
2. Select cells B2:B11 and type the following array formula:
   =1*MID(A2,MATCH(FALSE,ISERROR (1*MID(A2,ROW($1:$10),1)),0),255).
3. Press **<Ctrl+Shift+Enter>**.

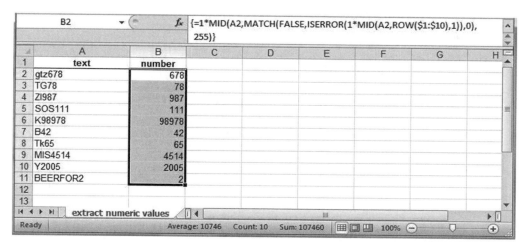

FIGURE 11–22

USE THE MAX AND COUNTIF FUNCTIONS TO DETERMINE WHETHER ALL NUMBERS ARE UNIQUE

This tip lets you check whether or not all listed numbers are unique. In this example, you use the MAX and COUNTIF functions in combination with an array formula.

▶ **To Determine Whether All Listed Numbers are Unique:**

1. In column A list some numbers.
2. Select cell C2 and type the following array formula:
   =MAX(COUNTIF(A2:A11,A2:A11))=1.
3. Press **<Ctrl+Shift+Enter>**.
4. Select cells A2:A11.
5. From the **Home** tab, go to the **Styles** bar and click on **Conditional Formatting**.
6. Choose **New Rule**.
7. In the **Select a Rule Type** dialog select **Use a formula to determine which cells to format**.
8. In the **Edit** box type the following formula:
   =COUNTIF($A$2:$A$11,A2)>1.
9. Click **Format,** select a color from the **Fill** tab, and click **OK**.
10. Click **OK**.

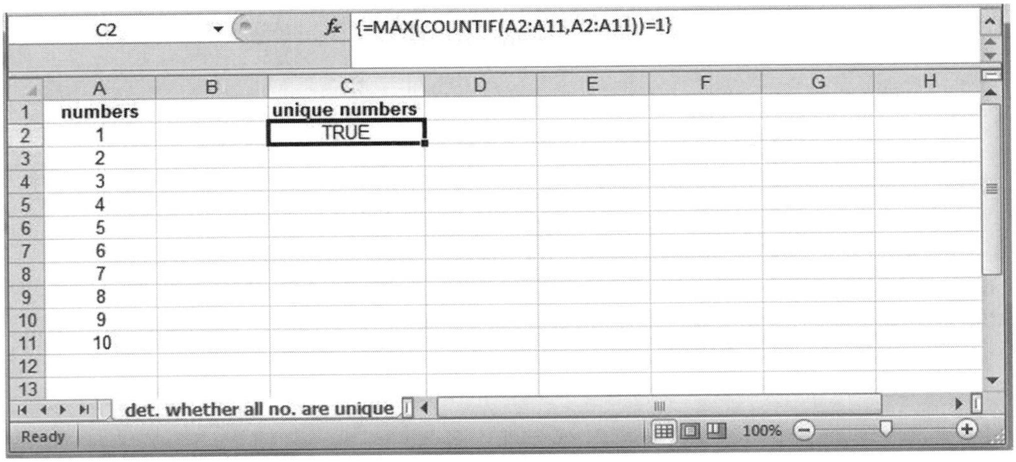

	C2			f_x	{=MAX(COUNTIF(A2:A11,A2:A11))=1}			
	A	B	C	D	E	F	G	H
1	numbers		unique numbers					
2	1		TRUE					
3	2							
4	3							
5	4							
6	5							
7	6							
8	7							
9	8							
10	9							
11	10							
12								
13								

det. whether all no. are unique

Ready   100%

FIGURE 11–23

NOTE *If any numbers are listed more than once, they will be shaded and cell C2 will display FALSE.*

USE THE TRANSPOSE FUNCTION TO COPY A RANGE FROM VERTICAL TO HORIZONTAL OR VICE VERSA

Sometimes it is very useful to copy a vertical range of cells to a horizontal range or vice versa. Just copy a range, select a cell outside the range, and click Paste Special on the Edit menu. Checkmark the Transpose option and click OK. The copied range will be shifted by its vertical or horizontal orientation. To use the same functionality but keep the original references to the copied range, use the TRANSPOSE function in an array formula. Follow this tip to transpose the following table below the range A1:G3.

▶ **To Transpose a Range and Keep Original Cell References:**

1. In a worksheet, copy the data in cells A1:G3, as shown in Figure 11–24.
2. Select cells B7:B12 and type the following array formula:
   =TRANSPOSE(B1:G1).
3. Press **<Ctrl+Shift+Enter>**.
4. Select cells C6:C12 and type the following array formula:
   =TRANSPOSE(A2:G2).

5. Press **<Ctrl+Shift+Enter>**.
6. Select cells D6:D12 and type the following array formula:
   =TRANSPOSE(A3:G3).
7. Press **<Ctrl+Shift+Enter>**.

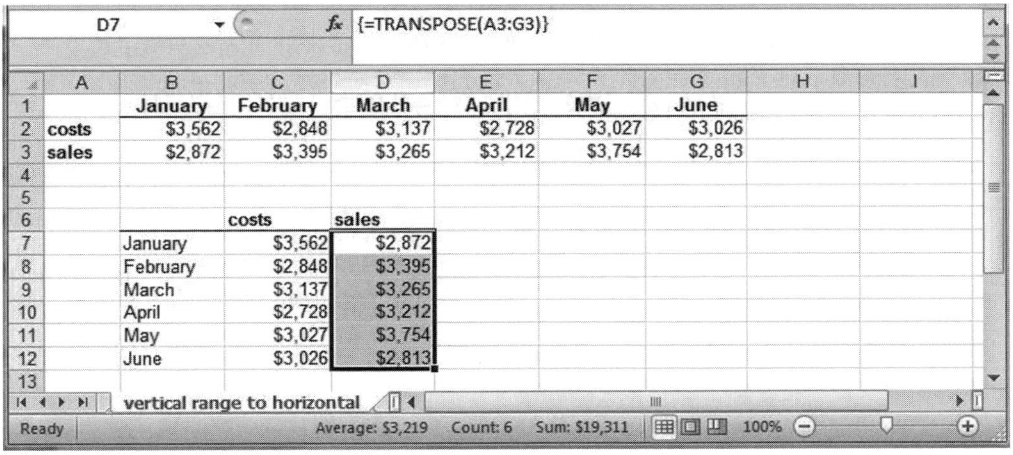

	D7			fx	{=TRANSPOSE(A3:G3)}				

	A	B	C	D	E	F	G	H	I
1		January	February	March	April	May	June		
2	costs	$3,562	$2,848	$3,137	$2,728	$3,027	$3,026		
3	sales	$2,872	$3,395	$3,265	$3,212	$3,754	$2,813		
4									
5									
6			costs	sales					
7		January	$3,562	$2,872					
8		February	$2,848	$3,395					
9		March	$3,137	$3,265					
10		April	$2,728	$3,212					
11		May	$3,027	$3,754					
12		June	$3,026	$2,813					
13									

vertical range to horizontal

Ready   Average: $3,219   Count: 6   Sum: $19,311   100%

FIGURE 11–24

NOTE   *The order of an array will always be the same; only the vertical and horizontal orientation is shifted.*

USE THE FREQUENCY FUNCTION TO CALCULATE THE NUMBER OF SOLD PRODUCTS FOR EACH GROUP

The table in Figure 11–25 lists the number of products sold daily. To do some market analysis and check consumer behavior, group the list and count the different consumption patterns. Use the FREQUENCY function entered as an array formula to count the frequency by different groups.

▶ **To Calculate Frequency and Check Purchasing Habits:**

1. In column A, enter dates in ascending order.
2. In column B, list the number of products sold daily.

3. Define the different groups in cells D2:D5.
4. Select cells E2:E6 and type the following array formula:
   =FREQUENCY(B2:B11,$D$2:$D$11).
5. Press **<Ctrl+Shift+Enter>**.

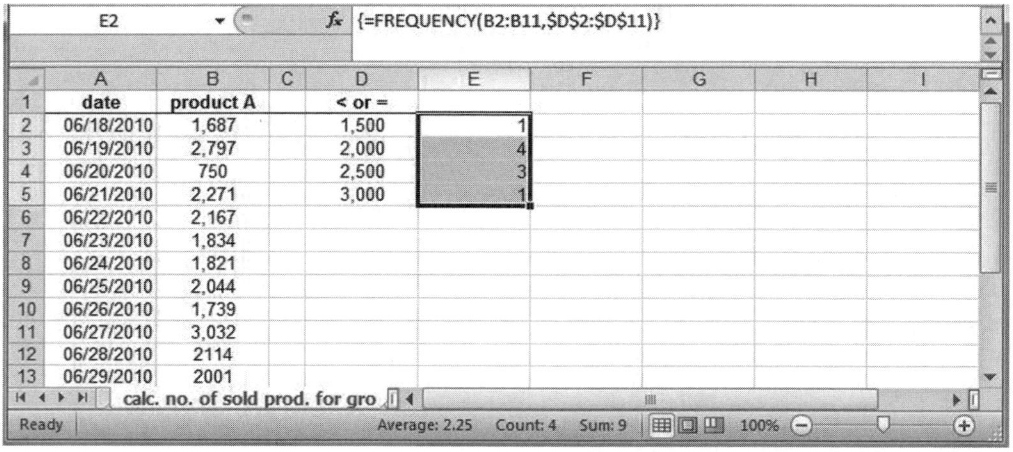

	E2			f_x	{=FREQUENCY(B2:B11,$D$2:$D$11)}				
	A	B	C	D	E	F	G	H	I
1	date	product A		< or =					
2	06/18/2010	1,687		1,500	1				
3	06/19/2010	2,797		2,000	4				
4	06/20/2010	750		2,500	3				
5	06/21/2010	2,271		3,000	1				
6	06/22/2010	2,167							
7	06/23/2010	1,834							
8	06/24/2010	1,821							
9	06/25/2010	2,044							
10	06/26/2010	1,739							
11	06/27/2010	3,032							
12	06/28/2010	2114							
13	06/29/2010	2001							

calc. no. of sold prod. for gro

Ready   Average: 2.25   Count: 4   Sum: 9   100%

FIGURE 11–25

NOTE   *FREQUENCY ignores blank cells and text.*

Chapter 12 SPECIAL SOLUTIONS WITH FORMULAS

USE THE COUNTIF **FUNCTION TO PREVENT DUPLICATE INPUT THROUGH VALIDATION**

This tip shows an easy way to prevent duplicate input in the range A1:A100. Use the Validation option and enter a custom formula to get the desired functionality for the specified range in a worksheet.

▶ **To Prevent Duplicate Input:**

1. Select cells A1:A100.
2. On the **Data** tab, in the **Data Tools** group, click **Data Validation**.
3. In the **Data Validation** dialog box, click the **Settings** tab, and select **Custom** in the **Allow** drop-down box.
4. In the **Formula** box, type the formula **=COUNTIF($A:$A,A1)=1**.
5. Select the **Error Alert** tab.
6. Enter a custom error message.
7. Click **OK**.

When a user attempts to enter duplicate data, an error message will appear.

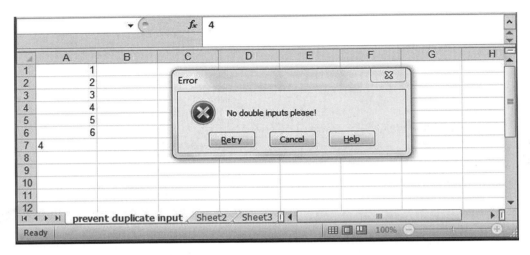

FIGURE 12–1

> **NOTE** *To remove data validation, select the desired range, click Validation on the Data menu, select the Settings tab, and then click Clear All.*

USE THE EXACT FUNCTION TO ALLOW ONLY UPPERCASE CHARACTERS

This example shows how to allow only uppercase characters in a specified range. Use the data validation option in combination with a custom formula.

▶ **To Allow only Uppercase Characters:**

1. Select cells A1:A100.
2. On the **Data** tab, in the **Data Tools** group, click **Data Validation**.
3. In the **Data Validation** dialog box, click the **Settings** tab, and select **Custom** in the **Allow** drop-down box.
4. In the **Formula** box, type the formula **=EXACT(A1,UPPER(A1))**.
5. Select the **Error Alert** tab.
6. Enter a custom error message.
7. Click **OK**.

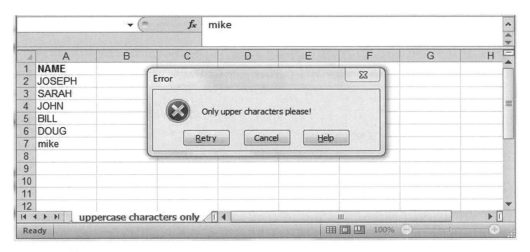

FIGURE 12–2

NOTE *If you want to allow only lowercase characters, use the formula =EXACT(A1,LOWER(A1)).*

USE VALIDATION TO ALLOW DATA INPUT BY A SPECIFIC CRITERION

A range is defined to allow data input as long as it is not locked through a criterion specified in cell D1. Allow data input only if the value 1 is entered in cell D1. Again, we use data validation in combination with a custom-defined formula to get the solution for this exercise.

▶ **To Allow Data Input by One Specified Criteria:**

1. Enter data in cells A1:A10 as shown in Figure 12–3, and select cells A1:A10.
2. On the **Data** tab, in the **Data Tools** group, click **Data Validation**.
3. In the **Data Validation** dialog box, click the **Settings** tab, and select **Custom** in the **Allow** drop-down box.
4. Type the formula **=$D$1=1**.
5. Select the **Error Alert** tab.
6. Enter a custom error message.
7. Click **OK**.

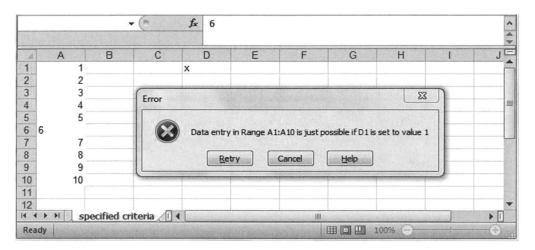

FIGURE 12–3

NOTE *This formula only allows data to be changed if cell D1 contains the value 1.*

USE CONTROLS WITH FORMULAS

The table shown in Figure 12–4 contains an address list with company names and a contact person for each company. Imagine that we can use a drop-down box to select a company, and all corresponding data about the company automatically displays in specified cells. Just open a new worksheet and copy the table below to learn more about using drop-down boxes in combination with functions.

	A	B	C	D	E	F	G
1	company	first name	last name	country			
2	Smith Enterprise	Doug	Morgan	USA			
3	Beach club	Walter	Sanders	New Zealand			
4	Waters	Ben	King	Australia			
5	Sugar and Salt	Leon	Becker	Canada			
6							
7							

FIGURE 12–4

▶ **To Assign a Name to the Range of Data:**

1. Select cells A2:D5 (as shown in figure 12–4).
2. Click the Name box at the left end of the formula bar (which shows "A2") and enter **data**. This name represents all the data inside the range A2:D5.
3. Press **<Enter>**.
4. Select the cells A2:A5.
5. Assign a name to this header row by entering **company** in the Name box.
6. Press **<Enter>.**

▶ **To Display Addresses by Selecting them from a Drop-Down Box:**

1. Insert a new worksheet in the same Excel file and display the **Developer** toolbar by selecting the **File** tab. Click **Options** and choose **Customize ribbon**.
2. In the **Main tabs** tick **Developer.** A new tab will appear in the tab ribbon.
3. In this new tab go to the **Controls** box and click **Insert**.
4. From **Form Controls** choose **Combo Box**.
5. Move the mouse cursor to the desired location inside the worksheet. Click and drag the combo box to the desired size.
6. Click with the right mouse button on the combo box and select **Format Control**.
7. Select the **Control** tab and type **company** in the **Input range** field.
8. In the **Cell link** field, enter **E2**.
9. Check the **3D shading** box.
10. Press **OK**.
11. Select cell B6 and type the formula **=INDEX(data,$E$2,2)** to display the first name.
12. Select cell C6 and type the formula **=INDEX(data,$E$2,3)** to display the last name.
13. Select cell B7 and type the formula **=INDEX(data,$E$2,4)** to display the country.

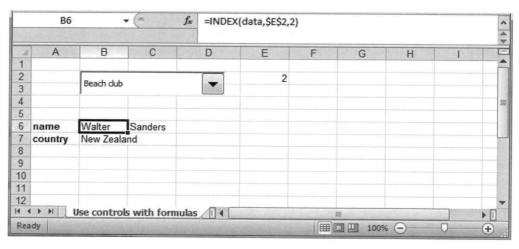

FIGURE 12–5

NOTE *If the index in cell E2 is not visible, move the combo box so it doesn't cover this cell or change the displayed font style color from Automatic (black) to white.*

USE GOAL SEEK AS A POWERFUL ANALYSIS TOOL

Goal Seek is a standard function found on the Tools menu that takes several criteria into consideration and helps find the correct value of a calculation. This example shows the quality control of a production run. The monitoring process sorts out products that don't meet the expected quality standards. The first time we check the quality, we find that 5% of the production does not meet quality standards, and the second time, we find that 2% of the production fails to meet standards. How many more products have to be produced to reach the required amount of 1030?

▶ **Use Goal Seek to Determine the Total Amount of Production Needed:**

1. In cell C3 enter **1030** as the production goal.
2. In cell C4 type the formula **=C3*0.05**.
3. In cell C5 enter the formula **=C3-C4** to calculate how many products are needed to reach the production goal.

4. In cell C6 type the formula **=C5*0.02**.
5. Calculate the final sum in cell C7 with the formula **=C5-C6**.

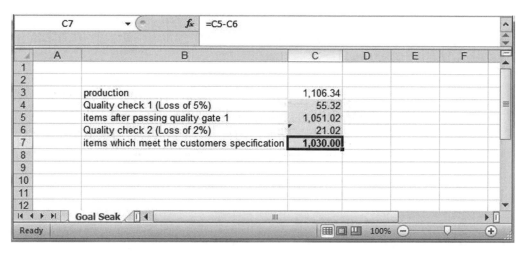

	C4		f_x	=C3*0.05			
	A	B		C	D	E	F
1							
2							
3		production		1,030.00			
4		Quality check 1 (Loss of 5%)		51.50			
5		items after passing quality gate 1		978.50			
6		Quality check 2 (Loss of 2%)		19.57			
7		items which meet the customers specification		958.93			
8							

FIGURE 12–6

6. On the **Data** tab, in the **Data Tools** group, click **What-If Analysis**, and then click **Goal Seek**.
7. In the **Set cell** box, enter **C7**, enter **1030** in the **To value** box, and enter **C3** in the **By changing cell** box.
8. Press **OK**.

	C7		f_x	=C5-C6			
	A	B		C	D	E	F
1							
2							
3		production		1,106.34			
4		Quality check 1 (Loss of 5%)		55.32			
5		items after passing quality gate 1		1,051.02			
6		Quality check 2 (Loss of 2%)		21.02			
7		items which meet the customers specification		1,030.00			
8							
9							
10							
11							
12							

Goal Seak

Ready   100%

FIGURE 12–7

USE A CUSTOM FUNCTION TO SHADE ALL CELLS CONTAINING FORMULAS

The remaining tips in this chapter describe the usage of Visual Basic Application (VBA) macros to enhance and optimize Excel worksheets. For the first example, we'll write a macro that shades all cells containing formulas.

▶ **To Shade All Cells with Formulas:**

1. Press **<Alt+F11>** to open the Visual Basic Editor.
2. On the **Insert** menu, click **Module**.
3. Type the following macro:

```
Sub ColorThem()
Selection.SpecialCells (xlCellTypeFormulas).Select
    With Selection.Interior
        .ColorIndex = 44
        .Pattern = xlSolid
    End With
End Sub
```

4. From the Excel **Tools** menu, select **Macro | Macros**.
5. Select the **ColorThem** macro and click **Run**.

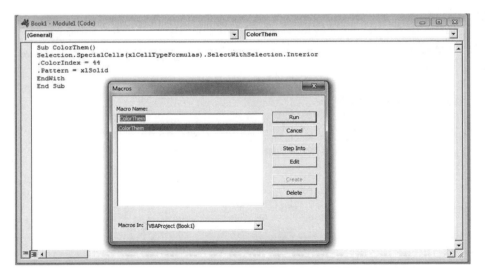

FIGURE 12–8

USE A CUSTOM FUNCTION TO CHANGE ALL CELLS WITH FORMULAS TO VALUES

This macro changes all cells with formulas to cells containing values. Note that all formulas will be deleted. This is a common need when copying tables where we need just the results of a calculation and no formulas or individual formatting.

▶ **To Change all Formulas into Values:**

1. Press **<Alt+F11>**.
2. On the **Insert** menu, click **Module**.
3. Type the following macro:

```
Sub ChangeToValue()
Dim rng As Range

With ActiveSheet
 For Each rng In .UsedRange
  rng.Value = rng.Value
Next rng
End With
End Sub
```

NOTE *To start the macro from the Visual Basic Editor, click anywhere within the macro code and press <F5>.*

USE A CUSTOM FUNCTION TO DOCUMENT AND DISPLAY ALL CELLS CONTAINING FORMULAS

This powerful macro will document in an Immediate window all cells containing formulas. When executed, each cell that contains a formula is listed by its cell address, along with the formula and the current value.

▶ **To Determine and Document All Formulas in the Current Worksheet:**

1. Press **<Alt+F11>**.
2. On the **Insert** menu, click **Module**.

3. Type the following macro:

```
Sub DocFormulasWks()
Dim rng As Range

With ActiveSheet
 For Each rng In .UsedRange
  If rng.HasFormula = True Then
    Debug.Print "Addr.:" & rng.Address
    Debug.Print "Form.:" & rng.Formula
    Debug.Print "Value:" & rng.Value
  End If
Next rng
End With
End Sub
```

4. With the cursor in the macro start it by pressing F5.
5. Click **View** and choose **Immediate window**.

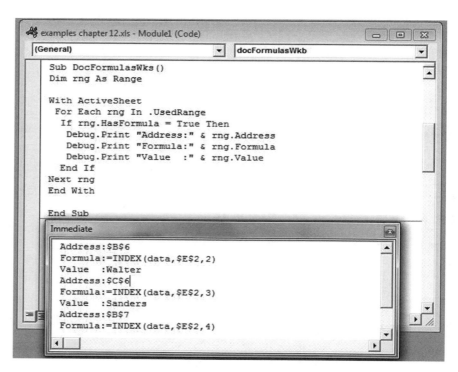

FIGURE 12–9

NOTE *If you want to document all formulas in the entire workbook, use the following macro:*

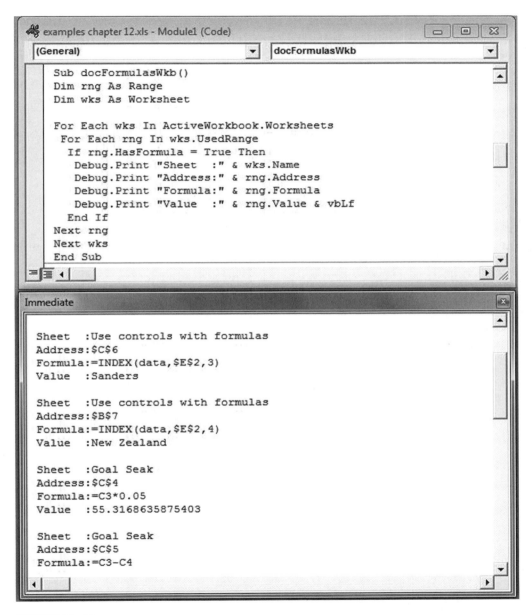

```
Sub docFormulasWkb()
Dim rng As Range
Dim wks As Worksheet

For Each wks In ActiveWorkbook.Worksheets
  For Each rng In wks.UsedRange
   If rng.HasFormula = True Then
    Debug.Print "Sheet   :" & wks.Name
    Debug.Print "Address:" & rng.Address
    Debug.Print "Formula:" & rng.Formula
    Debug.Print "Value   :" & rng.Value & vbLf
   End If
Next rng
Next wks
End Sub
```

```
Sheet   :Use controls with formulas
Address:$C$6
Formula:=INDEX(data,$E$2,3)
Value   :Sanders

Sheet   :Use controls with formulas
Address:$B$7
Formula:=INDEX(data,$E$2,4)
Value   :New Zealand

Sheet   :Goal Seak
Address:$C$4
Formula:=C3*0.05
Value   :55.3168635875403

Sheet   :Goal Seak
Address:$C$5
Formula:=C3-C4
```

FIGURE 12–10

```
Sub docFormulasWkb()
Dim rng As Range
Dim wks As Worksheet

For Each wks In ActiveWorkbook.Worksheets
 For Each rng In wks.UsedRange
  If rng.HasFormula = True Then
   Debug.Print "Sheet:" & wks.Name
   Debug.Print "Address:"&rng.Address
   Debug.Print "Formula:"&rng.Formula
   Debug.Print "Value:" & rng.Value
  End If
 Next rng
Next wks
End Sub
```

USE A CUSTOM FUNCTION TO DELETE EXTERNAL LINKS IN A WORKSHEET

To distinguish between cells containing formulas and cells containing external links, all cells need to be checked. If a cell contains a "[" or "]", it is a cell with a hyperlink to another workbook.

▶ **To Delete all External Links in a Worksheet:**

1. Press **<Alt+F11>**.
2. In the **Insert** menu, click **Module**.
3. Type the following macro:

```
Sub DeleteExLinks()
Dim rng As Range

With ActiveSheet
 For Each rng In .UsedRange
   If InStr(rng.Formula, "[") > 0 Then
        rng.Value = rng.Value
   End If
Next rng
End With
End Sub
```

NOTE *Starting this macro will delete all external links and only values will be displayed.*

USE A CUSTOM FUNCTION TO DELETE EXTERNAL LINKS IN A WORKBOOK

Like the previous macro, this macro will delete all external links; however, they will be deleted in the entire workbook, not just the current worksheet. This macro will look up all existing worksheets of a workbook and delete the external links while changing them to values.

▶ **To Delete all External Links in a Workbook:**

1. Press **<Alt+F11>**.
2. In the **Insert** menu, click **Module**.
3. Type the following macro:

```
Sub DeleteExLinksWkb()
Dim rng As Range
Dim wks As Worksheet

For Each wks In ActiveWorkbook.Worksheets
 For Each rng In wks.UsedRange
   If InStr(rng.Formula, "[") > 0  Then
        rng.Value = rng.Value
   End If
 Next rng
Next wks
End Sub
```

USE A CUSTOM FUNCTION TO ENTER ALL FORMULAS INTO AN ADDITIONAL WORKSHEET

This example inserts a new worksheet with the name *Documentation*. Once started, all formulas inside the active workbook will be documented.

▶ **To Find all Formulas and Enter them into a Worksheet:**

1. Press **<Alt+F11>**.
2. In the **Insert** menu, click **Module**.

3. Type the following macro:

```
Sub NewSheetWithFormulas()
Dim rng As Range
Dim wks As Worksheet
Dim i As Integer

With Sheets("Documentation")
i = 1
For Each wks In _
  ActiveWorkbook.Worksheets

 For Each rng In wks.UsedRange
  If rng.HasFormula = True Then
   .Cells(i, 1).Value = wks.Name
   .Cells(i, 2).Value = rng.Address
   .Cells(i, 3).Value = " " & rng.Formula
   .Cells(i, 4).Value = rng.Value
     i = i+1
  End If
 Next rng
Next wks
End With
End Sub
```

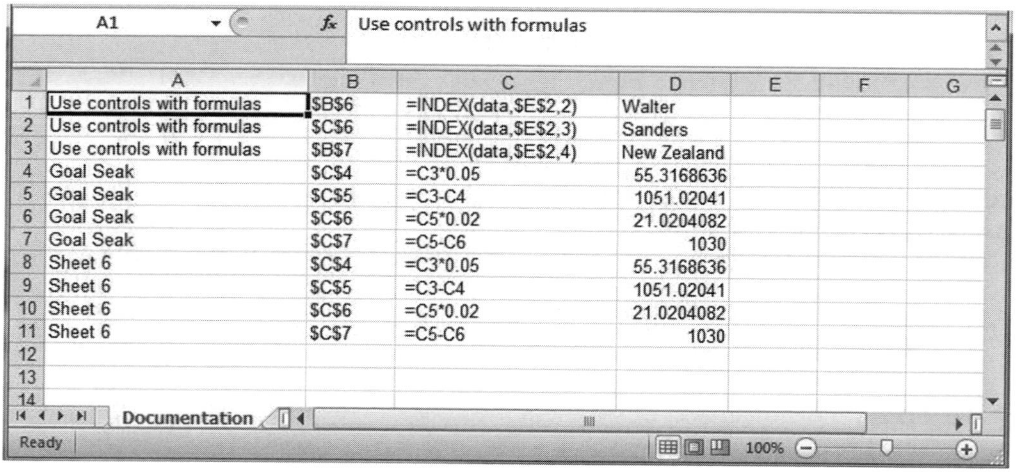

	A	B	C	D	E	F	G
	A1	▼	*fx*	Use controls with formulas			
1	Use controls with formulas	$B$6	=INDEX(data,$E$2,2)	Walter			
2	Use controls with formulas	$C$6	=INDEX(data,$E$2,3)	Sanders			
3	Use controls with formulas	$B$7	=INDEX(data,$E$2,4)	New Zealand			
4	Goal Seak	$C$4	=C3*0.05	55.3168636			
5	Goal Seak	$C$5	=C3-C4	1051.02041			
6	Goal Seak	$C$6	=C5*0.02	21.0204082			
7	Goal Seak	$C$7	=C5-C6	1030			
8	Sheet 6	$C$4	=C3*0.05	55.3168636			
9	Sheet 6	$C$5	=C3-C4	1051.02041			
10	Sheet 6	$C$6	=C5*0.02	21.0204082			
11	Sheet 6	$C$7	=C5-C6	1030			
12							
13							
14							

Documentation

Ready   100%

FIGURE 12–11

13 USER-DEFINED FUNCTIONS

USE A USER-DEFINED FUNCTION TO COPY THE NAME OF A WORKSHEET INTO A CELL

To copy the name of a worksheet into a cell, you have to create a user-defined function.

▶ **To Copy the Name of a Worksheet into a Cell:**

1. Press **<Alt+F11>** to open the Visual Basic Editor.
2. From the **Insert** menu, click **Module**.
3. Type the following function:

```
Function TabName()
   TabName = ActiveSheet.Name
End Function
```

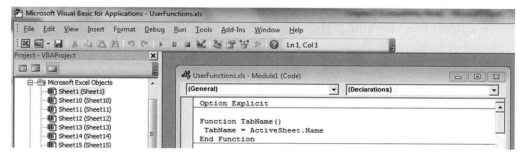

FIGURE 13–1

4. Close the VBA Editor by pressing **\<Alt+Q\>**, and in cell A1 type the following function: **=TabName()**.
5. Press **\<Enter\>**.

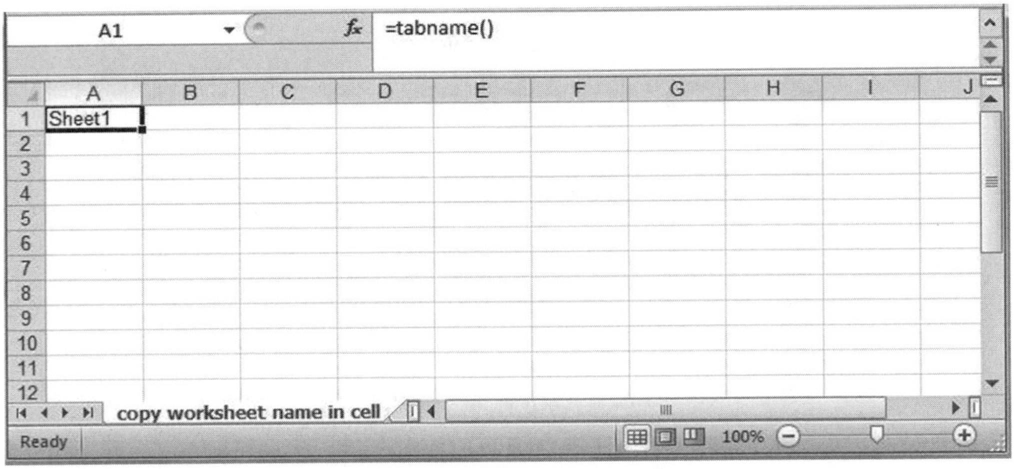

FIGURE 13–2

USE A USER-DEFINED FUNCTION TO COPY THE NAME OF A WORKBOOK INTO A CELL

To determine the name of a workbook, including the path and current worksheet name, you can type the function **=CELL("Filename")** in cell A2. Another way to determine the name is to write a user-defined function, as shown here.

▶ **To Display the Workbook Name in a Cell:**

1. Press **\<Alt+F11\>** to open the Visual Basic Editor.
2. From the **Insert** menu, click **Module**.
3. Type the following function:

```
Function WkbName()
   WkbName = ActiveWorkbook.Name
End Function
```

4. Close the VBA Editor by pressing **<Alt+Q>** and in cell A3 type the following function: **=WkbName()**.
5. Press **<Enter>**.

USE A USER-DEFINED FUNCTION TO GET THE PATH OF A WORKBOOK

Continue with the same worksheet for this task. Here, we want to determine the path of the active workbook.

▶ **To Find the Path of a Workbook:**

1. Press **<Alt+F11>** to open the Visual Basic Editor.
2. From the **Insert** menu, click **Module**.
3. Type the following function:

```
Function WkbPath()
   WkbPath = ActiveWorkbook.Path
End Function
```

4. Close the VBA Editor by pressing **<Alt+Q>** and in cell A4 type the following function: **=WkbPath()**.
5. Press **<Enter>**.

USE A USER-DEFINED FUNCTION TO GET THE FULL NAME OF A WORKBOOK

We have learned how to determine the filename and path for a workbook. To get both at the same time, we could combine the two text strings. Another, more convenient way, however, is to use a user-defined function that delivers both the name and path of the active workbook.

▶ **To Determine the Full Filename and Path of the Workbook:**

1. Press **<Alt+F11>** to open the Visual Basic Editor.
2. From the **Insert** menu, click **Module**.

3. Type the following function:

```
Function WkbFull()
  WkbFull = ActiveWorkbook.FullName
End Function
```

4. Close the VBA Editor by pressing **<Alt+Q>**, and in cell A5 type the following function: **=WkbFull()**.
5. Press **<Enter>**.

USE A USER-DEFINED FUNCTION TO DETERMINE THE CURRENT USER OF WINDOWS OR EXCEL

This tip explains how to determine the current user of Windows and/or Excel. Once again, you will write a user-defined function. In this case, the function will return the name of the current user.

▶ **To Get the Current Windows User:**

1. Press **<Alt+F11>** to open up the Visual Basic Editor.
2. From the **Insert** menu, click **Module**.
3. Type the following function:

```
Function User()
  User = Environ("Username")
End Function
```

4. Close the VBA Editor and type the following formula in any cell: **=User()**.
5. Press **<Enter>**.

▶ **To Get the Current Excel User:**

1. Press **<Alt+F11>** to open up the Visual Basic Editor.
2. From the **Insert** menu, click **Module**.
3. Type the following function:

```
Function ExcelUser()
  ExcelUser = Application.UserName
End Function
```

4. Return to the worksheet and type the following formula in any cell:
   =ExcelUser().
5. Press **<Enter>**.

To get the name of the current Excel user, you can also use Tools | Options | General/username.

USE A USER-DEFINED FUNCTION TO DISPLAY FORMULAS OF A SPECIFIC CELL

Using this tip, you can look up the formula text of any cell. It is similar to the keyboard shortcut <Ctrl+#>. Generate a worksheet containing data and formulas, and then enter the user-defined function shown below.

▶ **To Make Formulas Visible:**

1. Press **<Alt+F11>** to open up the Visual Basic Editor.
2. From the **Insert** menu, click **Module**.
3. Type the following function:

```
Function FormT(rng As Range)
  FormT = " " & rng.Formula
End Function
```

4. Return to the worksheet and type the following formula in any cell:
   =FormT(A5).
5. Press **<Enter>**.

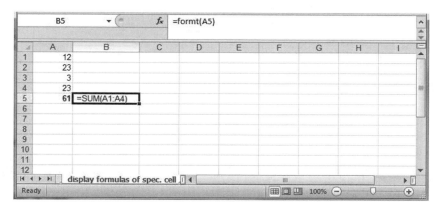

FIGURE 13–3

USE A USER-DEFINED FUNCTION TO CHECK WHETHER A CELL CONTAINS A FORMULA

The function described here checks whether or not a cell contains a formula. Open a new worksheet, list some values in the range A1:A4, and sum them up in cell A5. Generate a new user-defined function and use it for the range B1:B5.

▶ **To Check Whether a Cell Contains a Formula:**

1. Press **<Alt+F11>** to open the Visual Basic Editor.
2. From the **Insert** menu, click **Module**.
3. Type the following function:

```
Function FormYes(rng As Range)
   FormYes = rng.HasFormula
End Function
```

4. Close the VBA Editor by pressing **<Alt+Q>**, and in cell B1 type the following function: **=FormYes(A1)**.
5. Copy it down to cell B5 by dragging the cell handle in the bottom-right corner of cell B1.

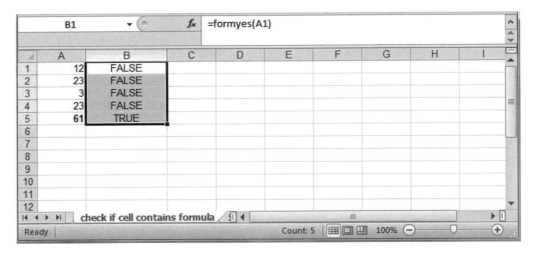

FIGURE 13–4

USE A USER-DEFINED FUNCTION TO CHECK WHETHER A CELL CONTAINS DATA VALIDATION

When a worksheet contains data validation, sometimes it can be useful to find all cells with data validation. One way to check for this is to select the Edit menu and click Go To. Click Special, and select Data validation and All. It is also possible to create a user-defined function to do this. First, open up a new worksheet and define a date validation for cell A1 that starts with 1/1/2005 and ends with 12/31/2005. Then perform the following steps.

▶ **To Check Whether a Cell Contains Data Validation:**

1. Press **<Alt+F11>** to open the Visual Basic Editor.
2. From the **Insert** menu, click **Module**.
3. Type the following function:

```
Function Valid(rng As Range)
Dim intV As Integer
  On Error GoTo errorM
    intV = rng.Validation.Type
    Valid = True
    Exit Function
  errorM:
    Valid = False
End Function
```

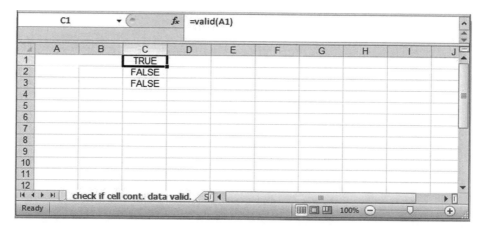

FIGURE 13–5

4. Return to the worksheet and type the formula **=Valid(A1)** in cell C1.
5. Press **<Enter>**.

USE A USER-DEFINED FUNCTION TO FIND ALL COMMENTS

Cells with comments have red indicator triangles in the upper-right corners.
Usually the comments are hidden and only appear if the mouse pointer is
rested over that particular cell. It is also possible to hide the red indicator.
One way to review all comments is to click Comments in the View menu.
It is also possible to create a user-defined function that returns True if a
comment is found.

▶ **To Check Whether a Cell Contains a Comment:**

1. Press **<Alt+F11>** to open the Visual Basic Editor.
2. From the **Insert** menu, click **Module**.
3. Type the following function:

```
Function ComT(rng As Range)
On Error GoTo errorM
If Len(rng.Comment.Text) > 0 Then _
   ComT = True
Exit Function
errorM:
   ComT = False
End Function
```

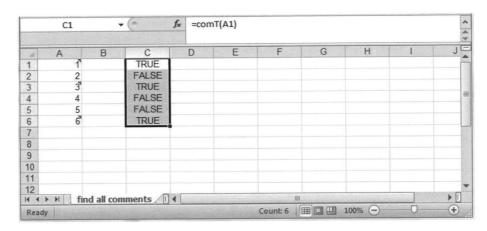

FIGURE 13–6

4. Close the VBA Editor by pressing **<Alt+Q>**, select cells C1:C5, and type the formula **=ComT(A1)**.
5. Press **<Ctrl+Enter>**.

USE A USER-DEFINED FUNCTION TO SUM ALL SHADED CELLS

This tip shows how to sum all shaded cells. Copy to your worksheet the values in range A1:A5, as shown in Figure 13–6. Format two of the cells with the color red and define a special user-defined function to sum them up.

▶ **To Sum All Shaded Cells:**

1. Press **<Alt+F11>** to open the Visual Basic Editor.
2. From the **Insert** menu, click **Module**.
3. Type the following function:

```
Function SumColor(Area As Range, Ci As Integer)
Dim sng As Single, rng As Range
For Each rng In Area
  If rng.Interior.ColorIndex = Ci Then sng = sng+rng.Value
Next rng
  SumColor = sng
End Function
```

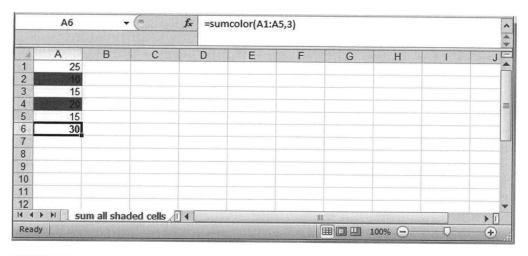

FIGURE 13–7

4. Return to cell C6 of the worksheet and type the formula **=SumColor(A1:A5,3)**.

5. Press **<Enter>**.

NOTE *The integer value Ci is the search criteria for the background color (e.g., 1 = black, 2 = white, 3 = red, 4 = green, 5 = blue, etc.).*

USE A USER-DEFINED FUNCTION TO SUM ALL CELLS WITH A SHADED FONT

As learned from the previous tip, it is quite easy to sum up cells that are shaded. Here we will sum up all cells formatted with the font color blue. Use the worksheet from the previous tip, changing the font style of two values to the color blue. Create a new user-defined function as described below.

▶ **To Sum All Cells with a Particular Font Color:**

1. Press **<Alt+F11>** to open the Visual Basic Editor.
2. From the **Insert** menu, click **Module**.
3. Type the following function:

```
Function SumColorF(Area As Range, Ci As Integer)
Dim sng As Single, rng As Range
For Each rng In Area
  If rng.Font.ColorIndex = Ci Then sng = sng+rng.Value
Next rng
  SumColorF = sng
End Function
```

4. Return to the worksheet and in cell A6 type the following formula: **=SumColorF(A1:A5,5)**.

5. Press **<Enter>**.

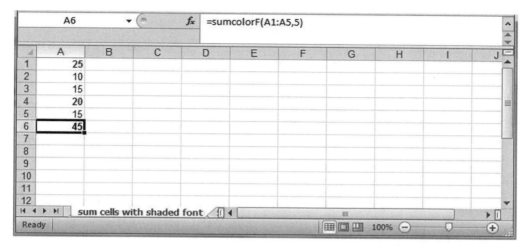

FIGURE 13–8

> **NOTE** *The integer value Ci is the search criteria for the font color (e.g., 1 = black, 2 = white, 3 = red, 4 = green, 5 = blue).*

USE A USER-DEFINED FUNCTION TO DELETE LEADING ZEROS FOR SPECIFIED CELLS

In this example, we delete all leading zeros with a user-defined function. Insert a new worksheet and type some numbers with leading zeros. You will need to enter an apostrophe before the first digit and continue with zeros. Create a user-defined function as shown below to delete those zeros.

▶ **To Delete All Leading Zeros:**

1. Press **<Alt+F11>** to open the Visual Basic Editor.
2. From the **Insert** menu, click **Module**.
3. Type the following function:

```
Function KillZeros(rng As Range)
Dim intS As Integer
intS = rng
```

```
While intS-Int(intS) > 0
  intS = intS * 10
Wend
KillZeros = intS
End Function
```

4. Close the VBA Editor by pressing **<Alt+Q>**.
5. Select cells B1:B5 and type the formula **=KillZeros(A1)**.
6. Press **<Ctrl+Enter>**.

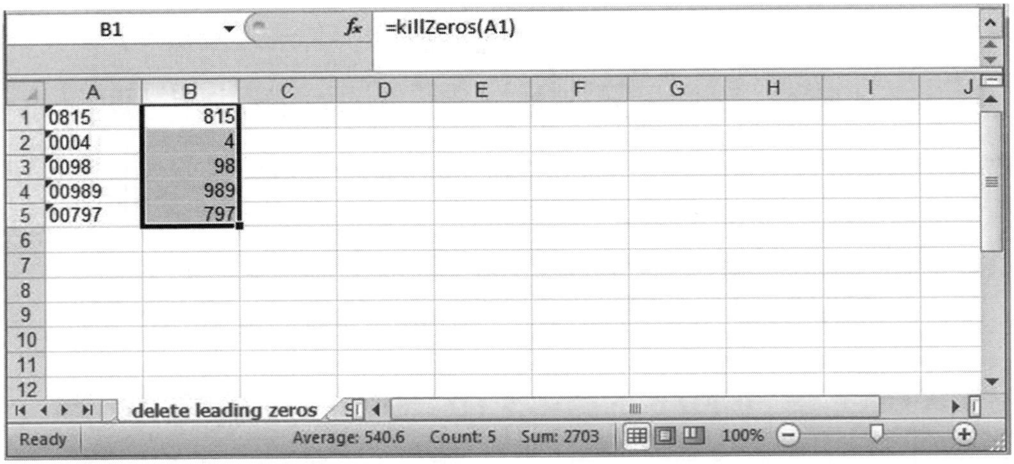

FIGURE 13–9

USE A USER-DEFINED FUNCTION TO DELETE ALL LETTERS IN SPECIFIED CELLS

With this tip you can easily delete all letters of specified cells. Doing so manually would take a long time with a large list, but you can automate this process with a user-defined function. Copy the table shown in Figure 13–9 to a new worksheet, create the user-defined function, and test it.

▶ **To Delete All Letters in Specified Cells:**

1. Press **<Alt+F11>** to open the Visual Basic Editor.
2. From the **Insert** menu, click **Module**.

3. Type the following function:

```
Function LetterOut(rng As Range)
Dim i As Integer
For i = 1 To Len(rng)
  Select Case Asc (Mid(rng.Value, i, 1))
    Case 0 To 64, 123 To 197
      LetterOut = LetterOut & Mid(rng.Value, i, 1)
  End Select
Next i
End Function
```

4. Return to the worksheet, select cells B1:B5, and type the formula **=LetterOut(A1)**.
5. Press **<Ctrl+Enter>**.

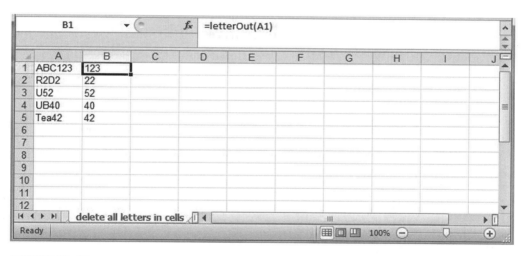

FIGURE 13-10

USE A USER-DEFINED FUNCTION TO DELETE ALL NUMBERS IN SPECIFIED CELLS

Similar to the previous tip, this task deletes all numbers in specified cells. Again, without the help of a user-defined function or a special macro, this would be a difficult job and take a lot of time. A more convenient way to perform this task is with a user-defined function.

▶ **To Delete All Numbers in Specified Cells:**

1. Press **<Alt+F11>** to open the Visual Basic Editor.
2. From the **Insert** menu, click **Module**.
3. Type the following function:

```
Function NumberOut(rng As Range)
Dim i As Integer
For i = 1 To Len(rng)
  Select Case Asc (Mid(rng.Value, i, 1))
    Case 0 To 64, 123 To 197
      Case Else
      NumberOut = NumberOut & _
      Mid(rng.Value, i, 1)
  End Select
Next i
End Function
```

4. Return to the worksheet, select cells B1:B5, and type the formula **=NumberOut(A1)**.
5. Press **<Ctrl+Enter>**.

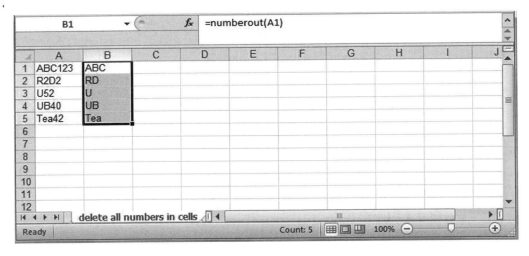

FIGURE 13–11

USE A USER-DEFINED FUNCTION TO DETERMINE THE POSITION OF THE FIRST NUMBER

The user-defined function described here determines the position of the first number in a cell.

▶ **To Determine the Position of the First Number:**

1. Type any data with letters and numbers in cells A1:A5.
2. Press **<Alt+F11>** to open the Visual Basic Editor.
3. From the **Insert** menu, click **Module**.
4. Type the following function:

```
Function FirstNum(rng As Range)
Dim i As Integer

For i = 1 To Len(rng.Value)
  Select Case Mid(rng.Value, i, 1)
    Case 0 To 9
      FirstNum = i
      Exit Function
  End Select
Next i
End Function
```

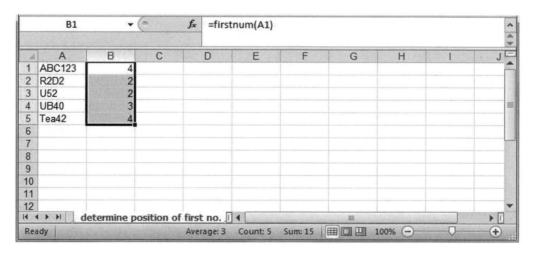

FIGURE 13–12

5. Close the VBA Editor by pressing **<Alt+Q>**.
6. Select cells B1:B5 and type the formula **=FirstNum(A1)**.
7. Press **<Ctrl+Enter>**.

USE A USER-DEFINED FUNCTION TO CALCULATE THE CROSS SUM OF A CELL

With this tip, you can calculate the cross sum of a cell. Create a table like the one in Figure 13–12 and type any numeric data in cells A1:A5.

▶ **To Calculate the Cross Sum of a Cell:**

1. Press **<Alt+F11>** to open the Visual Basic Editor.
2. From the **Insert** menu, click **Module**.
3. Type the following function:

```
Function Qs(rng As Range)
Dim i As Integer

For i = 1 To Len(rng.Value)
  Qs = Qs+Cint (Mid(rng.Value, i, 1))
Next i
End Function
```

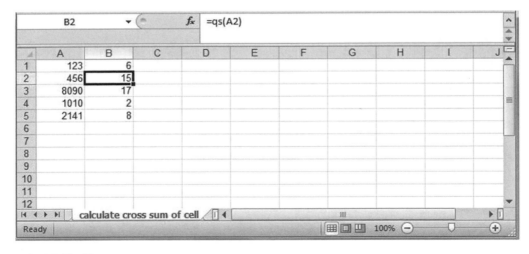

FIGURE 13–13

4. Close the VBA Editor by pressing **<Alt+Q>**.
5. Select cells B1:B5 and type the formula **=Qs(A1)**.
6. Press **<Ctrl+Enter>**.

USE A USER-DEFINED FUNCTION TO SUM EACH CELL'S CROSS SUM IN A RANGE

Continuing with the previous example, now we want to sum up each cell's cross sum in a range. Create a table like the one in Figure 13–13 and calculate cross sums in a specified range with a new user-defined function.

▶ **To Sum up Each Cell's Cross Sum in a Range:**

1. Press **<Alt+F11>** to open the Visual Basic Editor.
2. From the **Insert** menu, click **Module**.
3. Type the following function:

```
Function QsE(Area As Range)
Dim i As Integer
Dim rng As Range

For Each rng In Area
  For i = 1 To Len(rng.Value)
    QsE = QsE+CInt  (Mid(rng.Value, i, 1))
  Next i
Next rng
End Function
```

4. Close the VBA Editor by pressing **<Alt+Q>**.
5. In cell B1 type the following formula: **=QsE(A1:A5)**.
6. Press **<Enter>**.

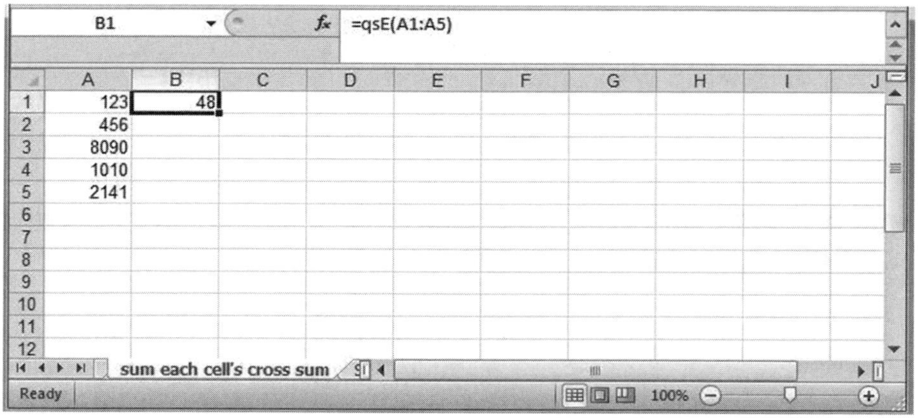

FIGURE 13–14

USE A USER-DEFINED FUNCTION TO CHECK WHETHER A WORKSHEET IS EMPTY

Sometimes it is necessary to check whether a worksheet is really empty or still contains hidden formulas. To do this, choose Worksheet from the Insert menu to add a new worksheet to the current workbook and write a user-defined function in the Visual Basic Editor as described below.

▶ **To Check Whether a Worksheet is Empty:**

1. Press **<Alt+F11>** to open the Visual Basic Editor.
2. From the **Insert** menu, click **Module**.
3. Type the following function:

```
Function ShEmpty(s As String) As Boolean
If Application.CountA (Sheets(s).UsedRange) = 0 Then
  ShEmpty = True
Else
ShEmpty = False
End If
End Function
```

4. Close the VBA Editor by pressing **<Alt+Q>**.
5. Select any cell in the worksheet and type the formula **=ShEmpty("Sheet15")**. Be sure to replace "Sheet15" with the sheet name you want to check.
6. Press **<Enter>**.

USE A USER-DEFINED FUNCTION TO CHECK WHETHER A WORKSHEET IS PROTECTED

The function described here checks whether a worksheet is protected. First, you need to create a worksheet and protect it, then write a user-defined function to test it.

▶ **To Check Whether a Worksheet is Protected:**

1. Press **<Alt+F11>** to open the Visual Basic Editor.
2. From the **Insert** menu, click **Module**.
3. Type the following function:

```
Function ShProt(s As String) As Boolean
On Error GoTo errorM

If Sheets(s).ProtectContents = True Then
  ShProt = True
End If
Exit Function

errorM:
  ShProt = False
End Function
```

4. Close the VBA Editor by pressing **<Alt+Q>**.
5. Select any cell in the worksheet and type the formula **=shProt("Sheet15")**. Be sure to replace "Sheet15" with the sheet name whose protection you want to check.
6. Press **<Enter>**.

USE A USER-DEFINED FUNCTION TO CREATE YOUR OWN AUTOTEXT

The last tip in this chapter provides a way to use AutoText inside your worksheet. This functionality can be useful for a number of different Excel-based tasks.

▶ **To Create Your Own AutoText:**

1. Press **<Alt+F11>** to open the Visual Basic Editor.
2. From the **Insert** menu, click **Module**.
3. Type the following function:

```
Function AuTxt(rng As Range) As String
  Select Case rng.Value
    Case 1
      AuTxt = "fire"
    Case 2
      AuTxt = "water"
    Case 3
      AuTxt = "heaven"
    Case Else
      AuTxt = "invalid text"
  End Select
End Function
```

4. Return to the worksheet. Select cells B1:B4 or a much larger range and type the formula **=AuTxt(A1)**.
5. Press **<Ctrl+Enter>**.

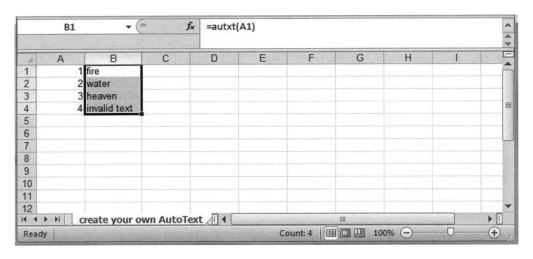

FIGURE 13–15

Chapter **14** EXAMPLES

This chapter is about how to use the Excel formulas and functions that have been discussed and to gain some more experience with them as well. With these exercises, you need to determine which functions are best to solve the task. Try to solve the tasks, and consult the previous chapters if necessary.

CALCULATING AVERAGE FUEL CONSUMPTION

Figure 14–1 lists the miles driven and the number of gallons used. What is the average consumption for 100 miles?

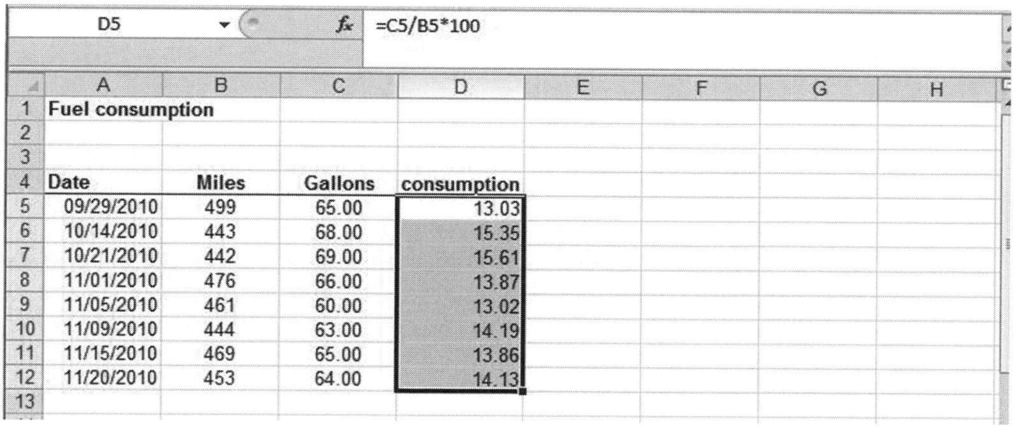

	D5	▾	f_x	=C5/B5*100				
	A	B	C	D	E	F	G	H
1	Fuel consumption							
2								
3								
4	Date	Miles	Gallons	consumption				
5	09/29/2010	499	65.00	13.03				
6	10/14/2010	443	68.00	15.35				
7	10/21/2010	442	69.00	15.61				
8	11/01/2010	476	66.00	13.87				
9	11/05/2010	461	60.00	13.02				
10	11/09/2010	444	63.00	14.19				
11	11/15/2010	469	65.00	13.86				
12	11/20/2010	453	64.00	14.13				
13								

FIGURE 14–1

▶ **To Determine Average Fuel Consumption:**

1. In a worksheet, copy the data shown in cells A4:D12 in Figure 14–1.
2. Select cells D5:D12.
3. Type the formula **=C5/B5*100**.
4. Press **<Ctrl+Enter>**.
5. Calculate the average consumption by selecting cell D15 and typing the formula **=AVERAGE(D5:D12)**.
6. Press **<Enter>**.

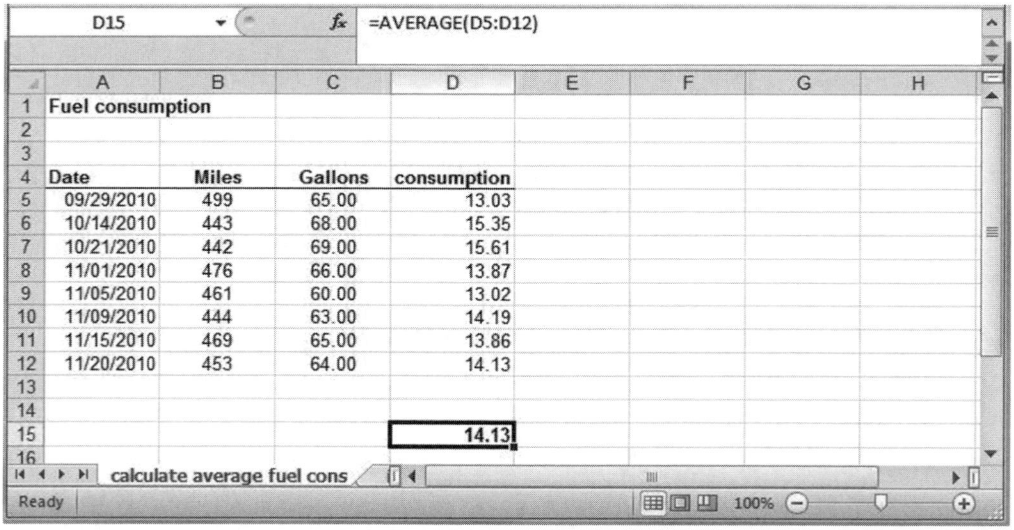

	D15	▾	f_x	=AVERAGE(D5:D12)					
	A	B	C	D	E	F	G	H	
1	Fuel consumption								
2									
3									
4	Date	Miles	Gallons	consumption					
5	09/29/2010	499	65.00	13.03					
6	10/14/2010	443	68.00	15.35					
7	10/21/2010	442	69.00	15.61					
8	11/01/2010	476	66.00	13.87					
9	11/05/2010	461	60.00	13.02					
10	11/09/2010	444	63.00	14.19					
11	11/15/2010	469	65.00	13.86					
12	11/20/2010	453	64.00	14.13					
13									
14									
15				14.13					
16									

calculate average fuel cons

Ready   100%

FIGURE 14–2

Extend the task to indicate the lowest and highest gas consumption. Both values should be formatted individually. The highest value needs to be shaded in red and the lowest shaded in green. In addition, the whole row rather than just the individual cell should be shaded. These requirements can be solved with conditional formatting.

1. Select cells A5:D12.
2. From the **Home** tab, go to the **Styles** bar and click on **Conditional Formatting**.

3. Choose **New Rule**.
4. In the **Select a Rule Type** dialog select **Use a formula to determine which cells to format**.
5. In the **Edit** box type the following formula:
   =$D5=MAX($D$5:$D$12).
6. Click **Format,** select a color from the **Fill** tab when the cell value meets the condition, and click **OK**.
7. Repeat step 2 and choose **Manage Rule**.
8. Click **New Rule** and insert the following formula:
   =$D5=MIN($D$5:$D$12).
9. Repeat step 9.
10. Click **OK**.

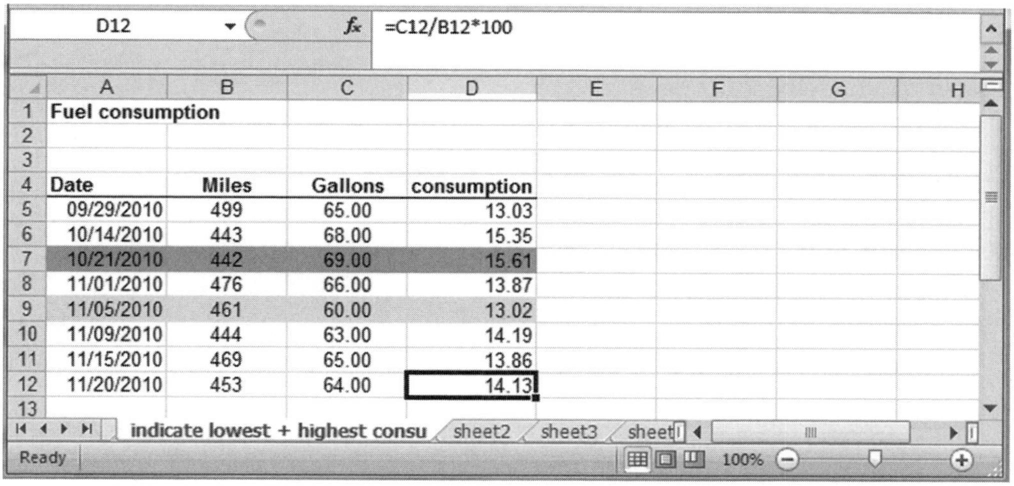

	D12			f_x	=C12/B12*100				
	A	B	C	D	E	F	G	H	
1	Fuel consumption								
2									
3									
4	Date	Miles	Gallons	consumption					
5	09/29/2010	499	65.00	13.03					
6	10/14/2010	443	68.00	15.35					
7	10/21/2010	442	69.00	15.61					
8	11/01/2010	476	66.00	13.87					
9	11/05/2010	461	60.00	13.02					
10	11/09/2010	444	63.00	14.19					
11	11/15/2010	469	65.00	13.86					
12	11/20/2010	453	64.00	14.13					
13									

indicate lowest + highest consu / sheet2 / sheet3 / sheet□

Ready   100%

FIGURE 14–3

CALCULATING NET AND CORRESPONDING GROSS PRICES

Figure 14–4 shows a gross price and a net price. Calculate the corresponding values using a tax rate of 7%.

FIGURE 14–4

The net price needs to be calculated in cell C5.

▶ To Calculate the Net Price:

    1. Select cell C5.
    2. Type the formula **=B5+(B5*A5)** and press **<Enter>**.

The gross price needs to be calculated in cell B7.

▶ To Calculate the Gross Price:

    1. Select cell B7.
    2. Type the formula **=C7/(1+A7)**.
    3. Press **<Enter>**.

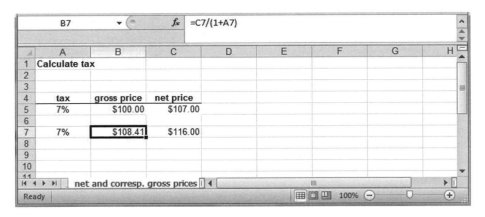

FIGURE 14–5

DETERMINING THE ECONOMIC VALUE OF A PRODUCT

The table in Figure 14–6 lists the cost, price, and profit margin of various products. Determine which product is most profitable and use conditional formatting to format it.

	E5			f_x =D5/C5					
	A	B	C	D	E	F	G	H	
1	determine the economic value of a product								
2									
3									
4		Product	cost	price	margin				
5		product 1	$15,911	$17,249	1.08409277				
6		product 2	$19,320	$16,982	0.87898551				
7		product 3	$18,078	$19,297	1.06743003				
8		product 4	$17,967	$19,137	1.06511939				
9		product 5	$18,743	$16,831	0.89798858				
10		product 6	$16,364	$17,699	1.08158152				
11		product 7	$16,697	$18,833	1.12792717				
12		product 8	$16,282	$18,330	1.12578307				
13									

FIGURE 14–6

▶ **To Determine the Economic Value:**

1. Using the information in Figure 14–6, select cells E5:E12.
2. Type the formula **=D5/C5**.
3. Press **<Ctrl+Enter>**.
4. Select cells B5:E12.
5. From the **Home** tab, go to the **Styles** bar and click on **Conditional Formatting**.
6. Choose **New Rule**.
7. In the **Select a Rule Type** dialog select **Use a formula to determine which cells to format**.
8. In the **Edit** box type the following formula:
   =$E5=MAX($E$5:$E$12).
9. Click **Format**, select a color from the **Fill** tab, and click **OK**.
10. Click **OK**.

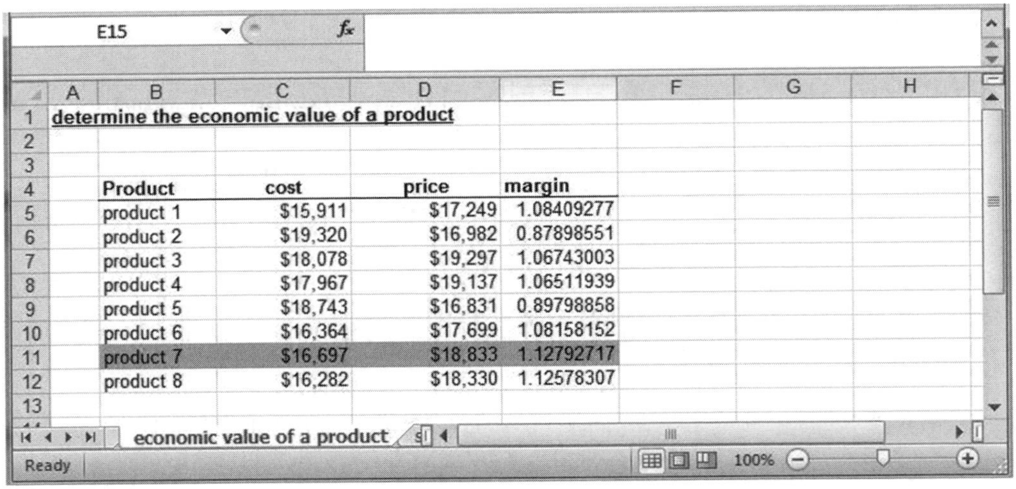

	A	B	C	D	E	F	G	H
	E15			f_x				
1	determine the economic value of a product							
2								
3								
4	Product		cost	price	margin			
5	product 1		$15,911	$17,249	1.08409277			
6	product 2		$19,320	$16,982	0.87898551			
7	product 3		$18,078	$19,297	1.06743003			
8	product 4		$17,967	$19,137	1.06511939			
9	product 5		$18,743	$16,831	0.89798858			
10	product 6		$16,364	$17,699	1.08158152			
11	product 7		$16,697	$18,833	1.12792717			
12	product 8		$16,282	$18,330	1.12578307			
13								

economic value of a product

Ready   100%

FIGURE 14–7

CALCULATING THE FINAL PRICE OF A PRODUCT, TAKING INTO ACCOUNT REBATES AND PRICE REDUCTIONS

Take a look at the price table in Figure 14–8. The net price of a tractor is listed along with an agreed-upon rebate and a price reduction because of minor defects. To calculate the gross price, those reductions need to be taken into account and then the taxes must be added. Your task is to calculate the final price of the tractor.

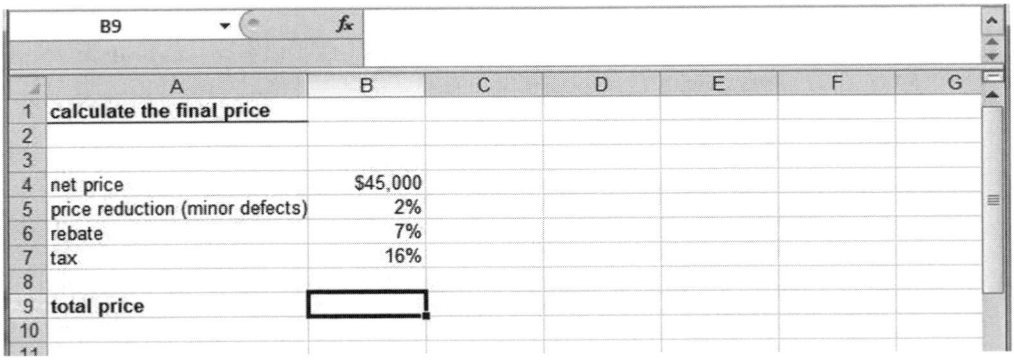

	A	B	C	D	E	F	G
	B9		f_x				
1	calculate the final price						
2							
3							
4	net price	$45,000					
5	price reduction (minor defects)	2%					
6	rebate	7%					
7	tax	16%					
8							
9	total price						
10							

FIGURE 14–8

► **To Calculate the Final Price:**

    1. Select cell B9.
    2. Enter the following formula: **=B4*0.98*0.93*1.16**.
    3. Press **<Enter>**.

The order of parameters is not important when multiplying.

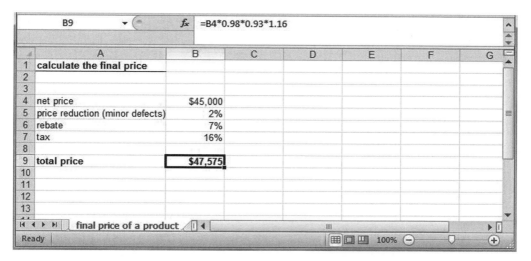

FIGURE 14–9

SEARCHING FOR DATA THAT MEETS SPECIFIC CRITERIA

Figure 14–10 lists dates and corresponding sales. Your task is to sum up all sales that are more than $500.

	A	B	C	D	E	F	G	H
1	to specify criteria to be found inside a set of data							
2								
3								
4								
5	start date	09/30/2010						
6	sales	$500						
7								
8	date	sales	function					
9	09/25/2010	$841.00						
10	09/26/2010	$822.00						
11	09/27/2010	$390.00						
12	09/28/2010	$557.00						
13	09/29/2010	$331.00						
14	09/30/2010	$348.00						
15	10/01/2010	$458.00						
16	10/02/2010	$658.00						
17	10/03/2010	$411.00						
18	10/04/2010	$296.00						
19	10/05/2010	$883.00						
20	10/06/2010	$452.00						
21	10/07/2010	$683.00						
22	10/08/2010	$70.00						
23	10/09/2010	$109.00						

FIGURE 14–10

There are various ways to solve this task. One solution is to mark the values that fit the given criteria.

1. Select cells C9:C23.
2. Type the formula **=AND(A9>$B$5,B9>$B$6)**.
3. Press **<Ctrl+Enter>**.
4. Select cell C25.
5. Type the formula **=SUMIF(C9:C23,TRUE,B9:B23)**.
6. Press **<Enter>**.

If you'd like to use the built-in data filter, filter column C for the entry TRUE:

1. Select cell C8.
2. Select **Filter | AutoFilter** from the Data menu.
3. In cell C8, select **TRUE** from the drop-down box to filter the list.

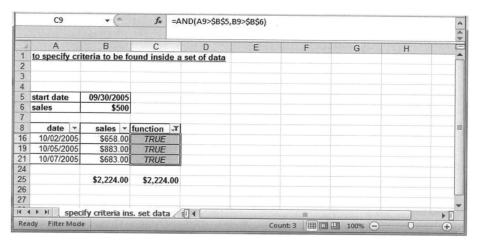

FIGURE 14–11

NOTE   *When you calculate the sum of a filtered list, usually the hidden cells are added as well. Therefore, use the SUBTOTAL function rather than the SUM function. The easiest way to do this is to place the mouse cursor in the target cell and click on the AutoSum symbol in the Standard menu. Excel automatically recognizes the filtered list and uses the correct function, which in this case is SUBTOTAL.*

SEPARATING CITIES FROM ZIP CODES

The table in Figure 14–12 lists zip codes and their corresponding cities. This information should be separated and shown in two separate columns.

	A	B	C	D	E	F	G
1	separate cities from zip codes						
2							
3							
4	zip code / city	zip code	city				
5	94102 San Francisco						
6	95150 San Jose						
7	96140 Carnelian Bay						
8	91350 Santa Clarita						
9	10019 New York						
10	90049 Los Angeles						
11	70123 New Orleans						
12	33139 Miami Beach						
13							

FIGURE 14–12

▶ **To Separate Data:**

1. Select cells B5:B12.
2. Type the formula **=LEFT(A5,SEARCH(" ",A5)-1)**.
3. Press **<Ctrl+Enter>**.
4. Select cells C5:C12.
5. Type the formula **=RIGHT(A5,LEN(A5)-(SEARCH(" ",A5)))**.
6. Press **<Ctrl+Enter>**.

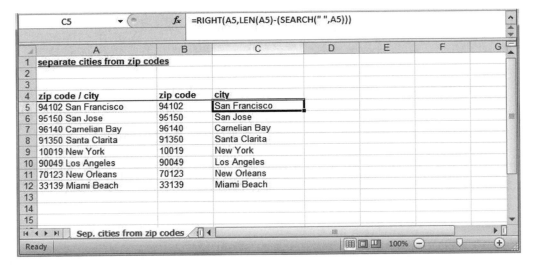

FIGURE 14–13

ELIMINATING SPECIFIC CHARACTERS

Various telephone numbers are listed in the following table and formatted in a variety of ways. Some contain hyphens or slashes, while others contain spaces.

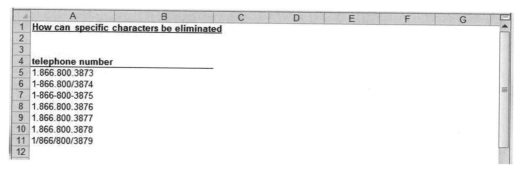

FIGURE 14–14

▶ **To Eliminate Specific Characters:**

    1. Select cells B5:B11.
    2. Type the formula **=SUBSTITUTE(SUBSTITUTE (SUBSTITUTE(A5,"-",""),".",""),"/","")**.
    3. Press **<Ctrl+Enter>**.

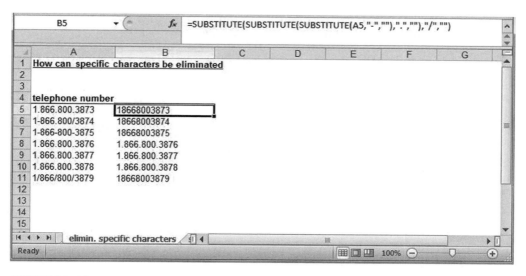

FIGURE 14–15

COMBINING TEXT, DATES, AND TIMESTAMPS

In this example there is text that should be combined with dates and times and presented in a single cell. Excel needs to be "tricked" to produce the correct result.

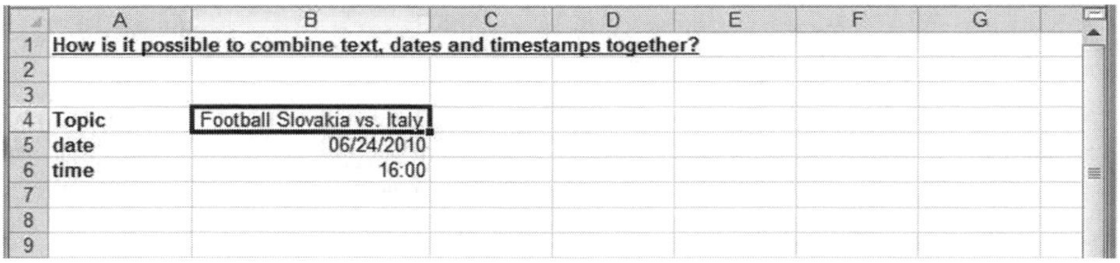

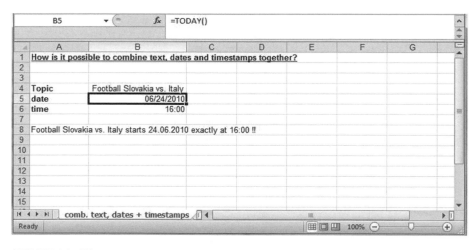

FIGURE 14–16

▶ **To Combine Dates, Times, and Text:**

1. Select cell A8.
2. Type the formula **="Attention " & B4 & " starts " & TEXT(B5;"DD.MM.YYYY") & " exactly at " & TEXT(B6;"hh:mm") & " !!"**.
3. Press **<Enter>**.

FIGURE 14–17

DETERMINING THE LAST DAY OF A MONTH

The table in Figure 14–18 contains a number of dates. Your task is to determine the day of the week that falls on the last day of the month for each date, taking into account the length of each month.

	A	B	C	D	E	F	G	H
1	How can the last day of a month be determined							
2								
3								
4								
5	date	offset	last day of month	weekday				
6	10/06/2010	3						
7	04/13/2010	-3						
8	03/24/2010	-1						
9	05/08/2010	6						
10	06/17/2010	-3						
11	07/25/2010	2						
12	09/29/2010	3						
13								

FIGURE 14–18

To solve this task you will need to install the Analysis ToolPak add-in for Excel, if it has not already been installed. From the Tools menu, select Add-Ins. In the dialog that appears, select Analysis ToolPak and confirm with OK. Now you can proceed as described:

1. Using the data shown in cells A5:D12 of Figure 4–18, select cells C6:C12.
2. Type the formula **=EOMONTH(A6,B6)**.
3. Press **<Ctrl+Enter>**.
4. Select cells D6:D12.
5. Type the formula **=C6**.
6. Press **<Ctrl+Enter>**.
7. In the **Home** tab go to the **Cells** bar and click on **Format**.
8. Select **Format Cells** and then the **Custom** option in the **Number** tab.
9. Type **DDDD**.
10. Press **OK**.

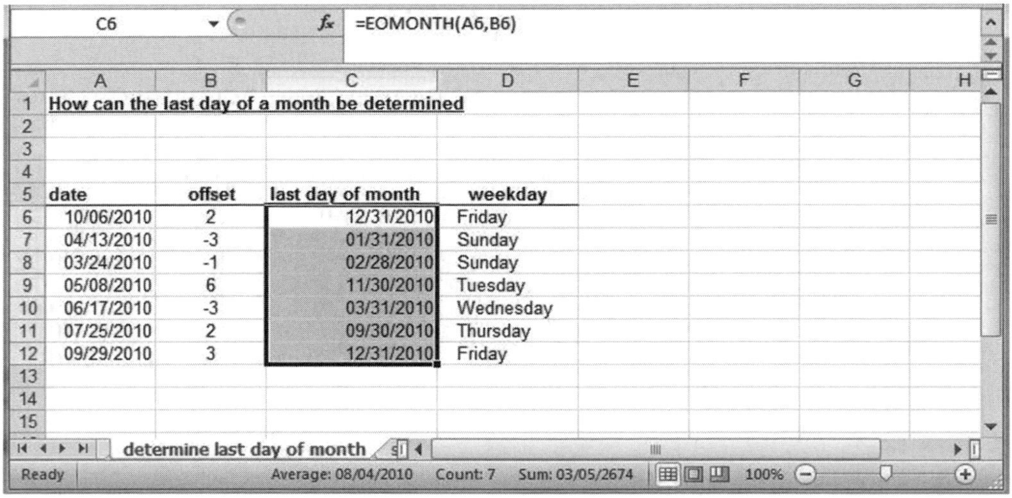

	C6		f_x	=EOMONTH(A6,B6)			

	A	B	C	D	E	F	G	H
1	How can the last day of a month be determined							
2								
3								
4								
5	date	offset	last day of month	weekday				
6	10/06/2010	2	12/31/2010	Friday				
7	04/13/2010	-3	01/31/2010	Sunday				
8	03/24/2010	-1	02/28/2010	Sunday				
9	05/08/2010	6	11/30/2010	Tuesday				
10	06/17/2010	-3	03/31/2010	Wednesday				
11	07/25/2010	2	09/30/2010	Thursday				
12	09/29/2010	3	12/31/2010	Friday				
13								
14								
15								

determine last day of month

Ready   Average: 08/04/2010   Count: 7   Sum: 03/05/2674   100%

FIGURE 14–19

DETERMINING THE NUMBER OF AVAILABLE WORKDAYS

This task shows the timeframe of a project. There are weekends between the start date and end date, which are usually not workdays. Only the actual workdays need to be determined. Excel supports this task with a specific table function called NETWORKDAYS, which can be found in the Analysis ToolPak add-in.

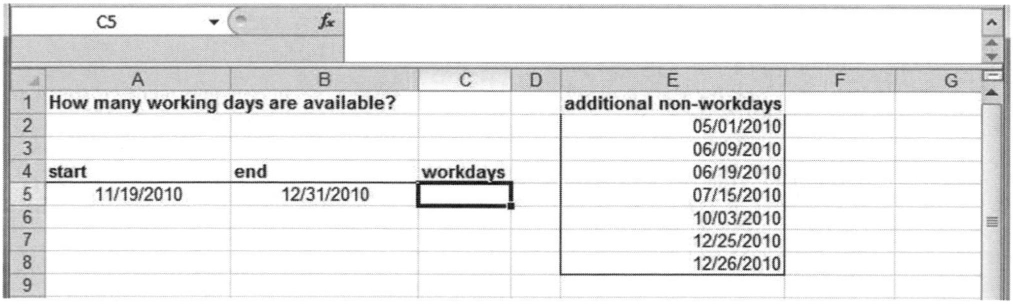

	C5		f_x				

	A	B	C	D	E	F	G
1	How many working days are available?				additional non-workdays		
2					05/01/2010		
3					06/09/2010		
4	start	end	workdays		06/19/2010		
5	11/19/2010	12/31/2010			07/15/2010		
6					10/03/2010		
7					12/25/2010		
8					12/26/2010		
9							

FIGURE 14–20

In addition to finding the weekends, the NETWORKDAYS function can be used to find holidays. To solve this extended task, some holidays have been entered in cells E2:E8. Of course, it is possible to extend this list for additional non-workdays, such as company parties and various promotions.

Determine the available workdays for the given time frame, taking into account additional non-workdays:

1. Select cell C5.
2. Type the formula **=NETWORKDAYS(A5,B5,E2:E8)**.
3. Press **<Enter>**.

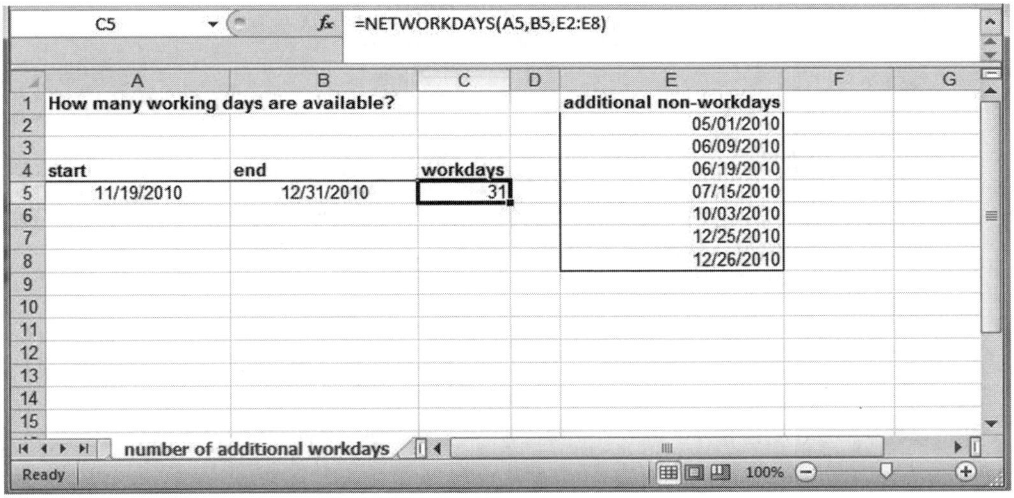

	A	B	C	D	E	F	G
	C5			f_x	=NETWORKDAYS(A5,B5,E2:E8)		
1	How many working days are available?				additional non-workdays		
2					05/01/2010		
3					06/09/2010		
4	start	end			06/19/2010		
5	11/19/2010	12/31/2010	workdays		07/15/2010		
			31		07/15/2010		
6					10/03/2010		
7					12/25/2010		
8					12/26/2010		
9							
10							
11							
12							
13							
14							
15							

number of additional workdays

Ready   100%

FIGURE 14–21

NOTE *The WORKDAY function is similar to the NETWORKDAYS function. WORKDAY needs a start date and the number of workdays and will calculate the end date, taking into account weekends and holidays.*

DETERMINING A PERSON'S EXACT AGE

Figure 14–22 shows a list of various birthdates. Your task is to determine the exact age for each person in years, months, and days.

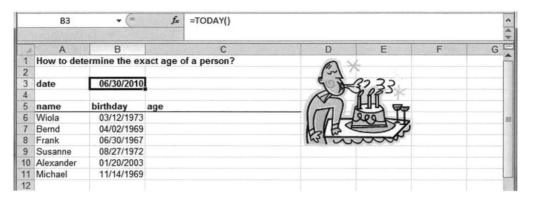

FIGURE 14-22

▶ **To Determine the Age of a Person:**

    1. Select cells C6:C11.

    2. Type the formula **=DATEDIF(B6,$B$3,"Y") &**
       " years and " & DATEDIF(B6,$B$3,"YM") & " months and " &
       DATEDIF(B6,$B$3,"MD") & " days".

    3. Press **<Ctrl+Enter>**.

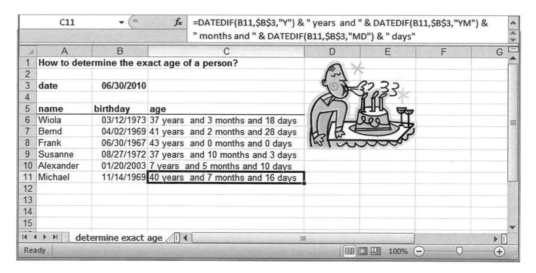

FIGURE 14-23

DETERMINING THE NUMBER OF VALUES IN A SPECIFIC RANGE

Figure 14–24 shows a table containing different values. Your task is to count the number of values that are between 50 and 100. This task can be solved easily with an array formula.

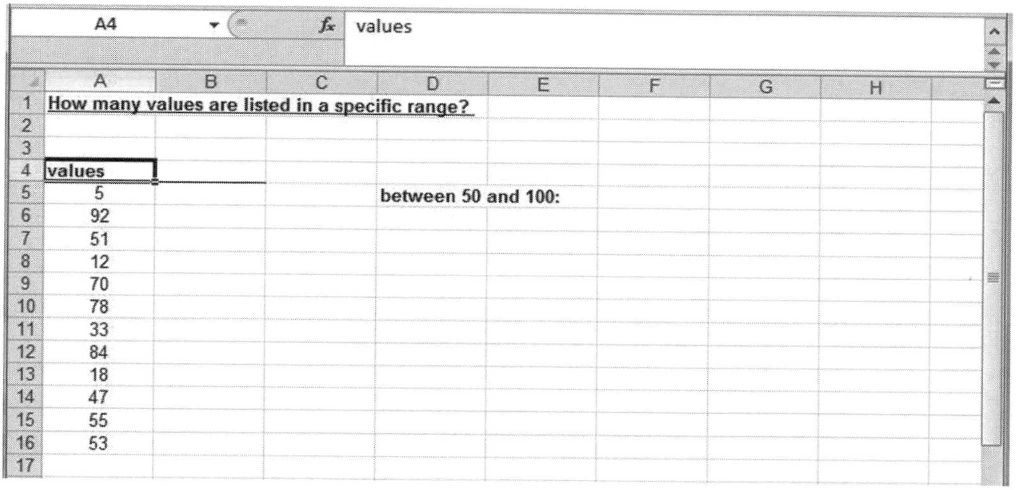

A4		f_x	values					
	A	B	C	D	E	F	G	H
1	How many values are listed in a specific range?							
2								
3								
4	values							
5	5			between 50 and 100:				
6	92							
7	51							
8	12							
9	70							
10	78							
11	33							
12	84							
13	18							
14	47							
15	55							
16	53							
17								

FIGURE 14–24

▶ **To Determine the Number of Values in a Specific Range:**

1. Select cell D6.
2. Type the array formula **=SUM((A5:A16>=50)*(A5:A16<=100))**.
3. Press **<Ctrl+Shift+Enter>**.

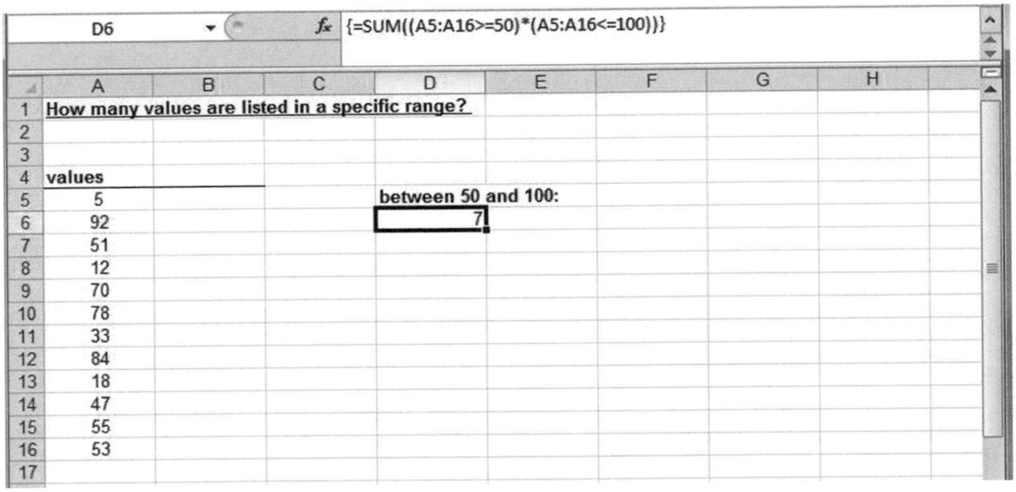

	D6		▾	f_x {=SUM((A5:A16>=50)*(A5:A16<=100))}				

⊿	A	B	C	D	E	F	G	H
1	How many values are listed in a specific range?							
2								
3								
4	values							
5	5			between 50 and 100:				
6	92			7				
7	51							
8	12							
9	70							
10	78							
11	33							
12	84							
13	18							
14	47							
15	55							
16	53							
17								

FIGURE 14–25

NOTE *The curly brackets in the formula are generated automatically with the keyboard combination <Ctrl+Shift+Enter>. Enter the brackets this way rather than entering them manually.*

If the values in a certain range need to be added instead of counted, use this solution:

1. Select cell D7.
2. Type the array formula
   =SUM(IF(A5:A16>=50,IF(A5:A16<100,A5:A16))).
3. Press **<Ctrl+Shift+Enter>**.

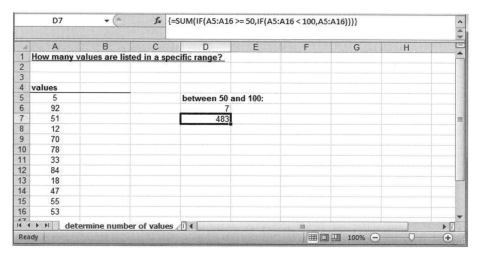

FIGURE 14–26

DETERMINING THE WEEKLY SALES FOR EACH DEPARTMENT

This example involves an unsorted list of sales by individual employees from different departments. Your task is to calculate the weekly sales for each department.

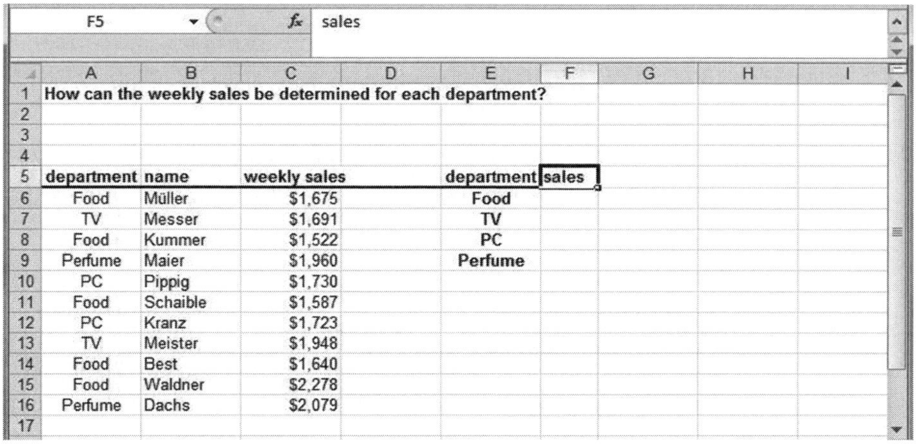

FIGURE 14–27

▶ **To Determine Weekly Sales:**

    1. Using the data shown in Figure 14–27, select cells F6:F9.
    2. Type the formula **=SUMIF($A$6:$A$16,E6,$C$6:$C$16)**.
    3. Press **<Ctrl+Enter>**.

	F9			*fx*	=SUMIF($A$6:$A$16,E9,$C$6:$C$16)				

	A	B	C	D	E	F	G	H	I
1	How can the weekly sales be determined for each department?								
2									
3									
4									
5	department	name	weekly sales		department	sales			
6	Food	Müller	$1,675		Food	$8,702			
7	TV	Messer	$1,691		TV	$3,639			
8	Food	Kummer	$1,522		PC	$3,453			
9	Perfume	Maier	$1,960		Perfume	$4,039			
10	PC	Pippig	$1,730						
11	Food	Schaible	$1,587						
12	PC	Kranz	$1,723						
13	TV	Meister	$1,948						
14	Food	Best	$1,640						
15	Food	Waldner	$2,278						
16	Perfume	Dachs	$2,079						
17									

FIGURE 14–28

Because of the different sizes of each department, the weekly sales figures do not really indicate anything about the performance of each salesperson. As an example, the Food department has more salespeople than the Perfume department. To break down the average sales in each department, you need to take into account the number of employees for each department. Now let's determine the average weekly sales per employee for each department and shade the department with the best performance.

    1. Select cells G6:G9.
    2. Type the formula **=F6/COUNTIF($A$6:$A$16,E6)**.
    3. Press **<Ctrl+Enter>**.
    4. Select cells E6:G9.
    5. From the **Home** tab, go to the **Styles** bar and click on **Conditional Formatting**.
    6. Choose **New Rule**.
    7. In the **Select a Rule Type** dialog select **Use a formula to determine which cells to format**.

8. In the **Edit** box type the following formula:
   =$G6=MAX($G$6:$G$9).
9. Click **Format,** select a color from the **Fill** tab, and click **OK**.
10. Click **OK**.

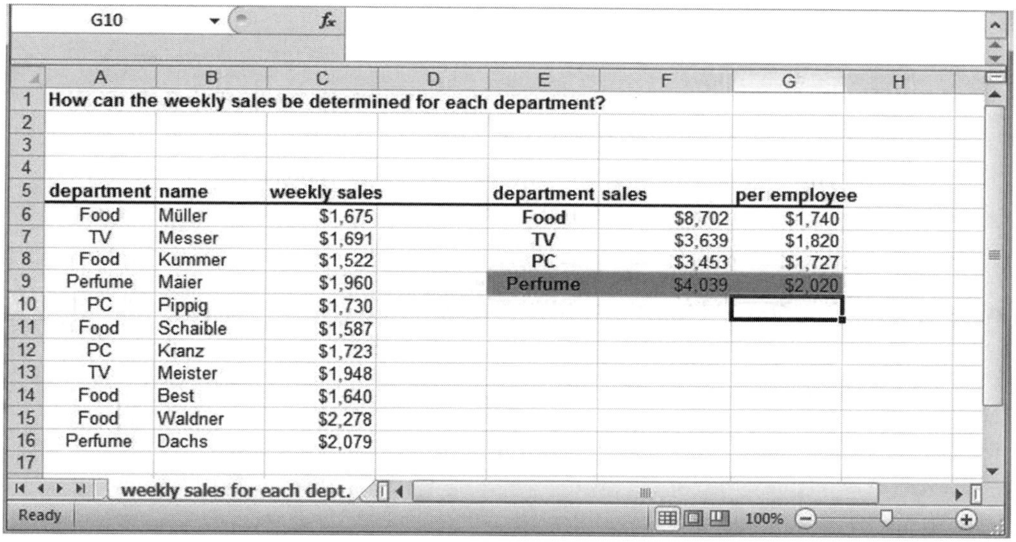

	A	B	C	D	E	F	G	H
1	How can the weekly sales be determined for each department?							
2								
3								
4								
5	department	name	weekly sales		department	sales	per employee	
6	Food	Müller	$1,675		Food	$8,702	$1,740	
7	TV	Messer	$1,691		TV	$3,639	$1,820	
8	Food	Kummer	$1,522		PC	$3,453	$1,727	
9	Perfume	Maier	$1,960		Perfume	$4,039	$2,020	
10	PC	Pippig	$1,730					
11	Food	Schaible	$1,587					
12	PC	Kranz	$1,723					
13	TV	Meister	$1,948					
14	Food	Best	$1,640					
15	Food	Waldner	$2,278					
16	Perfume	Dachs	$2,079					
17								

(Name box shows G10; sheet tab: weekly sales for each dept.)

FIGURE 14–29

ROUNDING A VALUE TO THE NEAREST 5 CENTS

In this example, the dollar values need to be rounded to the nearest number divisible by 5; i.e., the rounded number must end with 0 or 5. There are various functions inside Excel for rounding values, but the best function for this task is the MROUND function. It can only be used if the Analysis ToolPak add-in has been installed.

	A	B	C	D	E	F	G	H
1	How can a value be rounded to the nearest five cents?							
2								
3								
4	value	rounded						
5	$ 120.37							
6	$ 11.97							
7	$ 121.11							
8	$ 45.03							
9	$ 99.99							
10	$ 89.51							
11	$ 89.49							
12								

FIGURE 14–30

▶ **To Round to a Value That Ends with 0 or 5:**

     1. Select cells B5:B11.
     2. Type the formula **=MROUND(A5, 0.05)**.
     3. Press **<Ctrl+Enter>**.

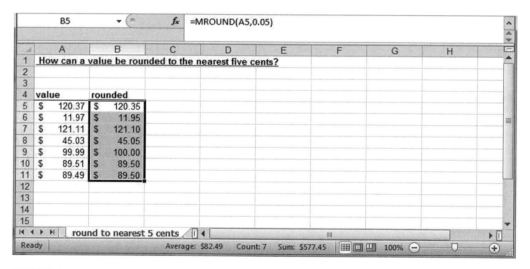

FIGURE 14–31

DETERMINING THE INVENTORY VALUE

Figure 14–32 shows a list of items that are in stock, along with their cost and current quantity. Your task is to calculate the total value of the items in inventory.

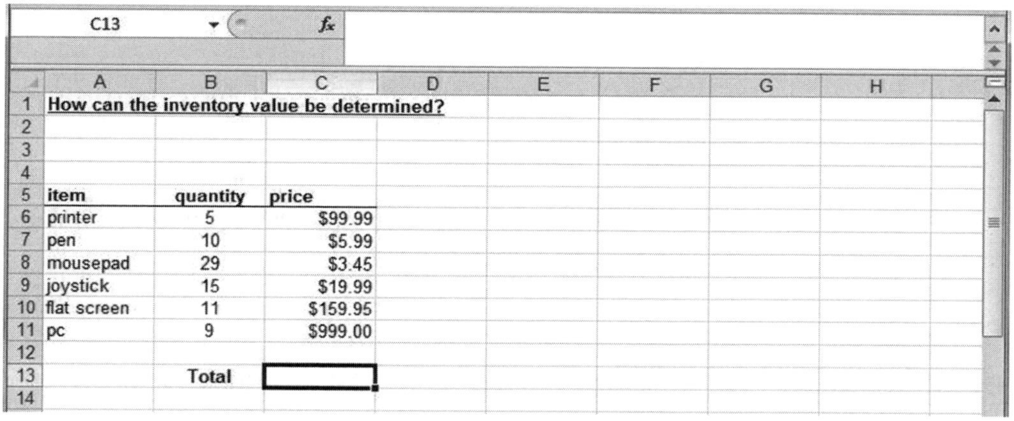

	A	B	C	D	E	F	G	H
	C13		f_x					
1	How can the inventory value be determined?							
2								
3								
4								
5	item	quantity	price					
6	printer	5	$99.99					
7	pen	10	$5.99					
8	mousepad	29	$3.45					
9	joystick	15	$19.99					
10	flat screen	11	$159.95					
11	pc	9	$999.00					
12								
13		Total						
14								

FIGURE 14–32

It is certainly possible to solve this task by adding an additional column to calculate a total for each item and sum those values. But there is a much easier way!

▶ **To Determine the Value of the Inventory:**

1. Using the data in Figure 14–32, select cell C13.
2. Type the formula **=SUMPRODUCT(B6:B11,C6:C11)**.
3. Press **<Enter>**.

	C13			f_x	=SUMPRODUCT(B6:B11,C6:C11)			
	A	B	C	D	E	F	G	H
1	How can the inventory value be determined?							
2								
3								
4								
5	item	quantity	price					
6	printer	5	$99.99					
7	pen	10	$5.99					
8	mousepad	29	$3.45					
9	joystick	15	$19.99					
10	flat screen	11	$159.95					
11	pc	9	$999.00					
12								
13		Total	$11,710.20					
14								
15								

determine inventory value

Ready   100%

FIGURE 14–33

DETERMINING THE TOP SALESPERSON FOR A MONTH

Figure 14–34 presents a list of salespeople and their monthly sales volume. Your task is to determine the best sales each month and mark it in the list.

	A	B	C	D	E	F	G	H	I
	F14			f_x					
1	How to determine top salesperson for a month								
2									
3			sales						
4		$7,273	$7,627	$6,911	$7,524				
5	name	january	february	march	april				
6	Just	$7,273	$7,627	$5,581	$5,659				
7	Kiebel	$3,870	$4,299	$6,911	$3,937				
8	Schmette	$3,001	$6,654	$4,881	$6,891				
9	Dürr	$3,740	$4,815	$5,285	$6,981				
10	Kohler	$3,980	$5,454	$3,504	$3,284				
11	Rudolf	$5,570	$7,354	$5,514	$7,133				
12	Brenner	$5,129	$4,051	$4,822	$7,524				
13	Best	$4,453	$7,272	$5,616	$5,689				
14	Wimmer	$5,330	$5,966	$5,863	$3,819				
15									

FIGURE 14–34

► **To Determine the Top Salesperson:**

1. Using the data shown in Figure 14–33, select cells B4:E4.
2. Type the formula **=MAX(B6:B14)**.
3. Press **<Ctrl+Enter>**.
4. Select cells B6:E14.
5. From the **Home** tab, go to the **Styles** bar and click on **Conditional Formatting**.
6. Choose **New Rule**.
7. In the **Select a Rule Type** dialog select **Use a formula to determine which cells to format**.
8. In the **Edit** box type the following formula: **=B6=B$4**.
9. Click **Format**, select a color from the **Fill** tab, and click **OK**.
10. Click **OK**.

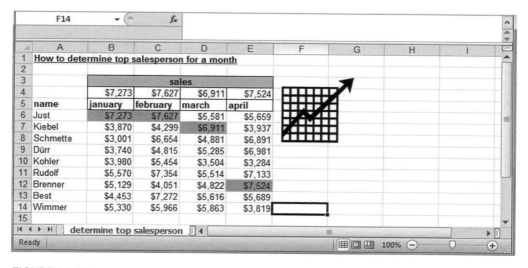

	A	B	C	D	E	F	G	H	I
1	How to determine top salesperson for a month								
2									
3				sales					
4		$7,273	$7,627	$6,911	$7,524				
5	name	january	february	march	april				
6	Just	$7,273	$7,627	$5,581	$5,659				
7	Kiebel	$3,870	$4,299	$6,911	$3,937				
8	Schmette	$3,001	$6,654	$4,881	$6,891				
9	Dürr	$3,740	$4,815	$5,285	$6,981				
10	Kohler	$3,980	$5,454	$3,504	$3,284				
11	Rudolf	$5,570	$7,354	$5,514	$7,133				
12	Brenner	$5,129	$4,051	$4,822	$7,524				
13	Best	$4,453	$7,272	$5,616	$5,689				
14	Wimmer	$5,330	$5,966	$5,863	$3,819				
15									

determine top salesperson

FIGURE 14–35

DETERMINING THE THREE HIGHEST VALUES IN A LIST

A particular area has a speed limit of 20 miles per hour. All drivers who have exceeded that speed limit are listed in the following Excel table. Your task is to determine and mark the three fastest drivers who will receive a ticket for speeding.

	A	B	C	D	E	F	G	H
1	How to determine the three highest values in a list							
2								
3		radar control			allowed	20.0 m/h		
4	date	time	speed	difference				
5	03/19/2010	14:55	36.0 m/h	16.0 m/h				
6	03/19/2010	15:01	41.0 m/h	21.0 m/h				
7	03/19/2010	15:15	75.0 m/h	55.0 m/h				
8	03/19/2010	15:17	34.0 m/h	14.0 m/h				
9	03/19/2010	15:19	59.0 m/h	39.0 m/h				
10	03/19/2010	15:25	85.0 m/h	65.0 m/h		miles/hour		
11	03/19/2010	15:30	43.0 m/h	23.0 m/h	1			
12	03/19/2010	15:45	52.0 m/h	32.0 m/h	2			
13	03/19/2010	15:52	48.5 m/h	28.5 m/h	3			
14	03/19/2010	15:59	72.0 m/h	52.0 m/h				
15								

FIGURE 14–36

▶ **To Determine the Fastest Driver:**

1. Using the data shown in Figure 14–36, select cells F11:F13.
2. Type the formula **=LARGE($C$5:$C$14, E11)**.
3. Press **<Ctrl+Enter>**.
4. Select cells A5:D14.
5. From the **Home** tab, go to the **Styles** bar and click on **Conditional Formatting**.
6. Choose **New Rule**.
7. In the **Select a Rule Type** dialog select **Use a formula to determine which cells to format**.
8. In the **Edit** box type the following formula: **=$C5=$F$11.**
9. Click **Format,** select a color from the **Fill** tab, and click **OK**.
10. Insert Condition 2 and Condition 3 as shown in Figure 14–37 by clicking **New Rule**.

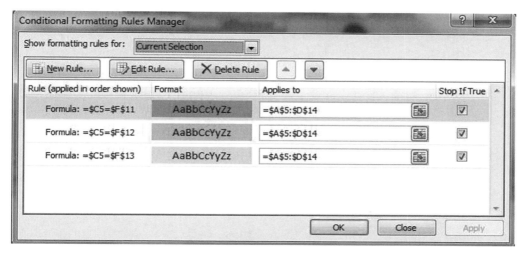

FIGURE 14–37

11. Click **OK**.

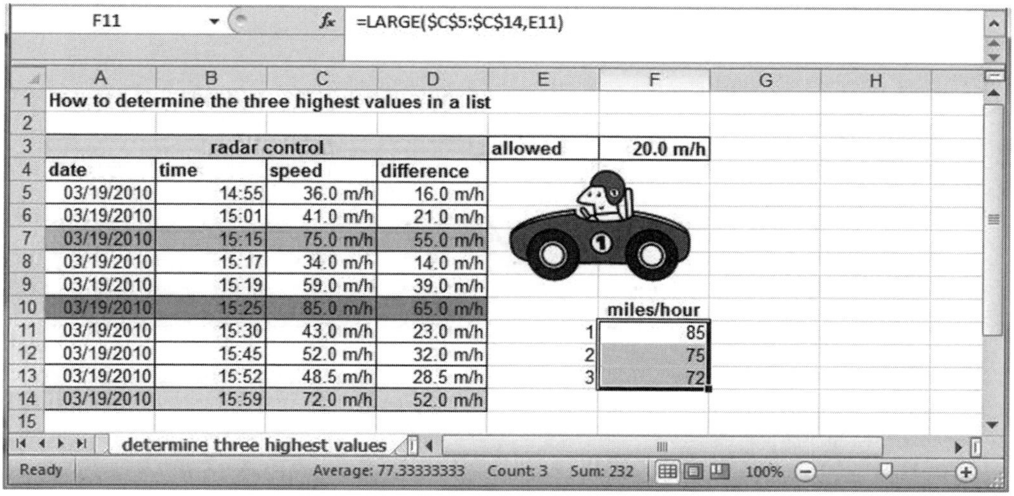

FIGURE 14–38

DETERMINING THE AMOUNT TO INVEST

To determine how much to invest, there are various factors that need to be taken into account. First of all, you need to know if the cost of the investment will be covered by its yearly return. You also need to know the length of the investment and the interest rate. All this information can be compared by using the PV formula.

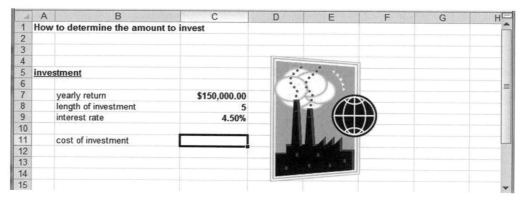

FIGURE 14–39

▶ **To Determine the Cost of an Investment:**

1. Using the data shown in Figure 14–39, select cell C11.
2. Type the formula **=-PV(C9,C8,C7)**.
3. Press **<Enter>**.

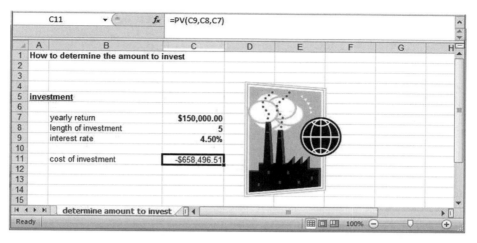

FIGURE 14–40

DETERMINING HOW MANY ITEMS ARE IN VARIOUS CATEGORIES

It is possible to use different solutions to come up with the solution for this task, including Pivot tables and the SUBTOTAL, COUNTIF, or DCOUNTA functions. Here we use the DCOUNTA function.

	A	B	C	D	E	F
1	How is it possible to determine how many items are in various categories?					
2						
3	Art.Nr.	item	category	maker		
4			components			
5						
6						
7	Art.Nr.	item	category	maker		
8	X101-001	OfficeConnect Fast Ethernet NIC	network	3COM		
9	X101-027	Internet Keyboard dt. PS2 W32	components	LOGITECH		
10	X101-011	IBM Ethernet 10/100 TX PCI f.NF	network	IBM		
11	X101-012	IBM EtherJet 10/100 PC Card RJ45	network	IBM		
12	X101-024	HP TOP HD 9GB Ultra3 HDD 7,2K	components	HP		
13	X101-042	HP ScanJet 7490C	components	HP		
14	X101-041	HP ScanJet 5370C	components	HP		
15	X101-040	HP ScanJet 4300C	components	HP		
16	X101-023	HP HD 6.4GB IDE Disk Drive Ultra ATA/66	components	HP		
17	X101-039	HP DeskJet 980Cxi	components	HP		
18	X101-038	HP DeskJet 930CM	components	HP		
19	X101-037	HP DeskJet 840C	components	HP		

FIGURE 14–41

▶ **To Count All Items in the Components Category:**

1. Using the data shown in Figure 14–41, select cell C4.
2. Type **Components**.
3. Select cell C5.
4. Type the formula **=DCOUNTA($A$7:$E$52,C7,$A$3:$E$4)**.
5. Press **<Enter>**.

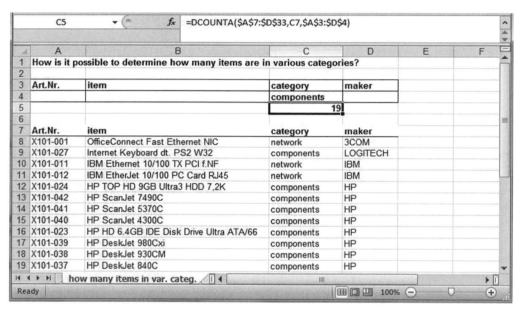

FIGURE 14–42

FINDING A SPECIFIC VALUE IN A COMPLEX LIST

Different flights are listed in the table in Figure 14–43. When a passenger enters a flight number, the corresponding flight information should be shown.

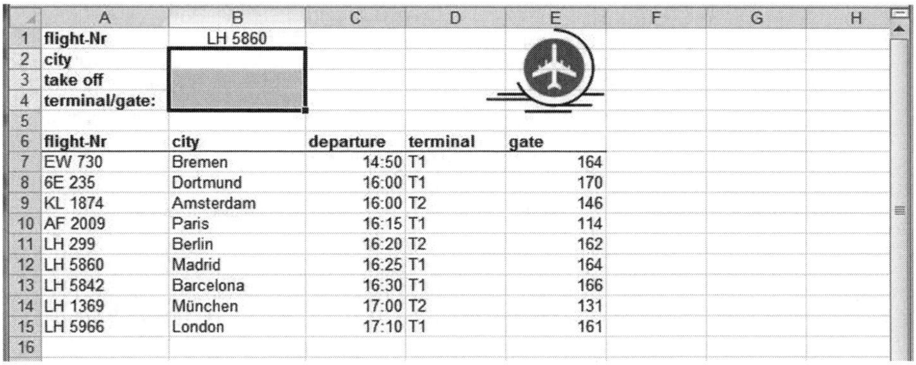

FIGURE 14–43

As seen in the Figure 14–43, a list of flights starts in row 7. The search field to enter the required flight number is cell B1. Cells B2:B4 display the corresponding flight information if available.

▶ **To Display Specific Values from a List:**

1. Select cell B2.
2. Type the formula **=VLOOKUP($B$1,$A$6:$E$15,2,FALSE)**.
3. Select cell B3.
4. Type the formula **=VLOOKUP($B$1,$A$6:$E$15,3,FALSE)**.
5. Select cell B4.
6. Type the formula **=VLOOKUP($B$1,$A$6:$E$15,4,FALSE) & " / " & VLOOKUP($B$1,$A$6:$E$15,5;FALSE)**.

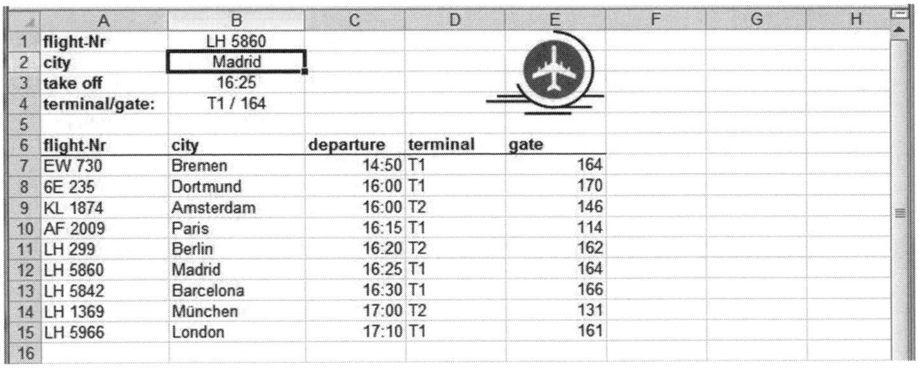

FIGURE 14–44

If you need to shade the corresponding row in the range A7:E15, use Excel's conditional formatting feature as described here:

1. Select cells A7:E15.
2. From the **Home** tab, go to the **Styles** bar and click on **Conditional Formatting**.
3. Choose **New Rule**.
4. In the **Select a Rule Type** dialog select **Use a formula to determine which cells to format**.
5. In the **Edit** box type the following formula: **=$A7=$B$1.**
6. Click **Format,** select a color from the **Fill** tab, and click **OK.**
7. Click **OK**.

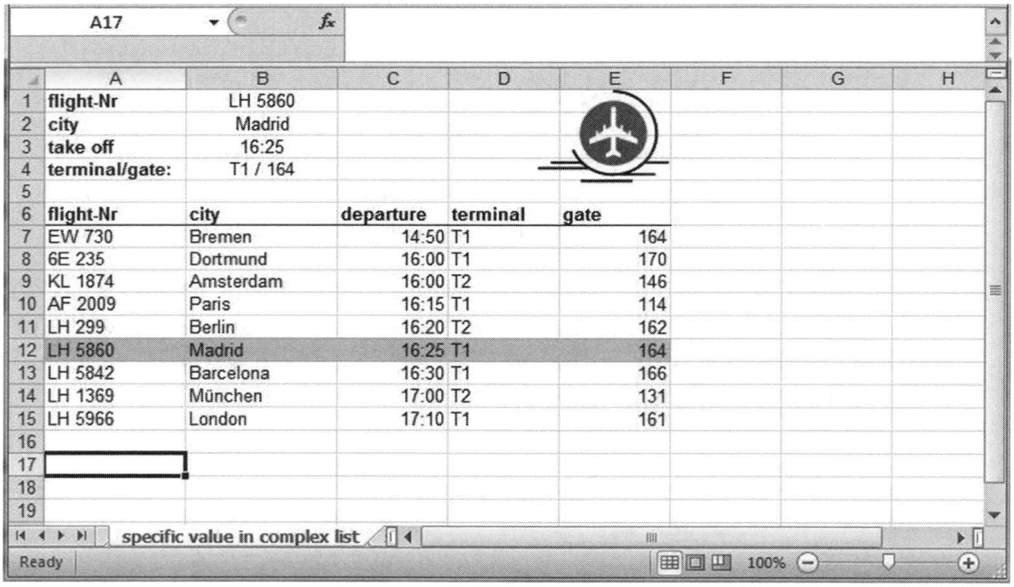

	A	B	C	D	E	F	G	H
1	flight-Nr	LH 5860						
2	city	Madrid						
3	take off	16:25						
4	terminal/gate:	T1 / 164						
5								
6	flight-Nr	city	departure	terminal	gate			
7	EW 730	Bremen	14:50	T1	164			
8	6E 235	Dortmund	16:00	T1	170			
9	KL 1874	Amsterdam	16:00	T2	146			
10	AF 2009	Paris	16:15	T1	114			
11	LH 299	Berlin	16:20	T2	162			
12	LH 5860	Madrid	16:25	T1	164			
13	LH 5842	Barcelona	16:30	T1	166			
14	LH 1369	München	17:00	T2	131			
15	LH 5966	London	17:10	T1	161			
16								
17								
18								
19								

specific value in complex list

FIGURE 14–45

DYNAMICALLY SHOWING COSTS AND SALES PER DAY

The table in Figure 14–46 contains cost and sales values per day. After entering the desired date, the corresponding cost and sales values should be found and displayed.

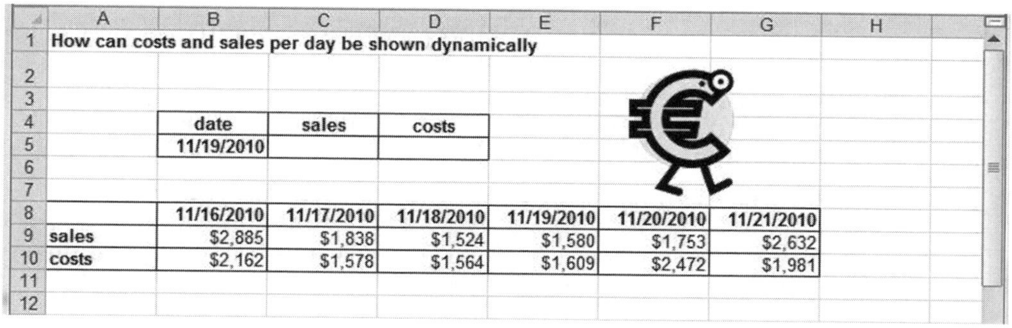

FIGURE 14–46

▶ **To Dynamically Show Costs and Sales Per Day:**

1. Using the data shown in Figure 14–46, select cell C5.
2. Type the formula **=HLOOKUP($B$5;$B$8:$G$10;2;FALSE)**.
3. Press **<Enter>**.
4. Select cell D5.
5. Type the formula **=HLOOKUP($B$5;$B$8:$G$10;3;FALSE)**.
6. Press **<Enter>**.

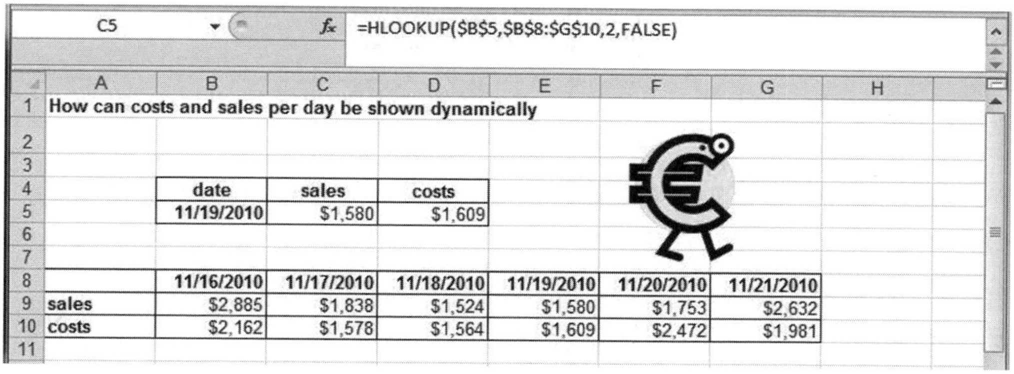

FIGURE 14–47

For this example, it is also good to use conditional formatting to mark the results in the table, as shown in Figure 14–48:

1. Select cells B8:G10.
2. From the **Home** tab, go to the **Styles** bar and click on **Conditional Formatting**.
3. Choose **New Rule**.
4. In the **Select a Rule Type** dialog select **Use a formula to determine which cells to format**.
5. In the **Edit** box type the following formula: **=B$8=$B$5.**
6. Click **Format,** select a color from the **Fill** tab and click **OK**.
7. Click **OK**.

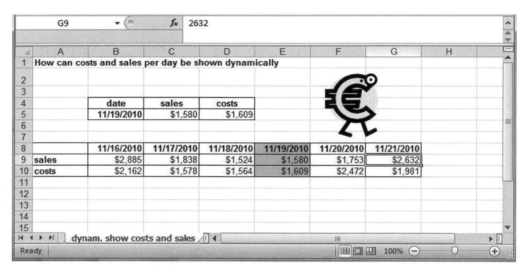

FIGURE 14–48

EXTRACTING EVERY FOURTH VALUE FROM A LIST

A list of measurements taken every two minutes is shown in Figure 14–49. Your task is to extract every fourth value from the list and transfer that value to another list.

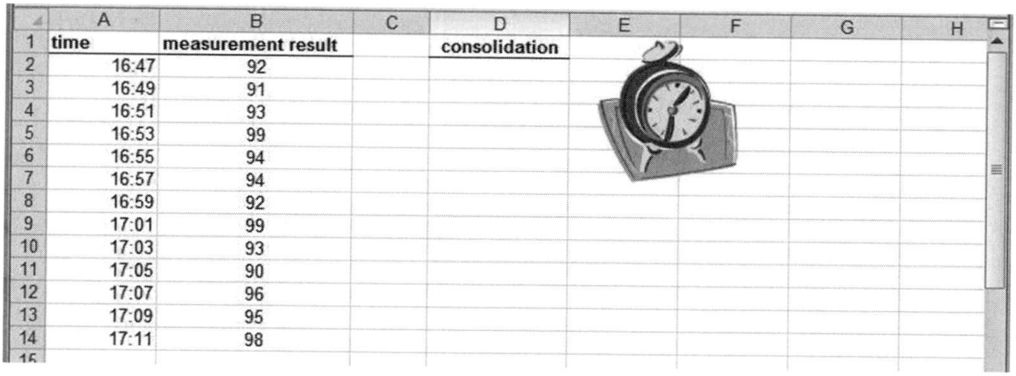

	A	B	C	D	E	F	G	H
1	time	measurement result		consolidation				
2	16:47	92						
3	16:49	91						
4	16:51	93						
5	16:53	99						
6	16:55	94						
7	16:57	94						
8	16:59	92						
9	17:01	99						
10	17:03	93						
11	17:05	90						
12	17:07	96						
13	17:09	95						
14	17:11	98						

FIGURE 14–49

▶ **To Extract Every Fourth Value:**

1. Using the data shown in Figure 14–49, select cells D2:D5.
2. Type the formula **=OFFSET($B$2,(ROW()-2)*4,0)**.
3. Press **<Ctrl+Enter>**.

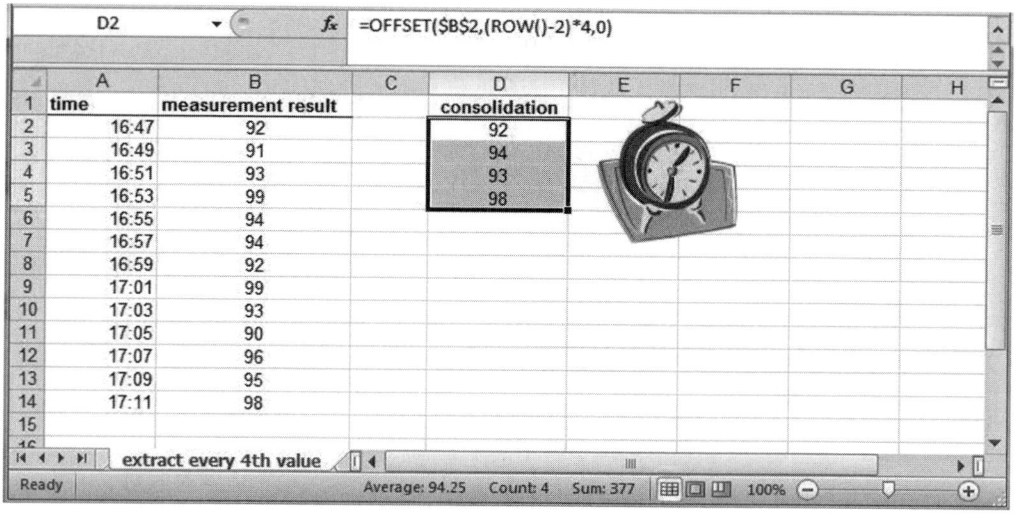

D2   fx =OFFSET($B$2,(ROW()-2)*4,0)

	A	B	C	D	E	F	G	H
1	time	measurement result		consolidation				
2	16:47	92		92				
3	16:49	91		94				
4	16:51	93		93				
5	16:53	99		98				
6	16:55	94						
7	16:57	94						
8	16:59	92						
9	17:01	99						
10	17:03	93						
11	17:05	90						
12	17:07	96						
13	17:09	95						
14	17:11	98						

extract every 4th value

Ready   Average: 94.25   Count: 4   Sum: 377   100%

FIGURE 14–50

INDEX